P9-CBE-799

FRENCH LESSONS IN AFRICA

FRENCH LESSONS IN AFRICA

Travels with my Briefcase Through French Africa

PETER BIDDLECOMBE

LITTLE, BROWN AND COMPANY

A *Little, Brown* Book

First published in Great Britain in 1993 by
Little, Brown and Company

A CIP catalogue record for this book is available from the British
Library.

ISBN 0 316 90329 9

Typeset by Leaper & Gard Ltd, Bristol
Printed in England by Clays Ltd, St Ives plc

Little, Brown and Company (UK) Limited
165 Great Dover Street
London SE1 4YA

FRENCH LESSONS IN AFRICA

SENEGAL
MALI
NIGER
BURKINA FASO
BENIN
TOGO
CÔTE d'IVOIRE
NIGERIA
CAMEROON

ZAIRE

Contents

FOREWORD

I was in the bar of the Meridien Hotel in London with a delegation from French Africa I had just met at Heathrow. The minister leading the delegation had gone up to unpack; the ambassador from Paris had arrived two days earlier and was still telephoning his friends all over the world at the government's expense; other delegation members were milling around, swopping stories. The security men were already in the restaurant ordering entire chateaubriands for themselves, the sign of an authentic secret agent all over francophone Africa.

The telephone rang, and the barman signalled to me. The minister wanted me to go up to his suite straightaway. The minister was standing staring at his open suitcase. For his first visit to London, as head of his government's delegation, his servants had packed his boubou, two shirts – and a tent.

If the French Africans don't understand the Anglo Saxons, then the Anglophones certainly don't understand the Francophones. The green cheese on the other side of the moon is probably more familiar to the English than the 10 million square kilometres of French sub-Sahara Africa that make up one third of the continent and one fifth of the population.

I've been in meetings where businessmen are amazed that not all Africans speak English. I've been closeted with civil servants who have assured me in triplicate that the currency in French Africa is as soft as a damp Venezuelan ten bob note. I've met politicians and cabinet ministers who have been astonished that for some reason Francophones prefer a Cheval Blanc 1947 to a bottle of house claret.

French Africa may not be the most important place in the

world, but to me it is one of the most exciting. And it is no wonder. The Anglophones arrived in Africa carrying the Bible and Bagehot. The French arrived carrying bottles of champagne and baguettes. The British set out to create England in Africa, down to the warm gin and tonics served in dirty glasses in seedy old-fashioned clubs. The French set out to make Africa as French as the fourth leg of the Eiffel Tower.

For some reason nobody has tried to explain the workings of one to the other. For the last ten years I have been working and travelling – and waiting for planes – all over French Africa. It has been the happiest thirty years of my life: the people, the places, the *joie de vivre*, and learning to run for planes across scorching tarmacs in the midday sun in case the seat you reserved four months ago in Le Crillon in Paris is taken by a witch doctor wearing Pierre Cardin shoes beneath his robes, and sporting an Audemars Piguet watch before you can finish writing the Foreword to . . .

Peter Biddlecombe
Departure Lounge
Ouagadougou International Airport

BENIN

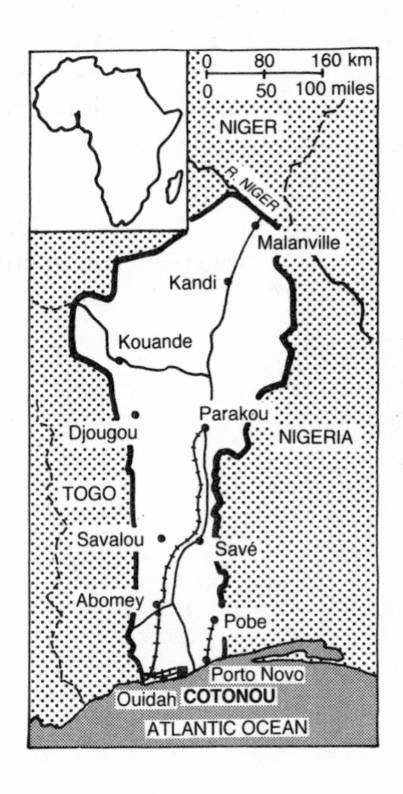
0 80 160 km
0 50 100 miles
NIGER
R. NIGER
Malanville
Kandi
Kouande
Parakou
NIGERIA
Djougou
TOGO
Savalou
Savé
Abomey
Pobe
Porto Novo
Ouidah
COTONOU
ATLANTIC OCEAN

It is eerie – not ghostly, or spooky, or creepy; just somehow eerie. At first it looks like any other African town: houses of red mud; dirt roads; goat dung blowing in the wind; people sitting around. A fat old lady is slumped over a stall, an old man stretched out on a bench, children are playing near a water pump. There are columns of driver ants, broken-down cars gathering sand, and a sense of desolation.

You see a fetish. Then you see fetishes everywhere. On tiny mounds outside houses, on walls, above doors, inside strange mini-igloos the size of dog kennels, behind ragged curtains, peeping from behind sheets of corrugated iron, hidden by cardboard boxes. Everywhere.

Look down one street and you see a straggly procession of ten or twelve women and a few men smeared with white paint, one banging a drum. They are going to a fetish ceremony. Look down another, and maybe twenty-five women are waiting outside a house for another ceremony to begin. You drive further into the tiny, dusty town; everybody seems to be just sitting around. Even the children are sitting, or slowly wandering around. The heat is intense. You're struck by the desolation, the misery and horror of the place. For this is Ouidah, the once notorious slave capital of the world, which supplied all the men for the mines and plantations of Brazil, Haiti and the Southern States. Scratch a Brazilian, they say, and you will find Ouidah, the Portuguese for help, written on his soul. Ouidah is an African Auschwitz. As if that is not enough, it is also probably the only town in the world almost totally dedicated to fetishes, good luck charms and white magic. The black magic you find in Brazil, and especially in Haiti, was white magic when it left Ouidah. You don't have to come to Ouidah to understand why it became black magic when it reached the other side.

The other thing that struck me was the age of the fetishers and worshippers. I expected gnarled old men, great fat old women. Sure they were there. But people seemed younger than I had expected. Some of the fetish priests were almost boys. I saw one priest putting the knife to a goat's neck and briskly dispatching a dozen chickens. He must have been in his early twenties. It was uncanny.

In the centre of the town, just 40 kilometres from the capital, Cotonou, I was also surprised to see staring opposite each other the Sacred Serpent Temple and – the Catholic Church of the Immaculate Conception. And yet somehow, it seemed appropriate. I turned to the Serpent Temple. Children appeared from nowhere, smeared with sand and dirt and food. Some came running up to greet you, others hung back. Then from a gap in the mud brick wall came an old man, of seventy or eighty. Thin and wiry; a grizzly, scabby beard; shiny head; twisted, filthy teeth. He was buttoning up his trousers. He said he was the protector of le Temple des Serpents. He was called Kargongou, but he said I could call him Robert.

He walked to the entrance, three steps up to a tiny platform. The temple had a backyard with three mini-igloos, one larger igloo and an old cage like a chicken run. It was no bigger than a double garage. There was dust and sand and rubbish everywhere. In front of one black and greasy mini-igloo were fetishes; some big, some small, some well-made, others bits of stick or rubbish. In front of the larger igloo was a curtain behind which you could see better-class fetishes and offerings.

Robert took me to the chicken run. It was full of six-foot long pythons. Some were curled up in corners; a group huddled together under sheets of cardboard. He picked them up and caressed them. One crawled round his neck, spitting its tongue out within inches of his face. He didn't seem at all worried. Some of the children went into the cage and played with the snakes.

I asked him if this was the only snake temple in Ouidah.

'Oh no, we have three snake temples, monsieur.'

'And only one Catholic church.'

He laughed. His teeth broke all over his face.

'What do the snakes do during the day?'

'They sleep, monsieur. During the night we let them go to hunt. They eat rats.'

'Do they go into the Catholic church?'

'Oui, monsieur. They go everywhere. They come back very fat.'

'You mean fetish snakes eat Catholic rats?'

He laughed. The children jumped up and down. After that we were great friends. We walked around his temple but I resisted the opportunity to pick up the snakes; when it comes to snakes I'm with the Book of Genesis, although I know pythons are pretty harmless, even the African python, which can grow as long as twenty feet. One python was discovered in Bingerville in the Côte d'Ivoire in 1932 which measured over thirty feet. In Nigeria they even house-train them and keep them as rat catchers. But I didn't want them crawling over me.

He told me about the two other snake temples in Ouidah. Did I want to visit them as well? There were about fifty different fetish cults as well. I could also visit them. Instead I asked how many Catholics there were.

'About 4,000. There are lots here.'

'Do the Catholics go to fetish ceremonies and the fetishers go to church?'

'Oui, monsieur. We do everything,' he said.

He wanted to show me the church but there were so many people coming out, laughing and talking, that we couldn't get past them. Instead we went to his sister's house at the back of the church. It was another serpent temple – dark, about the size of a double garage. Along the far wall were ramshackle kitchen tables, each with a greasy tablecloth, red or blue. On top of each was a bizarre collection of rotting food, bottles of beer and spirits, candles, vases, fetishes and pictures of angels and saints. One table was covered with woollen dusters; on top were half a dozen fetishes and a picture of Our Lady as well as two pictures of an energetic saint on his knees in the middle of a field. Alongside it I noticed another table with plates of bones and tiny skulls and claws.

I sat on a chair in the corner and tried to disappear. It was stifling. There were no windows. The only air coming in was through some gaps in the wall where bricks had fallen out. An old man was sitting under a canopy on the floor banging on an improvised drum, his eyes closed. Around him women were sitting swaying on the floor, practically covered with nets and beads and shells, some holding iron bells. A younger man at the back was blowing what looked like a bone whistle.

'Are they in a trance?' I asked Robert.

'They are filled with the fetish. The fetish has entered their body. They are not in this world any more.'

'How long will they stay in a trance?'

'One week, two weeks, it depends on the fetish.'

'But how can they stay like that for a whole week? Do they eat?'

'The people give them food for the fetish, and drink.'

'What does the fetish drink?'

'Spirits.'

The drummer was still drumming the same rhythm. An enormous fat lady came in dressed in white. She started swaying slowly around the room. Others followed. Some seemed to be acting as guides, stopping people from bumping into each other. The drumming became faster, louder, stronger. They started clapping. Some women started murmuring or singing. One old lady shrieked and collapsed. I practically jumped out of my skin.

'The fetish,' whispered Robert.

I slumped back in the chair. Now the drumming became faster, the dancing more vigorous. I wanted to stay; I also wanted to leave. But before we could move more women came in, stomping slowly in a trance, the first carrying a chicken, upside down, flapping its wings. The drum is now louder than ever. More women begin shrieking and crying. Then all of a sudden the chicken is torn apart – its wings and legs pulled out, its head broken off. There are blood and feathers everywhere. Everyone now turns to the dead chicken and collapses on the floor around it, trying to smear themselves with its blood. I can't get past them to the door. I am fascinated, but I still want to leave. Robert whispers, like an experienced churchgoer, that the ceremony is nearly over. I reluctantly settle back hoping there won't be a second collection.

The women are now smeared with blood, some with it running all over their faces, others with just a few drops on their hands. The drumming is slower and lighter. One woman, thin and ancient, begins to back out of the door on her hands and knees. The others follow. I spot a gap in the queue and rush for the door. The last thing I want is to be trapped in a snake temple in Ouidah with a fat lady fetisher jammed on her hands and knees in the door.

Benin, and along the coast east into Nigeria and west into Togo, is virtually the home of voodoo, which comes from Vodun, the fetish equivalent of a guardian angel. The vodun is your personal protector who keeps you fit, and ensures you have a house over your head. You thank him by making offerings or sacrifices.

After the temple the Portuguese fort is conventional; horrific, but a National Trust type visit. You walk along the battlements built in 1721, inspect the tombs of the soldiers who died defending themselves against the Africans, and pick your way through sand and mounds of dry grass and tiny vegetable gardens being tended by workers from the fort. Inside you are given a quick history of the slave trade. Africans destined for Brazil or Haiti would arrive terrified. Their families would have been slaughtered. They would have manacles around their necks. They would be brutally beaten. They would be bleeding and hungry. Presiding over everything would have been Francisco Felix de Souza, the famous white Brazilian slave trader.

But don't forget the slave trade was not just supplying slaves to the merciless slave traders. To the African chief it was a vital factor in running the country, almost the basis of the economy. Slaves did all the work and virtually ran the country. Big farms and royal plantations couldn't work without them. They kept the army on their toes; slave raids were seen as a means of training the troops. It was a means of getting rid of troublemakers, witches, thieves and undesirables. Slaves were used for human sacrifice for which the local kings were notorious. And, of course, they were currency. When urged to switch to ivory one chief is alleged to have said it was easier to catch slaves than elephants. Another Benin chief, King Glele, went a stage further, claiming it was part of their culture. In 1863 he told Commodore E. Wilmot of the West African Squadron that it was the custom of his ancestors. He could not break with tradition without bringing disaster on his people. Abolition would ruin the country.

Even when slavery was abolished, many chiefs continued to round up and export slaves for more money than before. Many of the people captured in the raids and disturbances that continued to break out along the West African coast in the nineteenth century ended up as slaves in spite of the ban. The chiefs even established a series of alternative shipping methods. If the British were policing one port they shipped the slaves out of another.

The sun was now high in the sky. Everything smelt even more decayed. I could hear the drums. Processions were beginning to form for more fetish ceremonies. I walked across the market square. An old man carrying a metal drum shuffled up to me.

'Est-ce que vous avez vu les cérémonies?' he asked me.

'Déjà voodoo,' I mumbled as I climbed back into my car and headed for Cotonou.

The huts or tatas look as though they were designed by Gucci for a less than primitive Club Mediterranée. Outside they are quite splendid; tall and round like slim, elegant oast houses, about fifty yards apart – the distance, the villagers told me, you can shoot an arrow. Inside they are genuine African machines for living in. The ground floor is for earthenware jars, household pets and animals being fattened for slaughter; hunting trophies hang from the walls. Upstairs are the bedrooms and a terrace for washing and cooking. There is even a loft divided into equal parts where they keep the food. On top is a removable straw roof. Connecting everything is a ladder sculpted out of a tree trunk. Inside, the tatas, which are made of mud, are remarkably cool.

I climbed the spiral staircase and clambered out on to the

roof. It was evening and the valley was cool and quiet. We sat talking and thinking. I then climbed back inside. They gave me a straw mat to sleep on.

In French the villagers call them *chateaux* and you can understand why. They are a far cry from the usual four-square, mud-block houses you see all over Africa. These have style and grace, like the Somba themselves. For I was in Atacora, the sprawling province in the north-west of Benin where up to independence in 1960 everybody clung to their old beliefs, and went traditionally naked. As a result even today everything is still highly organised and ritualised and basic.

Every morning the men march out to the fields together. They swing their hoes high and bring them crashing down into the soil. Each is in his own furrow, all working together but at the same time keenly working alone. The rivalry may be friendly, but it is there. After the ploughing the women arrive. Breaking up the ground is masculine work, but fertility and procreation are left to the women. To ask a man to plant the seeds, say the Somba, is to ask a man to become pregnant.

The head of the family I was staying with still wore the traditional skull cap made of straw and decorated with cowrie shells and a thick mop of loose hair; he had three wives and eight children, even though he was just twenty-three years old and a graduate from Benin University.

'Why did you come back?' I asked him.

'My father died. I am now the head of the family.'

'But didn't you like university?'

'Of course. But my place is with my family.'

I was heading for the Borgu plain. I wanted to meet the Bariba, who live along the top of Benin, from Nigeria in the west to Togo in the east. They sounded as if they had it all organised. All the cooking was done by women; servants catered to your every need; and they believe that horses and riding are the most important thing in the world. For them, horses are not just a symbol of power and wealth; they are given the place of honour. They are never used as pack animals. All the heavy work and the heavy loads are for women. The horses are painted and decorated and virtually worshipped. The most important thing to a Bariba was not a big house or sumptuous robes, but a magnificent horse with a beautifully carved and decorated saddle. It is the only society in the world where all the arts and crafts work – of tailors, leatherworkers, woodworkers, metalworkers – are devoted to horses. And the most important craftsman is the blacksmith. This, I thought, was a society worth joining.

On the way I had stopped at Natitingou, the regional capital, which today is a city of flowers. Shops, houses, even the small factories making concentrates and fruit juices are bedecked with blooms. The marketplace is busy. There are fruit and vegetables everywhere; the tomatoes are the size of cooking apples, there are piles of tobacco leaves woven together. A row of market women or Mamas were selling wax prints, baskets, batswings. But that wasn't always the case. I've been in Natitingou in the middle of Benin's Marxist–Leninist revolution when everything was drab; Chinese jeeps toured the streets, everybody carried Kalashnikovs, everything was tense. Practically every 100 yards there were roadblocks and checkpoints. The bars were empty apart from the occasional soldier or policeman. Today things are different.

Benin is always changing its mind. Between 1963 and 1969 they wandered through five military coups d'état, ten attempted coups, seven successful coups, twelve governments, ten heads of state and six constitutions. The old president, Lt. Col. Mathieu Kerekou, a Catholic from the north, seized power in league with a group of middle- and junior-ranking soldiers in October 1972 insisting salvation lay with the East. He gave the country a Marxist–Leninist revolution, down to abolishing Christmas and Easter and changing the name of the country from Dahomey to Benin.

At one time they also switched the European school calendar to that of Eastern Europe. The French, aghast, offered to send 300 French teachers to Benin to put things right. Kerekou, it was rumoured, thanked them very much; they would like to accept the teachers but unfortunately they had nowhere to accommodate them. Perhaps France would also like to provide the houses, he said. And they did. Benin then changed back to the French school year.

The result of all this instability has been a slow but steady decline compared to other francophone countries, until today. In 1986 the president suddenly changed his mind again and began turning away from the East to the West and rejoining the rest of the world. Some said he was pushed by forces inside the country, others that he was gently chided by Paris in return for their support in the IMF structural adjustment negotiations. Either way recent African meetings of heads of state show Kerekou far more sociable and relaxed than for a long time.

At the summit of the sixteen-nation Economic Community of West African States in 1988, for example, he was positively chummy with Togo's President Eyadema and the Côte d'Ivoire's everlasting Houphouet-Boigny. Shortly afterwards, Benin's ambassador in Paris, Idrissou Souler Issifou, appeared in Abidjan for an off-the-record meeting with a number of Beninois exiles. Rumour had it that they were being offered a place in a government of national unity. But there was no deal. Issifou returned home emptyhanded and was promptly sacked by Kerekou. In his place, Kerekou appointed his own directeur du cabinet – Taweman, who comes from the same Atacora region as the president but, more important, is a civilian. Taweman also had his cousin, Boni Yoto, made directeur de protocol at the Paris embassy. So he had his own direct line of information right at the heart of the embassy.

After that, the decline accelerated fast. Finally the country just ran out of money. Salaries were not paid. Banks had to close. Kerekou even raided the government's social security funds. 'But that's unfair,' cried old age pensioners. They needed the money.

'Other people are suffering,' he told a delegation while I was in Cotonou. 'Government salaries have not been paid for three months. Everybody must suffer. If you don't like it you will have to shoot me,' he told the OAPs. And they tramped out empty-handed.

Shortly afterwards I arranged for a British television crew to film him.

'In Africa we have no ideologies. Look. Here in this pocket,' he said slapping his jacket, 'I have Communism. In this pocket,' slapping the other side, 'I have socialism. Here is capitalism. If the Communists give me money for my country, I am a Communist. If the capitalists give me money, I am a capitalist. You want me to wear a Communist mask, I wear a Communist mask. It is simple. I will do anything to bring money into my country.'

But it was too late. December 1989 saw crowds of students, lecturers and civil servants take to the streets. In one of the poorest countries in the world – the average income is only US $300 a year – they had not been paid for up to six months. Buildings were looted. The air-conditioning system and lavatories were taken from the Chinese-financed sports complex. Shots were fired at the president's bodyguards. Kerekou, under pressure from the French, and, more important, the IMF which was holding back US $470 million in loans, promptly called a national conference to discuss the matter. But, literally weeping into his mouchoir, he was quickly outmanoeuvred by the opposition in what he has since called a 'civilian coup d'état'. The conference voted in a Togolese, Nicephore Soglo, a World Bank official, as prime minister and voted out Marxist–Leninism in favour of multi-party democracy.

'This is a devastated economy,' Soglo said. 'The World Bank says it will take seven to ten years to put right. I have been told to do it in twelve months.'

Kerekou began talking about his love of bicycling, contemplating no doubt the results of the first free elections in March 1991.

Benin is long and narrow, about two thirds the size of Portugal. It is 700 kilometres long but has less than 100 kilometres of coast. Much of the land is good for farming: oil palms, coffee, cotton and tobacco grow in the plateau. In the far north it is savanna, which is good for cattle. In many ways the Beninois, when they are not worshipping their fetishes, are the herdsmen of West Africa – at least the Bariba and Somba are. The Fon, now the largest group in the country, were the original inhabitants of Abomey, the City of Amazons, which between the fifteenth and nineteenth centuries was one of the most famous art and cultural cities in West Africa.

Sir Richard Burton, the great Victorian explorer, thought that Benin was 'more civilised than Great Britain'. Not because 'they still hang even women', but because they did it in private, inside the prisons, and the job was carried out by women. Whereas in Britain, he wrote in his memoirs, 'in 1864 we hanged four murderers on the same gibbet before 100,000 gaping souls at Liverpool'. He also praised them because they didn't hang for trifling offences, only for serious ones.

In the nineteenth century, Benin was the most efficient, strongest and probably most brutal country along the West African coast. So tough, in fact, that it was one of the last to be attacked, if that is the right word, by missionaries, who tackled the softer markets first. When they ventured in they saw them as devils, and urged the British to protect surrounding tribes from them although in 1600 the Edo city in Benin had, according to one European visitor, 'great broad streets, not paved, which seem to be seven or eight times broader than the Warmoes Street in Amsterdam,' with houses 'standing in good order, one close and even with the other, as the houses in Holland.'

By order of the Fon kings, descendants of the panther god Agassou, statues and the famous embroidered tapestries could only be made inside the palace walls. Outside, people were only allowed to carve wood. The palace covered forty hectares and was surrounded by walls ten metres high and no less than two metres thick. Inside there were estimated to be more than 10,000 inhabitants including ministers, eunuchs and the famous Amazonian bodyguards. The kings always chose women as their bodyguard because they were thought to be more loyal than men. Now the Fon are spread throughout the country. The third largest group, the Yorubas, are found around Porto Novo, a former Yoruba Kingdom, along the border with Nigeria. Along the coast are the Mina.

When I first went to Benin it was Karl Marx in the sunshine. North Koreans were everywhere. These days Kerekou is slowly loosening the ties on the economy, cutting back on the number of state enterprises, introducing more private investment. He released the former head of state, Alphonse Alley, although still nobody mentions the young army captain, Adabaou Kossa, who organised one of the near-successful coups of recent years, though students distribute T-shirts with his picture on them.

Anti-imperialist invective and Marxist propaganda have

disappeared from the columns of *Ehuzu*, the pro-government newspaper, which has even called for the 'exploitation of all the positive factors which capitalism has provided for humanity in the realm of science and economics.' After years of East European socialism, with a heavy dose of North Korea's Kim Il Sung, they are ready to become capitalists. Not hell-for-leather, rip-roaring capitalists in the Nigerian sense, but quiet, relaxed, restrained capitalists.

We had breakfast in the courtyard outside the tata. Around the edge were fetish mounds – on one a freshly killed chicken. Blood was pouring out of its neck into a hollow. I have killed chickens myself at home, but somehow this seemed more personal. After breakfast one of the old men took me to another tata where we had breakfast again, but this time it was more like lunch. The family gave us a large stew and insisted we had everything. Inside the houses everybody was practically naked apart from loincloths. One old lady had a small white stone hanging by a thread through a hole in her lip. When she spoke it moved up and down.

The eldest son, Yaya, took me to Taneka-Koko, a fetish village, now deserted because it had become impossible to grow anything in the surrounding fields. The streets were paved with stones, sand blew everywhere, the huts were empty. The only person I could see still living there was the fetisher, the witch-doctor. He was tall and thin with almost a straw turban on his head. He was carrying a long white pipe. He was determined to stay.

'It is my duty. We cannot abandon our ancestors. We must continue to pay our respects to our families.'

'But how do you live if you cannot grow food?'

'People will look after me. I have no worries.'

'Wouldn't you like to be with your family, your brothers?'

'It is important that I stay here.'

He showed me the tomb of his predecessor, Orou Deki. He was obviously determined that he should be buried in the same way. It was his destiny.

Further on we visited another village, Taneka-Berri, this one bustling with people. Everybody began filing into the village square and forming a big semi-circle. The women looked dull compared to the men, who seemed to be wearing their Sunday best, except for one old man, who was led by a little boy of four or five. He was obviously losing hold, but that was no reason why he should miss the celebrations. Many of the men were wearing hats like tea cosies topped with what looked like cats' tails.

A fetisher hobbled into the centre of the half-circle. An attendant followed carrying an umbrella to shade him. Practically everybody helped him to sit down. Settled comfortably into his chair he started smoking a long white pipe, similar to the one the fetisher had been smoking in Taneka-Koko. It was obviously their trademark.

Six young men appeared, naked bar a few beads and bangles. Their heads were shaved apart from a small tuft of hair in the centre. They had beads around their necks and bands of leather around their ankles and legs. They were obviously in good shape, and carried small whips. They knelt in the sand in front of the fetisher, whips in the left hand. He seemed to be asking them questions. Some replied quietly, others threw themselves face down in the sand. The atmosphere was becoming tense. People stopped speaking. The musicians had finished playing. I asked Yaya what was happening.

'It is a circumcision,' he said – the initiation ceremony admitting young men into the Somba tribe.

'How old are they?'

'About sixteen. Maybe eighteen.'

'Does every boy go through this ceremony?'

'If they want to be admitted as full members of the tribe, yes.'

'Are these young men all villagers?'

'They are all from this village. Some work on the land with their families, others in the town. Some even come back from France for the ceremony. It is our tradition.'

I was wondering whether to ask if we could go but luckily Yaya went on: 'We cannot stay for the whole ceremony. That takes two days. It is secret, for members of the tribe only. The fetisher agreed to let us see the start because he knows you are interested in our traditions. But you cannot stay.'

All over francophone Africa, I'd come across examples of the ease with which young people were able to live in two cultures. Often, young men returned from studying in Douala or Montreal or Paris for tribal ceremonies. Some would hold degrees, maybe speak several languages. But they were able to make the adjustment. Whether they did this because they genuinely believed in the ceremonies or whether from a sense of family or loyalty, I don't know. My guess is a mixture of the two. Anyhow the last thing I fancied was watching a circumcision.

I made my way quickly back to the Hotel Tata Sombo, a superb luxury hotel built in the shape of the local tatas. I was more than ever determined to become a Bariba and not a Somba.

I was driving back from Abomey, the old capital of the Dahomey empire which at one time had been home to King Glele. We had been visiting a hospital which had over 200 beds, one operating theatre and an x-ray room which had not been used for over three years. Unlike many hospitals in Africa they actually had more than enough x-ray plates, but the room was built in such a way that the operator couldn't see the patient nor the patient the operator, so that all the x-rays were useless. The toilets were nearly 200 metres from the hospital. The old, the maimed, the sick and the dying had to drag themselves along a muddy path and join a long queue.

'This is crazy,' I said to the hospital chaplain, a member of a French medical missionary society. 'What are you doing about it?'

'Our masters in Brussels are studying the situation,' he said.

'Your society?'

'Non, the EC,' he sighed. 'The feasibility study should be completed in two years. After that we have to wait for the allocation of resources. Then we go out to tender. Then . . .'

'But that will take years,' I said. He shrugged, which was not quite what I expected from a Christian missionary.

Of all the priests I've met in francophone Africa, the Italians and Portuguese seem most at home. The French and Germans seem either too intellectual or bored by the routine and lack of challenge. The only priest I've ever met who actually hated being in Africa was an Irish missionary who'd been working all over West Africa for nearly forty years. 'If only they would expel me,' he sighed, 'you'd see me dance a jig on the runway.'

But that's unusual. Normally they're immensely dedicated men who have quite happily devoted their lives to teaching Africans – even showing them how to play football. Their living conditions are anything from basic to adequate. They rarely have even the luxury of an air-conditioner; they open the windows. They work all hours of the day teaching, visiting, travelling and, the parish priests, conducting services and prayer groups. The Irish priest would drive over 600 miles a week visiting outlying mission stations, saying mass, administering the sacraments, even carrying out simple medical work, which probably accounted for his attitude.

A Belgian priest I know in Benin, Father Louis, was doing the same thing. One evening after a long day waiting for meetings we were having a meal. Did he enjoy life, I asked him.

'It's God's work,' he replied.

'But socially, what is it like? Are people friendly? Do they drop in for a chat? Do you have whist drives and bingo like at home?'

He smiled a long smile and poured another glass of mineral water. Maybe I shouldn't have asked, I thought. 'It is lonely,' he said slowly. 'You don't have much contact with the local people, I mean social contact.'

'Is that you or them?'

'I think it's circumstances.'

'You have nothing in common, apart from your religion?'

'Perhaps.' We went into his study, painted white, a little dusty, papers and books arranged neatly on shelves. I spotted a recent biography of Thomas Merton, an American Trappist monk who became a pop-hero in the days of Vietnam.

'It's a question of culture,' he said sinking into a broken armchair. 'We come from two different worlds. It's difficult to bring the two together.'

'Have you ever been tempted to go native?'

'You mean wear desert clothes, ride camels and sleep in a tent? No, never. Some priests have, but I've never wanted to.'

'How about the other way? How many go European?'

'More and more. When I first came here nobody wanted to wear a suit or a collar and tie. Now many officials wear a suit on formal occasions. They know Paris, London, Rome better than I do. But at home they tend to relax in their traditional clothes.'

'What about the children?'

'They have problems. They are in the middle. The problem is it isn't a straight choice between one culture and another, but between one that is out-of-date, old-fashioned and very traditional and one that is modern.'

'And young people always like the modern.'

'Exactly,' he said. 'The dilemma seems to be particularly difficult for the girls. The boys seem able to face the problem better.'

He was a friendly, understanding, gentle man. I still wondered why he found it difficult to mix with people in the town. He knew everybody, had seen many of them grow up, spoke the language.

'First,' he said, 'I'm a priest. We lead different lives, have different purposes in life. We see things differently. Second, I'm not one of them. Third, I understand their culture but I'm not part of it.'

'Do priests have the same problems in other countries?' I wondered.

He laughed. 'I've known priests in Paris who've had very lonely lives. Others have had the time of their lives.'

'But if there are these social problems,' I said, 'why don't they send local priests here instead of Europeans?'

'They've tried. But they don't want to come.' I was surprised. 'They prefer the cities and towns. There are lots of local priests, enough to look after this little parish,' he said sweeping his arms across the room, 'but nobody wants to come here.'

'But aren't you all under a vow of obedience? Surely, if you're told to go somewhere you've got to go.'

'But they're not told. Politics,' he smiled.

'Even in the church?'

He smiled. I was obviously getting dangerously near the bone. But I didn't understand why he was here and local priests were not.

'Circumstances, not politics,' he corrected himself. 'People here believe in fetishes, they're animists. Lots of local priests are from other parts of the country. They're Catholics, under a vow of obedience. But still in their local culture there is this apprehension. The authorities don't tell them to come here . . .'

'For fear of them refusing?'

'For fear of upsetting the balance. It's a question of time. Eventually. But not now.'

'But isn't that odd. In other parts of Africa the church is almost at war with the state. Look at South Africa . . .'

'But look at Zaire. The church has given in to Mobutu. The mass has been Zaireanised.'

'You mean the Katanga mass?'

'The priests don't dress as priests any more, they look like traditional chiefs. They are called the chiefs of God's people. Even Christ is referred to as the Supreme Ancestor. In Sudan the Muslim north is fighting the Christian south. In Nigeria. In Senegal. In Côte d'Ivoire. In Kenya the president has thrown out lots of missionaries, even though they were doing a lot of good for the country.'

'But he kept the nuns.'

'He said he could trust them. He couldn't trust the men.'

I asked about the Muslims, who are about as numerous as the Catholics – each share around 20 percent of the population. They are concentrated in the north. But the poorer the north and the richer the south becomes the more people will want to become Muslims rather than Christians.

'Islam, let's face it, is a much easier religion to accept than Christianity. It's pretty general. It talks about the oneness of God, it stresses the role of the Prophet Mohammed, but after that it's a pretty broad church.'

'A bit like the Church of England.' We laughed.

'That's not too far off,' he said seriously. 'Because Islam makes everybody feel part of a wider family.'

'But so surely does Christianity?'

'I agree, but only in a religious sense. Muslims feel part of an active family of nations. It's religion, politics, a way of life, a language. It's money.' He was searching for the right word. 'It's more . . . relevant. But in a temporal sense only.'

'And ethically?'

'Very relaxed. They have their rules, but they don't seem so coded as our commandments. They also seem to be more relaxed in their interpretations. More emphasis seems to be given to personal interpretation, and the more imaginative the interpretation the better.'

I had read about the Pope's visit to Africa, and wondered what difference it had made, if any. After all, many other priests I'd met in Africa kept reminding me that Robert Moffat, Dr Livingstone's father-in-law and one of the great nineteenth-century missionaries, was fond of saying that Satan had scored 'a fatal success in erasing every vestige of religious impression' from the mind of the African.

'Enormous difference. Everybody was very excited. It made a lasting impact.'

'Did you get any new members?'

'They estimate that conversions increased by as much as 25 percent.'

'And do they stay?'

'So far, most of them.'

'And what effect did it have on existing members?'

'Made them much more determined, much more conscious of their faith and,' he twisted around to look out of the window, 'and much more conscious they were part of a great big family. It's not just me, it's the whole wide world.'

We seemed to be getting on well. He didn't seem to mind my questions. I had often wondered how many Africans were really Christians. Sure they said they were, but many still believed in voodoo and white magic and many things a European Christian would find hard to reconcile.

'The answer is, I don't know,' he said thoughtfully. 'Certainly our people are very fervent, very committed. But I know what you mean. The question is, are the other things they believe in tradition or superstition? Are we saying that you can't be a good Catholic if you refuse to walk under a ladder? Because that rules out most Christians.'

'But can you equate not walking under ladders with voodoo and white magic – even having more than one wife?'

'Superstition is all about believing in other forces and influences. Same as voodoo.' It was a valid point. 'In some old

Catholic families they sprinkle holy water on their cars before using them. Africans will do the same with spirits or wine. As far as morals are concerned, we mustn't forget their culture and their concepts of family life. In Africa they respect the family unit far more than we do. They help each other more. They respect and look after their parents more. When it comes to families they are far more Christian than we are.'

'Sure,' I agreed. 'But I've been in African homes where they still have voodoo dolls and images.'

'And don't Christian homes have statues of the saints and crucifixes? Maybe that's a form of superstition. The longer I'm here, the less certain I am of anything.'

I told him about the ceremony at Ouidah. He capped it with stories about fetishers and the hold they have on people even today. At a building site recently in Cotonou, work had been stopped for nearly three weeks by the fetisher because one man had been killed and he insisted everybody placate the gods.

He told me about another company which suddenly found petty cash, light bulbs and office furniture disappearing. They wanted to call in the police, but the staff insisted they call in the fetisher. The fetisher arrived in his robes and asked for an office so that he could talk to each of the staff in turn. 'He sat them down and pulled a piece of grass across their throats. They were innocent. But the grass stuck at one boy's throat. It wouldn't go past his neck. The boy collapsed screaming on the floor and the fetisher said he did it. Anyhow the thefts stopped after that.'

If a Catholic priest could be as flexible as this, I wondered how easy it was to make converts.

'Normally it's very difficult,' he said slowly, 'largely because it's difficult for me to contact the ordinary people, and difficult for them to make contact with us. When you get something like the Pope's visit, of course, you can pick up thousands of converts. At other times they tend to come in batches. In Europe you get converts one at a time; in Africa, if one member of a family wants to become a Catholic, they all come.'

'The village chief syndrome.'

'If you like. Africans are very much inclined to follow other people, especially people in a position of authority or influence.'

'And do you find they stay?'

'If the top man sets the example, yes.'

'And if he doesn't?'

He smiled, got up and made more coffee.

'Do you like Africa?' I asked, 'and the Africans?'

'One must do one's duty,' he replied.

'But you would prefer to be somewhere else?'

'I am happy here.'

'But you might be happier somewhere else?'

'We will all be happier somewhere else.'

I wondered how he ended up in Africa.

'I was sent. We are under a vow of obedience.'

We then spoke about our favourite authors, other religious orders, what was happening in Europe, the future for Africa. I didn't ask any more personal questions. I guessed he had said more than he wanted to say already.

Sirens wailing, horns blaring, motorcycles screeching, we had just swerved and skidded and death-defied our way through the centre of Cotonou to deliver a group of francophone presidents to the airport. And now we were doing what the Africans are good at: waiting.

As soon as they hit the airport the presidents, like schoolchildren on the last day of term, tumbled into the salon d'honneur. Guards of honour shuffled to attention. Military bands coughed and stood ready to play interminable national anthems. Presidential jets screamed into life. And then – nothing. Five minutes. Ten minutes. The guards began to look less honourable. The bands got more *sotto.* Only the local president directeur-general of Total looked pleased as the jets continued to burn up all that lovely, expensive fuel which would ensure record figures for his masters in Paris. Twenty minutes and the whole airport was beginning to wilt. Swords were scattered over the red carpet, musical instruments upside down on the tarmac. The PDG was now dreaming of the promotion he was bound to get as a result of the best figures ever achieved by an African subsidiary.

I strolled through the non-existing security cordon which had been thrown around the airport only minutes before. 'So what's happening?' I asked the captain of the guard of honour. 'Or not happening?' He gave me an experienced shrug. 'They playing cards?' He smiled.

'So what do we do now?'

'Wait.'

Most of the guard of honour were sprawled over the red carpet by now. The band had virtually disintegrated. The PDG was dreaming of retirement.

'How long do we wait?' I asked the captain.

'We wait,' he said honourably.

A group of diplomats were oozing towards the salon d'honneur, led by the Russian ambassador, as cool and smooth and professional as any French ambassador in francophone Africa. I'm amazed how French the Russians look nowadays; they dress immaculately, behave immaculately, and speak French immaculately. Their wives no longer look like Siberian guards; they are elegant, charming and delightful. It is as if the Kremlin has started shipping Mikhail and Raisa Gorbachev lookalikes all over Africa.

And the Russians have one enormous advantage over everybody else in Africa: caviar. And they know how to use it. At Russian embassies all over francophone Africa, the tables are groaning under mountains of real, black and grey caviar. Then there are trays of smoked salmon and smoked sturgeon and shrimps and a neverending supply of sliced ham and salted cucumbers. What there isn't, of course, is vodka. Gone are the days when you could sink eight, nine, ten of those little glasses at a Russian reception and fall into your taxi dreaming of hot summer nights in Georgia. Instead it's flat Russian lemonade, warm Soviet Pepsi or just their awful mineral water. At Christmas even the poorest country in francophone Africa resembles the caviar counter at Zug, the luxury store in Moscow. If they could sell the caviar whizzing backwards and forwards in embassy cars they could probably solve their debt problems overnight.

Next to the Russian was the Chinese ambassador. The Chinese diplomats are like the North Koreans – everywhere. Maybe not as much as they used to be, but there, although you never see them except at receptions and late at night in casinos. They are all very quiet, determined and secretive. But they all speak their own brand of French. The embassies tend to be small and inadequate and generally tucked away at the far end of town. Inside many are more like warehouses; the walls lined with shelves of rice, dried fish, cooking oil and samples of everything from paraffin lamps to cheap shirts and shorts and shoes. They have none of the niceties of diplomatic life. The North Koreans are a little more human although their embassies tend to be full of leather-bound books written by Kim Il Sung.

Chinese journalists, like all journalists, are more relaxed. They like to talk and drink although they have problems mingling with the local scene. They are also intensely hard-working. One journalist from the New China News Agency I met in Benin told me he had to file over 2,000 words back to his office every day. From London or even New York that could be a problem some days, but from Cotonou? Every day? I kept asking him what he found to write about, but I never understood. Probably something to do with his Chinese–French accent.

British diplomats by comparison are either very stuffy or very casual. One diplomat I know insisted on travelling everywhere in a battered old Bentley, so decrepit that he had net curtains fitted inside the windows so that people couldn't see what condition it was in.

'Got no alternative, old man. Been on to the FO for years,' he told me. 'Tried to get one of the Rolls they left behind in Harare after Independence. Nothing doing. London said the only way to get it to us was shipping it back to Blighty then out here again. Said it would cost more than the thing was worth so I'm stuck with the curtains.'

The result, of course, was to attract even more attention. People are used to broken-down cars in Africa. At home senior government ministers happily drive around in old wrecks they would not be seen dead even looking at in Europe. But a wreck with curtains, that was something else.

'It's ridiculous,' the diplomat's wife told me, 'but he made me put the curtains in. I kept telling him it was silly, but he said it's the only way he can force London to give him a new car.'

At the other extreme, some British diplomats make you want to curl up and pretend to be North Korean. I don't mean the usual baby-kissing and let's-all-join-in-the-traditional-dancing, although that's bad enough. I mean throwing handfuls of coins in the air and making children scramble in the dust for them. Or during official banquets grabbing the microphone and singing 'When the Saints Come Marching In'. (I kid you not. I was there.)

The crew of the armoured car now began gingerly to open the back door of the vehicle; the ambulance crew did the same thing. Once they had assured themselves the air was fit for breathing, the soldiers leapt out and joined us, leaving their weapons behind. For my sake, I was grateful. What the presidents inside, probably well into their second game of bezique by now, would have thought, I don't know. Everybody shook hands in the spirit of companions in distress.

'Does this happen often?' I asked one soldier.

'Only at summit meetings,' he said in a remarkably civilised accent. 'You can speak in German,' he added. 'I speak German.'

'No. I'm Chinese,' I said. They laughed. The whole crew turned out to have been trained in a special school for African secret service men just outside Leipzig.

'How long does it take?'

'Six months.'

'To teach you everything?'

'Everything: protection; detection; investigation; self-defence.'

'How to kill? Poisoned umbrellas . . .?'

'Encoding, decoding . . . They said we were sehr gut. Normally it takes two years.'

'You shouldn't have been so good. You could have stayed away two years.'

'Too cold,' he shivered. 'Prefer Africa.'

'So have you improved things since you've been back? Better security? The president safer?'

'Naturellement,' he said shyly, as if he couldn't kill a fly.

'So you can guarantee security? One hundred percent?'

'Bien sûr. Well. Most of the time,' he corrected himself, which was disarming for a secret service man.

'Why, what happened?'

The soldier beside him slapped him on the back, they slapped each other's hands, spun round on their heels and burst out laughing.

'So what happened?' I repeated. 'The president escaped?' The rest of the crew now joined in the hand-slapping and spinning round and laughing. One man was almost bent double.

'The other week we were in Lagos,' said the soldier. 'Security everywhere. The president goes into a big meeting. We park the cars in the garage. The officials tell us the meeting will last all day. They say we can go into town. So we went into town.'

'What happened?' They all burst out laughing again.

'The president left the meeting early,' said the soldier, exploding all over with laughter.

'So what did he do?' I asked, trying to enter into the hilarity.

'He went to the garage to get us, but when he went into the garage the doors locked behind him. Security.'

'You mean he couldn't get out?' I said.

'Bien sûr.' They all burst out laughing again.

'But that's serious. What did he do?'

'There was a telephone in the garage. The president asked the operator to send someone to let him out. But the operator didn't believe him, because she thought the president was in the conference. She thought it was a mechanic. She told him to stop being crazy and cut him off. The president kept calling and she kept cutting him off.'

'He must have been hopping mad,' I said, knowing what Mrs Thatcher was like if she was kept waiting for five seconds. 'What did he do?'

'He kept calling other numbers in the conference centre. Nobody believed him. They thought it was a joke.'

By now we were surrounded by the entire guard of honour and half the military band. The only people still working were the presidential airline pilots and the PDG's Swiss banker.

'Well, how did he get out?'

'Somebody called the police, and they went down there to see who was causing all the trouble.'

'And they let him out?'

'No. They didn't recognise him. They thought he was some kind of troublemaker.' The laughter erupted all over again.

'They said the president was in the conference. He was obviously an imposter. If he was really the president they said he wouldn't be in the garage by himself making phone calls.'

This was something you couldn't invent. 'So how did he get out?'

'One of the soldiers said he would check; then they discovered the mistake. Everybody apologised. They were all embarrassed.'

'And what did the president say to you?' I asked, imagining instant postings to embassies in Outer Mongolia.

'He laughed and laughed and laughed.'

I couldn't believe it. 'He is a good man,' said the soldier, and the whole airport descended into more laughter.

At that moment the doors swung open, the presidents spilled out, the bands began playing national anthems with all the precision of the Brigade of Guards, the guard of honour sprang to attention and the planes began rolling up to collect their solitary passengers. The only people who did not remain on the tarmac to wave goodbye were the PDG and his Swiss banker.

The telephone rang. 'I'm sorry I didn't call you on time,' said the voice. I looked at my watch. It was 7.20 am. I had asked for a call at 5.30. 'I forgot.'

'That's all right. Thank you for calling me now.' Within ten minutes I was in reception. Within ten seconds I was surrounded by all the shoeshine boys of Cotonou.

'Oui, oui, demain matin,' I shouted, leaping into a town taxi.

Within 13.5 minutes I was waiting in a tiny office in the middle of town for a meeting with one of the Couve de Murvilles, an old established French family, a cross between the Rothschilds and the Kennedys, which has provided France with ministers, a prime minister and fulfilled numerous other roles of state. I was seeing Claude Schaeffer who was running a tiny (in terms of clients) but substantial (in terms of assets) private bank in Paris. He had promised to tell me about the French banking connections with francophone Africa which many people say is a far more effective system of control than any form of colonialisation.

He was tall, slim, with crinkly fair hair, about forty and impeccably dressed. There was a cup of coffee on his desk waiting for me.

'I'm sorry, I haven't time to talk to you now,' he said as we shook hands.

'I know. I'm sorry,' I stuttered. 'I asked for a call at 5.30 but . . .'

'So you'll have to come with me. We can talk as we go. I've got lots of people to see. You might find it interesting.'

He pocketed his gold Waterman, buttoned his jacket, adjusted his tie and we were off. This, I thought, was better than sitting in an office. Outside he walked past a gleaming Peugeot 504 and we climbed into an old Toyota with an even older driver. 'Always use this when visiting clients,' he said. This was going to be an interesting day.

We drove down the Avenue Clozel towards the Ancien Pont which crosses the Lagune de Cotonou, weaving in and out of the traffic, skidding around corners, braking and accelerating and hooting for all the world like a Parisian taxi.

Cotonou is a fishing village which has become a town but insists on calling itself a city. It's like a giant jigsaw puzzle with half the pieces missing. Opposite the Ministry of Foreign Affairs with its flying-saucer-shaped annex perched twenty foot in the air are empty patches of ground. Take the road where the embassies are situated and opposite are fields. Stand in the middle of the road and look at the Sheraton Hotel and you could be in the Sahel looking at a mirage.

The town hall spreads itself comfortably behind a rambling brick wall in a sea of sand. Inside, the offices are enormous with papers stacked everywhere. Most desks boast the statutory radio you find in offices throughout francophone Africa. On the desk of the colonel who runs the police is a short bamboo cane which, in one of the poorest countries of the world, has to serve as his baton. The president's house, a restrained, white, two-storey structure, looks at ease in the middle of the town amazingly without guards or any form of protection.

A few years ago Cotonou was making a fortune. When Nigeria was booming, everybody was desperate to get their goods in, but Nigeria couldn't cope. Port Harcourt, the big harbour near Lagos, was bursting at the seams. Ships were forced to wait up to four weeks to get in. Many's the time they had to jettison cargoes which had rotted away in the time they were held up. Ships loaded with cement had to be abandoned because the powder had set solid and couldn't be moved. Some very smart operators even began chartering ships knowing the cargoes would have to be abandoned in order to collect the insurance, worth far more than the original goods. The Beninois and especially the Mina, the fishermen who live all along the coast as far as Lomé, Togo, with their knowledge of the shoreline and its dangerous currents, provided a back door into their giant neighbour. Cotonou became a boom town. They handled the big cargoes, the Mina handled the small stuff. But today Nigeria has gone into reverse, Cotonou has stepped back to the old lazy days and the Mina have gone back to fishing.

'So tell me,' I said as we roared down Avenue Seikou Toure, 'do the French banks really control French Africa? I mean it's really financial colonialisation, isn't it?'

'First, the facts,' he said crisply. 'France is a friend of Africa. Probably her best friend. The Americans are not interested. The British are not interested. We are interested culturally, politically and militarily. We send our troops to Chad. Nobody else does. We have agreements with African governments. If they need us, we're there. Like Togo. President Eyadema only had to pick up the telephone. French troops were in Lome.'

'And commercially.'

'And, of course, commercially.'

We had now turned into a side street and were negotiating lakes and craters in the hard sand. 'Politically, therefore, Africa is important to France,' he continued. 'Now aid, assistance, co-operation, whatever you call it. France spends a lot of money in Africa. Our aid programme is enormous. We reschedule our debts to Africa again and again. Mrs Thatcher said she was not interested in Africa because all the Africans do is criticise her policy on South Africa and ask for money. We don't mind if Africa asks us for money. We give it to them.'

'But it's not all one way. After all ...'

'Of course. Because these countries were part of France, because we assist them so much, they must help us.'

'And the best way they can help is by buying French goods.'

'Voilà, c'est ça,' he cried as we skidded to a halt outside a tiny white washed house cowering under an enormous bougainvillaea tree. 'Monsieur Azakpo. Very important. Always pay him a courtesy call.'

As soon as he got out of the car, dogs started barking and running up to the gate. A scruffy dirty young girl opened the gate. We followed the dogs into the house, which seemed to consist of one room with a lean-to at the back. There were no decorations, practically no plaster on the walls, hardly any floor covering. In the far corner was an old bed and beside it a trestle table surrounded by metal boxes.

'Mon cher ami,' said a wizened old man wearing a vest and what could have been a pair of pyjamas or a boubou. 'Comment ça va? It is so nice to see you. A great honour.' He gestured towards the bed and we sat down. He shouted at the girl who came flip-flopping back into the room.

'The usual?' he enquired.

'Vous êtes très gentil,' Schaeffer whispered.

'Allez-y,' he barked at the girl, who ran. Within two seconds we were drinking Dom Perignon '79 from light flute glasses and picking at sweet biscuits. We talked about the weather, the economy, recent changes in the government, friends in Paris and Africa. They asked me about Mrs Thatcher and the Common Market. I told them my joke about the Channel Tunnel: 'C'est très important parce que France a été tres isolée pour trop longtemps.' The bottle was emptied, another offered but politely declined.

'You're obviously old friends,' I said as we climbed back into the Toyota which was getting desperately hot.

'Deals in currencies,' Schaeffer replied. 'Biggest money-changer in West Africa. Bristol Hotel, Lagos. Cow Lane, Accra, Togo, Mali, Senegal. He's everywhere.'

'You mean all those Senegalese at border crossings offering to change money into any currency you like?' He smiled.

'I've seen Senegalese all over the region changing French

francs into sterling; dollars into CFAs; even going from yen into naira, deutschmarks, Swiss francs and, once, Dutch guilders and back again. And big amounts too: 1,000, even 10,000 dollars. The only other moneychanger I've met was an American in Lomé who had a similar lifestyle. He had a big apartment in New York, but to look at him you wouldn't think he had two CFAs to rub together.

'He must launder a lot of money as well then.' We were now heading towards la Place de l'Etoile Rouge. 'They say a lot of mafia money comes into West Africa and gets absorbed somehow.' We stopped at traffic lights. 'From casinos, clubs, all over.'

'Now where was I?' he said. 'Oh yes. They must help us. We need overseas markets. French industry needs a big market. France is not big enough. After 1992 maybe, but now it's nothing. So what better than our old colonies? That, after all, is what colonisation is for. It wasn't politicians who discovered these countries and risked their lives exploring them, it was traders. So how could we keep these markets to ourselves? By tying them to France. And how do you do that?'

'By holding the purse strings.'

'By helping them control – ' he coughed, 'I mean manage their economies.'

'By linking their currencies to the French franc. By insisting they keep, what, 30–35 percent of their deposits with the Bank of France. By – '

'You can sneer,' he smiled. 'You could have done the same thing with your colonies.'

'I'm not sneering,' I said. 'I admire you. I think it was a good thing for France, and even better for Africa. They have hard currencies. People can do business with them.'

'Better than the naira and the cedi. Who wants them?'

'I agree,' I protested. 'I think it was a fantastic idea.' We turned in front of a poster advertising expensive French perfumes. 'But there's money in it for France,' I said.

'You mean interest rates?'

'Sure. You're getting cheap money.'

'Naturellement, mon cher. We get the African balances. That helps our balances. Our banks also get all the deposit accounts.'

'At cheap rates.'

'At fair rates!'

'But they are lower than you would get in France.'

'Because of the risk. There are risks in banking in Africa.'

'But you still pay low rates on your African accounts which gives you cheap money to play the world markets.'

'Business.' He gave a Gallic shrug.

'And don't you also charge much higher rates on overdrafts?'

'Sure. Don't forget the risks.'

I remembered a big story in *Le Canard Enchainé* about the enormous interest rates charged by French banks. Instead of around 9.5 percent they were charging 16–20 percent. There was a court case and the French supreme court agreed the banks had overcharged their customers by as much as F5–6 billion over a three-year period. *Le Canard* said the figure was nearer F60 billion, but the point was made. If that's how the French banks treat French customers you can imagine how they treat African customers.

'But surely if you paid higher rates wouldn't you attract more money into the region?' I asked.

'It's a question of balance,' he shrugged.

Officials in the West African Central Bank had told me that over US $500 million worth of local CFA currency was being illegally shipped out every year, about one-third of all the notes in circulation.

'You mean you're not unhappy all that money ends up in the French system?'

'You know all the questions.'

We were now racing down the Avenue de la Republique. Schaeffer was agreeing that the banks were charging high rates on money out and low rates on money in, but he didn't think it would last much longer because of the increased competition from other international banks. Originally the French had bought them off by inviting them to form joint ventures with them which, in effect, blocked them from coming in on their own. Now new, more aggressive banks were moving in, setting up on their own and taking a lot of business away from the French.

'Because they charge lower prices and pay better prices.'

'Exactement.'

Now we were outside a big three-storey house off la Place, with balconies on every floor. A tree was growing so low by the door that we had to bend down to get through. There was nobody inside which is unusual for any African house. We climbed to the first floor: one or two old photographs on the walls, plaster peeling off. On the second floor again nobody. As we climbed to the third floor we could hear a voice. Sitting at a big desk in the middle of an elegantly furnished room we saw Monsieur Gordon in the middle of a telephone row about deliveries. He was obviously very pleased to see Claude. Hugs, kisses, even two for me, then Davidoffs all round.

Again, the weather; what's it like in Paris? Washington was chilly. He'd just got back but next week was off to Tokyo. Then he told us about his telephone call. He was supplying the army with the instruments for their band which, he said, had been easy. Now they were asking for the music for all the national anthems in the world. Was this causing him a problem?

'You would never believe how much time it's cost me. I said to the conductor, Why every national anthem? When is the Sultan of Brunei going to come here? Why not just the obvious ones? But he says what happens if the minister says a president is coming and we don't know his anthem? I said, then I'll get the music for you. But he must have it now.' He slumped back in his chair. 'And what is he going to do when he gets all the music? Nothing. Probably stick the whole lot in a cupboard and forget they're there.' He threw his hands up in the air. 'Africans!'

And he was probably right. On the other hand, I've been at summit meetings in Africa attended by heads of state from all over, and the conductor had a point. You never know who's coming until they actually arrive. Claude sympathised, but said all that extra work obviously meant extra commissions.

'Oh no.' Monsieur Gordon rested his forehead on his desk. 'The captain says it's all included. Without the music the instruments are useless. And if he doesn't get the music he won't pay for the instruments.' We all laughed. It was a typical African story.

Outside, I asked Claude if that was Mr Gordon's speciality:

supplying musical instruments to the military. 'Pas du tout. He is a big dealer, in everything – fighter planes, helicopters, tanks. You want to build a new barracks, he'll arrange it. He's a very big businessman.'

'So why is he worrying about national anthems?'

'Because he can't afford to upset the minister.'

'But don't you make,' I coughed, 'special arrangements?'

'Of course,' he said matter-of-factly. 'But that's why you mustn't be seen to be not supplying the goods. You mustn't let people say you've only got the business because of your arrangements.'

'But everybody knows it.'

'But you mustn't give them the opportunity of saying it.'

'So how much do they take?'

'Twenty. Twenty-five. Thirty.'

'As much as that!'

'Sure, it's no problem, especially with defence. In Africa there is always money for defence, you should know that.'

I wanted to ask more about that, but I didn't want to lose the chance of talking about the financial hold of the French. 'We've been talking about consumer banks,' I said, 'but what about the commercial banks? That must be enormous business.'

'Enormous,' he said. 'And don't forget about the business with other banks and regional organisations and this and that fund and governments and ministries and post offices. Enormous.'

'So how does that work? You charge big fees, pay low interest rates?'

'Of course. They have no alternative. You're a small country, you've got to pay for planes or tanks . . .'

'Or food . . .'

'No, not food – special equipment. How can you pay it? You've got to pay through a French bank.'

'So how much do you charge?'

'Not much. Very reasonable. Because,' he looked left and right as if checking whether anybody was listening, 'because we – I mean they – I'm not that kind of banker, because they make their money other ways.' I was puzzled. 'By tying the money up in the system for days on end.'

'You mean taking ages to transfer the money so that they can put it on the overnight market and pocket the funds?'

'Exactement.'

'Which is why,' it suddenly dawned on me, 'my transfers from Africa can take two or three weeks – anywhere else, a day, maybe two days. The crooks. And all the time they are playing games with my money.'

'Then there's the interest rate dodge.'

'What's that?'

'You go into a bank, you put money on deposit. So when do they start paying interest?'

'From when you put the money in,' I said, not really seeing his point.

'Yes. But from when? From the following morning? From the day you put it in, or from the day it arrives in the deposit account?'

'I don't know,' I said, never having thought about it before.

'You put the money in at 10 in the morning. Do they pay you interest from 10 o'clock or from 11 o'clock? Or 12 o'clock? Or the following morning?'

It was beginning to dawn on me. 'Because the banks can again play games with your money. If you stick it in in the morning, they can play games with it in Tokyo in the afternoon.'

'Or New York, or London. So what do the banks do? They must have some rules. They say that any money in before 4 pm, the interest is calculated from that day. Any money in after 4 pm, the interest is calculated from the following day.'

'So?'

'So, mon cher innocent, nobody knows the rule except the banks. So what happens? You're a big French bank. You want to get a government account, or whatever. You say to the minister, You give me a million dollars, I'll calculate the interest from turnover. But today's interest. I'll . . .'

'I'll look after for you.'

'Exactement,' we both laughed.

'But surely,' something was occurring to me, 'surely it would show up in the records? Somebody could pick it up.'

'In Africa? Never. You can give them a cheque for a million

dollars and they will lose it, or never pay it in, or never be able to check which account it went into.'

'But if the French banks are that – flexible,' I said, 'what happens if nobody asks for anything?'

'The banks keep the money. There was a famous case once, in London, an American bank. They were forced to admit that in order to increase their profits for the year they hung on to some money from the Libyans for a couple of days because they didn't think the Libyans would notice. They put it in the overnight market and made millions.'

'But the Libyans discovered it.'

'The Libyans,' he chortled. 'No. It was discovered when the Americans froze all Libyan assets in the US and they sent people into the banks to check.'

We passed l'Hotel du Port and pulled up in front of what looked like an old shed. Inside they were making chest refrigerators. The motors came in from France, the freezing section and the shell were made locally and fitted and sold locally and exported as well. I could only see about eight people. Upstairs we met the director, a nice, quiet young man, very earnest, very academic, who invited us into the boardroom. On one end of the table was a model of a new building. 'Our new head office,' he said. I thought that he would have to sell a lot of refrigerators to build it.

Coffee and grande champagne cognac were brought in by a busy little French lady, grey-haired, fragile looking, but very confident, bossy almost. Knew Claude well although they addressed each other formally. She showed us a bunch of orders they had received for refrigerators from other countries. But, she said, they didn't have enough capital to buy the motors from France and everything else to meet the orders.

'You mean the banks won't lend you the money even though you've got the orders?' I asked her. 'Why not?'

'They say they want to see money in the bank, or shares, or property before they will lend the money.'

'This wasn't the first time I'd come across this problem. But it was interesting, as another example of the grip the French, sorry French banks, have on Africa. Claude said he would look into it. The most sumptuous lunch appeared; oyster mushrooms, lobster, champagne sorbet, boeuf bourgignon, and good wine.

We talked about Benin, the economy, how they were hoping to develop the private sector and attract outside investors. Then we talked about literature. Benin was once known as the latin quarter of Africa because it boasted more writers and poets and artists than any other francophone country. Wole Solinka, the Nigerian winner of the Nobel prize for literature may be Africa's greatest living writer but a Beninois was the first novelist ever published in West Africa – Felix Couchoro. Born in Ouidah in 1900, he spent most of his life working as a journalist in Togo. He wrote regularly for *La Dépêche Africaine*, a Parisian political publication, and in the mid-1920s started his own newspaper, *L'Eveil Togolaise*, which seems to have been remarkably evenhanded, publicising 'any abuse on the part of the administration' but 'asserting to the blacks, the rights of whites'. In 1941 he published *Amour de Féticheuse*, the first novel printed and published in West Africa, a somewhat steamy, melodramatic story of a wife betraying her wealthy respectable husband with the family slave. The plot drifts effortlessly into abortion, incest and multiple murder. His second novel, *L'Esclave*, made up in length what it lacked in excitement. Between then and 1968 he turned out no less than seventeen other novels.

But over the years, the Beninois writers and artists have packed their bags and left, most to Paris, some to Montreal, a few to Brazil. Today Benin is a country without books, without any form of serious communication and without any real practice in discussion and debate. But once the intellectuals return my bet is Benin will quickly regain its reputation as the cultural centre of Africa.

First, because no other country is as intellectual. 'We are polymaths,' a hotel secretary once told me, and it is difficult to disprove. Officials are often qualified twice over. The minister of tourism, for example, is a colonel in the army and a doctor of medicine. Second, because they are so far behind the rest of francophone Africa – at least ten years behind their neighbour Togo, maybe fifteen years behind the Côte d'Ivoire. But that does not mean the changes will not affect the world of action as well as the world of ideas. For maybe twenty years the rich residents of Porto-Novo, which still thinks it is the official capital, have let their city collapse. Now they have told the president they want to start rebuilding the city themselves, with their own money. Imagine what can happen to a country when that kind of enthusiasm catches on. And especially when that country is calm, polite, hardworking and hard drinking.

Our lavish lunch must have cost that little company half their year's profit, if they made any. But it didn't occur to me at the time.

In the afternoon we continued our tour: calling on a little textile company making imitation Pierre Cardin suits, three or four pharmacists, a travel agency and a mysterious Lebanese gentleman whom we met in one of the seedy hotels normally used by African workers and US Peace Corps volunteers. Around seven o'clock Claude dropped me back at my hotel. 'Got some more companies to see this evening,' he said, 'Night clubs. Interesting investments. Do you want to come?' But I was dining with a minister, so Claude gave me his card, saying I should look him up in Paris.

When I got back to my room that night after dinner, the telephone was ringing. 'I will call you tomorrow morning at 5.30, monsieur. This time I won't forget.'

'No thank you. That's kind. It's Sunday and I want to sleep in.'

'Bien sûr, monsieur. Pas de problème. Bonne nuit.'

And what happened at 5.30?

Ganvie is the Venice of West Africa. Over 20,000 people live in around 3,000 fragile bamboo huts and houses built high on stilts in the middle of Lake Nokue, a freshwater lagoon. No lighting, no electricity, but running water everywhere. All commonsense says it is crazy to live in huts on stilts in a lagoon when just down the river there are plenty of very pleasant, far healthier places to live. But the people of Ganvie like it where they are. It is where their ancestors lived, and where they want to live.

The drive from Cotonou – once you have beaten the

shoeshine boys – begins innocently enough. Past the Sheraton Hotel and, would you believe, its London bus, a relic from a cigarette promotion that went wrong. Past enormous muscle-bound statues to the martyrs of Benin's struggle for independence. Most of the statues in Benin and many of the official statues in West Africa come from North Korea. As a result all the presidents' statues not only bear a remarkable likeness but seem to have distinctly mongoloid features.

Now you pass the enormous sports stadium, also built by the North Koreans. An optimist lines the walls of the electricity station with mattresses, all sizes, all colours. Who buys a mattress from the wall of the Communauté Electrique de Benin? Apparently everybody. It's big business. Girls wander the streets, boxes of cigarettes on trays on their heads. Chickens squawk across the road. Old women sit on tree trunks staring at nothing.

Instead of hiring a car, I had decided to take a jungle taxi, one of the thousands of broken-down cars and vans that drive all over West Africa carrying everything from people to pigs, and from bags of rice and old clothes to whisky and even, according to rumours at the frontiers, gold being smuggled out of Ghana to countries with harder currencies. Now twelve more people clamber into the back of the taxi and there is no room to breathe.

Suddenly the old president comes hurtling by. A single motorcycle outrider leads the way, then the president's car, then maybe ten other cars. But no ambulance, no armoured car, though there have been various coup attempts over the years. This is not Gabon, where President Bongo drives around in a gold-plated Cadillac followed by a silver-plated ambulance. The dust settles. Everybody carries on.

President Kerekou, unlike many African presidents, shunned publicity. He gave only one press conference in fifteen years. One day I arrived in Cotonou he had just heard that a trader was selling textiles featuring his portrait. He had them all bought in and burnt, which is probably being a little too coy.

We pass one bar, l'Oasis, then Bar Chez Jerome. There is a sign saying, in English, 'Chicken House Restaurant'. A gang is starting to repair the roads. A man by the side of the road is selling louvred windows and heavy ornate doors. Cattle are sitting under the palm trees. Another car has broken down by a giant, faded Coca-Cola sign. Half of Cotonou has gathered around offering advice to the driver.

Then you see it. A fetish. But this is not your usual African fetish, this is a three-times life-size Charlie Chaplin figure complete with cane. Seen from Benin, one of the smallest countries in Africa, maybe everything is bigger.

Driving in other countries, you look at shrines on the hillside; vines rambling over picture-book cottages or, in London, mountains of litter. In Benin you look for legba and fetishes. For the drive from Cotonou along the coast towards Ganvie and Togo is voodoo country.

The buildings straggle out into unkempt fields. Old, broken-down cars are stacked in dusty metal mountains by the road-side. Huge tree trunks are flung in the gutter. Outside Chez Ben, a rickety hut of mud blocks, is a row of brand-new Honda motorcycles. Further along is a dress shop, L'Eternelle Couture, a big dusty building with the latest Paris fashions. At least that's what they tell you. Even in poor countries, women want new dresses or lengths of textile. Maybe they can only afford one length of cloth a year, but they are just as fussy about style, quality and price as New York society hostesses buying from Bloomingdales.

Textiles or Dutch wax prints are big business in francophone Africa. Originally virtually the monopoly of the Dutch who imported them from Java, today many are designed and made – in Manchester. A number of African countries have tried to produce their own, but apart from Zaire they have not had much success. For success depends not just on the designs – one successful design can sell millions of copies in weeks – but also on quality. I know businessmen working for textile companies who have turned grey dealing with the big women dealers throughout West Africa.

The road now turns to Pahon. There are three big Peugeot 504s in front making light work of the roads. Everybody in French Africa loves a Peugeot; Peugeots can take the most punishing roads, often at fairly high speeds and – this will come as a surprise to devotees of the Land Rover – with the air-conditioning working beautifully. Gone are the days when you saw British cars all over French Africa. An old Range Rover, abandoned in the centre of Lomé, stayed there for three years before it was finally taken away by the authorities. In all that time, nobody touched it; nobody took the wheels, or anything out of the engine. Nobody wants British cars. They are not built for the roads, not even Land Rovers, never mind Range Rovers. They are as uncomfortable as hell and the air-conditioning never works.

The palm trees are now fading out. The countryside is becoming like Ashdown Forest after one of their little forest fires. There is not much traffic. Occasionally you see a group of women waiting for a jungle taxi. We stop at Chez Toledo. I have a Coke. The boy behind the bar asks if I'd like anything to eat, and hands me a menu.

'What would you recommend? Do you have anything local?'

He recommends the 'spécialité gastronomique'.

'Oui, d'accord, je prends ça. Mais qu'est-ce que c'est ça?'

'C'est le chat, monsieur.'

I think of what they would say back home. But when in Africa ... The poor cat looked like a fancy rabbit stew. You could hardly recognise the meat, which tasted like hare. But there wasn't much of it. Cats in this part of the world don't live long enough to get plump. They are considered such a delicacy people can't wait for them to grow fat. Either their own or other people's – they think nothing of snatching a neighbour's cat for dinner. If you can't catch your neighbour's cat, you can always buy one in the market. They sell for around CFA 2,000 each, which in a country where the average monthly income is less than CFA 10,000 a month, puts it firmly in the luxury category. But why they should be so highly rated, I don't know. I certainly wouldn't worry if I never had cat again.

D'Agbanto is the start. You can tell you're entering the land of voodoo when you pass a mission catholique. Outside one village is an egon, a mini straw wigwam, with or without somebody hidden inside, who acts as a guardian, protecting you during the day and destroying the evil spirits at night. The fun is not knowing whether there is somebody inside. I've watched egons standing in a village for hours, then suddenly moving. Now there is a gravestone made out of cheap pink and green bathroom tiles. Everywhere there are fetishes, on the walls, over the doors, in mounds outside the doors.

Now we're in Ganvie. I take a canoe. The boy asks for a million francs, we settle for 1,000. Still cheaper than the safer, flat-bottomed boats owned by the local Mama Benz. We drifted between the frail bamboo huts. Children played casually everywhere, some climbing the bamboo poles. I wondered how many drowned every year. Nobody seemed to be worried; it was probably safer than playing in the street. Women were brushing out the huts or cooking. The men were smoking or just staring into thin air.

Ganvie, like Venice, is the result of war. Towards the end of the eighteenth century a group of Adja refugees fled their homeland in the north in fear of the Fon and the Dan-Home, and settled on the edge of Lake Nokue. At first they lived in houses built above the swamps, but gradually the water level rose and they had to live above the actual lake in houses on stilts sunk into the mud. Ganvie in the local Tofinu dialect comes from two words, 'gan' meaning 'we've escaped' and 'vie', 'community'. Ganvie, therefore, is the town that escaped.

I wanted to visit one of the homes. Benin's answer to Donald Campbell swung the canoe towards one of the bigger houses. I could hear music coming from inside, probably a radio – I wondered if it could possibly be a television. As we drew alongside five or six children came to the edge of the platform. A dog ran up and down between their feet. Smoke was coming from an earthenware pot inside the hut. I didn't want to go in without being invited so we hovered precariously, bumping up against the bamboo poles. After a few minutes an elderly man came out onto the platform. He had old jeans on, no shirt, no shoes. He looked as though he had just woken up. We introduced ourselves. The boy driving the canoe said he knew him, but I wasn't convinced. I asked whether it would be possible to have a look inside the house.

'Oui. Pourquoi-pas?' he said. But he didn't make any gesture to tie up the boat.

'Perhaps it is not convenient now,' I said. 'Perhaps we could come back later.' I had the feeling we were exchanging courtesies and he did not actually want me to come in. No wonder the French had never been able to persuade the locals to pay taxes. 'It is very kind of you,' I said. 'I would very much like to come back later. Thank you very much.'

'Merci beaucoup. A bientôt.'

It was a genuine African conversation, a cross between a union negotiation and a diplomatic two-step. You ask a question or make a proposal. The African disagrees or is uncertain, but doesn't want to offend you so he agrees. But it's a formality, he uses symbol words or codes. Like a diplomat saying yes when he means perhaps and perhaps when he means no. He has observed the rules of courtesy, but has conveyed his true feelings. The problem, of course, is interpreting the signals. But in spite of what many people say, this is not a particularly African approach. Cynical Europeans will always tell you, 'Ask an African if he can arrange for the sun to rise in the south and he will say, No problem. How can you deal with people like that?' Invariably they are the people who say 'We must have lunch some time' and not mean it, or 'The cheque is in the post'. When the Japanese do it we say they are inscrutable. When the Arabs do it we go into raptures about their courtesy and hospitality. Why should the Africans be criticised so much for saying things they don't mean?

I wondered how the people of Ganvie lived; how they earnt their keep. The answer, I discovered, walking around the lagoon, was by fishing and occasionally taking tourists on trips around the village. Women were selling fruit, vegetables and fish in their little market near where the boats were moored. Maybe they were busy when big coaches arrived from Cotonou or Togo. But tourism is still very small and low-key. They probably sold mainly to each other. Perhaps they were kept by the boy guides, who charged one million francs a trip. After all, they only need one punter to bite and they could afford to build St Mark's Square in the centre of the village.

As we headed back to the bank I could see fishermen checking the adjas, their special fish traps – patches of water fenced off with foliage stuck into the mud. As the water rises the fish swim in and start nibbling the leaves. As the water recedes they are trapped by the fencing and ready to be collected. Other fishermen were lassoing huge nets into the water.

I climbed out of the canoe alongside a woman grilling thick slices of meat. It smelt good. She offered me some. It tasted as though it had fermented inside a pregnant camel before being forcibly expelled.

'What is it?' I choked.

'Agouti.'

'What's agouti?' I said, spitting it out quickly.

'Rat,' the boy laughed.

From cat to rat in one day. This was going to play hell with my gastric juices. But in the interest of gastronomy I took another bite. Actually it was quite tasty, a little like the brown meat of a turkey or chicken in a curry sauce. Strictly speaking, of course, it's not rat at all. Agouti is really a giant guinea pig, a grass or cane eater, like the American grass-cutter or cane rat. Researchers at the University of Ibadan in Nigeria have discovered it has the right mix of protein, fat and minerals for human consumption and have been trying to rear it to between four and six kilos. I hope they succeed because it must be safer to eat than chicken. Have you seen the way Africans let their chickens wander all over the place pecking at everything – including the sewage? In any case, you can't visit Ganvie without eating agouti. It's like going to Venice and not having coffee in Florians.

'La Patrie ou la Mort,' said the sign as we came to the frontier with Togo. The roads had been very good, part of the new regional highway network being pushed through by the West African Economic Community which stretches from Mauritania down to Nigeria. One section was going to be a toll road, but they had not yet started collecting the money, which was most unAfrican. They usually collect tolls before they start building the roads.

Wood in wicker baskets or stacked in neat bundles lined the road. Branches from dying palm trees were being ferried by children. Other palm trees were standing without branches like giant cocktail sticks in the sand. In the distance I saw a tiny house made out of scrapwood and palm leaves with a giant television aerial on the roof. Which proves yet again either that it is wrong to judge by appearances or that the CIA have a listening post in West Africa. Not far away, in the middle of rough scrubland littered with tree trunks, was a gravestone, beautifully kept, with fresh flowers in a vase on top.

It was just gone nine o'clock. I was meeting a French journalist, an expert on Africa, coming across from Togo. We had agreed to meet between nine and ten, so I settled down to wait.

Entering Benin, especially if you're coming back across the border from Togo, is always a problem particularly if it is your first visit. You pass the Togo customs without any problems. You walk across no-man's-land and queue up for the Benin customs. After one hour, maybe two, in the blazing sunshine, it's your turn. You sit in front of the customs officer, smile and say Bonjour. You give him your passport, visa, two photographs, everything in order. The customs officer looks at the visa form quickly and hands everything straight back to you. 'Not in order,' he says.

The earth opens up in front of you. You know everything is in order. You have filled in a million similar forms in your life. 'Excuse me. I don't understand. Everything is in order.'

'I can't accept them. You can't enter Benin.'

You've got meetings, which took months to arrange. Then you've got a plane to catch. 'But I don't understand. Why aren't they in order?'

'The photograph is not the right size.'

'Not the right size?' you say slowly, trying to stifle the rage boiling up inside you. 'The form didn't say anything about the size of the photograph.'

'They are not the right size.'

Controlling every muscle in your face and every inflection in your voice, you say as casually as you can, 'But what is the right size?'

'They are not the right size.'

'But if you're refusing to let me in because they're not the right size then you must tell me what is the right size. I will cut them and make them the right size. No problem,' you sigh wearily.

'I don't know the right size . . .' Kafka was nothing compared to this. 'You'll have to go back into Togo, to Anécho, and have your photograph taken again. The photographer there knows the right size.'

Then it dawns on you. This is another African dodge. Why didn't I realise it earlier? It would have saved the blood pressure a bit. Do as the man says or you'll never get into Benin.

Back you go across the Togo customs post where they smile weakly at you. You search desperately for a town taxi. No taxis. You look around for a jungle taxi coming across the border. No bush taxis. Maybe a lorry will give you a lift. No lorries. An old man appears pushing a prehistoric motorcycle. You offer him a few pennies to take you back to Anécho, about twenty minutes by car. He is not interested. A little more. Now he begins to waver. Still there are no taxis in sight, no lorries. In desperation you empty your wallet into his hands. He grabs the lot, switches the engine on, throws you on the pillion and kicks the bike into action.

You asked him to drive fast, but this is too fast. You wish you'd asked for a crash helmet. You wish the road wasn't so bumpy. You wish dogs wouldn't keep running out of the bushes and snapping at the wheels. You just wish those damn photographs had been the right size.

Then you're at Anécho, the old colonial capital. You suddenly realise you haven't told the driver you want the local photographer but he is taking you there all the same. So this is all part of one big Benin sting and you're the innocent victim, yet again. You tumble into the photographer's dingy studio and explain your problem. Please could he take your picture and give you photographs the right size?

He leads you into another dingy room with a camera, a dirty white sheet hanging on the wall, a chair in front of it. You slump into the chair and stare at the camera. The photographer takes the picture. 'Marvellous. Fantastic. Thank you very much indeed.'

'Come back tomorrow. You will have the photographs.'

'Tomorrow? Tomorrow! You've meetings, appointments, lunch with the minister, a plane to catch. Another day, another country. Tomorrow! You say very calmly, 'Do you think you could possibly let me have them today? I can pay.'

'Ten thousand francs. You don't need the photographs. Just give the customs man this receipt. They'll let you through. Tell them I sent you.'

It is now 3.45. I've been waiting nearly seven hours. But at last I can see our expert on Africa, a grubby mass of sweat, dust and frustration shuffling across the border, muttering a string of obviously new words he has learnt in the local dialect. By now he is obviously also an expert on Benin border crossing customs.

'Welcome to Benin,' I wave cheerily.

He shouts back in a language I do not understand.

BURKINA FASO

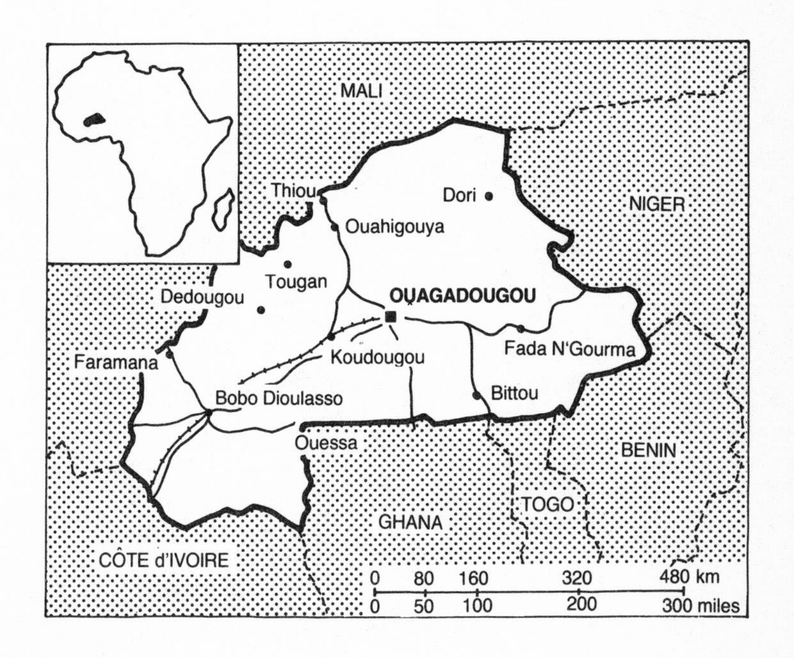

I checked into a strange-looking hotel, filled in the forms, handed over my passport. The receptionist disappeared. Five minutes later the manager came back. He gave me the key to my room, my passport – and an electric light bulb. 'There are no light bulbs in the hotel, sir,' he said. 'They keep being stolen. This is the bulb for your room.'

'Just one bulb?'

'That's all we have.'

'Thank you very much,' I said, looking forward to moving a heated light bulb every evening from the room to the bathroom and back.

'That'll be CFA 10,000.'

'What for?'

'Deposit on the light bulb.'

Burkina Faso is abject, heartbreaking poverty and hunger and disease. Everything that's gone wrong in Africa has gone wrong in Burkina Faso. When I first went there it was the poorest country on earth. Per capita income was less than $100 a year. It was probably only that because the computers were not programmed to calculate anything smaller. One child in seven died before it was one year old, one in six before it was five years old. Infant mortality was as high as 30 percent compared to just 1 percent in the USA. Average consumption was less than 200 calories a day. It was impossible to imagine how things could get worse. Life expectancy was just thirty-three years. It was like one vast refugee camp, except that in refugee camps you at least know there is somebody around to help you and feed you. In Upper Volta, as the country was then called, they didn't even have that. It was nothing, wrapped inside a vacuum, and starving.

After the major drought in the early 1970s, the children all had those swollen bellies and matchstick legs. Men and women were wasting away on pavements, on street corners, in groups under the trees. I saw a fight over a crust of bread somebody had thrown in the gutter in the capital, Ouagadougou, or 'Wagga' as it is known to old Africa hands.

Many children were so hungry they could no longer eat. They actually refused the food they needed to survive as if they had forgotten what eating and drinking was about. The extremest form of anorexia, it begins by the time a baby is six months old. If by then they have not received enough goodness and minerals and vitamins either naturally or artificially they are vulnerable. There is nothing anybody can do. They just wither away and die. Yet Burkina has resources: gold at Poura, antimony at Malatou, marble at Tiara, zinc and silver at Perkoa, manganese at Tamboogo and phosphate at Kodkari. It is also a major producer of mangoes, green peas and Irish potatoes.

Today things are getting a little better. 'The big problem is still anaemia,' a French nun told me on the flight to Ouaga. 'We see Africans lying in the sun all day and think, what a great life, no worries. The fact is, most of them just haven't the energy to do anything else. I often think that instead of pouring all these millions into Africa in the form of aid, we should simply ensure that the Africans have iron to cure their anaemia, and let them solve their own problems. I'm convinced that an anti-anaemia campaign would work wonders for Africa.'

I was sitting in the middle aisle, with two nuns on my left and two earnest American members of the World Assembly of God on my right. I decided to talk to the nuns. The younger was going out to replace the older who was going to retire, she whispered to me, after over fifty years in Africa.

'Well, why don't they do something about anaemia?' I asked the younger nun.

'I don't know. Too simple. Doesn't involve enough money. Not enough jobs for consultants . . .'

'... And probably because the last thing we want is for Africans to do things for themselves. Just think what chaos a self-sufficient Africa would cause for the world's agriculture and industry. So how bad is anaemia in countries like Burkina? What causes it?'

'Women. In fact women create most of the diseases in Africa,' the young nun replied quite briskly, which staggered me a little. I wondered whether she had been a prison warder who had discovered a late vocation. 'Women need a lot more iron than men and if they don't get it they become anaemic. When they become pregnant they need more still, and if they don't get it they become more anaemic. Then they get hookworm, which they pass on to their children. A child born of an anaemic mother has no chance, it will be infested with hookworm very quickly. They reckon that over 700 million people are infested with hookworm. It will be deficient in vitamins and especially folic acid. It will probably also get tropical diarrhoea. What chance has it got?'

'But plenty of children survive.'

'Sure, but they suffer from iron deficiency anaemia. They are always the lazy ones. No,' she corrected herself equally briskly, 'it's our fault for not looking after them. But they are the, let's say, lethargic ones. And they are the ones who are always getting other illnesses, which is not surprising because they've got no protection.'

'Well how do you treat anaemia? What can we do?'

'Give them a decent diet with plenty of iron and vitamins. Give them the strength they need.'

'Do you have iron tablets?'

'Yes. Tablets are the quickest and easiest solution. Iron can be administered by normal tablets or sustained release tablets. In acute cases we can pump in the iron by injection or, in the really bad cases, by infusion. Sometimes you can infuse all the iron the body needs and in some emergency cases you can top it up with a complete blood transfusion. But we don't do that often. First because, let's be honest, blood is expensive. Second, because tablets are really just as good.'

'How long before you get a reaction?'

'Usually about two weeks. We like to test patients who –'

Suddenly the plane reared and lurched forward. The sound of the engine switched from a quiet hum to a strained roar like a Land Rover driving over railway sleepers. Some women screamed. Children fell over. People started crossing themselves. Up front, I could see a gaunt old man looking for Mecca and kneeling in the aisle. An air hostess rushed to restrain him, but in so doing she let go of her drinks trolley. The trolley hurtled down the aisle and crashed into the edge of our row spilling whisky, gin, cognac and wine all over the timid, elderly nun. Her white habit was stained with the most ferocious in-flight cocktail.

'I'm sorry,' I said weakly. 'You are soaked. Is there anything I can do?'

'No thank you,' she said gently, summoning up all the Christian resources of her soul. 'It's all right.'

The prison warder next to me was completely indifferent to the suffering and embarrassment of her drenched sister. 'We like to test patients who start a course of iron tablets,' she continued, 'and usually after two weeks their haemoglobin level starts to increase. But the whole course takes about nine months. Once the haemoglobin levels start to rise the patient feels better, more active, more alert. But their iron stores are not fully replenished. The trouble is once they start to feel better they stop taking the tablets. They say they don't need them any more. Then they sell them. I know one man who sold them. I was mad. I said, "What did you do that for? You're not cured yet." He said his family were hungry. The tablets were the only thing he could sell to get money to buy food.'

'So what did you say?'

'What could I say? I gave him some more tablets,' she said, proving a Christian soul lurked behind that tough exterior.

'Which he then sold.'

'I know. But he is still helping to fight anaemia so long as he uses the money to buy food for his family.'

I wanted to ask her about other health problems in Africa; river blindness, yellow fever, leprosy, but they dimmed the lights for the film which, of course, was one of those French films you are not exactly happy watching sitting next to two nuns, one of whom is drenched through to her soul with alcohol. I buried my head in my book.

The film over, the fasten seat belts sign flashed on. We prepared to land. 'I'm looking for my wife,' said an imperious little man.

'Please sit down, monsieur,' said the hostess. 'We are coming in to land.'

'But where is she?' he demanded.

'Monsieur, she is here. Please, you must sit down.'

'I want to see my wife.' The temperature was rising rapidly.

'Monsieur, I will have to call the captain.'

'But where is she?' The man now pushed past the hostess and ran the length of our cabin. 'Anne-Marie,' he shouted. Half the crew pursued him. By now we had burst through the clouds. The airport was in the distance.

'You must go back to your seat,' they were all screaming, 'otherwise we'll have to call the captain.'

'Anne-Marie. Anne-Marie!' He was running up and down like a headless chicken. I could now see palm trees and the roofs of houses. The engines were changing sound. I'm sure I heard the undercarriage being lowered.

The chief steward came through the curtains, saw what was happening, turned and ran. Within seconds the plane shot up towards the stars. We jerked back in our seats, the engines leapt into top gear and the demented husband and his pursuers crashed down like ninepins: onto the floor, sideways onto other passengers, headlong into the gap to the emergency exit. The poor drink-stained nun sat through it all obviously with her mind on other things. By now we were horizontal again and circling the airport. The husband had been dragged back to his seat sobbing. 'My wife. Where is my wife?' he wailed.

I could hear the crew arguing with him. A voice now came on the loudspeaker, asking everybody to return to the seat they had been allocated at Paris or Rome and have their boarding passes ready for inspection. The plane erupted. Four hundred people started complaining it was impossible. They had thrown their cards away. They couldn't find them. Half the passengers stood up and started moaning in the lockers. The other half started returning to their original seats. The plane pitched to the left and then to the right. The voice screamed at everyone to return to their seats. But which seats? The original seats or the seats they had just left? The aisles were like the first day of a Harrods' sale. Normally sane, quiet people were now shouting and shoving and climbing over each other. The plane pitched and tossed. Everybody screamed. Except the elderly nun. She was just violently sick all over her already stained habit.

Everybody took this as some kind of sign and started praying noisily to their god. The nun was now whiter than her once-white habit. I tried to get the sick bag out of the pocket, but it was tucked into the in-flight magazine which was wired up by the headphones I had forgotten to hand in. And she erupted again giving a whole new meaning to the odour of sanctity. This time she screamed, jumped up and ran to the toilet at the back of the plane.

I turned and saw her wrestling with the trolley which was blocking the door. Sobbing and screaming, she pushed the trolley aside and opened the door. Then I heard the most terrifying scream of my life. The poor nun was now shaking and screaming at the top of her voice. I climbed over the prison warder and ran down the aisle. Slumped on the floor in that tiny gap between the toilet and washbasin was an enormous fat old lady. Obviously the missing wife. She had been trapped inside the toilet since the trolley had crashed down the aisle.

The screaming started all over again. Was the woman dead? I couldn't tell. Maybe she had had a heart attack. I didn't really want to find out. This was something for the crew. I retreated to my seat and let them take over. We circled the airport yet again, I could see the woman being lifted to her feet. At least she was alive. The pilot now came on the loudspeaker, imploring everybody to go back to their seats. He was running out of fuel; we had to land.

The poor nun was led gently back to her seat, looking like the floor of a public bar in the worst part of Liverpool on a Saturday night. The missing wife was helped back to her seat as the engines once again dropped into second gear. This was it. The engine dropped into first gear. The wings were hovering. The missing wife finally reached her seat. Then pandemonium broke loose again.

The distraught husband rushed to his wife. They collapsed

sobbing in each other's arms. The crew screamed at them to sit down. The chief steward dashed towards the cockpit. The cabin was suddenly full of screams and prayers. All the Muslims started searching for their prayer mats once more. The nun collapsed again into a dead sea of vomit. How we landed, I shall never know.

The next thing I remember is an old Italian priest whispering something about how Africa affects everyone in the end. But he was surprised it had affected the Reverend Mother. In all the fifty years she had worked in Africa, he had never known her touch a drop of alcohol.

What do you get if you cross a camel and a leopard? A giraffe – at least that's what the ancient Greeks used to say.

Once I travelled right through Parc d'Arly for three days with a group of French, British and American journalists and all we saw were giraffes: big giraffes, baby giraffes, lots and lots of in-between giraffes. No lions or panthers or baboons or buffaloes or hippos or crocodiles. Not even a heron. The game wardens with their 'poupous', homemade guns which looked more dangerous for them than for any adversary, kept telling us there were plenty just up the road.

Parc d'Arly is a bit like Dartmoor with trees – desolate and empty, almost dead. Driving through the stubble and the trees, you could hear nothing but the crack of dead branches. Goodness knows what the giraffes found to eat. The British complained about the sand, the heat, the dust. The French waxed lyrical about giraffes. The Americans complained there was no Coca Cola.

'Giraffes were discovered in 1826. As late as that,' said an enthusiastic French travel writer who looked like a recruiting sergeant for the Foreign Legion. 'The Egyptians sent one to Paris as a present to Charles X. Over 500,000 people turned out to see it.'

'I could murder a gin and tonic,' said a British journalist.

'Gee, I should have packed more Cokes,' said an American adventure writer.

'The giraffe was escorted by a full military guard of honour, two gendarmes on horseback, carriages. It was given six servants to look after it.'

'Why aren't there any pubs here? Can you imagine it? A pub, right here in the middle of nowhere. Serving g and ts.'

'What about a triple chocolate milk shake?'

'Balzac was a great fan of giraffes. He bred giraffes. He called them philosophers.'

'Haven't we got any drinks in the back?' said the Brit rummaging around the Land Rover.

'Did you know giraffes can gallop? They can get up to fifty kilometres an hour. It's a marvellous sight . . .'

'Next time I pack the drinks. I'm not going through this again.'

'Do you know the giraffe has a special valve in its neck to stop the blood leaving its head when it bends down to eat grass? Otherwise all the blood would quickly leave its head and kill it.'

'**** the giraffe.'

This trip, as we drove nearer and nearer to Parc d'Arly, with its 500,000 acres one of the biggest game reserves in Africa, we came across more villages, or rather shacks and corrugated iron, each with its bar selling beer only 30p a pint, cigarettes even cheaper.

'Cheap beer, cheap cigarettes, keeps the people quiet. Good for the army,' said the doctor who was with us.

Yet smoking is another major health problem throughout Africa. Consumption, of course, is still low: 300 per person per year compared with 3,000 in the developed world.

'Smoking just five cigarettes a day can lead to a monthly dietary deficiency of 8,000 calories,' he added.

Campement d'Arly, supposed to be a safari lodge, was more like a jungle shanty town. The facilities were worse than spartan. I turned on the bathroom tap and out came a stream of insects. Furniture was basic, food and drink there was none. But not to worry, we were told, the minister of tourism was flying in for dinner and bringing smoked salmon and caviar and champagne. Perhaps we would like to wait for him in the dining room. I headed for the bar instead. As I walked through reception a group of tourists suddenly arrived from nowhere. Their safari had hit problems and they had been diverted to d'Arly at the last minute.

'I want a single overlooking the pool.'

'No, that's too near the disco. I'll never get any sleep.'

'Can you get a doctor? My wife is sick.'

'Look, I don't care what it costs, get me a charter plane. I'm never coming here again.'

'I demand to see the manager.'

'Where's the bar?'

I got to the bar, ordered a whisky soda and sat down with an American already into his third cognac. Other old Africa hands strolled in: two Frenchmen; a German; a Swede or German, it was difficult to tell; a Belgian. First, we guessed how long we were going to have to wait. Then, of course, how it was much worse in Nouakchott or Bamako or Ouaga or even Abidjan; how UTA or Air Afrique or Air Dakar was the worst airline in the world; and how in the hotel in Koudougou, Burkina's third largest town, you had to sleep on a concrete bench; how there was no soap or light bulbs in Ouahigouya, and how nobody was telling us how long we were going to be holed up in this lousy, godforsaken hotel when we all had so much work to do back in the office.

'But there's no point getting mad,' said the American.

'We're in Africa,' we all sighed.

'In the US they would say, We will give you some information at 10 o'clock. Then everybody knows where they are. This way, we don't know what we are doing.'

But if the Africans say one thing and mean another, it's not their fault. They got it from the French. I'm convinced the French are a success in Africa because they do nothing but chatter or say whatever they think people want to hear. The British, by comparison, hardly open their mouths. At receptions French diplomats chatter non-stop while the occasional Brit spends his time desperately searching for another Brit or trying to persuade the barman to mix him a gin and tonic.

African diplomats, however, can even outsmart the French. If it is a group meeting they do it by simply out-talking everybody in sight. Ask them to make the speech of welcome and they will speak long enough to ensure nobody has a chance to get a word in. I was at a meeting once with a group of journalists. The first question was fairly general and innocuous. The minister spoke for 44 minutes 32 seconds non-stop. Pure, modulated poetry flowed uninterrupted across the room. Nobody stirred or coughed or tried to stop him. When he finished everybody applauded. Then he thanked everybody for such a warm welcome – and fled. Nobody had a chance to ask nasty questions.

'Ssh,' he said. 'It's the CDR.' They were banging on the front door. 'They're always sniffing around.' It was about three o'clock in the morning. 'The secret police always come for you in the middle of the night.'

We were standing in front of a fridge packed with champagne and caviar in a tiny house at the back of the Pizzeria Vesuvio in Ouagadougou. Outside I could see lights flashing.

'If they discover us, we're finished.' I froze, staring at the fridge packed with everything forbidden and praying the CDR would go away.

The evening had started in one of the best restaurants in town, run by nuns. I was with the chef du cabinet of an important ministry. We were beginning to order when he suddenly stood up, said he wasn't hungry any more, apologised to the sisters and left by the back door. I followed quickly.

'What happened? Don't you feel well?' I had caught him up and we were walking quickly to the taxi.

'No. It's the CDR,' he said. 'I saw them outside the restaurant.'

'CDR?'

'The Committees for the Defence of the Revolution.' These were the days when Thomas Sankara, Africa's answer to John F. Kennedy, was in power. 'They are our equivalent of the Red Guards. They are all eager young men, not so bad as the Red Guards. Certainly not as violent. But they are inconvenient. They are supposed to maintain the purity of our revolution. Oh don't get me wrong, I agree with the president, with everything he is doing. The country is more united, people are working harder. I don't think anybody disagrees with him. It's just that the CDR are so enthusiastic.'

By now we had reached the taxi. It was obviously not the time to continue the conversation. I asked when the rains were coming, how the crops were doing, whether they would get two seasons again this year. We turned into a side street. The headlamps picked out a figure sleeping in front of the metal gates to the driveway. He jumped to his feet and opened the gates. The driver made no allowances; he maintained the same speed and we shot into the driveway in the split second the gates were opened.

'Who's that?' I asked. 'Do you make him stay there just to open the gates?'

'I keep telling him to go away, but he won't. He says he is the house boy. It's his job.'

'But did you hire him?'

'Of course not. He was here when I came. I told him I didn't need him. He said he was part of the house. He was there to work for me.'

'What does he do then?'

'He just opens the gates. He lets me out in the morning and back in again in the evening. What can I do? I feed him. He eats with the other servants. He helps himself to scraps and leftovers. He survives. That's what it's all about in a poor country.'

The role of the servant and his relationship to his employer or rather sponsor is a subject that fascinates me. I live in one of the richest countries in the world. Few people have servants. In francophone Africa, in some of the poorest countries of the world, everybody has servants or, at least, the people in any kind of position have servants. A factory foreman might have a servant. A journalist will have a servant. A chef du cabinet or technical consultant will have servants. A minister will probably have three or four servants living in the house, a servant to look after the car, maybe two to look after the garden, and a chauffeur.

How can they afford it? Why don't they spend the money feeding themselves? The answer, of course, is complicated – and simple. Africans have servants because they have always had servants. Throughout history African chiefs have been surrounded by advisers and retainers and slaves, sub-chiefs have had sub-servants, and so on.

In the villages, the traditional chiefs don't queue up at the water pipe; somebody does it for them. So it is in the towns today. You've only got to be earning a fraction over the basic minimum wage, around US $200 a year, and you can afford servants. Another reason, of course, is the sense of family. If one member of a family is doing well, he feels it is his duty to help other members, whether they be aunts, uncles, or third cousins of the wife of their thirty-sixth brother. Go a stage further and servants are a healthy way of injecting more money into the economy. Better six servants than a Swiss bank account.

'We said to Jean-Pierre, "No thank you, we already have our own servants." But he wouldn't listen,' said the chef du cabinet. 'I introduced him to the other servants, who have been with me for years. I thought they might try and get rid of him, as a threat to their jobs. But they all came back to me together. Michel, who has been with me for years, said they didn't think we could send him away because he belonged with the house not with me. They noticed that there was nobody to open the gates, so they had agreed he could stay and open the gates. I said, "But how are we going to pay him?" Michel said they had decided it was wrong to expect me to do it so they had agreed to give him some of their money and share their food with him.'

'And are the others looking after him?'

'I give him something. I could hardly refuse after the way Michel put it to me. But it's not much.'

'Do the other servants really give him money?'

'I don't know. I don't ask. If I ask and they do, then I'm going to be embarrassed. If I ask and they don't, they are going to be embarrassed. And in any case they won't necessarily tell me the truth. But I must say he's very good. He's by the gates twenty-four hours a day, seven days a week.'

In Africa a servant expects to be treated like a servant. He might be a cousin or a niece, but he or she is there to fetch and carry. None of this: 'We're all the same really, all one happy family.' An African might be a junior administrator third grade or a minister but when he gets home, he is king. As soon as they hear the car, the servants come running. They open the gates, the garage door. They wait to be handed a briefcase, escort their master into his home, provide a drink for him, bring him slippers. They run a bath, serve drinks, wait at table. If the phone rings they answer unless there is a special hotline. The master might go to his study to read his papers, or slump into an armchair and watch television. If he wants more champagne, he shouts. I have even seen a junior government official call a servant to change the channels over, when he had an automatic control box by his side. To us, brought up in our so-called egalitarian society, it might seem wrong. But to the African it is the natural extension of their centuries-old culture.

Safely inside his house, a three-room bungalow at the end of a dirt road where he lived with three servants – his wife was a teacher in Paris – the chef du cabinet opened some beer.

'You were telling me about the CDR. What do they do to maintain the purity of the revolution?'

He hesitated. For a moment I thought he didn't want to discuss it. 'In theory, they are a good idea,' he said slowly. 'Every revolution needs its officers, its purists. They are the people who make things work, like the street committees in Russia. We haven't many police or soldiers, so Sankara needs help. The CDR help him. Trouble is they are all volunteers, they don't get paid. We haven't any money. They are just so enthusiastic.'

'How?'

'Well, we have a curfew, so we all stay at home. It's not as if we have many places to go to. But the CDR insist on patrolling the streets from one in the morning. They make a lot of noise, deliberately, so you can hear them. Sometimes if you leave a light on they will come to your house and ask if you are going out or expecting somebody to come in late. Then they will tell you about the curfew. You tell them you just forgot to turn the light off. You shout at the boys and blame them. The CDR listen very carefully. They are always very polite. They write it all down in their book, then they go away.'

'I can't see anything wrong with that.'

'But they write it all down, don't you see?'

'So. They probably throw it away.'

'You don't know Burkina Faso, our bureaucracy. We keep everything. We read everything. It might take two years, maybe ten. I should know, we do the same in our ministry. Everything is read, signed and countersigned. It takes a long time, but we do it.'

He was obviously becoming nervous. I poured him another beer. He looked at it for a few seconds, then said, 'Forget the beer. I hate the stuff anyhow. What about a glass of champagne?' We'd reached the point of no return. He obviously wanted to talk. He fetched a bottle of Dom Perignon and crystal glasses.

'I'll tell you what it's like living here now. I'm all for the president, he's getting things done. I hope he is still here in twenty years. The trouble is the people around him. Of course he can't do everything himself, but they sometimes go too far. They know they do, I know they do. Trouble is you can't say so because they claim they are doing it in the name of the revolution. If you complain, they say you are against the revolution. Look, I could just as easily be in Abidjan or Paris; I choose to stay here because I believe in the revolution. What happens? I decide to work late, we've so much to do. Along comes one of the CDR, tells me I'm breaking the curfew and that I am no friend of the revolution.'

He sighed deeply, waved his arms. 'If I invite him in he will think I'm either trying to intimidate him or claiming special privileges. I apologise politely, and hope that because I'm polite and understanding he won't write it down and won't report it.'

'But surely in your position you can explain the situation?'

'That won't help. At the end of the day the CDR believe the CDR. That's what keeps them together. And everybody else believes the CDR or say they do because they know the country needs the CDR. They're just so inconvenient.'

'So, don't work at night. Don't turn the lights on. Keep the curfew.'

'But it doesn't end there. The CDR also report on you in the ministry. Nobody knows who they are. They are everywhere. It's like living in Russia or China.'

'What do they do in the ministry?' I asked.

He laughed. 'Oh they've got a marvellous idea. Every Wednesday they publish their own CDR bulletin in which they say who is working hard; who is not; who should be promoted; who should be fired. And if you're fired, whether you should be given another job, whether you should receive your pension. It keeps everybody on their toes. Trouble is they don't give any proof. They don't even have to give the truth. But everybody believes them.'

'Why? That's unfair.'

'Of course, but it's politics. Nobody can afford to criticise them; that would be criticising the revolution. The government doesn't criticise them because they are providing the kind of discipline the government wants. Supposing three or four innocent people lose their jobs. What's that against an efficient country? Overall the government needs the CDR. They ran a big campaign last year to get children inoculated against yellow fever, meningitis and measles. It was a big success. How can the government criticise or ignore them?'

The moving spirit, some say the éminence grise, behind the CDR was Captain Pierre Ouedraogo, he told me. At his beck and call he had 100 crack members, ready to work day and night for the success of the revolution. The élite of the élite had just come back from running political training courses for 12,000 new members. He opened a third bottle. One bottle would probably be enough for the CDR to report him to the People's Commission for the Prevention of Corruption. Two was obviously a gross violation of their ruling of December 12 1983 on lifestyles and the revolution. But three! That would give the chairman, Captain Henry Zongo, apoplexy. But there was more to come.

'Do you fancy some caviar?' he said, holding the door of the refrigerator. 'Beluga. The best.'

I admit I hesitated. 'Well, yes, of course. Thank you very much. This is fantastic,' I said as he heaped my plate. 'But where do you get it from? It must cost a fortune.'

'Not a penny. I get our diplomats to buy it. They get it cheap and send it back in the diplomatic bag. It's a great scheme.'

We both laughed and toasted the Russians. Then we toasted Dom Perignon. Then Captain Ouedraogo. Then Captain

Zongo. By now the bottle was empty. 'I'll get another,' he said. I followed him along the tiny passage to the kitchen. He opened the refrigerator door. The light came on. Then the CDR knocked on the door.

Mercedes and Paris fashions are back on the streets of Ouagadougou. Thomas Sankara is dead, killed with twelve officers in a vicious coup in October 1987. The new president is Blaise Compaore, previously one of the Sankara's best friends, and a former minister of state.

The IMF are talking about structural adjustment programmes. Public finances are being rationalised. State industries are being privatised. Foreign investors are being wooed. The middle classes, even in this poorest of countries, are behaving like the haut monde anywhere. The CDR have been replaced by the CR, the Committee for the Revolution. Sankara's widow and their two sons are in Gabon. Colleagues and former ministers have either emigrated or repented. But his memory lives on.

Thomas Sankara, le Rebelle, was one of the youngest, most dynamic, unpredictable, idiosyncratic and charismatic leaders francophone Africa has seen. From the moment he seized power in a bloodless coup in August 1983 at the age of thirty-four until he was gunned down by his nearest and dearest he captured the imagination of young people throughout Africa, stole the headlines from the continent's most respected leaders and outraged everybody.

To the French, he said things no other African leader would dare say. 'There is not a Burkinabe who does not remember an uncle or a father who died so that France could be free,' he told a Paris press conference. 'I would suggest you don't forget it either.'

To his colleagues and administration he preached austerity. Instead of using the presidential Mercedes he drove around in a little Renault. He hitched lifts to regional summit meetings in other presidents' jets. Once, in Nigeria for a summit meeting, when all the other presidents were arriving by Mercedes, in a glorious coup de theâtre he turned up by bus. He set up the

People's Commission for the Prevention of Corruption to root out 'the gangrene of corruption, a weapon used by imperialists and bourgeoisie to destroy from within revolutionary experiences wherever they develop', and told the first session that he had CFA 353,665 in the International Bank for Industry, Commerce and Agriculture and CFA 69,792 in the National Savings Bank; that his salary was CFA 138,736 a month and his wife's CFA 192,690; that gifts he had received as head of state came to CFA 850 million and had all been sent to the national budget department: that the cars he had been given had been handed over to the national vehicle compound.

He sent his government ministers to work on the farms 'to build a better Burkina' and their officials to school to learn about computers. He cut salaries by over 10 percent. He changed the name of the country from Upper Volta to Burkina Faso – the Land of Upright Men – to emphasise the point. Burkina is Mossi for 'the land of men of integrity', and Faso is Dioula for 'rule by the people'.

More important, he captured the hearts of his people. He debated like a Marxist – 'It is better to take one step with the people than ten without' – but he was a populist, and they loved him for it. He built solidarity compounds to teach beggars a trade. He ran 'Keep Burkina Beautiful' campaigns including 'pretty village' competitions. Sankara even set up Burkina's own rudimentary national health service. Every village elects a health committee, which builds a primary health post which, in turn, trains local health workers. At the end of 1984 he gave everybody a New Year's present. He told everybody they would not have to pay any rent for 1985 regardless of what their landlords said.

He outraged the aid organisations. 'Nobody is going to tell us what to do,' he told them, and increased Burkina's budget including capital spending by 8 percent and pushed up their debt–service ratios from 10 to 19 percent. He complained bitterly about their policies and supported his ministers when they did so, even down to the type of cheap water pumps they had to buy to bring water to the villages. Why should we buy five different types with the help of five different agencies, demanded Josephine Ouedraogo, the thirty-seven-year-old highly articulate Minister of Family Affairs and National Advancement, when they were all incompatible. Wouldn't it be more sensible if they were interchangeable? Then there would be no problem about spares. Sankara agreed.

To me Sankara was an innocent, a political boy scout. He knew what he wanted to do, but he didn't understand people. He didn't believe in original sin. He thought all people were good and honest and, with a little bit of encouragement, eager to do their best. He thought civil servants would welcome the opportunity of working on the land, that banning trade union activity as 'reactionary' would galvanise the work force. He believed that school leavers and graduates would welcome his political seminars as more important for the country than getting a job and earning money. In the end, for all his ambitious health, education, farming, anti-desertification and human rights programmes, which admittedly began to benefit the majority of the population, he fell foul of the influential minority, the people who run the government and the army which protects the government. Too many people became too nervous, for themselves and for the effect Sankara's policies were having on the international community. They decided he had to go. Did they have to kill him?

I was in Togo when the coup took place. People coming out of Burkina said (a) it was an accident, (b) they had to kill Sankara because he was planning to kill them, (c) the army took the decision into their own hands.

Today under thirty-six-year-old 'Beau' – some say Brutus – Blaise Compaore, Burkina Faso is turning sharply to the right. Compaore has a Mercedes and a bullet-proof Alpha Romeo; he has his own Boeing 727, admittedly paid for by Gadaffi and now and then leased out to Michael Jackson. Thanks to the Germans, government officials are again being whisked around Ouaga by Mercedes. A new presidential mansion is being built. Civil servants and workers have had pay rises. Village elders and traditional chiefs are again being consulted. The price of beer has been lowered.

'The aim of the revolution is not that everyone should be poor but that everyone should be rich,' says Compaore. The government is behaving like a government and you can hear the sighs of relief all over West Africa and as far away as Paris and Washington. For Compaore is, with his immaculate uniforms and suits and expensive tassled shoes, acting and talking like a president, although I can't understand what he is saying in English let alone in French.

While Sankara spoke of revolution, Compaore speaks of 'rectification'. In one breath he says, 'We must work hard and talk less.' In the next he is talking about 'seeking to achieve a real extension of democracy and by applying vigorously the principle of centralised democracy, criticism and self-criticism and all organisational principles through open and frank debates, the Popular Front aims at protecting our people from other deviations . . .'

Whether you understand him or not, he is obviously saying and doing the right things. Slowly he seems to be bringing all the different groups and interests in the country into the government. He is organising the youth. Instead of knocking on people's doors at three in the morning they are building roads and bridges and working on farms.

For the first few months Compaore, who is married to a niece of Houphouet-Boigny, went everywhere, especially overseas, surrounded by soldiers. But he learnt to relax very quickly, and was soon going around with the minimum fuss and surprisingly little protection. I saw him during the West African economic community summit in Lomé in 1988 wandering around with just one aide, driving in unmarked cars, and dropping in unannounced for chats with journalists. Since then he has established himself as a serious regional politician and brought Burkina back into the mainstream.

Last time I was in Ouaga, I went to see the dynamic Jeanne Ouedraogo, who in Sankara's days was designing and producing Faso Dan Fani, 'the Clothes of the Revolution'. Burkina Faso, she told the government, was producing 34,000 tonnes of cotton a year. Revenues had been falling because of low prices on the international market. Why not produce more Burkina-made products to boost domestic cotton production? Sankara was happy to oblige. The National Revolutionary Council decreed that all government officials must wear Faso Dan Fani. Madame Ouedraogo could just have churned out

Chairman Mao suits by the thousand. Instead she designed haute couture tunics and trousers in a wide range of colours and designs: CFA 4,000 for trousers and tunic, CFA 40,000 for an evening dress. Not only were people happy to be forced to wear such exciting clothes, it also created a brand-new export business. From Côte d'Ivoire, from Mali, from Niger, even from Paris orders came rolling in. Production soared. More people were taken on. A big factory and design centre was built. At one time Madame Ouedraogo was employing over 350 workers. Faso Dan Fani was as fashionable as Gucci. But no more. Today the two most popular designs are Femme Milliardaire and Mon mari sort, je sors, which says it all.

While waiting to see her, I met a Nigerian businessman living in Ouaga. 'So how is he doing?' I asked.

'Better. More organised. More businesslike. Not so exciting.'

'And what do people think?'

'People are still very guarded. But you've only got to look at the houses being built. They call it Aid City because it's all being done with aid money.' He laughed. 'Look at the cars, the goods in the shops ...'

It was certainly the smart end of Ouagadougou, where all the new money had come directly or indirectly through the aid organisations: to consultants, advisers, transport companies, construction firms, rice traders, suppliers of office equipment, people renting out accommodation. But it's fascinating seeing the impact a little spending has on a tiny, close-knit, desperately poor society and how it spreads. Not only the traders benefit; so do their servants and families. They might only get CFA 10,000 a month but in a country where the average income is US $200 a year that's big money.

'But most people are still hungry.'

'Sure. But they are now doing something about it. Before they were making speeches.'

'And people accept that?'

'I think so. Everything takes time.'

I often wonder whether the World Bank should up-date Machiavelli's *The Prince* and give it to new presidents. They insist on job descriptions for every other job under the African sun, why not for the biggest jobs of all? After all the problems a new president faces are enormous.

First, they must consolidate the changeover. Hundreds may say they will support them, but they can probably directly rely on only ten or twelve key people. The rest will follow because they need the job. A few may cause trouble; they have to be accepted, accommodated or neutralised. This is why different presidents, for example, have changed the names of their countries on taking office. A new country, a new start. And lots of contracts printing passports, identity cards, currency notes . . .

Second, they must unite the country. Some, like Sankara, try to do this by inspiration. Others, like Togo's President Eyadema, construct a party machine in which everybody, students, businessmen, trade unions, traditional chiefs, women and so on, is represented.

Third, they must create a sense of belonging and identity and commitment. In Europe we've had hundreds of years to grow attached to our patches of land. In Africa they have only just started. On top of that their nations were largely artificially created by old men scribbling on dusty maps in Berlin over a hundred years ago. They need national anthems, school songs, football teams. Some countries, like Zaire, insist everybody wears national dress or, as in Congo, little red scarves. Côte d'Ivoire simply created the richest and fastest-growing economy in the region although it's having problems.

Fourth, they have to create a sense of history and tradition. Again in Europe we have a million things to commemorate every day. In Africa they are still creating their history. To us some of their anniversaries and traditions may appear insignificant, but Africa is doing now what we have been doing over centuries.

Fifth, they have to give people something to be proud of: statues, monuments, palaces, even cathedrals are all part of the fabric of a country. It is absurd to say that they are essential in Europe but not in Africa.

The Nigerian thought that Compaore was between stages two and three. He had consolidated the changeover and was now uniting the country and trying to create a sense of belonging and commitment.

'So will it last longer than Sankara?'

'Oh I think so,' he said. 'It feels sensible.'

After I left Madame Ouedraogo's I tried to find my friend's house at the back of the Pizzeria Vesuvio but things looked different in daylight. Either that or the house had been razed to the ground by the CDR. When I finally saw him, he had been transferred to the Ministry of Foreign Affairs and was staying as a guest of the French government at the sumptuous Crillon in Paris. 'Having plenty of champagne and caviar?' I asked. 'No time,' he replied. 'Too busy.'

He opened the freezer door and revealed the usual bottles of champagne. But this time alongside the champagne were two flasks which looked distinctly medical.

'Blood,' he explained.

'Expecting Bokassa for lunch?'

'Everybody has their own blood bank now – at least every expat, and many of the locals. It's too risky otherwise: dirty needles; AIDS. Nobody in their right mind would go into a local hospital. Instead of curing you, they are likely to kill you.'

I was with a French architect, Jean-Marie Steinhoff, a short, fat, balding man who spoke as if he had a mouthful of croissants. He was in Burkina Faso working with the Association pour le Développement Naturel d'une Architecture et d'un Urbanisme Africain. He was trying to develop special medical buildings which could be constructed with local materials. The French government had told him that travellers and expats in sub-Sahara Africa were a hundred times more likely to get AIDS from receiving medical treatment than in Europe. A number of people had already returned to France after getting AIDS as a result of medical treatment.

Blood is obviously a problem. In some countries the health authorities pay for blood. For many Africans, donating blood is their only source of income, but hospitals are unable to screen the blood because they can't afford the equipment.

'We've all got our own blood supplies, but you never know whether that will be enough or, even worse, whether you will be able to get to your fridge if anything happens,' he said. 'So we are trying to organise our own blood register, to get all the expats together to draw up our own list of donors. Some expat companies have already done this among their staff, but we are trying to extend it. The more people in the scheme, the better.'

'And the bigger the risk,' I said.

'No. Because everybody will be screened before their blood is accepted.'

'Does that mean that only people with good blood will be allowed to work in bad countries?'

'No, of course not, but we want everybody to know where they stand.'

Monsieur Steinhoff was working on a building project in Batie-Nord, a tiny village about 450 kilometres from Ouaga. He was going to inspect the work and asked if I wanted to go along. I had heard a lot about such projects and agreed. If they could make it work in Burkina, they could make it work anywhere in Africa.

Burkina Faso may be poor, but it is rich in vernacular architecture – architecture created by the people, for the people and using local materials – as opposed to much of Western architecture which is created by the planners for the planners using the most expensive imports. Throughout the country, and especially way out in the villages, they have managed to achieve all the things we have failed to achieve architecturally: low-rise buildings within high density developments; gradual transitions from public to private areas; interior private courtyards; expandable units; proper play space for children; and the integration of old people with the rest of the community.

'They think they are primitive, but they are far more advanced than we are,' a student at the school of architecture in Dakar, Senegal had once told me. 'Yet today they are destroying their architectural heritage and putting up modern houses with concrete blocks and corrugated iron roofs because they think that's progress.'

He was part of a team surveying architectural styles in Burkina. 'The interesting thing,' he said, 'is that the local language doesn't have words for door, bedroom, kitchen. They refer to the entrance as the mouth of the house, the walls as its arms, the main building as the head, and so on. Which forces them to build their homes in human, not architectural terms.'

They have also adapted their buildings to suit their lifestyle and environment, where we have to adapt our lifestyles to live in high-rise buildings or work in enormous impersonal office blocks. 'At Tangassoks, for example, the Kassena have built their houses so that to get in you have to stoop down, then stand upright, then step over a low wall. This gives them protection against rain, stops animals coming in and makes it difficult for robbers to slip in,' he said.

'But won't that change as their circumstances change; as they begin to fence in their animals?' I asked.

'Bien sûr. It's already happening. The young people coming back from the towns build different houses from their parents. And in Yuka, for instance, the style of the houses has changed since they stopped fighting their neighbours. In the old days the Nankana houses were big and heavy with tiny entrance ways to stop anybody getting in. Today they are lighter, the doors are bigger, they've even started including windows.'

About seven in the morning I left with M. Steinhoff. 'So why are you in Burkina Faso?' I asked.

'Tradition. My grandfather was here as an administrator. Burkina – Upper Volta then – was part of the eastern region of French Sudan. My father came here. Tradition.'

Under the French, Dakar – the capital of French West Africa – governed eight countries and Togo, at the time a 'trusteeship territory' of the United Nations. French Equatorial Africa, on the other hand, had its governor-general in Brazzaville, now capital of the Congo, and covered another four countries together with another UN trusteeship, Cameroon. At the top was the Minister for the Colonies, a member of the French government. Under him came the governor-general. And under him came the governors of each country and their provincial and district officers.

The old administrators divided their area into 118 cercles or, I suppose, counties. Each cercle had to contribute 175 million francs in taxes and 21 million days work a year. How it was organised was left to the local commandants. Robert Delavignette, High Commissioner for French Cameroon, said they were like the natural daughters of a mother who refused to have anything to do with them: they were expected to survive on their own. He also explains in his book, *Freedom and Authority in French West Africa*, how the French sent out farmers experienced in working oxen and ploughs only to discover the Africans knew nothing about either. They used animals for sacrifice, not for working on the land. Fields were chosen not because they were fertile or suitable for different crops but because that's what the witchdoctor said. And they worked not as long as they had to but as long as the village decided they should.

The African chiefs came under the district officers. Depending on the chief, he either had a say in the running of his village or just took orders. Either way neither he nor his villagers had any say in how their country was run, but to be fair, the French encouraged the Africans to become French citizens. Once they had become French they were entitled to share in the administration of their country, be made a district or provincial officer or even governor, as well as vote in elections to the French Assembly. Trouble was few Africans became French, partly because few knew about the offer, partly because they had to be over eighteen, monogamous, educated in French, have completed their military service with the French and been in French employment for ten years. But at least it was possible . . .

'Don't forget,' said M. Steinhoff, 'we came to independence by a different route. In anglophone Africa it was simple, each country wanted independence. In francophone Africa it was more complicated.'

'You mean la plus grande France?'

'Certainly,' he continued. 'Houphouet, Senghor and the others thought they were bringing their parties and countries into France; that they were going to become part of France. Then gradually things changed. France after Vietnam and after its problems in Tunisia and Morocco seemed to lose confidence. They didn't seem as interested in having Africa as part of France. At the same time, the Africans saw what was happening with the anglophone countries and thought, Why go for part independence as part of France when we can have full independence on our own?'

'Makes sense.'

'Except that some leaders, especially Sekou Toure of Guinee, went a stage further. He wanted the French to grant independence to their two colonial empires, French West Africa and French Equatorial Africa, in their own right.'

'But of course the French were against it.'

'You bet. What chance would they have stood faced with two big French African power blocks? They preferred to give independence to fourteen separate little countries.'

'Then came Algeria ...'

'And the return of de Gaulle. Once he had given independence to Algeria there was nothing stopping the others, although the French had more ties with their old colonies than the British.'

'Like the CFA franc.'

'Defence agreements, ministries of co-operation, that kind of thing.'

We passed a stall selling slim-line masks produced by the Mossi. In Africa, it's a case of by their masks thou shalt know them. The Senufu in Côte d'Ivoire also produce slim, stylised masks. In Ghana, Benin, Nigeria and on through Cameroon and Zaire the masks become rounder and more confident. Perhaps it's because Ghanaians and Beninois are slim while the Zaireans are, well, different. In Ouaga once during their famous Do-Do Carnival which some say is a celebration of a Hausa tradition going back hundreds of years, others an excuse to celebrate the end of Ramadan three days early, I met a Belgian schoolteacher who was collecting masks of people saying their prayers.

The Mossi, one of the great West African tribes whose royal dynasty stretches back over 500 years and who compose about half the population, had it great until the French arrived. From the fifteenth century their kings ruled in Ouagadougou, Ouahigouya and elsewhere. But in 1896 their king fled to Dagomba, and from then on things got worse. First, the French forced the Mossi to work their big plantations in Côte d'Ivoire. Then the French changed the system, and sent them voluntarily to work the same plantations. Today instead of being forced or volunteered many still decide to work in Côte d'Ivoire or Ghana or Nigeria. The logic of economic necessity. They are free of both systems, but as you can see from the number of masks for sale, they need the work.

The road was getting more difficult, with enormous ruts and boulders. Then in the middle of nowhere we came across a group of people, men and women, young and old, sitting in an open-air classroom learning to read and write.

All over Burkina Faso I've seen peasants who a few weeks before couldn't read or write chalking up columns of accounts. It is going to take the Ministry of Peasant Affairs ten years before everybody is literate, but they have started. In one year alone they built 1,256 classrooms. Trouble is the more successful they are the more problems they create. As Sankara used to say, 'When we ask a province to build four schools, they end up building twelve, and we have to provide the chairs, tables, chalk and schoolmasters. But,' he added, 'perhaps it is better that the people are committed and enthusiastic, than if they pull back.'

Attendance rates at schools have jumped from 12 to 24 percent in one year, but behind the enthusiasm is the old Burkinabe trader's mentality. 'Before, the peasants didn't realise they were being cheated every time they sold their grain to the national cereal board. They were just given a piece of paper,' one official told me. 'Now they can check the amount they are paid against the weight. It's amazing how quickly people want to learn when they realise they can make money.'

'And,' I added, 'it stops the officials at the cereals board from cheating the peasants.'

'The country benefits,' he said.

'But does everybody want to learn? What about the women?'

'Of course. It is part of our revolution,' he said. 'But there are problems. Men don't like their wives coming to classes given by a male teacher. They get very worked up about that. Then, the women do all the hard work. If they come to classes, there is nobody to bring the water, prepare the food, look after the children. We also find that the women bring their children with them; there are no babysitters. You can imagine what it's like with dozens of children running around. It's very difficult.'

'But not impossible.'

'No. We're determined to succeed because if women can

read they can carry out simple health care, which saves a lot of problems for our health authorities and, of course, saves lives.'

We passed a group of huts surrounded by fetishes. Burkina Faso is a land of magic, of spirits, of secret cults, even of human sacrifices. Serious businessmen and politicians have warned me to be careful of certain villages or roads and never, never to sleep out in a village. The ancient Mossi resisted the spread of Islam, and most today still follow their animist religion. The same is true of the Gourmantches in the east, the Gourounsis along the border with Ghana, the Bobos in the south, the Senoufos along the Mali and Côte d'Ivoire border, and the still secretive and very traditional Lobis along the Ghana and Côte d'Ivoire borders.

In Ouaga I met a local Burkinabe who specialised in supplying the bits and pieces for the animist religion, and asked him if he knew anything about human sacrifices. Did he ever come across human fetishes?

He was matter-of-fact. 'There is a man in Nzerekore. He has human heads.'

'Where does he get them from?' I asked, a little taken aback.

'It is business. I don't ask him. I just tell him I have a customer, he gives me the heads.'

'Does he have people killed just to get their heads?'

'He probably gets them from dead bodies, cuts them up, probably the bones as well.'

'How much does a human head cost?'

'It depends on the age of person, whether it's a man or a woman or a child, what condition it's in. And, of course, it depends on who wants it.'

'How much would you charge me for a human head? An average one, not too young, not too old.'

'You I charge CFA 10,000.'

'But that's expensive.'

'Of course. I've got to live.' He was getting agitated.

'All right then,' I said, 'but you'll have to take my American Express card.' He walked away muttering something nasty. But I had made certain of one thing. If he is ever offered my head, he'll pay handsomely for it.

The heating gauge on the car was now firmly in the red.

Jean-Marie swung off the track and we parked under trees on the edge of a village somewhere near Possi. We walked across the patch of sand which served as a village green. Underneath a clump of trees was a wooden hut built on the sand – the local bar. We ordered a beer and came outside to sit on the rickety chairs. A smart young man introduced himself. He was working at the Institute for International Crops Research just outside Ouaga. They had started by researching ways of improving the yields of Africa's three major subsistence food crops, millet, cassava and sorghum. If you can't persuade African farmers to grow more productive crops, he said, you might as well make sure they get the best out of the ones they want to grow. Trouble was, the government and local farmers didn't like the results coming out of the Institute. For according to the young man, who looked like a teenage Sidney Poitier and smelt of those little refreshing tissues Air Afrique give you on long flights, all their research proved that as far as Africa was concerned millet was just about the last crop that any farmer should produce. Cassava, the whitish root, was better although yields were almost 50 percent lower in Africa than elsewhere. With new hybrids they have developed, he said, the Institute believed they could push up yields by a staggering eighteen times. In one experiment in Oyo, yields had gone up by 300 percent.

I asked an old man sitting nearby for his view. He shook his head. 'So what's your harvest like?' I asked him.

'Bad. Locusts.'

He blamed it on the government's mini-war with Mali. After a series of border clashes, the two governments had agreed a ten kilometre no-man's-land either side of the border. Which sounds fine, but in practice meant a ban on all aircraft – including planes spraying against grasshoppers. By the time the farmers had told their préfets and the préfets had told the ministry of agriculture and the ministry had been to the president, the grasshoppers had laid their eggs and it was too late. And with a female capable of producing nearly twenty million descendants in five months you can imagine the problem.

'If countries were ruled by farmers we would not have these problems,' he said.

I asked how they kept the locusts under control. 'We try, but we can't,' he said. 'But what about the Food and Agriculture Organisation? Don't they help?'

'They do their best for us. They try to discover the breeding grounds, they set up early warning control systems, spray all the time. It doesn't really help. Only one thing kills locusts,' he said. 'A drought.'

'But a drought will kill people and cattle as well,' I said.

'That's Africa.' He pulled a dirty bottle out of his pocket and took a gulp at it.

'What's that?' I asked. 'Whisky?'

'Medicine,' he said. It looked grey and very greasy.

'What for?' He grinned.

'I've met witchdoctors, or doctors in natural medicine all over West Africa. Lots of their herbs and natural remedies come from Burkina Faso, especially bosca senegalensis which features in many of their cures. After being out in the cold for so long, traditional medicine is becoming more respectable. The World Health Organisation in Geneva, for example, is co-ordinating research programmes into traditional medicine with universities and medical institutes around the world. For not only do they and other institutes see traditional medicine helping in the battle against disease, they also see it as a way of dramatically cutting the national drug import bills of many African countries as well as helping to increase their export earnings.

A new cough syrup recently developed by Dakar University's faculty of medicine, based on the Senegalese gueira plant could, for example, sell at half the price of an imported medicine and save nearly US $500,000 in foreign exchange. Other savings could be made by using the indigofer arrecta leaves boiled and drunk as tea to cure diabetes; cryptolepsis for malaria and an assortment of herbal medicines for asthma and sickle cell diseases. But traditional medicine faces two problems: first, credibility, although plant extracts are already used in 25 percent of all drugs; second, lack of development funds. Things are changing slowly. In some countries, Cameroon in particular, governments are setting up professional associations of traditional doctors to 'mobilise a new strategy to rectify the errors of the past and to remove all charlatans and crooks' from their ranks. But it will take time.

In the meantime there are many impressive traditional doctors, among them Komlan Amevor, an amazingly sprightly fifty-year-old Togolese modern medicine man who is gaining international scientific recognition for his knowledge and practice of herbal medicine. The president of Togo's National Association of Therapeutic Medicine and a member of their Association for Scientific Research, he studied at the University of Sussex from 1982–1985 and obtained his doctorate in natural medicine under Prof. Dr S.A. Buchanan, one of Britain's leading experts. He has written a definitive study on herbal medicine and diabetes. He lectures regularly. But he is more at home with his plants and herbal medicines. 'Of course there are charlatans,' he told me once at his surgery. 'They travel all over the country selling fake medicines and bogus herbal remedies.'

But it is becoming more difficult for them to survive. Governments are introducing stricter controls; patients are becoming more knowledgeable and selective. At the same time serious medicine is beginning to take a greater interest in the subject.

The WHO's Collaborative Centre for Traditional Medicine at the College Pharmacy, University of Illinois in Chicago, for example, is building up a worldwide computer database on natural medicines. Over 3,500 medicinal plants have been identified by the Chemical Science Faculty of the National University of Asuncion in Paraguay. The Institute of Pharmaceutical Biology in Munich is concentrating on herbs which cure heart and liver disorders, while the Medical and Pharmaceutical University in Toyama, Japan, is analysing the effect of herbs on everything from blood pressure to cancer.

As a scientist, Mr Amevor welcomes the daylight streaming into this once hidden world. For he is as much at home in his laboratory as he is roaming around Burkina looking for bosca senegalese. But most of all he prefers the time he spends in his tiny surgery treating the hundreds of people who queue up every day to be cured.

I asked him to tell me some of his cures. For sterility, he

recommends women take a dash of trichilia roka with a squirt of lemon every day for fourteen days or maybe the roots of the erythrina senegalensis in a litre of water every day for four days. For diabetes, it could be 25 grams of eligenia jamolana three times a day, and nothing is better for a headache than the bark of the newbuldia laevis ground to a powder with a sprinkling of piper guinneense fruit. Inhale that and within two minutes your headache is gone.

'Everything depends on being able to recognise the true symptoms. Once you have done that there is no reason why you cannot be cured by traditional medicines. There are different kinds of sterility, of diabetes. Once you know the symptoms you can make the tumour disappear, or dissolve the sugar in the system,' he told me.

And, of course, it depends on the right medicines. Not for Mr Amevor the mail order catalogues from international drug companies and the research seminars in Paris and Monte Carlo. He spends over four weeks every year searching for plants and herbs. Within a few minutes from his surgery in Rue Bedou near Lomé airport he can find hygrophilia auriculata. But for tamarindus indica he has to travel to the far north of Togo, for coccinia grandis to Niger. Afromosia laxiflorahe can only be found in Côte d'Ivoire and boscia senegalese in Burkina. With the demand for his services increasing all the time, he is trying to develop a network of herbal correspondents to keep him supplied.

Once you have the right medicine you have to decide the right quantities and formulae. Tapinanthus, for example, which is found everywhere in Africa and especially south of the Sahara, can be used for everything from female infertility to respiratory illness to mental disorders. Too much and witch-doctors can use it to induce trances. Too little, and it is as much use as taking Lucozade for a broken leg. Then you have to decide whether the medicines should be taken as powders, creams, pills or simply inhaled. Another doctor I met in Togo was so successful he had built up his own fetish hospital where he was looking after European as well as African patients.

Last time I saw Mr Amevor, I met Papa Pierre, an old soldier from Gabon, who had fought with the French in the First

World War. He was sitting in the shade outside the surgery wearing his only suit and his four campaign medals. It was around 80 degrees. Already he had been waiting for nearly two hours. Thousands, young and old, all over West Africa wait hours to see their local witchdoctor.

Papa Pierre wanted something to make him feel vigorous again. Mr Amevor's recommendation: the roots of the cassia sieberiana and some hymenocardia acida, mixed in water, heated with a little sugar and taken every morning for seven days.

The old Burkinabe farmer now drank the whole dirty, greasy bottle of medicine. He looked as though he was on fire. He danced a little jig then shuffled off into the trees.

I got up and looked at the car; the heating gauge was back to normal. We decided to continue, but after a few desperately slow kilometres we gave up. The road had all but disappeared into one enormous pothole. We turned back for Ouaga, hot, sweaty and caked in sand and dirt. Jean-Marie dropped me back at my hotel. I was desperate for a drink. I opened the fridge door – but suddenly I didn't feel thirsty any more.

If you really want to know what's going on in a country – the real country, not the government machine or the export community – don't ask the taxi drivers. They only talk to journalists. In any case, they'll only tell you what you want to hear. Ask the nuns. They know better than anyone whether the retail price index is rising or falling; whether the IMF is squeezing the economy too much; and whether there is going to be grumbling about price increases, riots or even coup attempts. They know it all, and they love to gossip. Not because they are political. I've never met a political nun. But because they are so wrapped up with the people in their clinics and schools. They know if the rains are a day late; if there are more locusts about than in previous years; if the price of sorghum is going up or down. They can tell you if the government's austerity programme is beginning to bite, and who is suffering most. I know some nuns who can tell you what the average family in the bush has to eat and which ministers feed their pet dogs better than their staff. Their contacts are enormous, their sources of information amazing. And unlike taxi drivers they always tell the truth.

After the episode on the plane, I decided to visit the nuns and see how they were getting on. Far from worrying about post-disaster depression they seemed more interested in getting ready for FESPACO, the bi-annual pan-African film festival. For Ouaga is to the developing world what Cannes is to the developed. It is the home of the Centre National du Cinéma, the Consortium Interafricain de Distribution Cinématographique, the Société de Production, and the Institut Africain d'Education Cinématographique, the only film school in francophone Africa. And film festivals anywhere are good for business, especially for restaurants run by nuns.

They were all talking about Idrissa Ouedraogo, a thirty-three-year-old Burkinabe director whose film, *Yam Daabo* (*The Choice*), an everyday story of love, jealousy and family hatred, had just been shown at Cannes, the first film from Burkina to be screened there.

When it started, FESPACO only managed to screen fifteen films from four countries. Today they screen no less then 250 films from twenty-five countries and attract over 40,000 people. There is an international jury and a comprehensive fringe programme featuring seminars discussing everything from 'cinema and cultural identity' to 'oral traditions and the new media'.

The brainchild of Madame Alimata Salembere, a former television presenter in Burkina and France, the festival is firmly supported by the government. Sankara used to wax lyrical about the importance of the African cinema and how it must be protected against cultural aggression. Compaore is more businesslike about it, but nonetheless enthusiastic.

The trouble is it's an industry without a market. For in spite of the growing number of African film makers, led by Souleymane Cisse, the Malian director who won the prix du jury at Cannes in 1987 for his film *Yeelen* – the *Financial Times* called it the first masterpiece of African cinema – African films are rarely seen in Africa, Europe or the States. Perhaps because, as the *FT* said about *Yeelen*, that are 'like watching a ballet from outer space performed underwater without subtitles.' A Cameroonian actor, Gerard Essomba, has been doing his best to change this by trying to persuade governments the cinema is a huge untapped source of revenue and foreign investment so they should pump in public funds to get the cameras rolling. Not surprisingly, none of them is biting. So African cinema looks like being more Out of Africa than inside.

But instead of going to the pictures one of the sisters had to go to Kongoussi, the capital of Bam province about 100 kilometres away. I didn't fancy watching a ballet from outer space so I asked if I could go with her.

Ouagadougou is one of Africa's oldest cities. It is pleasant, relaxed and friendly. Very sandy. Lots of trees. All divided up into squares. As we drove along, I asked if the nuns in Ouaga, like those I had met all over francophone Africa, knew what was going on.

'The children come to our schools, the mothers come to our clinics. They tell us everything,' she said. 'They tell us whether they are getting enough to eat, whether they are working too hard. They tell us what the girls are selling their goods for in the street and whether people can afford the prices.'

'And do they tell you if they can't?' I asked.

'They don't have to. There's not much spare on these people. If they are going hungry, we can tell. The father of one of our boys is chauffeur to a minister. We know what his programme is for next week. At Christmas we can tell you how many pots of caviar he got from the Russian ambassador,' she said with a twinkle.

'What's it like when times are hard?'

'Terrible. They become very quiet, as if they are withdrawing into themselves and want to be alone. They are not very lively people; God knows they don't have the energy to go running around. They are barely able to survive. But once that survival limit starts to drop they are very quickly in trouble. We sense it. If there is trouble coming you can almost feel the tension. These people can teach us a lot. They have nothing, but they survive and they have their dignity.'

'What gets them really uptight?'

'Any increase in the price of bread. They seem able to take

anything else. If petrol goes up they just walk. They don't mind as much as we would. But bread affects everybody. One of our sisters has just come from Lagos. She said the same thing happens there. As soon as the government even thinks of doing anything about bread prices, it's as if an electric current goes through the whole country. People try not to talk to each other.'

'You mean a word out of place . . .' I told her about my word out of place. I'm always careful of beggars. Some are so deformed you can't refuse, but the abled-bodied down-and-outs are different. But once I saw a poor wizened old man, a big scar on his cheek, wearing a sweaty brown robe, kneeling by the entrance to a petrol station in Niger, his skullcap on the pavement beside him. I dropped a couple of hundred CFAs into his hat and muttered, Bonjour monsieur. He jumped up and chased me down the street. I thought he was going to attack me for only giving him a pittance, but he said he was a director of the Central Bank and was saying his prayers and certainly didn't need any financial assistance from me.

'Oh definitely,' she smiled. 'A wrong word and the place could explode.'

As we turned into one village and stopped in the market square a young boy with one arm and no legs was propelling himself along on a primitive skateboard. Roughly 10 percent of the country's population was mentally or physically disabled, the nun told me. Around 25 percent were affected by disabilities either directly or indirectly, by having to look after somebody disabled. Yet, she said, nearly half the disabilities could have been prevented. 'Forty percent of cases of cerebral palsy can be prevented. Eighty percent of blind people can be cured,' she said. 'Guineaworm – from 60 percent incidence it can be cut to zero in two seasons.'

'But why aren't they?'

'Money. It doesn't cost much, compared to how much is spent on other things. A piece of nylon cloth, that's all you need to reduce the transmission of guineaworm. But the money is not there so we have to cope with the consequences.'

And they were coping very well. 'First, we must immunise people. Then we must prevent accidents. It's amazing how many people are disabled for life just because they didn't take enough care or because the little factories they were working in did not take enough care of them. There aren't many factories in Africa, but I am convinced the rate of industrial accidents is higher than in any other country. And we must also improve the standard of medical treatment; many people, plenty of babies and children are injured as a result of treatment. Many disabilities are caused because mothers are not looked after properly before or after they give birth. Babies are injured because of the way they are born and the way they are treated afterwards.'

I wondered what conditions were like for the handicapped. 'We are trying to get disabled people to play an active part in the community. It's difficult, but possible,' she said. 'Not every disabled person wants to sit on a street corner selling matches. We want them to lead as normal a life as they can. Maybe it's more difficult in Africa, but it is important that we try. We must stop people thinking of what they can't do. They can't play football, or carry heavy loads. We have to get people, disabled and able-bodied, thinking of what they *can* do. A disabled man might not be able to walk but he can make wood carvings or jewellery or answer the telephone.'

'How do you find them? How do you decide who to train?'

'As always, we must get the children. If you get people when they are young you can help them shape their lives. It's too easy for a disabled child to disappear into the shadows of his family. The family don't know how to look after him. If we find him we can help him accept his disability and make the most of his life.'

I know many statistics on Africa, but Sister was the first to tell me the ratio of patients per psychiatrist. 'In the United States,' she said, 'there are 80 patients per psychiatrist. In Nigeria there are 20,000. But in sub-Sahara Africa there are 600,000 patients per psychiatrist. Don't you think that's shocking?'

To be honest, it had never occurred to me. My mother had been a mental nurse and I had grown up visiting patients in mental institutions. But I never thought of psychiatrists and Africa.

'Some people say that 1 percent of the world population

suffers from some form of severe psychiatric disorder. That means 40 million people need mental health care. Other people say 18 percent – 720 million people – have a psychiatric disorder. Yet there is virtually no one to look after them – especially in Africa.' What about neurology? 'The problem is just as great, but there are even fewer specialists. It's impossible.'

'But surely in Africa people are looked after by their families?'

'Of course, and the level of care is usually very good, certainly compared with the way we treat our people. But it is not clinical care.'

'Have you the resources to provide clinical care? Surely not?'

'That doesn't mean we mustn't try. Trouble is nobody is interested in mental health care. People will give you tractors and steelworks and maybe schoolbooks, but nobody will donate a psychiatric hospital. In fact if you offered a psychiatric hospital to an African country they would probably turn you down. The governments want to look the other way as much as the donors.'

'But isn't it a question of priorities? Feed the body, then feed the mind.'

'You can find arguments for anything. My point is there are millions of people in the bush needing proper clinical attention. At the moment, they are kept in the corner of the hut.'

She was right. I've seen old men shouting at trees and cursing the sky. I went to a government reception once which featured a folklore group. In the middle of the group was a very old man with a fly whisk in his hand and an old hat on his head. Apart from that he was stark naked. A young boy, maybe his grandson, was leading him. The man was obviously in need of treatment, but it was interesting to see how he was being looked after by his family.

'The amazing thing is it doesn't cost a fortune to treat the majority of cases. Tranquillisers, anticonvulsants, even antidepressants are relatively cheap. You don't even need a doctor to administer them, they can be given by health workers. Chloropromazine, used for acute schizophrenia, is cheap and easy to administer. It would make a world of difference to maybe millions of people. But there isn't enough money for even a limited supply. And nobody cares. Everyone is interested in defence and weapons; they want schools and colleges; they want money for agriculture. Sure, they're important. All I'm saying is that some money should be found to help these poor people.'

I asked whether the witchdoctors could help. 'A great deal, but not in any systematic way. Witchdoctors mix herbs and potions. Usually nothing happens, but sometimes they hit lucky. If they do, they are a great help. But more important are the midwives, not just for delivering babies but for the health of the family as a whole. Most women now have either a trained midwife or a village midwife. The good ones have a look at the rest of the family, maybe even other families in the village. They are often the only trained medical people the villagers ever see. We are trying to develop this contact to help identify the psychiatric problems; then see whether we can develop some form of basic mental health care service.'

I asked her how local people had reacted to the coup.

'I told you when times are tense everybody is very polite for fear of upsetting each other. The same is true of people driving. If prices are being increased and everybody feels angry, they tend to drive much more slowly and carefully.'

'For fear of having an accident?'

'And causing a row. Or worse, injuring or killing somebody.'

'You mean, a car crash could have that effect?'

'Oh certainly. One word and the whole town could be on the streets. It's very frightening.'

'What can you do about it?'

'Pray. And stay out of trouble. That's how we lost one of our cars. One of the nuns knocked a cyclist over last time things were tense. Didn't injure him, didn't really damage the bicycle, but the man was very angry. The crowd surrounded the car and started shouting at the Sister. She went up to the cyclist, apologised and gave him the car as a present.'

'Gave him the car!'

'It was the best thing to do. The cyclist was no longer angry. The crowd calmed down. They saw Sister had more than apologised. It took their breath away. They tried to talk her out of it, but she insisted.'

'So one of your Sisters saved the government,' I said.

'She preserved the peace. That's what counts.'

CAMEROON

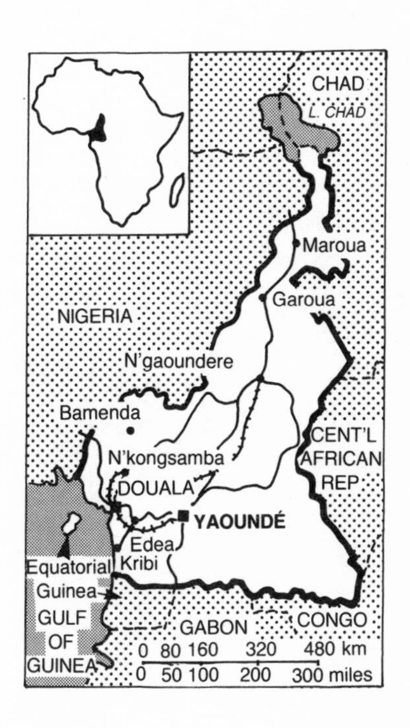

CHAD
L. CHAD
Maroua
Garoua
NIGERIA
N'gaoundere
Bamenda
N'kongsamba
DOUALA
YAOUNDÉ
Edea
Kribi
CENT'L
AFRICAN
REP
Equatorial
Guinea
GULF
OF
GUINEA
GABON
CONGO
0 80 160 320 480 km
0 50 100 200 300 miles

An enormous German rottweiler, thick and muscular, came bounding down the path towards me. I froze instantly. Dogs I like, but this was a Hund out of Hell. Definitely not verbraucher freundlich.

'Ist zoft. Like bébé,' shouted an enormous Brunhilde. 'Voodn't arm vlea.'

'Natürlich,' I mumbled. For my sins I had met a group of German birdwatchers at the airport at Douala. It was their first visit to Cameroon, where they were hoping to spot the rare Shelley's Eagle Owl. Cameroon being an old German colony – Kamerun – they thought everybody would speak German. When I saw them they were looking utterly helpless, so I asked if they needed help. In spite of my bad French and bad German I was immediately adopted. I steered them through customs, organised taxis, helped them change their money and packed them off to their hotel. 'Zoo kindt. Ist zoo kindt,' they kept saying.

No sooner had I checked into the Akwa Palace than I received a telephone call from the local German African bird expert thanking me for helping his friends – he had been delayed by police checks from getting to the airport on time – and inviting me to dinner. He would send a car at six o'clock. And at six a big white Mercedes arrived driven by Douala's answer to Oddjob. Birdwatching was obviously a profitable business. We drove out towards Garoua. I ended up somewhere round the back of the bus station in a grand house surrounded by practically the whole German community of Cameroon. Our host, a fat little Bavarian, was the local director for a big German explosives manufacturer. I kept asking if he was selling a lot of explosives which struck me as a more useful political indicator for Africa than many other figures reeled off by economists, but he insisted on talking about his dog. They had brought him out from Stuttgart for protection, but at first he was just too successful.

'Nobody kom near us,' he told me, 'zay terrified, not used to dogs. Zoon as zay zee him zay vlee. Zee boys always haff lunch in yard. But ven Wastl zee zem he ran towards zem. Zay vlee leaving food. He eat their lunch. Vun boy tries, how you zay, own back. He leave food behind – sehr hot. Covered with spicy zauce. Virst time he eat it down in one go. It explode inside him.'

'Boy-eez. Verry bat,' said Brunhilde. 'He start howling. He trink lots of wasser. Boys sehr delighted. But next day he back for more.'

'They left some more for him?'

'Now they all friends. Wastl now used to food. He eats hot sauces. They luff him. They no more frightened of him.'

But did anybody ever try to eat him, I wondered, because in many parts of Africa dog meat is rated a delicacy. 'Mein Gott, nein. Eat Wastl. Never. Zee idea,' he said.

Did he ever try and eat anything himself? 'We have lots problems at first. He just luff zose little goats zat run around. He chase them, he dig teeth in, give zem shake, break zair necks.'

'Didn't their owners complain?' I asked.

'Nein.'

'You mean they were frightened to say anything?'

He hesitated. 'Well, ja, I suppose.'

'So how many did he kill?'

'Don't know. Vier or fünf.' Which probably meant eight or ten. To the struggling African it represented quite a slice of their income. For many families look upon their petites chèvres much as European peasant farmers look upon their pigs: they're easy to look after, cheap to feed but can produce a good meal. Perhaps more important to many African families, their little goats can double up as voodoo sacrifices. Many a throat is cut to mark the opening of a new house or luxury hotel. I wondered how they managed to stop this friendly dog of theirs wiping out generations of African culture.

'We tried keeping him in house but it make him mad,' said Wastl's Vater. 'Then we try locking him in garden but ee keep leaping over vall. We not keep him in a cage. Zat's nicht gut life for him.'

'But it's no life for the little goats either,' I said.

'But ee not kill zem now. Wastl teach people here to be gut farmers. Zay all happy now, everybody luff im.' This was getting complicated. 'People tink if vee not lock Wastl up, zay lock zair goats up ozzervise zay get kilt. Und vor virst time zay start veeding zem properly, not letting zem run around eating scraps ...'

'So the goats get fatter faster ...'

'Und start breeding. Vich means zay haff enough for themselves, enough to take to market.'

It was an amazing story, how one savage hound could transform a little community. I was almost tempted to give him a pat on the head for his services to Afrikapolitik. But I resisted the temptation. He still looked sehr vicked to me.

There was a West German parliamentary delegation in town and we were all invited to meet them at a reception. The East Germans had been there the previous week trying to persuade the government to open an embassy. In return, they were promising to open their own embassy in Yaounde. They were also talking about big aid programmes, teams of agricultural advisers and squads of technical assistants. The West Germans, as a result, were out to trump everything and throwing in scholarships, exchange visits, even a couple of state visits.

The leader of the delegation, a particularly earnest member of parliament, was accompanied by three dedicated civil servants. When we joined them, the MP was talking about his visit to President Biya. He said he was impressed by the presence of the man, his grasp of international affairs and his attention to detail. He also said he liked the 'soo-it' the president was wearing. I didn't blink, let alone say a word. Who am I to talk about pronunciation? Not so a junior protocol official from the foreign ministry.

'It's not pronounced soo-it,' he said. 'It's pronounced suit.'

There was silence. The German drew himself up to his full Prussian dignity. 'Let me tell you,' he replied in clipped, Oxford English, 'I studied at Heidelberg University and it is soo-it.'

'It looks like soo-it,' said the protocol official, 'but it is pronounced suit.' Then he turned to me. 'You're English. Tell him it's suit.'

Before I could even think of ignoring his plea, the German went berserk. 'Nobody has ever corrected my English before. I have been speaking English for twenty-five years, all over the world. My professor was Herr Doktor Bauer. He told me it was soo-it. Soo-it it is.'

'What do you say?' repeated the protocol official, impervious to this tirade.

'I'm afraid,' I said in my best casual manner, 'soo-it is not a soo-itable English pronunciation.'

'It cannot be,' shouted the German, oblivious to my wit, 'You are wrong. Professor Doktor Bauer was an expert on English. He translated Shakespeare. Soo-it. It is soo-it. You are wrong.' Then he turned and I swear with the slightest click of the heels disappeared out of the room.

'Typical German,' said a Cameroonian government minister. 'You can't tell them anything.'

'You not understand,' said the explosives manufacturer. 'Zat vas German joke. He knows it suit. Natürlich. Ho ho.'

'A German joke is no laughing matter,' I said.

'English,' he said slapping me on the back. 'Sehr funny.'

'I know German joke,' said another Cameroonian. 'So during the last war there was this big beauty competition in Germany,' he began. 'They wanted to elect a Miss Germany. So they asked all the contestants what was their ambition. They all said, Make love to Adolf Hitler . . .' The Germans looked at each other and spluttered nervously. I wondered whether to disappear. 'So there was a big cheer each time one of the girls said, Make love to Adolf Hitler.' The Cameroonian ploughed on. 'So this girl comes on stage and the master of ceremonies asks who she would most like to make love to. She says, Winston Churchill.' The Germans choked with stifled laughter.

'So the master of ceremonies says, "Why Winston Churchill?" And she says, "Because he said he would do it on the beaches, he would do it in the air, he would ..."' The whole room explodes with laughter. '"... Do it in the streets, he would do it in the fields and ...'" the Cameroonian paused for breath, '"he would never withdraw."'

There was an even greater explosion, which could probably have been heard all over Bavaria.

After that, we started discussing the Germans, how they behaved in Africa; how difficult they were to work with; how detailed everything had to be compared to the French who seemed pretty relaxed. Then, everybody started praising the English. Not for anything we did in Africa, just for being English.

Standing next to me was a German businessman who had been running plantations all over Cameroon for over twenty years. His family had even lived there when it was Kamerun. He knew Africa inside out, but he kept coming back to Cameroon. This time he was trying to sell the government solar-powered mills. I asked why he liked the country.

'The people are quiet. They leave you alone,' he said. 'None of this sickly sweet hollow stuff.'

'You mean protocol à la française?' I said.

'Can't stand it. The people here are very serious. They are also nervous and unsure of themselves. They have done very well, but they know they are living in the shadow of Nigeria. The border with Nigeria is long and wide open. The Yarubas come and go as they please. They are scared of the Yarubas. Put them in a room with a Yaruba and they won't say a word. They think they'll be eaten alive. Which they probably would be. For generations they have been wary of Yarubas. It must be difficult for them to shake it off.'

'Is it just the Yarubas who make them think twice?'

'No, it's really all strangers. They are very scared of robbers. The rich turn their homes into virtual fortresses.'

That day's *Cameroon Tribune* had said there had been thirty-six armed robberies and nine murders in the previous three months. Robbers were bursting into banks wild-west style, guns blazing. Tourists had been gunned down in the street. A British Telecom engineer had been chased to his hotel and stabbed to death at the door.

'These insincere and lawless men went on striking terror here and there perhaps because they benefited from the protection of some highly placed persons,' it said. But the police had already arrested twenty of the most dangerous criminals, including Oum alias Jackson, the leader of the gang. Still at large, however, were Ngwa Yves, Dani Backo, Pom Pon alias Maux de Têtes and Fonkoua Albert alias Bebey Mambou alias Chocolate alias Chinois, Cameroon's most wanted man.

Violence is something the francophones are only just beginning to experience. In the streets, that is. In the home, survey after survey shows wife beating is still very popular. A few years ago muggings and break-ins were unheard of. Now, probably because of the lack of money in the economy, the return of especially many young people from Europe and elsewhere, the growth of a more obvious middle class and maybe even the influx of expats and tourists, it's becoming more evident. As in everything francophone, Abidjan seems to be setting the pace. Any member of the French community knows somebody who has been robbed or attacked. Officially, of course, the government denies everything. Armed assaults, they maintain, are down on the previous year. Unofficially, they are worried about the increasing numbers of small arms which are cheap and easy to obtain. They are also terrified in case the tens of thousands of Shia Muslims in their midst get restless.

The Cameroonians were maybe not as professional as the Ivoirians so what were they like as businessmen, I asked.

'Very good. Straightforward. Not like the Zairois who are only interested in what's in it for themselves. The very big businessmen, like James Onobiono, are as good as businessmen anywhere. And they don't care who they do business with. Zaire, Angola . . .'

'South Africa?'

'Then they are very careful. They are not as open as, say, the Zairois. But they'll do business with them. Trading. Nothing big. Shipping.'

I had heard rumours about companies laundering South African goods. This seemed as good a time as any to try and find out if the stories were true. 'You mean simple re-labelling, re-packaging jobs,' I said. 'False papers, false documentation, that kind of thing?'

He grinned broadly. 'No. You don't do that kind of thing in Cameroon. Côte d'Ivoire, Benin, yes, even Dakar. But you don't try that here.'

'Because you'd get caught?'

'No. Because they won't do it.'

'You mean they're honest?'

'They don't seem to look for the angles. Probably because there aren't the same number of Lebanese as in other countries.'

I'm always interested in dodges, from the academic point of view of course. I asked about re-labelling. It's a common trick to ship into an African country, say, thousands of T-shirts from China, get local out-workers to turn up the hem and stitch in a label saying it was made in the country, and ship it to the US or Europe as a local product and escape all duties. In Mali or Niger or Mauritania it would obviously be suspicious, but in Côte d'Ivoire, Senegal or even Cameroon you could get away with it.

'Sure, it's done,' he said, 'but nowadays you've got to be a bit clever. Governments are more switched on. Foreign embassies are watching out.'

'You mean spying?'

'Yes, spying. Everybody is protecting their own markets. The Americans are not going to let you ruin their market without trying to do something about it.'

'But how can they stop you?'

'Easy. If I suddenly ship in a million T-shirts and re-label them everybody is going to know. The following day I'll get a visit from the American ambassador, who'll inform US customs. They'll simply ban all imports. You've got to be subtle.'

'How can you be subtle?'

'First, you go to a country which is already making T-shirts. Millions of them. Such as Malta,' he said. 'The T-shirt capital of the world after China.'

'And then?'

'You fix to ship in, say, four containers a week of T-shirts.

You give them to the local textile factories. They'll do it because it's business.'

'But why won't the Americans find out?'

'Because it's a tiny proportion of the millions they are already producing legally. The factory staff won't know, customs officials won't realise. The only people who will know are the people running the factory. And they will do it because it means extra money for them, paid offshore. And the people who put the deal together. And an innocent importer/exporter who handles the paperwork.'

'How does that work?'

'Well you can't just bring that kind of quantity into a country or take it out again without the documentation. Somebody has to launder it, as they say.'

'So how is that done?'

'Through Switzerland. You place an order on the manufacturer, some factory in China or Hong Kong. You ask them to deliver to wherever. They deliver. You then get your customer to place their order on another company –'

'In Switzerland, or the Isle of Man . . .'

'Then they place another order on the African company. The African company supplies and all the paperwork shows that it is a genuine export.'

Later, I talked to an art dealer from Bonn and an official with the German Development Service. The art dealer wanted to talk about his gallery which was devoted to works of art from the Third World; the official about their experiment building low-cost health clinics with local materials.

'People think African art is nothing but masks and statues. That is not true. There are many young African painters experimenting and developing their individual styles. Our gallery, Boutique du Tiers-Monde, is helping to give them a wider audience, to encourage people to take their work seriously.'

The GDS official was much more difficult to understand. He kept talking about vernacular buildings and indigenous materials and technology-sound construction and standardised low-rise concrete-frame systems. But what I think he was trying to say was interesting. Instead of importing all the latest building materials from Europe at an enormous price just to put up simple buildings, why not use local materials? It was quicker, simpler and much cheaper.

Using this system he told me he had just built a clinic in Batie-Nord, Burkina Faso. I told him about my visit to Ouagadougou. A well had been dug in the December so that the villagers could make their own bricks. Three brickmakers and four bricklayers were trained. On January 3 they had started work. The mud bricks were stabilised with Portland cement and made by hand using a mechanical press. Instead of straight doors and windows, everything was arched so that lintels were not required. Instead the bricks formed arches. By April 4, the building was finished.

'But more important even than the building is the confidence and skills it brings to the local people. One of our bricklayers has now set himself up as a contractor and is putting up buildings all over the country.'

Nobody can say the Germans were not interested in doing their best in Africa. Within a few years of moving into Togo in 1884, for example, they had built nearly 800 miles of roads and 324 schools and installed a telephone service. They even came up with a scheme to irrigate the Sahara by – now listen to this – building a dam at either end of the Mediterranean, one at Gibraltar, the other in the Bosphorus. The Mediterranean would link Europe to Africa and be renamed Atlantropa. North Africa and the Sahara would be fertile again and produce £1 billion worth of crops a year. Germany would then build a railway network covering Europe, Atlantropa and Africa linking Berlin with Cape Town.

Many Africans today rate them as good colonisers although very strict and tough. I've met some old Cameroonians and Togolese who even served in the German army. One Togolese in Anécho, near where the Germans signed their treaty with local chiefs, even showed me the medals he won during the First World War. 'Good masters. Good organisation. Everybody worked. The Germans are very good,' he told me. 'Very good at building – thick, strong walls. Even today they can't knock down the buildings put up by the Germans.'

When the Germans first arrived in Africa they had no

experience of either running colonies or the Africans. At first they treated the Cameroonians as slaves of the mighty German empire, a conquered people with no rights. Some Africans might have liked it that way but the German people didn't. In 1907 there was uproar in the German parliament and the whole system was humanised. The Germans decided to start running their colonies along British lines. Which might have been good for the Africans or not.

By 1914, however, Germany was at war with its teacher of colonial administration. In Togo, Britain and France defeated Germany within days. In Cameroon it took until 1916. Both countries then came under temporary British and French administration. In 1919 they were handed over to the League of Nations, which in turn entrusted them to the British and the French. Somehow, the larger eastern sections of the two countries came under the French as well as the railway systems built by the Germans to open up the interiors. The French set up separate organisations to administer their sections. The British ran Togoland as if it was part of the Gold Coast and Cameroon as if it was part of Nigeria. Come the 1939–45 war the League of Nations ceased to exist and the two countries were administered by France and Britain as trustees for the United Nations. Problems came in 1956. The UN decided each country should have a referendum to decide its future. British Togoland voted to join Ghana. French Togoland remained French and in 1960 was given complete independence by France. In Cameroon it was more complicated.

Because it was an old League of Nations mandate, which in 1946 became a UN trusteeship, instead of demanding independence from France like all the other francophones were doing, Cameroon was asking France to carry out its 'missionary trust' and release it from its apron strings. But no deal. French settlers were against it, France was against it. There the matter rested until 1948 when a young trade union leader, Reuben Um Nyobe, launched his Union of the Populations of Cameroon, one of the first African nationalist parties. The French wanted it destroyed. They harassed the leaders so much as well as banning their meetings that they drove Um Nyobe and his supporters to switch from peaceful to violent means to achieve their aim. Far from helping their cause, this split the country along tribal lines. Um Nyobe fought a low-key guerilla action from bases in forests in the south of the country while the rest, including Ahmadou Ahidjo and his Movement for the Union of Cameroon, either looked the other way or supported the French. Um Nyobe was killed by a French military patrol in 1958. Two years later Ahidjo won 60 out of 100 seats in the parliamentary election and became president.

But today I get the impression Germany can't make up its mind what to do about Africa. They feel they *should* be in Africa, but they are not happy about what they are doing, about what people are saying about them. The only German I have ever come across who was happy about Africa was Franz-Josef Strauss, who seemed to revel in being Germany's unofficial minister for Africa and a super-frontman for Bavarian industry, building breweries here, landing construction contracts there and fixing trade deals everywhere.

Finally they brought some food round – weisswurst, flown in specially from Munich, and blutwurst, which somebody had once told me resembled 'a cross-section through a dead dachshund'. I grabbed a slice and bit into it. They were right.

'Luff und piss. Dat is all I need. Verstehen sie?'

I turned round sharply. I wondered what Brunhilde was talking about. 'Luff und piss,' she was saying to the slightly flustered Cameroonian minister. 'A-pee-noos. I want a-pee-noos,' she breathed all over him. He looked at me for help. I fled.

I was now introduced to a German businessman who had been dealing with Cameroon for fifteen years. I asked him what they were like as businessmen.

'They are very good traders. It's been in their blood for generations. The Bamileke are among the best in the world; they can stand up alongside your Ibos, Americans, Jews, Lebanese. But they don't understand anything else, like banking. Of course they understand current accounts and deposits, but they don't understand how you can use banks. I know big businessmen, billionaires, who keep everything on deposit. I know one man who wants to buy a plane. He saves up money in the bank, then he buys it – cash. He doesn't understand anything about financing and gearing and leverage.'

'Shares and stock markets?'

'Not an idea. They don't really want to understand it. They want to keep everything cash or on deposit or in property. Sure they use Swiss banks, Japanese banks, but it is still primitive financing.'

We freshened our glasses. 'I was negotiating to buy an African company recently,' he told me. 'Nice business, been running twenty years, turnover about US $1 million. Making losses, but it had potential. I could turn it round and make money. I go to the chairman, who owns the company and has built it up. He says he wants to sell, he can't afford to keep losing money. We go round and round in circles. He tells me about his children, his village, how he started in business, the ministers he knows, everything but about the business. Eventually I ask how much he wants for it. He said US $20 million.'

'But that's crazy.'

'Exactly. Do you know what he said? He said he should have taken US $1 million out of the company each year he'd been running it, but it never made enough. This was his chance to get the money.'

'But about the assets, how much it's making, its losses ...'

'Not interested. All mumbo-jumbo to him.'

'So what did you do?'

'I offered him US $200,000.'

'What did he say?'

'He rang and said he'd take it. But he noticed that my secretary had made a mistake typing the figures.'

The party over, as the fleet of Mercedes came to a stop outside Wastl's house, three men were racing up the street shrieking. Brunhilde and husband dashed into the house. I caught up with them in the lounge standing over the Hund out of Hell who was slumped in the corner choking all over the carpet.

'Mine littel hund. Zey haf kilt him,' shrieked Brunhilde.

'He's gasping for breath,' I said. 'He's got something caught in his throat.'

Papa prised his mouth open and pushed his fingers inside. 'Das ist right. Zere ist zomtink zair,' he said.

'Try and dislodge it.'

'Ist stook,' he said. 'Nicht possible.' The dog was whimpering and reaching. I thought his eyes were going to pop out of his head. 'Got it,' he said. 'Ist coming.' Then out on the carpet plopped five or six greasy lumps, like half-chewed lumps of blutwurst.

'Zat ist food,' he said, picking one up and examining it.

'Ist nicht food,' blurted Brunhilde. 'I gif him never food like zis.'

I kicked one of the lumps over.

'Vingers. Zay ist vingers,' she shrieked. 'Zay tried kill my bébé mit der vingers!'

The railway station in Douala is unbelievably modern, like a cross between a space station and an Ivoirian cathedral. Everything is clean and bright, and so new they have not had time to put up signs. Not only is it impossible to find out which train I need, I can't even find the platform. Eventually by asking and asking I get my bearings. I follow an old man, who keeps stopping to look at an imaginary watch on his wrist, down a flight of stairs. Halfway down, I spot a dilapidated, filthy, wooden-box railway carriage and instinctively think all the thoughts I shouldn't think. But another two steps and I see the most modern, most glamorous train I have ever seen. A smart young lady takes my ticket and escorts me to my seat. Am I dreaming?

This is Cameroon's new, up-to-date, privatised railway line to Yaounde, the capital in the north, financed by the Canadians and built by the Italians. In the old days there was only a narrow muddy road linking Douala and Yaounde, which was often closed because of the rains. In 1985 they built a road which cut travelling time to three hours. Now this superb railway.

The train slowly fills up. Every passenger is escorted to their seat and wished a good trip. African trains were never like this. A businessman sitting opposite me sees my amazement. 'It's all privatised,' he whispers. 'Even the reception and hostesses. They all come from a private company.' He buries his head in his papers.

For me Cameroon is a serious country; hardworking, dour,

and very staid compared to other francophone nations. Which probably has something to do with their Teutonic heritage. You can buy bread in the market, order a beer in a restaurant or even have a letter typed for you at one of the big open-air typing pools that spring up outside government offices in Yaounde and nobody will say a word to you. They take your money and give you your change without as much as a bonjour or merci. Even the children begging in the streets just shuffle up and stand waiting to be recognised. In other countries, they shout and plead. At the most in Cameroon they will murmur a polite 'Cadeau' and whisper a fragile 'Merci, monsieur'.

It is now 6.15 am. On the dot, the train puffs away from the station. If only my train to London was like this: beautiful upholstery, no dust, most definitely no cigarettes or ash. The staff are friendly and helpful and courteous. And so are the passengers. The conductor comes along and says bonjour to us. We all bonjour him back. Nothing like the 6.50 from Buxted, East Sussex. Out of the window – which is actually clean; no graffiti or rude words – I can see people hurrying to work. They scramble over the tracks, dodge between moving trains and duck between the carriages. Further away, the roads are filling up with buses and cars. Everywhere there are people, some striding out, others shuffling along unwillingly. Few seem to be talking to each other. Douala seems to lack the joie de vivre of other francophone cities. All along the line are flimsy huts and wooden houses. Old cars are piled up everywhere. Enormous puddles flow between the houses and the cars and the junk. The rain must have been heavier than I thought.

The ticket collector comes along, smart in his new uniform. He asks whether we want to visit the Panoramique. 'The dining car, sir. Breakfast is now being served.'

The wooden shacks have given way to lush vegetation. The train is still not going very fast, but it is sounding its horn all the time.

'Our people are not used to trains yet,' says the businessman opposite who can obviously read my thoughts. 'The driver is telling them we are coming. You cannot be too sure.'

We go straight through the first station. Old warehouses slip by on either side. Some more tin shacks. The view is now opening up and I can see right across Douala: tall office buildings, wide, straight roads. The city looks efficient, which is probably half the battle.

Now the train begins to pick up speed. The ticket collector insists on showing us how the little table works. Then he declares that the seats are not good enough and runs off to find us better ones, despite our protests that we are very comfortable. I feel the train definitely going faster; we're heading for open country. Back comes the inspector. He apologises; he can't find any other seats. Then he says that on behalf of the company he would like to treat us to breakfast. Would we do him the honour of joining him? How could anybody refuse an invitation to breakfast by a railway ticket inspector? Usually I'm on my knees pleading with them to serve me.

The restaurant car isn't the Orient Express, but it is bright, clean, almost functional. The service is superb, and no wonder. Standing behind the counter are four girls and two boys. I only have to say, 'coffee' and it is there; croissants too. I wish I had ordered a grand traditional English breakfast, for I'm certain it would have appeared, piping hot, before I could have got the words out. The inspector, beaming with pride, told me again how long it had been operating, how it was quicker than flying to Yaounde and, by the way, had anybody shown us how to operate the sunblinds.

A senior official at the Douala Chamber of Commerce joined me for breakfast. He put down on the table *Swing*, a French comic book he was obviously reading. It was a bit like seeing the head of the Africa section of the London Chamber of Commerce reading *Superman.* He was a very educated man, fluent in three or four languages, had travelled the world, yet he was still reading comics. Later I discovered this was far from unusual in Cameroon. BDs, or bandes dessinées, are very popular among adults in francophone Africa and in mainland France. The most popular is Tintin, who is in fact Belgian. His BDs sell like gâteaux chauds everywhere. Others include Gaston la Gaffe, some frightful office boy, and worse still Robert Bidochon, a Gallic Andy Capp. Of BDs for women the worst is Carmen Cru, an old lady who is forever getting into trouble. There are even some BDs printed in Italy which, I am told, are very adult indeed. We spoke about the train – everybody was so proud of the service. He didn't want to fly ever again.

The train was now passing huge terraced embankments, which petered out into forests. Cameroon is recognised for its rainforests. Korup, which covers 125,000 hectares, about the size of Greater London, in the south west, is not only Africa's oldest tropical rainforest but according to the World Wildlife Fund the richest and most important of the 158 in the continent. It is home to thousands of plant species – 90 medicinal and chemical substances have been identified to date in plants from Korup, 28 of them unknown to scientists; 500 different trees, 17 also previously unknown; 150 different species of freshwater fish and goodness knows how many endangered species. Pygmy kingfishers, giant hornbills, snake birds, even the rare whitenosed monkey, they are all in Korup. So everybody is desperate to preserve it even though it means, according to the WWF, resettling about 1,000 people whose families have lived in the forest for generations. 'Their way of life, involving farming, hunting, smuggling and distilling is incompatible with the park's conservation objectives,' they say. So they will have to go to villages which, I have been told, look like army camps.

The forest now disappeared. The land cleared. We were at Loungahe. The train pulled up. Another train, a local connecting service, was standing the other side of the platform. One or two people got off, one or two got on, which made a change from Adlestrop. Everybody else carried on eating croissants and drinking coffee. The train starts up again with a burst of speed, and almost immediately stops. There are squeals and screeches. My coffee spills over the table, soaks the comic book and splashes all over my friend from the Chamber of Commerce. In a British train nobody would say a word. Here everybody is giggling. An old lady is helped up from the floor, crying with laughter. A girl wearing Walkman earphones remains sprawled across two eager young men upon whom she has fallen. The inspector comes along apologising but nobody believes him and very soon we are off again.

We are now passing through the middle of nowhere; green

vegetation, scrubland, the occasional shack. Now and then women sitting in the sunshine doing nothing, children playing with stones and sticks. How do they live? What do they do? What do they eat? Do the children go to school? What are their prospects? How long are they going to survive? Do they know they are living in a world of nuclear weapons, video cassettes and wine coolers? The train begins to slow down and we pull into Edea. 'We call it Aluminium City,' says my friend, and you can see why. In the distance are giant aluminium smelters and an enormous paper pulp plant. Across the river is a huge hydroelectric works.

Women come along the track with trays of food on their head: manioc strips, a Cameroonian speciality; oranges, coconuts, bananas. Everyone trying to earn the salesman of the year award. I give in and buy some manioc which tastes, well, different. My window is then besieged by so many other women that I get off the train on the other side and wander around the station. It's dull and overcast, not the kind of weather you expect in Africa. Then I notice everyone is carrying an umbrella. It's a bit like London Bridge in April. A whistle blows and I race back to the train. Somebody has turned the music up in the restaurant car and people are dancing. Everybody is drinking. My friend is sitting on the floor between two chairs reading another comic. It looks like the best nightclub in Cameroon.

As I go back to my seat, I hear the ticket inspector on the intercom: 'To our dear passengers, we are pleased to announce your train is seven minutes early. Thank you for your attention.' Which is fine, I think, except for the people arriving at the station in seven minutes' time ... The businessman has finished his papers and is eager to talk. He tells me about his tribe, and the president's, the Bamilekes.

'We are the businessmen,' he says proudly. 'We are like the Ibos in Nigeria.'

'But people don't like the Ibos,' I say. 'They are frightened of them.'

'But we are not frightening,' he laughs. 'Here everything is balanced. We are good businessmen, another tribe are good administrators, others are good teachers.'

I asked who the big businessmen are.

'Onobiono; Soppo Priso; Fotso.'

I asked him to tell me about them. 'Onobiono is a genius,' he said. 'He was a professeur of mathematics in Paris when he was twenty-three. He now runs Sitabac, the big cigarette company. He's worth millions and he's only thirty-eight. He advises the government on economic affairs.'

Since then I've met Onobiono; he is tall, slim, elegant, smokes long, thin cigars and talks flowingly with his hands and ever so politely. He always speaks longer than anyone else. And he is into everything: cigarettes, construction, transport, banking, and desperately eager to get into pharmaceuticals. Sitabac has around 60 percent of the cigarette market. He exports about 30 percent of Cameroon's cocoa and 15 percent of the coffee. His insurance company is growing rapidly. His bank, the local Douala branch of Bank of America, he is turning into the International Bank of Africa. In ten years he has built up an empire with a turnover of more than US $250 million and employing nearly 3,500 people. Unlike most African businessmen, who are usually traders, he is finance orientated. He is international. He is not just interested in a Cameroonian empire, he wants to conquer Africa.

'Africans and Africa must be open. We must be competitive. We must not avoid any challenge in the business field,' he told me once in his small cramped office suite in Douala. He wants an African Stock Exchange, a special African investment corporation to back African businessmen, more cross-border investment, greater integration of national economies.

'Will it happen?'

'Of course it will. It is evolution. Business is evolving in Africa.'

The problem is the lack of managers. Most of Africa's biggest businessmen are there because they had the idea – or somebody gave it to them; they had the connections, backed their judgement and, in many cases, brought in professional managers to make it happen. In this respect French Africa is more open and more realistic about exports than maybe anglophone Africa.

Soppo Priso, the businessman told me, was in pharmaceuticals;

Fotso owned a big brewery. Both were much older than Onobiono and of the three, despite the theory, only Fotso was a Bamileke.

I wondered what he thought of overseas businessmen. He didn't like the Americans. He couldn't understand their accent and they never had enough time. The Japanese he liked very much because they were more interested in delivering the goods than being paid. The Germans, he said, were too specific about detail, but they were very efficient. If you did business with British companies you had to wait maybe three months before they could get agreement from their Export Credit Guarantee Department. The Germans could get Hermes, their export credit organisation to give the go-ahead the same day.

'It's true,' he insisted when I expressed incredulity. 'I've been with German businessmen on a Sunday afternoon and they have telephoned Hermes and got their approval straightaway.'

Certainly all the other export credit organisations seem to help their exporters do more business in French Africa than Britain's ECGD. In fact, if the Foreign Office seems to be working for the Russians, ECGD seems to be working for the French and Germans. For again and again British companies have landed big contracts in francophone Africa, often against fierce international competition, only to discover that ECGD refuses to back them. The contract goes yet again to the French even though in a number of cases the Department of Trade has been rooting for the home team. The problem seems to be lack of co-ordination and information. Lack of co-ordination because if the Foreign Office, the Department of Trade and the British Overseas Trade Board have decided that French Africa is a target market, somebody should tell ECGD so that they can assist British exporters, not hinder them. Lack of information, because all too often ECGD will refuse to back deals with francophone companies because they have no record of them, or the records they have are wildly out of date. I've come across several cases where ECGD have turned down requests for companies among the biggest and most profitable in Africa because they have no record of their existence let alone their latest balance sheets.

COFAS, the French export credit insurance operation,

seems content to insure practically everything even, perhaps surprisingly, British deals in French Africa, providing the application is made by their French subsidiary or through a French agent. After all, either way they maintain their connection.

The Germans are a little more cautious. Hermes, the private company which runs the government's export insurance programme, will insure most deals in francophone Africa largely because they concentrate on risks the conventional insurance companies will not touch. And francophone Africa is risk territory to German companies, who are now shipping over 80 percent of exports to secure OECD countries. Surprisingly for Germans, they have even started bending the rules a little to get the business. In the old days if a company had failed to pay up just four months after invoice, the shutters came down with a bang. All further cover was refused not only to the company but to the country, and Hermes paid out in full to its client company. Today they will wait up to a year before bringing the barriers down, and it can be postponed further for special circumstances. Even if the barriers come down, there is no longer that automatic block on all further deals. Deny it though they do, the deciding factor seems to be the number of German jobs involved. If putting the barriers down means a loss of German jobs then Hermes will be as understanding as the most understanding Frenchman.

'So what do you think of the British?' I asked. He laughed.

The train halted at Eseka, high in the mountains surrounded by clouds. Cattle with enormous horns sat by the line staring at us. Years after the Lake Nyos tragedy in August 1986 in which toxic gases killed over 1,700 people and about as many cattle – the country's worst-ever natural disaster – scientists still can't make up their minds about the cause or whether Cameroon's killer mountains are still dangerous. Some say, mostly the French, that the gas was ejected by volcanic action. Others, mostly Americans, claim it was released as a result of hot and cold water mixing at the bottom of the lake. Some say there are still dangerous concentrations of carbon dioxide in the lake which could explode at any time. Others say the area is safe again for habitation. Either way most of the 4,000 survivors are still living in tents in vast camps. One of them, Bole Butake, whose village was only 40 kilometres from the lake, turned the disaster into a stage play, *Lake God*, which he started nine days afterwards during a writing course in Iowa.

I congratulated my companion on the fantastic railway service. 'The problem is the restaurant car,' he said, to my astonishment. 'You can't rely on it being on the train.'

'I don't understand,' I said, 'Of course it's on the train.'

'But there is only one restaurant car on the whole system.' He then told me a long, sad and very African story involving national staff agreements, about switching the restaurant car to different trains so more people could see it – but this meant no one could rely on it, so people were opting to travel by air, so ticket sales were down, which meant they couldn't afford another restaurant car. It was awful. I had thought the train was too good to be true.

I was wondering whether to persuade him to take on the unions, fight for a new management structure, launch a big marketing campaign but I felt it would be like intruding upon someone's private grief. I turned to pick up my briefcase and in came my friend from the Chamber of Commerce.

'I've come to say goodbye,' he said. 'I'm getting off at the next stop.'

'But I thought you were going to Yaounde.'

'I changed my mind. I thought I would go to my village and visit my family.'

'What about your meetings in Yaounde?' I couldn't help saying.

'I'll come back next week. No problem,' he said laughing.

So much for modern management techniques, efficient business systems. But I didn't say a word. 'Tell me about your village,' I said instead. 'Have you far to go?'

'About 100 kilometres. I go by bus.'

I imagined the usual jungle taxi, a small truck packed to overflowing with people, animals, chickens and packages. 'How long does it take?'

'About two hours.'

'Two hours in this heat. You're going to be exhausted.'

'Oh no,' he said, 'it's air-conditioned.'

'Air-conditioned!'

'Yes. And the bus has now got video.'

'You're joking,' I said. 'I've never seen a jungle taxi with air-conditioning, let alone video.'

My friend burst into hysterical laughter. I thought he was going to have a fit. 'Jungle taxis!' he wheezed. 'The government have privatised the bus services.'

Well now, I admit I was stunned. Would Mrs Thatcher have believed it? Out here – private buses; air-conditioning; videos. We don't have that in England. It was almost as great a shock as the day I asked an old farmer in a tiny Cameroonian village whether the rains would be late this year and he said, 'Well according to the satellite picture this morning ...' At the next stop I got out and saw the buses for myself. I know there's no reason why they shouldn't have posh private buses but it came as a bit of a surprise. Back on the train, I was stopped by a ticket inspector with four policemen in attendance. They were looking for fare dodgers.

'No,' they said, when I asked if it was a big problem, 'people always pay their fares. We keep looking in case one day they start dodging.'

'But wait a minute,' it occurred to me, 'this is a private train. Why should the government spend money to make certain private trains get paid?'

'It is the regulation,' they said and were gone.

The businessman was now fast asleep. I started to check my papers for my meetings in Yaounde. Suddenly the whole train shuddered and screeched to a halt. My briefcase fell on the floor. Papers flew everywhere. The businessman shot out of his seat and landed on my briefcase smashing it to pieces.

'Another one of those market women,' he grumbled picking himself up. 'Always happens as soon as we get close to Yaounde. The women walk along the railway line. It's easier and quicker than struggling through the bush. Problem is the driver doesn't see them till the last minute.'

'You mean they'll walk to Yaounde and back on the track with all their goods on their head? Isn't it dangerous?'

'Not now everybody knows they are doing it. At first, yes. But now it's all right.'

'Why don't they put fences along the line?'

'Do you know how much that would cost?'

'A lot. But it would save people's lives.'

'And how long do you think the fence would last?'

'A couple of days,' I said, realising the African dimension. It would no sooner be up than it would be torn up and re-distributed all over the region – and you would have the problem as before.

'So you agree. It's best to leave things as they are, even if the occasional person gets injured or even killed.'

'I agree,' I said.

The train was now drawing into Yaounde. Stretched either side of us were row after row of sandy tin roofs. We passed the state printing company and a collection of giant oil tanks. By now there were hundreds of men, women, girls streaming across the lines on the way to work. There were probably more on the tracks, jumping over the lines, stumbling over the sleepers and dodging between carriages of trains waiting at red lights, than walking along the road.

'But that must be dangerous,' I said in amazement.

'More dangerous than the roads?'

I couldn't say a word.

It was seven o'clock in the morning. I had been waiting to see the minister for an hour. I'd studied the Cameroon newspapers and their photographs of mutilated skeletons, pendus and foetus sanguinolents. One actually showed a body split in two by a train. Another had a picture of the body of a young woman en putrefaction which had been left at a bus stop in Douala for five days, the report said, without anybody noticing it.

I picked up yet another copy of a magazine about North Korea's Kim Il Sung in relief. 'Loyalty to the leader ... is an immaculate ideological and emotional value ... the Leader is ... the supreme brain ... Communist revolutionaries are raised in the bosom of the Leader ... and enjoy an eternal life.'

I went back to the newspapers. This time I read the stories about corruption. One was pure *News of the World*. Bars flowing with champagne, homes the size of chateaux, ceilings dripping with chandeliers. Luxury homes all over the world, honest hardworking wives, young exciting girlfriends. The newspaper even explained how it was done.

'A small bottle of orangeade would be made to cost five times its usual price; a ream of paper which was not necessarily delivered, hiked up to a third of the agriculture ministry's budget for office stationery,' it said. They even allocated CFA 500 million for an agricultural show, spent as little as possible and shared the money amongst themselves. 'Is the time for general housekeeping definitely at hand?' asked the paper in not-quite-ringing editorial tones.

Once when I was in Cameroon a provincial delegate of posts and telecommunications revealed a favourite trick of African post office workers: sending their private mail as official government correspondence. Out of over ten million letters stamped 'official', he discovered – although he didn't explain how – that about four million were 'private correspondence circulating under cover of the state's seal'.

He should count himself lucky. In other countries of francophone Africa his counterparts are wrestling with far more serious problems such as the actual pilfering of the post. Clothes, books, food, medicines, and, of course, cash and cheques, are regularly stolen by post office workers often desperately trying to survive on little or no wages. Which is probably why it is so difficult to send anything to Africa.

The meeting I was currently so patiently waiting for was in fact to discuss corruption. The minister had rung me the previous evening, and suggested six o'clock. 'Before things start hotting up,' he said.

At 6.00 am I arrived at his office and found a delegation from Chad already waiting for him with a personal message from their President Hissene Habre. Within two minutes they were admitted. I sat outside.

Every waiting room in francophone Africa has copies of *La Corée Aujourdhui, Le Sport en URSS,* a dozen magazines from North Korea and, of course, an ancient battered copy of *The Thoughts of Kim Il Sung.* If I was Kim Il Sung, however, I'd be feeling pretty sore. For the North Koreans have poured a lot of money into French Africa, built congress halls and sports stadia, funded aid projects and supplied thousands of advisers who work in the most appalling conditions, and have got back very little in return either politically, diplomatically or commercially. Their books and magazines are read only by the likes of me, and as far as Kim Il Sung is concerned I'm sure I don't count.

Occasionally you may see *Afrika*, the German government's official African magazine, or maybe something published by the European Development Fund. Only once have I seen anything from the US; an old-fashioned gestetnered newsletter addressed to 'The Waiting Room, La Présidence', which I found in the ministry of public works. Never have I seen anything from the UK; not from the COI, nor the BBC, nor the British Council. And most definitely nothing bearing the slightest connection with the local – or should I say, nearest – British embassy, let alone the government in Whitehall.

6.05: a policeman puts his head around the door, looks as though he is checking the furniture is in place and disappears. I go back to Kim Il Sung.

Waiting of course is a way of life in Africa. 'Come and see me at 4 o'clock,' you're told. You're impressed. All the stories about Africa were wrong. Here is somebody who behaves as we behave. You arrive on the dot, give your card to reception. Promptly a secretary arrives and escorts you along a corridor. All very businesslike. You're shown into a room. You go in, hand extended – but you don't see the minister. Instead you see ten, maybe twenty other people who have also been told to come at 4 o'clock.

The Africans, like the Arabs, do business as a family. Everybody comes at the same time. People are then seen either singly or in groups. Often you wait your turn, go into the room, are offered a seat. Then nothing. You wait till the minister finishes what he is writing. He might glare at you over his glasses. He might take telephone calls, or receive other visitors. Eventually your turn comes.

In most of francophone Africa, presidents and ministers have a weekly audience. Anybody can go, any subjects can be discussed. But you have to wait, so people start queuing hours before the audience is scheduled to begin, so that what should take half an hour ends up by taking all day. But that's not seeing things from the African point of view.

'Why do you tell everybody to come at the same time when you know you can't see them all together?' I asked one minister in Zaire.

'That is our custom. That is our culture.'

'But it means a lot of people spend a lot of time just waiting.'

'In the villages everything is decided by the chiefs. They all discuss things, make decisions. Time is not important. It is taking the right decisions that is important. This way also shows that anybody can come to our offices – businessmen or village people. We are the servants of the people.'

'But not everybody is seen.'

'Our way, everybody has the opportunity to be seen either by themselves or in a group. Your way, it depends on fixing an appointment and you can only have so many appointments in a day.'

When you're seen, you're in the hands of the individual. Some Africans spit out decisions with the speed of a machinegun. Others brood and meditate and agonise. But at least the waiting is over.

6.15: I've now read all the magazines, and even re-read a story in an old *Cameroon Tribune* about a fire at a 'herbal home' of a famous traditional doctor who said that the 500 spirits guarding the temple 'were on leave' at the time of the disaster. I study the furniture: very Citizens' Advice Bureau, Sunderland, late 1930s.

6.20: the policeman gives me yesterday's newspaper. I haven't been forgotten. Or is he trying to tell me I am going to have to wait much longer?

6.25: in burst four huge women, laughing and shouting. They are the market women who control just about everything from the market stalls to the taxis. Many people say they virtually control the whole economy, and are more important to the government than the IMF. Which seems pretty far-fetched, but no sooner have they entered than the minister appears and shakes hands with them all – even kisses them. The Chadians are quickly dismissed and the women ushered into his office.

The policeman brings me an old copy of *Jeune Afrique*. I ask about the market women. He says the minister for trade has just banned beauty products which women use to lighten their skin and which had caused severe burns. Two women had actually died as a result.

'But why are the market women against the ban?' I ask.

'They make big profit selling them.'

'But that's shocking.'

He shrugs and goes out.

6.30: I am now talking to a French businessman who is making a fortune selling hi-tech morse code machines to African governments. 'They might not have enough money to feed themselves, but they always have money for security,' he says. I said I thought morse code was old-fashioned boy scout stuff, not exactly frontiers of technology. He explains that you tap your message out like you used to in the boy scouts. The machine then compresses the morse code into a message only a few seconds long. You then transmit the message by radio or telephone back to base. Because the message is so short, it doesn't cost you much and it is also more difficult to intercept, in fact virtually impossible because you have to monitor a possible transmitter twenty-four hours a day when the message might take four seconds. Like trying to find a needle in an electronic haystack.

We talk about African waiting rooms we have known. Once, he said, he had a meeting with the president of Gabon at nine in the morning. At 10.45 a secretary told him he would have to wait another three hours. 'Les affaires d'état?' he asked. 'Well, actually,' she whispered, 'it's the latest two episodes of Falcon-crest. The videos have just arrived and the president can't wait to see what happens.'

In some parts of Africa, mind you, in Togo for example, where the President starts work at 5 o'clock, ministers are fired if they are not in their offices by 7. One minister who continued, despite warnings, coming in about 7.30, found the president in his chair one morning. He was out.

The trouble is that in Africa time-keeping and courtesy overlap, and more often than not courtesy gets the upper hand. So instead of saying, 'Sorry, can't make it. Let's fix the meeting tomorrow,' an official will say, 'Yes, 4.30 pm' and hope that things sort themselves out. If the worst comes to the worst he can have everybody in his office at the same time, which is extremely difficult if two competitors are sitting opposite each other. Another reason is efficiency. I know that sounds strange, but a country that leaves everything to the last minute is a country on its toes.

6.45: a girl of seventeen or so slips through the door. She gives the policeman a piece of paper with her name on. He takes it straight in to the minister, returns in thirty seconds and takes the girl in with him. She is there for maybe two minutes. As she leaves I see her rolling up some notes and squeezing them into her handbag. Obviously another example of how Africans who make it support their far-flung families. The worst extreme is the telephone call to the company insisting they put brothers or cousins on their payroll and nothing else. I know one big state enterprise in Côte d'Ivoire where a minister has placed two sons in senior positions just by leaning on the management. They have a big office and a salary, but no responsibilities. I asked the director of the company if he objected.

'Not at all, it's protection,' he told me. 'If I have problems with customs or another minister, I ring up the minister direct. He solves the problems for me. It's worth it. But I don't tell him that. He still thinks I'm doing him a big favour. It also means I don't have to worry about making too much money. He'll look after me. It's not fair, but it works.'

6.50: a bit of luck. In come three other ministers; Foreign Affairs, Justice and Industry. I was hoping to see them, sometime, but wondering how I could arrange it. They've all got meetings all day and tomorrow. We talk, decide and agree. Very workmanlike. In five minutes I achieved what would take in many other countries, maybe, three different one-hour meetings.

7.10: a group of Nigerian journalists have just arrived and gone straight in. They are staying at the same hotel as me, and they weren't even up when I left it. The policeman returns with a book about Cameroon – or Kamerun, or Camaroons as Laurens van der Post says or Comeroons as the Irish say. They have over 200 different languages each with its own culture; three different colonial heritages, British, German and French; and a country which ranges from desert to tropical rainforest. It's like visiting three countries in one. In the capital, Yaounde, you are in France. Along the coast to Victoria you are in England. And in one or two areas you are in Germany. Ten years ago you would also have thought you were in China; the shops were full of Chinese goods, Chinese construction work was everywhere, there were Chinese on every street corner. But today it is firmly in the French Commonwealth.

Cameroon also had its own strong man, the notoriously glacial Ahmadou Ahidjo, a northerner who ruled almost single-handed from before independence in 1960 to November 1982 when he took everybody by surprise and resigned on the grounds of ill-health. At first everybody thought it was a hoax. France practically had a collective heart attack. But it was true. He handed over to his longtime prime minister, Paul Biya, a southerner. A less colourful character, but a man with a reputation for honesty and efficiency, he has kept the country on an even keel in spite of problems with neighbours: Equatorial Guinea where the regime of Nguema Masie Biyoto degenerated into barbarism; Nigeria with its coups; Central Africa with the notorious Bokassa; and Chad and its never-ending civil war.

In 1983, however, Ahidjo who remained as leader of the party suddenly announced that Cameroon under Biya was a police state. Telephones were being tapped, people were being interrogated. He was going to take over again. He even said he had been tricked into resigning by his French doctors who lied about his health. Biya and his supporters smiled sweetly and wondered aloud whether Ahidjo was saying such things as he had been forbidden from transferring his enormous fortune from Cameroon to the south of France where he was living. He was sentenced to death by a court, then quickly reprieved by Biya. But there were riots; the presidential guard mutinied; it was a little shaky, although everything was quickly back to normal. So much so that Biya felt confident enough halfway through his state visit to England to cancel everything and fly to Gleneagles to play golf.

Cameroon has maintained an average annual growth rate of a staggering 6 percent from 1982–87. Per capita income is nearly US $1200. But in recent years the economy has hit big problems. Other African countries have enormous debts and nothing in the bank. Cameroon, however, is one of the richest countries in Africa. But there was no money in the system. The government had decided to withdraw all its deposits from the banks, so that the banks had no money to play with. Industry, therefore, had no money, and if companies had no money, their employees had no money. The country was grinding to a halt. Everybody was forced to spend only on absolute essentials. Farmers were paying for seed for next year, but not for spraying for this year. Companies were paying for essential spare parts, but not for new equipment.

The more money was withdrawn from the system, and the longer it went on, the more impossible things became. At one stage the government actually admitted that it owed over CFA 150 billion to the business community.

The problem arose because the president didn't want to borrow. Borrowing money seemed to be an admission of failure. Instead they spent their savings, which created the problems.

Some politicians said that under no circumstances should the president talk to the IMF. Another group said he should. The super sophisticates, however, were whispering that the president had already seen the IMF, had negotiated the deal and was waiting for the right moment to invite them in so that he could throw out their proposals as an affront to the national dignity and renegotiate the deal already agreed in private.

Finally the government decided to act. They cut the budget by a draconian 18 percent. Taxes were increased and new taxes introduced, especially a super petrol tax which did not go down well; everybody had thought that because they had their own petrol – like the UK, they are not members of OPEC – the prices would come down. A string of state enterprises were put up to be privatised. They increased sentences on tax dodgers. They even started to cut out all the perks, such as free electricity for electrical workers; free telephones for telephone workers and, of course, free cars and chauffeurs for whoever could get hold of them. It was called a 'war against pajeros', the luxury Japanese car officials use for private as well as public duties.

The National Assembly then took a deep breath and asked the government to negotiate a loan of CFA 250 billion, 'on conditions that would safeguard the state's financial interests as well as its economic and political sovereignty'. All over the country you could hear businessmen breathing a sigh of relief. At last the government had recognised the problem and begun taking the right steps.

'I don't understand what all the fuss was about,' one banker told me. 'Their debts are only US $2.5 billion. Zaire gets through that in a week.'

In spite of recent problems President Biya still seems to be in charge. His election in 1988 was unanimous. Some people say it was because, although he called the elections six months before the end of his term of office, he only gave rivals a week to get their nomination papers signed by 500 supporters in each of the ten regions and submitted to the central committee. Others, naturally, say he was the best man for the job. When he took over everybody complained about his lack of political experience. Today nobody even dares think about it, for slowly and steadily he has been liberalising and democratising Cameroon. Open debate is encouraged although the occasional radio programme is banned. A choice of candidates is allowed at local elections, although instead of choosing between individual candidates voters must choose between different lists of ten candidates. Multipartyism is being phased in over the next ten years.

Overseas, Biya is a friend to all and a brother to every other president, but definitely not to the former president Ahidjo. As far as Europe is concerned, he is playing France off against Germany and the French are not amused. In Africa, he is now great friends with Nigeria, and a driving force behind the Economic Community of Central African States.

7.35: in comes a tiny, spindly man with a shock of hair like an Italian concert pianist. He gave me a funny handshake, which made me think. So, nothing to lose, I said, 'You're a Freemason.' He nodded and laughed. I had never come across a Mason in francophone Africa, and was eager to find out everything I could. I remembered they always ask about their mothers' age. 'How old is your mother?' I said.

'Peace, prosperity and co-operation. Number 4-3-7-1,' he replied. I was into the secret circle. He started showing me booklets and programmes and menus all about the Masons, complete with pictures of the officers wearing ceremonial robes and aprons.

'Are you very active here?' I asked.

'We meet regularly. We believe in keeping in touch with our brothers.'

'Do you do a lot of work for charity? In England the Masons do a lot.'

'Our resources are limited, but we do what we can. We help each other, our families and friends. That is our priority.'

'Presumably you are part of the French Masons,' I said.

'Some of our lodges are related to France, but some are related to Germany and some to Britain, particularly Northern Ireland. It is a result of colonial times.'

'Do you all meet as one local national lodge?' I asked.

'No. We know each other and we meet from time to time, but we cannot meet as one lodge. All our relations are with our Mother Lodge. That is the line of contact.' Colonies may come and go but colonialism, I thought, lives on in the Masons.

'Do you have much contact with the British Masons?'

'Yes. The Master comes to visit us, and they send representatives to our meetings.'

'But isn't that expensive?'

'We must keep together. We also have English Masons living here who come to our meetings and maintain the contact.'

'What do you do at the meetings?'

'We have our ceremonies, we talk about our activities.'

'Do you help each other get good jobs and big contracts and make lots of money? That's what the Masons do in England.'

He sat back and smiled broadly. 'We do everything we can to help each other,' he said.

I continued asking about Masons in Africa while looking through the documents he had piled on the table. I hadn't recognised any big names so I asked, indirectly I hoped, 'Presumably some of the ministers are Masons?'

'I suppose,' he said.

'It might help. Being a minister and a Mason. You must get lots of opportunities for meeting people.'

'You must.'

Obviously there was no point asking for names. I went back to the question of overseas contacts. 'Who is your favourite partner?'

'If we have a favourite, it's the English. They produce the best ceremonials. They make better cloaks and sashes and honours and regalia. Much better than the French. And better prices, too.'

Would you believe it? Another export earner! Wonder whether the Department of Trade could separate out the export earnings from selling Masonic bits and pieces around the world.

'I have an idea,' he said. 'Maybe you could help me.' Suddenly he was showering me with sales catalogues for Lodge paraphernalia. He wafted through them, ticking items. 'You're going back to London,' he said. 'Wonder whether you could buy these for us at the Masons' shop. I haven't got anybody who can do that for me.' Which is how I became a go-between for the Freemasons in francophone Africa.

8.23: the policeman spoke: 'The minister says he cannot see you today. You must come back tomorrow.'

Back at the hotel I described what had happened to a leading Cameroonian businessman. 'You were kept waiting because you didn't give the policeman anything,' said he.

'But I wanted to talk to the minister about corruption. How could I give the policeman anything?'

'For the books he kept bringing you, not for letting you see the minister. Why else do you think he kept bringing all those books and magazines? You should have thanked him.'

'But I thought . . .'

'Africa,' he said slowly. 'You're in Africa.'

'Bon soir.'

'Good evening.'

'Comment ça va?'

'Very well thank you.'

'Et votre femme?'

'Not bad.'

'Et les enfants?'

'Very bad, I'm afraid. One has pneumonia, one has food poisoning and my eldest daughter has run off with a politician.'

'Très bon. C'est ça. Bonne soirée.'

That's how cocktail party conversations start in officially bilingual Cameroon. For amongst all the countries in francophone Africa, Cameroon boasts that its official languages are both French and English; French because you cannot be considered civilised unless you speak French and English because the two big provinces, the North West and the South West, refuse to be civilised.

In practice, however, all but a handful of anglophone diehards eat, think and breathe French. Government officials will deny it; they stress that Cameroon is bilingual. Ignore them. Ce n'est pas vrai. I was with a senior director of the Société National d'Investiments one evening in Yaounde's Bar Portée Trente-neuf discussing a feasibility study I had submitted in English three weeks earlier, but he didn't seem to know what I was talking about. 'You've read the proposal?' I asked nervously.

'It was in English?'

'You said I could submit it in English or French. They were the two languages specified on the tender documentation.'

'Yes, of course.'

'You mean I should have submitted it in French?'

'Well . . .'

'You mean French is more equal than English?'

'Well . . .'

'You mean nobody understands English?'

'Well . . .'

'But it's better in French?'

'Put it this way,' he confessed, 'it's more practical. Of course English is an official language. But it's easier to read French.'

'So anything in French is always read first, and if you find what you are looking for in French, you don't bother to read anything in English?'

'Yes.'

'So if I want to do business in Cameroon I should submit everything in French whatever the regulations say?'

'No. You can of course submit everything in English. English is one of our official languages.'

'But if I want to stand a chance of winning any contracts . . .'

'Then French, of course, is much easier for us.'

Which is another reason why the French continue to have such a hold over Cameroon. But we're not the only ones to fall at the first hurdle. The Germans, he told me, always submit their proposals in English as well.

I set off round the crowded room to investigate further the bilinguality of Cameroon. I soon bumped into some local journalists, and asked their views. Cameroon was bilingual in theory only, they replied. Everybody thought, wrote and spoke French although the French were having big problems keeping French French and not English. Just before the Olympic Games, they said, the French embassy gave them all a book of French sporting terms.

'Instead of in-fighting we were supposed to say corps à corps.'

'And did you?'

'No. We said in-fighting. Nobody would understand us if we said corps à corps.'

'What other things were forbidden?'

'Sponsorship. Instead it was parrainage. And fair play. They wanted us to say franc-jeu. But we didn't.'

'That's not franc-jeu,' I said.

'And they also don't like us using words like radio trottoir or vidange or . . .'

'Or jumbo-jet or walkman.'

'So what do you say?'

'Un avion gros porteur.'

'And walkman is un baladeur.'

'And we can't have brain-storming sessions any more.'

'They're now les remue-messinges.'

'And hot money is les capitaux fébriles.'

'D'accord, d'accord. Je comprends,' I said.

'You mustn't say d'accord,' they said. 'That's old-fashioned. You must say d'ac. That's modern.'

'D'ac,' I said. Cries for champagne, and the waiter appeared.

'My brothers them oh, my sisters them oh, my papa them oh,' he beamed at us.

'So what kind of language is that?' I asked.

'Pidgin,' he said.

'How many people speak pidgin?'

'Everybody,' he said. 'Everybody speak pidgin my brothers them oh.'

This was too much for me. Besides I'd had too much champagne. 'Excuse me,' I said. 'I must go to the messieurs.'

'The what?' they said.

'The messieurs. The gentlemen.'

'Now that's interesting,' said someone. 'Why is it d'ac to say gentlemen in English but not messieurs in French?'

'So what do you say?' I asked, perhaps at that moment out of more than academic interest.

'Sometimes men.'

'I once saw a sign saying divers.'

'And in Paris on one occasion . . .' I didn't wait to find out.

The plane had been turned back – twice. Twice the pilot had warned us about 'zee stronk vesterly vinds'. Twice the air hostesses had told us about the lifejackets. Finally they decided we would have to spend the night in Douala. They trundled us all into buses, drove us back into town and dumped us at the Akwa Palace Hotel.

At intervals throughout the day I called the airline. No news. Instead of hanging around Douala for maybe another day I decided to go to Limbe, the one-time fashionable seaside resort for Douala.

The next morning I set off through the suburbs of Douala, which are much like suburbs anywhere. Drab. Now I edge through a street market which has flooded its banks and flowed all over the street. The sun is rising slowly, but everything is still covered in mist. The traffic is worse than ever; we hardly move an inch in twenty minutes. Crowds are all around us. But there is little reaction from other drivers. Most have turned their engines off and fallen asleep; one has even gone to sleep on the roof of his van. More civilised than traffic jams in London or New York or Lagos.

The driver of the car alongside asks me about the Mount Cameroon race. Once a year Guinness sponsor a gruelling 27 km race down the side of the mountain. For two years it was won by an Englishman. Last year it was won by a Cameroonian, a tiny twenty-three-year-old student, in just under four hours. This year, with over 200 competitors from all over the world, everybody was wondering whether the Englishman would fight back or the student win again. The Cameroonian driver said the Englishman would win, I said the Cameroonian. At last we moved on.

Now we are travelling through open bush – or the Cameroonian equivalent, more like scrubland: a few tatty trees, lots of long dry grass, the occasional hut of palm leaves and rush-matting. A tiny village, a huddle of huts and a small clearing in the grass for village meetings. Now we fly past a petrol station – how much business can they possibly do here? Cameroon seems to be much neater and tidier than many francophone countries. Funny I haven't seen any women carrying containers of water; instead there are dozens of boys dragging ramshackle green metal carts that look as though they started life as bicycle trailers. Obviously a sign of progress.

We came to a roadblock. There are roadblocks all over Africa, some official, most unofficial. Like the unofficial road repair gangs who block the road so that when you stop you find you have to contribute towards the cost of the road repairs. Or the more sinister rope or metal barrier across the road. When you stop you are surrounded by an eager group of villagers who would be only too pleased to move the barrier if ... In Niger and Mali, I've come across the even more fearsome group of soldiers who've not been paid for three months and have had nothing to eat since last week and ... But this roadblock was marvellous. The soldiers jumped to attention, smiled, saluted and waved us past. We didn't even stop.

The driver now took us through rubber plantations. Cameroon is big in rubber. Not the biggest, but by the year 2000 they plan to produce 100,000 tonnes a year – about 10 percent of the European market.

An old man is selling sugar cane at the roadside so we stop to buy some. Most people chew cane here. Many's the time I've settled down in the evening with a drink and been offered a couple of sticks of cane. To me, it's not very sugary or sweet. It's more stringy and watery-sweet.

Soon I can see a herd of cattle in the distance ambling all over the road. As we draw near I can see they are nothing but skin and bone. Rearing cattle in Africa is difficult but possible. I've seen some decent cattle in Zaire. Nothing like our Herefords or, my favourite, the Sussex. But these looked bad. Instead of taking five years to fatten up for slaughter they would probably take ten. And then they wouldn't be worth eating.

All along the road now there was nothing but palm trees as far as the eye could see, flowing up hills and cascading into valleys. Hundreds of thousands of them. Cameroon has always been big in palm kernels. Back in 1912, for example, according to a book I found in a secondhand bookshop in Rye, they were exporting over 15,000 tonnes a year, worth a handsome £220,300.

This is Cameroon Development Corporation territory, the biggest employer in the country after the state and responsible for everything from palm products, bananas, coconuts and rubber to tea and even pepper. Cameroon takes its agriculture seriously. Overall, it is self-sufficient in basic foodstuffs. By the year 2000 it plans to be totally self-sufficient. Covering nearly 100,000 hectares, CDC is responsible for a large slice of the action and over half the country's agricultural exports. Normally it is booming. But this year things were bleak. The economic crisis meant they couldn't afford the usual fertilisers. Lack of fertilising meant low yields; in many cases it wasn't even worth the cost of harvesting. From profits of over CFA 5 billion in 1986 they crashed to a loss of CFA 4.8 billion in 1987.

The barman at the restaurant where we stopped told me they'd even stopped work on some of the plantations. He said even the CDC had run out of money, and was getting rid of people. If it was like this in CDC country I wondered what it was like in other parts of Cameroon, especially the once neglected North West Province. Ten years ago the area, on the border with Nigeria, was destitute. Living conditions were impossible. Today, or at least yesterday, it was booming. Food production had soared a staggering 50 percent. Farms – over 70 percent are less than two hectares – were thriving. They were even exporting – unofficially, of course – to Nigeria. The reason: a US $45 million programme put together by the ministry of agriculture and aid organisations spearheaded by over 300 extension workers, a third of them women, who not only tell the farmer about new crops and farming techniques but actually help him choose which crops he wants and how he is going to grow them. Yields have soared, in the case of maize from 1.5 to over 3 tonnes per hectare. Proper storage techniques have cut wastages. Marketing has been streamlined.

The road approaching Limbe was littered with car wrecks and rubbish. The town was desolate, like a ghost town. I had a meeting at the Chamber of Commerce, a relatively smart, modern building which was barred and bolted. But one of the glass doors was smashed, so I climbed through and wandered around inside. It was like something out of Nevil Shute's *On the Beach.* Books and papers were still open on the desks; in the library somebody had left a book open on a table. It was called *Britain: Your trading partner in Africa* and published in 1934. It was eerie. I went back outside; even the street was empty. I walked round the back of the building, and I could hear schoolchildren in the distance practising hymns. Then from under a pile of corrugated iron sheets thrown against the side of the building out crawled a little boy.

'Where is everybody?' I asked him.

He just stared at me then crawled back under the corrugated iron. As I turned to walk away, he re-emerged with a rough-looking, dishevelled, slightly sinister-looking man of about thirty.

'I am the guardian,' he said. 'Can I help you?' Obviously one of the self-appointed guardians who latch on to buildings as watchman, door-opener, whatever they have to do in return for the most meagre living imaginable. It's better than starving.

'I'm looking for Mr Njike,' I said. Mr Njike was chairman of the Chamber of Commerce. Whenever I saw him he pleaded poverty, but somehow he managed to send his son to Winchester. 'He said he would meet me here at 10 am.'

'He's not here,' said the guardian, somewhat unnecessarily. He apparently knew neither Mr Njike's telephone number or address, so I left instructions that if my friend turned up he should tell him I was at the Atlantic Beach Hotel and ask him to come across. 'Yes,' he said and crawled back under the corrugated iron.

I drove back through the deserted town to the hotel which was right on the beach and, in the old days, was always packed. Crowds of expats would pour down from Douala for the weekend. Rich Cameroonians and even Nigerians would flood in to relax and gossip. Children would be climbing all over the rocks and squealing in the waves. The entrance, the bars, the restaurant would be full of boys selling masks and Cartier watches and ivory. Today it was empty. One old man had assembled his carvings in the carpark. Reception was deserted. I walked into the bar. Nobody. I crossed the little courtyard to the restaurant. Not a soul. I sat on the balcony overlooking the rocks. Nobody was on the beach. I opened my briefcase and checked the telex. It was the date agreed, the time and the place. I got out the newspaper and read a couple more stories about corruption.

Suddenly I jumped. A waiter was rearranging the tables. I was not alone in the world. 'Where is everybody?' I shouted across at him. 'The place is deserted.'

'Yes sir,' he said, flicking dust with a serviette. 'Nobody comes any more. People have no money.'

I walked across to him. 'How long has it been like this?'

'About a year.'

'So what's happened to all the staff?'

'All gone. There's only a few of us left. The old guard,' he smiled.

'Where have they gone?'

'Back to their villages.' The usual African reply.

'But what can they do there?'

'Help their families. Work on the land. Become farmers again.'

'Can they live? Can they make enough money?'

He shrugged his shoulders. 'This is Africa.'

In the West when people lose their jobs, they are cushioned. They get redundancy payments. If times are really hard they can pick up social security. Not so in Africa. If they are entitled to redundancy, they often don't receive it. Either they disappear the moment they are dismissed, or companies take so long to pay they forget all about it. Or, more often, companies don't have the money to pay. Employees, therefore, just disappear. Most go back to their families and hope for the best. Others try to get another job. A few try to emigrate – if they or their families have the money. They end up in France or Canada or Italy selling genuine Cartier watches.

The waiter carried on preparing the restaurant for guests who were not going to come. I wandered down to the beach. Years ago, I remembered, it was Douala-by-the-sea. You could meet ministers, civil servants, businessmen, traders – everybody you couldn't meet during the week. Deals would be done over a beer, agreements reached walking on the sand. A brisk swim would solve any disagreements. Today I only met a stray dog. I went back to the restaurant. All the tables were set for lunch.

I sat down and ordered a drink. Nobody came in. The waiter brought the menu, which still ran to over eight pages. I ordered two lobsters and a bottle of champagne. I might as well give them some business. Anyway, it was depressing and I had nothing else to do. Mr Njike just might turn up so I had to stay a couple of hours. The meal was superb: the lobsters light and succulent, the champagne properly chilled, light, fresh and very frothy. As I downed the last glass, the waiter came up to me. There was somebody to see me at reception. It wasn't my friend but his doctor, a nice, gentle old man, thin with lots of white hair, gold-rimmed spectacles and a nice light smile. He told me Mr Njike was not feeling well. He was sorry he could not come and see me, and had asked him to apologise. I thanked him and invited him to join me. He didn't want lunch, but he asked for a whisky.

The waiter brought it straightaway. 'There can't be many hotels in Africa serving Glenlivet,' I said.

'There aren't,' he said. 'That's my bottle. I keep it here just in case I'm invited to have a drink. I don't like wine or champagne. I like my whisky. Best drink in the world.'

The doctor, I quickly discovered, was Africa's biggest fan of Scotland. He was in love with everything Scottish, especially whisky.

'Studied in Edinburgh,' he told me. 'I try and go back there every year. Sometimes it's difficult, but things have to be very difficult to stop me.'

'Where do you go?'

'Everywhere. I like the cities and the little towns. I like the coast and the countryside, especially the mountains.'

'What do you do?'

'Drink and play golf,' he laughed. He rattled off a list of distilleries, then an equally long list of golf courses. Turnberry was his favourite. 'It's a wonderful course, very exciting, very challenging. And everyday it's different. The wind affects your play more there than at any course in the world.'

I told him it had just been acquired by the Japanese, but it didn't worry him. 'It's still Scotland,' he said. 'My trips to Scotland are my only extravagance. I think to myself, you work hard, you deserve it.'

I wondered whether I could ask him how he could afford it – a local doctor in a not particularly booming corner of Africa in the middle of a depression. I thought, why not, and ordered more drinks. 'You're a lucky man,' I said. 'Being able to visit Scotland every year. I couldn't afford it.'

'You don't get anything unless you work hard for it,' he replied.

'People around here must be pretty sick if you can make enough money to go every year.'

'Oh no,' he laughed, 'I don't make any money from being a doctor. Nobody has money here. If I relied on my patients I wouldn't be able to go to Douala, let alone Dundee.'

'Don't tell me,' I said, 'you're the son of a highland chief. You go back to meet the clan.'

The doctor laughed. 'Oh,' he said, 'you want to know how a poor country doctor can afford it? I'm also in trade. I make my money importing and buying and selling.'

'What do you import?'

'Whisky,' he said. 'I'm one of the biggest whisky importers in Cameroon.'

I was staggered. 'Why not?' he said. 'If I didn't import whisky I couldn't afford to stay here. Then what would the local people do? They would never get another doctor.'

'You mean nobody else would come?'

'Why should they? Doctors have to live as well as anybody else. Unless you had another income you couldn't afford it. Look, the government should pay us, but they don't. I can go for months without getting money from the government. How else am I supposed to live?'

'Does that mean that all doctors in Cameroon have another income?'

'Not all, that's impossible. But lots of them.'

'What do your patients say?'

'They don't know, or if they know they don't care. Just because I import whisky doesn't mean I'm a worse doctor. Do you know,' he asked, 'what the average life expectancy is around here? Forty-five for men and fifty for women,' he said. 'That means that all my friends and colleagues are dying. Every time I go away, I come back and find another friend is dead. They are still young, but they are dying.'

'Because they're not getting the right food?'

'Because they have never *had* the right food. They never had a chance. Look, in Europe you talk about the African debt problem. I'm living with its consequences.' He downed another dram and called for fresh supplies. 'In Europe you say Africa must repay its debts; to default would be to destroy their credit rating with the international financial community. That means that people go without their salaries – for three, four, even five months. They don't eat, they wear the same clothes for years. It means they can't spend. It means the whole town slowly grinds to a standstill. It means . . .' he drew a deep breath. 'It means death. They are just too exhausted to continue. They have nothing to look forward to.'

'You mean they just die.'

'I'm fifty-seven. I have friends of thirty or forty who look like old men; they have nothing inside them. Their wives are old women, their children grow up looking old. They have no strength, no energy. What hope have they?'

'But Cameroon is better off than other countries in Africa.'

'Better off, but still bad. We don't have famine, but we have hunger, lack of proper nourishment.'

We continued talking about the problems of an African country doctor; the amount of hidden poverty and hunger and sheer destitution in the villages, all masked by the official statistics. He told me of people who had lost their jobs in towns or on plantations and had gone back to their villages. The families, hardly able to support themselves, were forced to look after even more people.

'How do they do it?' I asked.

'They can't. They go without. They share nothing. What else can they do? They must help their families. But they have nothing. They starve.'

'Doesn't the government help?'

He waved his hands in the air in exasperation. 'As far as the government is concerned there is no problem. This is not Ethiopia. These people are dying in their houses, not in the desert.'

'Not in front of the television cameras.'

'Governments are only interested in big problems; this is small, a hidden problem. The government doesn't want to know about it.'

'But there must be something somebody can do. What about the aid organisations?'

'They're only interested in big problems.'

We walked across to the terrace overlooking the sea. 'There is something you can do to help,' said the doctor putting his hand on my shoulder. 'What? Tell me.'

'Buy another bottle of whisky,' he said. 'The more you buy, the more money I make, and the more I can help my patients.'

I bought three bottles. We drank one there and then. One I took back to Douala to celebrate the Mount Cameroon race. The other I presented to the doctor – a real whisky doctor.

CONGO

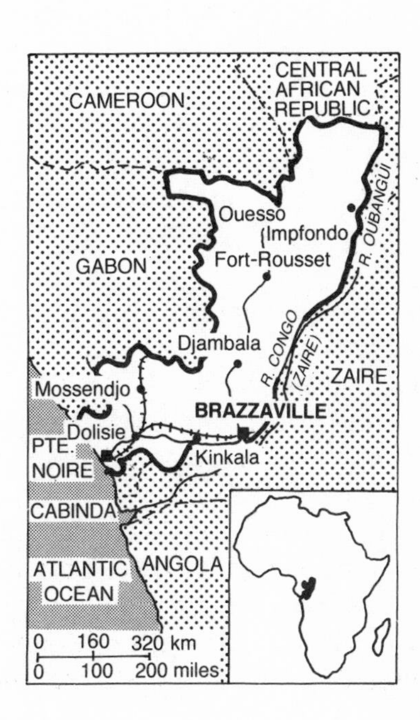

CENTRAL
AFRICAN
REPUBLIC
CAMEROON
Ouesso
Impfondo
GABON
Fort-Rousset
R. OUBANGUI
Djambala
R. CONGO
(ZAIRE)
ZAIRE
Mossendjo
BRAZZAVILLE
Dolisie
PTE.
NOIRE
Kinkala
CABINDA
ATLANTIC
OCEAN
ANGOLA
0 160 320 km
0 100 200 miles

'I've checked your bags straight through, monsieur. They'll be in Abidjan when you get there,' smiled the girl at the Air Afrique check-in desk in Paris.

'But I'm going to Brazzaville.'

'Oh yes,' she said, half in a trance, 'I mean, they'll be in – they'll be in – when you get to Abidjan.'

'But I'm not going to Abidjan, I'm going to –'

'Oh yes. They'll be in –'

'Forget it. Merci beaucoup.' I turned away praying to St Vitus, the patron saint of lost causes, the closest I could get to lost cases at the time.

Normally, thanks to my lucky 500-year-old plastic Niomuhine mask from Guinea which I bought off a Senegalese street trader in Dakar for only £157,243 – or which he and fifty-three other friends of mine forced on me inside a Dakar telephone box – I don't have any problems flying around francophone Africa. The planes are pretty good, apart from the occasional live pig in the aisle. The food is pretty good; better than anglophone Africa. I was once served baked beans three times during a flight on Kenya Airlines. I usually get leg room; I discovered that I'm usually rated ABP, able-bodied person, by the check-in girls, who therefore sit me next to the emergency exit – in case someone needs help. As for the flights, they are as punctual as British Airways on a foggy Bank holiday in the middle of a Spanish air traffic controllers' strike.

Mark you, there was one memorable flight into Ouagadougou. The only way to close the toilet door was to push your fingers through the half-open door and twiddle the latch outside, which looked as though it had come off a shed door. I half expected to see the ground when I pulled the chain. We were treated to stale croissants slapped on to greasy trays, covered in crumbs and sugar lumps, which looked as if they had been used continually since the Wright Brothers first took off.

When passengers complained, the stewardess, who was padding up and down the gangway in bare feet, darted into the toilet and returned with toilet rolls which she unrolled so that people could wipe their trays clean. Everybody immediately remembered a book they had to finish or a report they had promised to fax back to Paris. As we disembarked, instead of whispering us an indifferent bonjour she stood by the door emptying the untouched croissants, rolls and sugar lumps into a carrier bag.

But somehow when I checked in this time at Charles de Gaulle I guessed things might not go as usual. The police had just sealed off the section near the escalator and blown up a briefcase only to discover it belonged to a Beninois minister, invited by the French government on a goodwill mission.

The plane took off on time, give or take forty-three minutes. I had a seat in the middle of the central block and was surrounded by children. By the time we were over Lyon I was knee deep in Asterix comics, Tintin books and a game called Dazzling Debbie et Amis. All along the racks the whole length of the plane were baby cots. I asked for champagne, to be told this was a special holiday flight and all they had was orange juice. Sleep was impossible. The boy next to me kept eating the scented paper face towels and sucking the little air blower on the back of the seat in front.

Over Ouagadougou I suddenly became 'ton-ton' to every child on board. They wanted help in filling in their cartes de débarquement which I happily supplied. I put their professions down as CIA and KGB, apart from the air-sucker, whom I listed as 'Adjouant, Mossad', the Israeli secret service.

The plane, by now squawking louder than any maternity ward, landed with a thud. I looked at my genuine Rolex, another gift from my other 2,954 Senegalese friends, which had cost me only £3.75 but had taken two weeks to negotiate. It had stopped at 12.27 on Wednesday, April 31, 1853.

Customs was a pushover. All the officers were playing with a child's model of a Cadillac saloon which, I noticed, was labelled for the son of the American ambassador. By the time it got to him, it was going to look more like a scaled-down version of a New York taxi cab. All the policemen were shaking hands with 423 clergymen who had arrived three days early for a World Assembly of Churches jamboree.

Suddenly I was grabbed by a smart young man from protocol, sent by the ministry. He insisted I join him in the salon d'honneur. His staff would take care of formalities. Normally I avoid VIP suites on the basis that it is bad enough risking your luggage to the airline without risking it to the airport staff and protocol as well. I protested, but was led off to join a minister from Mozambique, two Italian nuns who were halfway through translating the bible into Lingala; a Swedish teacher who looked suspiciously like an undercover agent for Amnesty International and an elderly American couple. We introduced ourselves and waited.

The American couple grabbed the best chairs; the woman took out a book and started reading in a loud voice to her husband. 'At this mention of the dancing black man, Marcos fell to weeping, and after some moments, said softly, I was not generous with him, Gaveilaco, I deplored his way with women ...' I tried to look unconcerned. '... She works in our kitchen, Maria Victoria. But she's old enough now that people are beginning to talk ...'

After three chapters I asked protocol whether we were still waiting for the luggage or under a subtle form of house arrest. He smiled wearily and shook my hand. Around midnight, after I had three times been refused permission to telephone my lawyer and once had a request turned down for a food parcel, all the luggage arrived. Except mine. The nuns breathed a joyous Alleluia and ran towards a bearded friar lounging against the airport door. The Swede sidled up to a tall, thin, ascetic-looking German. The Americans waited until they had finished the chapter. 'His eyes are bad,' the wife said to me as she closed the book. 'I have to read everything to him.'

I turned to protocol. 'So I've lost my luggage. Now what do I do?'

'When you are in Congo, monsieur, there are no problems.'

Which is not how it looked from where I was sitting, in a shirt that had sweated and dried out four times in the VIP lounge alone, not to mention a suit that looked as though it had been praying to Mecca in a grease pit for the whole of Ramadan.

'So why don't we go and see someone about it?'

'No problem, monsieur.' But, of course, the airport was deserted. I started walking.

The striking thing about Brazzaville, even in the middle of the night searching for a hotel room, is its size. It seems much bigger, much greener and, somehow, much grander than you imagined. The roads are longer and wider, and there are more proper tarmac roads than in other francophone capitals. The buildings seem bigger. There are more big houses, set back in bigger compounds and surrounded by bigger walls.

Cathedrals in French Africa also seem bigger and more exciting than anglophone cathedrals, and I don't just mean the enormous churches Houphouet Boigney is putting up in Côte d'Ivoire. St Ann's Cathedral in Brazzaville is enormous, and powerful. The entrance is shaped like a huge stone canoe. Inside there are massive paintings. The choir can accommodate 200 people, the whole church over 5000.

Other capitals are like villages that have grown into towns. Brazza – as old Africa hands say – is a town about to become a city. It has the space and the layout, maybe because it used to be the capital for French Equatorial Africa. It was also General de Gaulle's African headquarters during the last war. While French West Africa – Senegal, Mauritania, Niger, Mali, Guinea, Burkina Faso, Côte d'Ivoire, Benin – sided with the Vichy government at least up until 1942, French Equatorial Africa – Gabon, Congo, Central Africa and Chad – supported the Free French. But in spite of that everyone is aware that they are living in the shadow of Kinshasa, the capital of Zaire, which stands tall and proud on the other side of the River Congo which here is known as Stanley Pool, Mary Kingsley's favourite African river.

Zaire used to be the Belgian Congo, and before that the Congo Free State. The Congo today is what used to be the French Congo. Sometimes it's known as Congo (Brazzaville), usually by the kind of Americans who boast that they stayed at a great little hotel in Paris called the George Cinq the Fifth.

Halfway into town I picked up a taxi. All the windows had been replaced with plywood in order, the driver said, to keep it cool. 'See the bright lights. That's Kinshasa,' said the driver. 'Look at the skyscrapers. One day we will have buildings like that.'

The two cities have always been rivals. When Kinshasa built its first skyscraper, a modest ten-storey office block, Brazzaville very quickly built one too. For years there were no telephone lines between them. Any call across the river had to travel via Paris. Above Stanley Pool, the river takes you as far as Bangui, the home of that infamous Emperor Bokassa in the Central African Republic, and Kisangani in Zaire. Downstream the river is virtually rapids all the way to the Atlantic.

'At night I like to go down to the river and look at the lights,' the driver said.

'Would you like to live there?' I asked.

'Never. Too big. Too violent. I go across by boat two or three times a month, but I would never live there. I like small towns, the peace and quiet.'

'But isn't there more action, more excitement over there?'

'Certainly. But the wrong kind. Here everything is calm.'

'But don't all cities hit problems once they reach a certain size?'

'True. I suppose we have got to grow. But not too big. We don't want the problems.

I arrived at the hotel as the first study mission from the World Assembly of Churches were leaving the boîte de nuit and collapsed into a staff room overlooking the garage. My original room had been given to an archdeacon from Uruguay because I was so late checking in the manager thought I wasn't on the plane.

At seven o'clock I was back at the airport; partly because I wanted to find my suitcase as quickly as possible, partly because the garage started work at twenty past four with the arrival of the slop wagon to take the day before yesterday's waste to the local pig farm. Yesterday's waste had already been recycled into salade traditionale.

Brazzaville was founded by an Italian count, Pierre Savorgnan de Brazza, who was also a naturalised French army officer. Working on his own and funding his own expeditions, he had already claimed Gabon. Now, backed by barefoot Senegalese soldiers, he founded Brazzaville. The land he claimed from the Bateke king, Makoko, in return for a sack of dirt. But according to Mary Kingsley, who was there at the time, both sides were happy with the deal:

'I have no hesitation in saying. . . . Brazza did a good thing for France that day. Makoko also did well, for he saved himself from the [Belgian] Congo Free State,' she wrote, and went on to praise de Brazza: 'It is impossible for anyone to fail to regard him with the greatest veneration, when one knows from personal acquaintance the make of the country and the dangerousness of the native population with which he has had to deal.' Which still holds true today, although it takes more than a sack of dirt to persuade the desk clerk at the Meridien to let you have a room for the night.

Even early in the morning the city is bustling. The centre is full of modern buildings. There are people everywhere: officials with files under their arms, women with loads on their heads, lots of children; not many policemen, hardly any military. Plenty of lazy young men hawking cassettes and cheap jewellery. And, surprisingly, lots of nuns, mostly white; Portuguese, Italian, French. One day I seemed to meet no one but nuns. At the airport, they were waiting with an elegant young Portuguese priest in a light brown blouson, would you believe, complete with brown slacks and tan shoes and smoking Gauloises. Very Vatican II. Outside the Chamber of Commerce in the town centre they were talking to a group of young mothers. In the port, packed with people delivering and collecting goods, or queuing for tickets to Bangui, more nuns were waiting for medical supplies to arrive. The only place I didn't see them was at the official residence of the papal nuncio which stands in gold and white splendour in the government district.

Nobody at the airport was interested in my problem. The boy in the airline office just kept shaking his head. The customs officer said it was not his responsibility. The airport manager said it was nothing to do with him; and didn't I know it was 'formellement interdit' to be in his office and if I wasn't out in trois secondes he would call the police. I telephoned Protocol at the ministry. They told me the minister had sent my official host to North Korea for another set of the 250 volumes of the *Thoughts* of Kim Il Sung. I was on my own. I spent three days going from airport to customs to airline to protocol before I found somebody I could talk to. By now the beggars were pushing coins into my hand and telling me to go to the mosque for a bowl of rice.

'Why didn't you report this straightaway?' said an elderly Dutchman at the airline office. I didn't say a word. He handed me a form which, roughly translated, began with the heading, 'In the name of God, please may we have your comments. Write in capital letters.'

'Come back at five. I will find your suitcase,' said the Dutchman. I thanked him, and walked up and down Avenue Lumumba for two hours hoping the sweat stains in my suit would dry out.

Along Avenue Lumumba, into Avenue de l'Independence and into the centre of town. There are absolutely no facilities for tourists: no postcards for sale, no tourist organisations, no guided tours. And no safari organisations, which is odd, because even in the sixteenth century, Leo Africanus or Al-Hassan Ibn Mohammed Al-Wezaz Al-Fasi to his friends, was raving about the wild life: 'Goates, sheepe, deere, Gugelle, conies, hares, civet-cats, and ostriches, are great swarmers of tigers, which are very hurtfull both to man and beast. The Zebra or Zabra of this countrey being about the bignes of a mule, is a beast of incomparable swiftnes ... Buffles, wilde asses, called by the Greekes Onagri, and Dantes ... range in heards up and downe the woods. Also here are infinite store of elephants ...'

Today it's the same, but better. Congo has pygmies and of course gorillas. But there is no way you can see them. Although I'm told if you talk to the French lady in the opticians she can arrange for you to go shooting.

'We have found your suitcase,' said a check-in clerk as I dripped through his office door.

'Merci, monsieur, merci beaucoup. Vous êtes –'

'It's in Nouatchott.'

'But I need it here. I've been . . .'

'You should have reported it earlier.'

'But there was nobody to report it to. Nobody wanted –'

'I am doing my best to help you.'

'I know, I'm very grateful,' I said taking a deep breath. 'How soon can you get it here?'

'I will have to ask Atlanta, monsieur.'

'Atlanta!'

'Atlanta is our worldwide headquarters for lost luggage.'

'So give them a call,' I said, suddenly excited at the thought of using a second handkerchief in four days.

'I can't do that, monsieur, because we have to send everything in by telex otherwise it clogs the system.'

'Well, let's send them a telex.'

'They are closed, monsieur. The time difference.'

'Well, send them a telex so it's there waiting when they open.'

'They close the telex down. You'll have to come back tomorrow.'

That night I moved into a proper bedroom. But at one in the morning I was moved back again. The manager said guests were complaining about the shower being used all night.

'Everything is all right, monsieur. It's on its way,' said the Dutchman when I sneaked into his office three seconds after it opened the following morning. 'I sent a telex to Brussels for forwarding to Atlanta.'

'And it worked?'

'It worked.'

'So when does it get here?'

'The day after tomorrow.'

'But I leave tomorrow evening,' I said.

'Can't you wait?'

'How would you like to spend four days in the same clothes?'

'The same clothes? You didn't tell me.'

'You mean you think I enjoy going around like this?'

'If you had told me I could have given you an allowance. We have a special allowance for people who lose their luggage.'

'I didn't lose it. You lost it.'

'I am trying to help you. Do you want to apply for our allowance?'

'Yes, please.'

He produced a roll of wallpaper. 'Name?'

'You know my name. You've been sending telexes –'

'I have to fill in the form,' he said sharply. And so we went through the form together: my date of birth, my mother's maiden name, the lot. 'Now, monsieur. Votre date de départ.'

'Demain matin. Dix heures.'

He put his pen down. 'Monsieur,' he said icily, 'if you are leaving tomorrow morning you are not entitled to the allowance. The allowance can only be paid if you are without your luggage for over twenty-four hours.'

'But I have been. I haven't had a clean shirt since –'

'But you did not tell me you wanted to claim for the allowance until now.'

'I didn't know there was an allowance,' I said, gripping the edge of his so far unblood-stained table. 'You've only just told me.'

'You've only just asked me. If you'd asked me before I would have helped you.' He paused, obviously counted up to dix, then spat out, 'Monsieur.'

'But how could I know there was an allowance –' I waved my hands weakly, took two deep breaths, counted up to vingt and continued. 'Okay. So why can't I have the allowance anyway? You know I've lost my suitcase . . .'

'Administration, monsieur. We must keep to the rules, mustn't we?'

'If you'd kept to the rules my luggage wouldn't have gone missing.'

'Oui, monsieur.' Another icy blast.

I rose and padded to the door. 'Just occurred to me. Can you confirm my ticket for the flight tomorrow?'

'Oui, monsieur. If you would like to wait outside the young lady will look after you.'

The girl punched away at the terminal. 'I am sorry, monsieur, the flight is full. You should have reconfirmed it earlier.'

'Oh, this is –' I started losing control. 'Let me see the manager.'

'He is on the phone, monsieur.'

'You didn't even bother to check.'

'I can tell by the light on the phone.'

'Well I've got to get the plane. I've been here since Sunday, all my papers are in my suitcase, it's been a complete waste of time. I've just got to –' Then it struck me. There's no point in reasoning with them. Look how far it had got me so far.

'Look!' I screamed, pointing at the manager's office. 'Fire! Vite!'

The girl turned round to look. I leant over the counter and grabbed a handful of those little flight confirmation slips. She turned round stonily. 'I think you had better leave, monsieur.'

I wrote my own flight confirmation details, and up-graded my ticket to first class. Then to stop Sabena realising what I had done, I went into Air Afrique and switched airlines and flights. That would make it more difficult for them to trace me. It's a trick I learnt in Abidjan when my ticket was stolen. The airline refused to issue me with another because they said that stolen tickets are switched from airline to airline so it becomes impossible to trace them. This was my chance to get my own back on the system.

I returned to the airport the following morning about five hours before departure. The girl checked me in without looking at the ticket. An elderly French supervisor said something about not being notified. I pretended I couldn't understand, and shuffled off to the first-class departure lounge to drink it dry. The flight was called, and at the gate I spotted them; on one side the Dutch airline manager, on the other, the official from protocol.

'Your suitcase, monsieur,' said the Dutchman and handed me my battered Delsey, covered in sand and grease. 'It wasn't lost after all. It just fell off the trolley on the way to the baggage hall. It's been here all the time. Have a good flight.'

'No problems, monsieur,' said Protocol. 'I told you when you are in Brazzaville there are no problems.'

I looked at my watch. It had just started working again.

Exactly 307 years after a total eclipse of the sun over the south of the Congo basin I was back in Brazzaville. How do I know? Because a nineteenth-century Hungarian explorer, Emil Torday, heard of the eclipse while talking to the elders of the Bushong people in the forests along the river. They were drinking palm wine and 'talking about the great events of various reigns and we came to their 98th king, Bo Kama Bomanchala. They said that nothing remarkable had happened during his reign except that one day at noon the sun went out and there was absolute darkness for a short while.' Torday describes how he jumped to his feet and 'lost all self-control. The elders thought that I had been stung by a scorpion.' He at last had an objective clue to dating the history of the Bushong people. Which proves the value of sitting and talking and drinking palm wine.

Which was why I was back in the Congo again for a conference although, knowing African conferences, they would probably be serving more than palm wine. The conference, like all African conferences, started late; partly because the camarade directeur adjoint at the registration desk was spending all his time trying laboriously to wrap up conference documents into a parcel.

Once the conference finally got going the speakers spent most of the reduced time complaining that they didn't have enough time to speak. Except one old lady on crutches who spent most of her allotted time being lifted in her wheelchair on to the platform and hobbling out of it to the rostrum to announce that she couldn't make her speech because it was in Zurich. Nobody sympathised, or asked what she was going to say; instead the chairman asked which airline was responsible. When she said Swissair the whole conference erupted in uproar. That the ice-cool, super-efficient Swiss could make a mistake and send a poor old lady's luggage around the world was too much. After years of apologising for the shortcomings of African airlines, this was muesli from heaven.

The conference was on improving productivity in sub-Sahara Africa – at least I think it was. As far as I could understand what few speeches the organisers managed to squeeze in between late coffee breaks and early lunches, everybody was talking about everything except improving productivity.

'Strikes me the only productivity in sub-Sahara Africa that is improving is the organisation of conferences,' I said to the woman next to me.

'That is an interesting concept,' she said. 'I will propose a study.'

The camarade directeur of the afternoon session, a Zairois banker, was speaking in English because he said fewer people seemed to fall asleep when English was spoken. 'Mon dieu,' whispered a Frenchman behind me, 'We are being overrun by saxophones.'

I didn't go back to the next session. Instead I went to visit some friends working for Congolese television. The government had just signed an agreement with the Soviet Union and they were hoping to go to Moscow for training.

To the Africans, Congo is Communist. Tell a minister anywhere in French Africa you are going to Congo and he will tell you, 'They are Communists. Prenez garde.' Which is not strictly true. Admittedly they all wear red scarves on ceremonial occasions and refer to businessmen as 'economic operators', but they are not Communists in the strict Marxist-Leninist sense.

When Major Marien Ngouabi and the army seized power in 1968 he formed the Parti Congolais du Travail on a Marxist-Leninist platform and the label stuck, even though with its enormous oil reserves it is potentially one of the richest countries in Africa. The assassination of Ngouabi in 1977 seems to have made them more determined than ever to stick with it although in many ways it is the most openly Catholic of all the francophone countries.

'It's the Poland of Africa,' one diplomat told me. 'They have this fierce loyalty to their faith. They don't always like it, or agree with it, but they are determined to keep it.'

'Their Catholic faith,' I said.

'No. Their Marxist-Leninism,' he replied.

In fact one of their early presidents was a Catholic priest, Abbé Fulbert Youlou, who was forced to resign in 1963 after two days of rioting in which the prison in Brazzaville was destroyed and a number of ministers' homes set on fire. French troops helped to keep order. But when the Abbé asked de Gaulle, whom he described as 'une créature divine. C'est dieu qui l'a fait exprès pour les Français,' for reinforcements, la créature divine refused. The Congolese army stepped in and appointed a new government. French troops, de Gaulle maintained, should be used to maintain public order not to shore up unpopular regimes, the same policy he had followed three years previously when he refused to send troops to Mali.

But today, in spite of calling each other camarade, Congo is no more a Marxist-Leninist state than Gorbachev's Soviet Russia. They do, however, have stronger leftwing views than most francophone countries: they are more anti-South Africa and anti-apartheid; more anti-Israel. But apart from one or two old guard ministers they are probably no more pro-Russian.

Ask any francophone African if he knows the UK – one or two have visited London; I once met a Zairois who learnt English in Glasgow; there is a deputé in Togo who even speaks Welsh. But I am always surprised at how many francophone Africans have visited the Soviet Union. The Russians seem to have a system for identifying potential high flyers while they are still students and whisking them off for a quick conference, or maybe even three months' study. It certainly gives them plenty of good contacts in government, in business, among students, but, I would guess, few recruits. Somehow the Africans, especially the francophones, find it difficult to adjust to the austere, regimented life of the Soviet Union. Not to mention the cold.

'It was interesting. I studied very hard. But it was too cold for me,' a junior Congolese diplomat told me. 'One day my brother forgot his hat and while he was waiting for the bus his ears got frostbite and just dropped off!' Others complain about the food, the way of life, the restrictions. One Congolese journalist told me, 'Until I went to Moscow I thought the Russians were interested in Africa, but they are not. They are only interested in where there is trouble. Not like the French.'

He spoke a little Russian so he was able to talk to ordinary Russians. 'In Africa, we are told by the Russians that we are important; that the Russian people are following our struggles. It's not true. The Russians don't know the different African countries, or our languages. They think we speak African. They don't know anything.'

He told me about Russian newspapers. 'Our newspapers are

always writing about Russia; Russian newspapers don't write anything about Africa. I read *Pravda* in Moscow every day – they hardly said anything about Africa. If an African president came to Moscow they reported that, but there was nothing about our problems, or how we are overcoming them.'

'But they must have written about some countries?'

'Yes, the ones they are involved in; the Socialist countries – Angola, Mozambique.'

'And South Africa?'

'Yes, but always in terms of the struggle against apartheid. They write a lot about South Africa, and Libya, but that's so they can criticise the United States. I did a survey; over three months they published thirty-three articles about Africa, and thirteen were about South Africa. And there is very little real news, only long articles about the history of the struggles of the working class in Africa, the oppression of the colonial powers, that kind of thing. Of course they have different news values from us. They also have very few journalists in Africa, unlike the Chinese. Then most big projects involve the Americans; the Russians are hardly going to write about the Americans helping Africa.'

'What about the help the Russians are giving Africa?'

'I expected them to write about themselves, but they don't seem to. Oh, you might see a report about a cocktail party in Luanda to celebrate the anniversary of the October Revolution – nothing else. Another thing,' he said, 'I thought they would write lots of articles celebrating our independence, like the *Financial Times* and the *International Herald Tribune*. But nothing. That surprised me because *Pravda* does not have to sell advertising to pay for a supplement.'

The Soviet Union never gives as much help to Africa as the West. The Russians will tell you this is because they believe that the problems in Africa were created by the West, and it is up to the West to solve them. On top of that the Soviet Union gives most of its aid to Ethiopia: around 60 percent of the US $3 billion voted for Africa as a whole. Congo only gets 2.6 percent, in spite of its credentials. Most of that money covers construction projects or mining and technical assistance. Occasionally the Russians send the francophones, especially Guinea,

Mali and Benin, plant and machinery. On one glorious occasion they delivered snow ploughs to the Côte d'Ivoire. Sometimes they also send advisers.

'So the Russians are not really interested in Africa?'

'I don't think the ordinary Russian is; he's got enough problems of his own. And the government are only interested in helping us throw off the colonial oppressor and in criticising America. Funny, but all the time they are criticising American policy in Africa. There is hardly a word about the French.'

'Which shows what a good job the French are doing in Africa. Did they ever write about the British in Africa?'

'They wrote about Britain as the colonial oppressor, but not in modern terms.'

The Russians have tried and failed to get a foothold in francophone Africa. The Africans like their caviar, but not much else.

There was no caviar at the Brazzaville hotel that evening. I was stuck behind a group of Americans. Daughters of the Revolution, following in the footsteps of Stanley, or John Rowlands as he was known in Denbigh, Wales until he arrived in New Orleans in 1857 and changed his name. For Stanley followed the Congo River from its source to the Atlantic.

'Bonsoir, mesdames. Qu'est-ce que vous –' began the waiter.

Without waiting for him to finish the most aggressive old lady shouted, 'Salad. Green. Verte.' She turned to her companions and said, 'That's the way to do it. You tell them straight.'

Another hesitated. 'But think how they prepare the salad. A friend of mine said she was in Tunisia once and the kitchens were next to the toilets. You just can't be too careful.'

'My daughter's professor went down with severe food poisoning after coming back from Africa. He was out of action for months.' The fourth added, 'And it's endemic with malaria, just everywhere. I didn't want to come but everybody said it would be an experience.'

The waiter was standing patiently in his best George V manner: interested, concerned and eager to please.

'Well we can't have nothing. I know I've got to lose weight, but I'm not going to starve.' The second Daughter of the Revolution turned to the waiter; 'Do you have steak? I'll have steak. Well done. Burnt. Cremated.'

Gradually everybody ordered: salads and steaks, the safe foods. Then it came to the drinks. The first lady was eager to try her French again. 'Local beer. Two cans. One unopened. Fermé,' she shouted, pleased with her ability to bridge the gap between two cultures. Everybody followed suit.

The third lady suddenly lunged at the waiter, jabbed her finger at his chest and shouted, 'Tea. English. Last. End. Fini.'

'Merci beaucoup, mesdames. Bon appetit.' The waiter retreated with the order. I heard him say in impeccable English, with a slight trace of an Oxford accent, 'Table 16, usual American menu: salads and steak.' If I was him I would have been hopping mad, but he obviously accepted it. Maybe the first time it had ruffled him, but it was now part of the job. I discovered afterwards that he had studied at the Sorbonne, and at university in Cameroon and in Montreal. He had a law degree and spoke French, English, German and Spanish. But this was the only job he could get.

'It's the American ambassador,' the minister told me, 'you'll have to wait outside. Don't worry, I'll get rid of him in five minutes.'

I took my glass of champagne outside to talk to the police on duty. As I did, the ambassador shuffled in with a lean, bronzed marine-looking type and a fit, blowsy Daughter of the Revolution. 'Three minutes late,' she was huffing. 'Wait until they want something from us.' Five minutes later, they were out and I was back in.

Congolese government offices are wonderful, like giant faded castles: long, low, dark with files and papers everywhere. An occasional fan whines overhead. The sun is blazing outside, but inside everything is cool.

The presidence, on the other hand, seems to owe more to the rational side of French culture than to the more usual sense of glory and destiny. It is a series of low-slung buildings like an army barracks. The only concession to splendour is the entrance, designed so that when you drive up to the main door you suddenly swing uphill and brake with a flourish. The waiting room is old-fashioned and dusty. Two big battered sofas run down the walls. A policeman, curled up fast asleep in a corner, didn't stir when I went in or when I left, which tells you how safe the Congo is. One wall has a giant mural depicting the history of the country to what looks like colonial times. Which, in a strongly socialist country, struck me as odd. The start of the picture is harmless enough – natives, hunting, straw huts. But the final part showed white men in khaki being carried in sedan chairs by crowds of natives.

I first met President Denis Sassou N'Guesso when he arrived at Heathrow for an official visit as president of the Organisation of African Unity. I had been responsible for the arrangements for his visit. Many African presidents look military, but Sassou N'Guesso is 100 percent military. Built like a commando, he always stands, even sits, at attention. He is brisk, brief, to the point. He gives you a feeling of power. He and Mrs Thatcher got on very well, which did not surprise me. He was just finishing his term as president of the OAU, and had been travelling for most of the previous year. He had hit the headlines for his uncompromising stand against South Africa. Now he was going back to, some said, discontent at home; there was even talk of an overthrow.

'Crazy people,' the minister said to me later at dinner that evening. 'They come in here, think they can tell me what to do. They want this, they want that. They're not serious.'

'But the Americans do a lot for Africa – aid, grants, the Peace Corps,' I said.

'Coca-Cola, hot dogs. They're not serious,' he repeated. 'They're so amateur,' he almost sneered. The Americans in Africa are, I agree, nowhere near as professional as the French. But I didn't think they were as bad as that.

'They think we know nothing. They come in, the biggest country in the world, the world policeman. They think they're always right; we've got to do as they say. They treat us like children.' He snorted. 'They are so silly. Listen, I'll tell you what I mean. The ambassador comes to see me – in my office, in my home. The first thing he does always is play with his fountain pen. He waves it around, pretends to write, then he puts it on the table between us – with the top pointing to me.'

I was baffled by this explanation of American stupidity. 'It's a microphone,' he said. 'He is recording everything I say. And he thinks I don't know. They're all crazy.'

'You're joking,' I said, but he wasn't.

'How do you know it's a microphone?'

'Because we've got the pen,' he said triumphantly.

'But how did you get it?' I asked.

'We have ways.'

'The French. They got it.' He smiled. 'The Israelis then.' He continued smiling.

'His Excellency,' he said pompously, 'of the United States of America, the greatest power on earth . . .' he paused. 'He left it behind.' And collapsed hysterical with laughter. I must admit, so did I. It was too silly for words.

'He left it behind,' he sobbed, 'on the table,' he mopped his brow, 'under some papers.'

'They're not serious,' he said, recovering his composure. 'Trust them?' He spat out the words. 'How can you trust them? They can't even trust themselves. They want us to share our secrets with them. How can we? They'd leave them all over the tables of the world,' he snapped.

I wondered how he realised the pen was not a pen. 'I didn't. I told my policeman to send it back to the ambassador. To me it was a pen. But he thought it was a bomb. We called the military. They told us it was a microphone.'

'Did you find out where they were transmitting everything?'

'To the ambassador's car, parked outside.'

They called in the French, who sent a specially trained team of counterintelligence agents to investigate. They discovered a vast communications operation based in the US embassy, he told me, capable of penetrating any building in the country and transmitting everything to Washington immediately. 'We always wondered why the Americans had so many people here. They kept telling us we were one of their priority countries in Africa. But now we really know why.'

'So presumably they got into the presidence, the military, wherever you had visiting heads of state . . .'

'They were probably listening in,' he continued. 'We've always had lots of American cars here. You'd see them outside hotels, outside people's homes. We thought they all had mistresses. But the French said to get a decent reception they had to have uninterrupted access, so when they were parked outside a house . . .'

I asked if they had called the ambassador in and complained. 'No. We wanted to, but the French said no.' 'Because now you can feed them wrong information.' 'Exactly.'

'And the French then sold you a load of expensive detecting equipment . . .'

'They did.'

'And a special negotiating room impossible for microphones and radios to get through.'

He looked at me quizzically. 'How did you know?'

'I heard it on my fountain pen,' I said. He looked at me, and for an instant I thought I had gone too far. But all of a sudden he exploded into another burst of hysteria.

'With his fountain pen,' he sobbed. 'With his fountain pen,' he cried into his handkerchief. It was enough to make Smiley smile.

It was one of Jean-Philippe's off days. 'I've spent nearly thirty years in Africa. I love Africa. I don't even go back to France any more. But, honestly, it can be the most inefficient, corrupt, impossible place on earth. You do everything you can for them. You give your life for them. And what do they do? They steal the money from right under your nose.' He sighed a big sigh. 'But I still can't help loving them. They're like children, they don't know they're doing wrong.'

'No sense of shame,' I said.

'That's right. You discuss everything with them. You agree. What do they do? They carry on as if nothing has happened, as if you never discussed anything. They're amazing.'

An old Portuguese missionary I once met in Zaire had told me something similar. 'We have some wonderful nurses in our hospital,' he said. 'They make a fuss of the patients, mother them. You couldn't ask for better. But when we leave them to look after themselves they fall to pieces. They forget to give them their medicines. They don't keep them clean. It is almost as if they do it deliberately because that way they know we'll come back.'

Jean-Philippe was an adviser with Caisse Centrale de Coopération Economique, the French government's shadowy but effective aid and technical assistance organisation. Some say it is the Elysée's backdoor method for keeping French Africa French. By providing the best advisers and most highly qualified consultants – and the aid – France ensures that African governments are not even tempted to look elsewhere. I think there is an element of that in their thinking, but I'm convinced the French are in Africa because they like Africa.

Jean-Philippe, for example. I first met him over ten years ago. Since then he has worked in three other francophone countries. He doesn't do it for the money; he would get much, much more in France. He doesn't do it for the glamour; not for him fast cars at the airport, sirens, intimate dinners with ministers, audiences with presidents that seem to greet even minor dignitaries nowadays from the World Bank or the IMF. And he certainly doesn't do it for a life of luxury, an elegant house, hundreds of servants. In Brazza he lives in a tiny, old-fashioned bungalow, a factory site with furniture that might have been rejected by an Oxfam shop, a dog with a bad leg that still hasn't healed after three years and a wife as devoted to Africa as he is.

I met him outside his office one evening. We were going to wander round the Poto Poto district, between the stalls and in and out of the bars and nightclubs. I had just got back from Italy and he said his favourite city was Florence. I told him they were digging up the Piazza della Signoria, probably the first main square ever built in Europe, and photographing and numbering each stone. The trouble was they had just discovered that the city employees were selling the paving stones off cheap to nuovi riechi as borders for swimming pools.

'They're lucky,' he said. 'Here the money just disappears.'

'How can it disappear?' I said. 'I've heard of money being recycled, borrowed, diverted, even stolen – not disappearing.'

'The money just disappears. There's no indication – you can't find it,' he said.

'So what's the solution?'

'First you've got to have proper accounts, then auditors.

You've got to have a bureaucracy that is not corrupt and will control things.'

'Do you think it's possible? After all, if in Florence ...'

'It's got to be.'

'Unless ...'

We jumped into his car and headed for Poto-Poto. 'I know $100,000 disappears every week,' he said. 'I've been through the books again and again. I've checked the orders, the invoicing, the receipts, the bank. Everything is in order. But somehow it disappears.' He laughed as we shot between two broken-down taxis. It was a game. 'You've got to admire them. The country has nothing at the moment. It's struggling to make ends meet. And here they are taking $100,000 a week and I don't know how they do it.'

'Everybody says Zaire is the worst country for corruption. I didn't think it was bad here.'

'Oh, it's not bad here. Here it's $100,000 a week. In Zaire it's $1 million a week. Mobutu is supposed to be the richest man in the world.'

'But they all say that.'

'It's true. Everybody puts up with it because we need the cobalt, the uranium. We can't afford to let the Russians get their hands on it. So Mobutu has ten, twenty billion dollars stashed away in Société Général or in Switzerland – it's cheap at the price.'

'How do you go about stealing a billion dollars? I can imagine how you would get, I don't know, a hundred thousand. You play games with invoices and so on. But a billion!'

'There's a million ways. I'm no expert but I reckon I know most of the tricks.'

'Apart from the hundred thousand you can't find.'

Jean-Philippe remembered he had to buy vegetables. Apparently the very best vegetables in Africa are to be bought from a fat old lady who has a stall inside the gates of the port.

The port is a heaving, thriving mass of people. Families queuing for the next boat to Bangui; traders waiting to cross the river to Kinshasa; women wandering around with trays of fish, food, textiles, secondhand shirts with designer labels, even live chickens on their heads eager to make just one sale in a day.

Then through the packed crowd comes a big Mercedes and somehow everybody breathes in and a space opens and it pulls up. Out gets an immaculately dressed old man, greying at the temples, very distinguished.

'Zairois,' an old lady mumbles. 'How do you know?' I asked. 'Very rich. All Zairois are rich.' 'Don't you have rich people in Congo?' 'We have rich people. But they keep quiet. Not like in Zaire.'

A student butted in. 'In Zaire, the businessmen have palaces, made of marble. I used to work there.'

He said that whenever he needed money he went across to Kinshasa. He knew the boatman so he had no problems. First, he got a job in a hotel. The Zairois don't like working in hotels, they all want to be managers. Then one evening the manager told him he had to go to one of the minister's private houses. They had been asked to serve a banquet. 'We went to this house just outside Kinshasa. It was enormous, like a church. There were big steps up to the front, all marble. We counted sixty. The security men told us that when the patron arrives home in the evening the staff have to stand on the steps to welcome him. And,' he drew a deep breath, 'there is one person on every step.'

'You're joking,' I said. 'They were making it up.'

The old lady shook her head and spat on the ground. Whether she just felt like it, or whether she was a social critic I wasn't certain. She was surrounded by woodcuts, one of which featured a patient stretched out on an operating theatre. At his head was an anaesthetist applying gas. The other figure was a surgeon neatly stitching him up. A veritable ballade en bois. An old man on the next stall was selling the most fantastic collection of Africa harps. Some were tiny and very fragile; others, like the famous Senegalese harp, were enormous.

'That's what he told me,' continued the student.

'But sixty people. *Hotels* don't have sixty people.'

'This was bigger than a hotel. And inside everything was big; big statues, big paintings – the bar was bigger than in a hotel. He said he could serve drinks from any country in the world. And the food: Russian caviar – they ate it with big spoons – and foie gras flown in from Paris. He used to charter a plane to bring in his own champagne . . .'

Jean-Philippe had bought the vegetables and we had pushed our way back to the car when I saw a fat old Mama Benz selling pills. Counterfeit drugs are a big problem throughout Africa. Not just for the pharmaceutical companies whose products are being copied, but for the poor Africans who are spending money they can ill afford for something that at best will do them no good and at worst may do them great harm. The middlemen, mostly Lebanese, make enormous sums either faking existing drugs or, worse still, buying up old and rejected drugs in the West and shipping them out to Africa and elsewhere.

'Excuse me, madame,' I said, 'I have a headache. Do you have anything for a headache?'

'Two white ones and a red one,' she said without even looking at me.

'It's very bad. Do you think that will do the trick?'

'Add a yellow as well,' she said. This type of marketplace diagnosis goes on all over Africa.

'You mustn't think all counterfeit drugs are bad,' Jean-Philippe told me. 'Some of them are good; maybe not *as* good but good enough. Don't forget in Africa we haven't got lots of money. So our choice is simple. A big drugs company comes along and says, Here is our new drug. It's fantastic. It costs US $10. That's expensive. Another company says, Here is our new drug. It is almost as good but it only costs US $5. I agree, with the second drug there might be a risk, but we are prepared to take the risk to treat twice as many patients. I know that's not what you do in Europe or the States, but this is Africa.' And after all, who wouldn't prefer even a ten-to-one chance of being cured than no chance at all?

Making cheap imitations is one thing; counterfeiting high-quality pharmaceuticals, copying trademarks and packaging, and charging the same price as for the real thing is much worse. I've been told about counterfeit drugs companies based in Africa but frankly I don't believe it. Most of the fake drugs, I am sure, come in from the Far East, and maybe Italy and the States.

I had some important correspondence to post to London. Normally I give my post to a secretary or a driver and leave it to them, but this was urgent. I asked Jean-Philippe to drop me off at the post office which, I had been told, closed at 5 pm. We got there around 4.30 to find the doors already shut. I would have put it down to faulty information, but Jean-Philippe said that if the workers wanted to go home early they just closed the doors regardless of regulations. If I really wanted to post my letter I should go around to the backdoor and see if anybody there could help.

Round the back we met a nice man who kept swatting imaginary mosquitoes. I explained I needed stamps, that I had to get some documents to London urgently. He took us in the back way, past mountains of mailbags, heaps of letters waiting to be sorted, swatting mosquitoes. We met a supervisor, an old man with fuzzy white hair.

'You need stamps?' he said. 'Go upstairs to the room with a red door.' I thanked him and tried to shake hands with the mosquito swatter, but it proved impossible. We ran up the stairs and opened the red door. Inside were about ten people and all the stamps I could want. Except they were stamps they were peeling off the envelopes to re-sell. This was why my letters never arrived, they were never sent. The staff took the stamps and threw the letters away.

I didn't know whether to pretend I didn't know what they were doing or to be direct. I decided on the latter. 'Now I know why my letters never arrive,' I said.

They just grinned. 'It helps the government,' the man by the window said. 'They don't have to pay us so much. It also means they don't have to buy so many lorries and vans. It's good for them. That's why we do it.' I just laughed. It was so outrageous – and so logical.

The man then said, 'You help us, we give you stamps. No charge. You agree?' For the next hour we helped to steam and peel and tear hundreds of stamps off letters and cards posted to Europe. At least I got my own letters posted.

'You were telling me how to steal a billion dollars,' I said as we walked back to the car.

'Well, the first and most obvious is the straight percentage deal. You know the idea. I may be a minister or whatever but I have a big family, lots of responsibility, that kind of thing.'

'What kind of percentage? Ten? Twelve and a half?'

'Goodness me, no. This is Africa. At least 20, maybe even 25. I've even heard of 50 percent. Goodness, if it were only 10 percent we wouldn't have such problems. It would be cheaper to give everybody a straight 10 percent and forget about corruption.'

'But how can you give such huge commissions?'

'You can't. It's as simple as that. But they do.'

'How is it paid?'

'Into a bank; usually Paris, sometimes New York. Not so often Switzerland, it's too obvious. Sometimes cash.'

'Fifty percent in *cash*?'

'I've seen trunks of cash dragged across hotel lobbies in the south of France, in Monte Carlo, even in the London Hilton.'

'In London!'

'I was in the lobby talking when I saw some officials from the embassy dragging this big trunk across the floor. They wouldn't let the porters touch it. I asked them, What's in it? A dead body? They said it was the commission of some deal a minister had just completed.'

'They all knew about it? They weren't trying to keep it quiet?'

'They're quite open about it. In some countries they throw parties to celebrate their latest deal.'

'So if you don't want cash, how else can you take it?'

'Buy a house in Europe, that's a favourite. I know a junior ministry of defence official who was given a big house in Onslow Square by a company that sold the army heavy lifting cranes, because he pushed the paperwork through for them. But that's old hat now, the big operators have all the houses they want. Now they are trying to set up their own big companies so they get their commission and part of the sub-contract work.'

'How?'

'Well, in the old days if a new building was to be put up they would take a commission and that would be that. Today they want a commission, and they want their architect to design it, and their construction company to build it.'

The Soleil, the red and white Brazza Express, was pulling into the station at the end of its run from Pointe-Noire on the Atlantic coast, the one-time booming oil and economic capital of the Congo. The old people will tell you that each railway sleeper represents the death of a Congolese; they were forced to build the line virtually with their bare hands. Next time, I promised myself, I would make the trip by train. I've met lots of people who have, and they all said it was an experience they would never forget.

'So how do they get their architects and so on in on the act?'

'By getting their wife or sister or secretary to form a company. They then establish a joint venture with a French or Belgian or Lebanese company. Then they give them the contract. Simple.'

'What do the aid organisations say?'

'Oh, they all know it's going on, but they can't say anything. They make certain they are the only local company bidding for the contract. No way is an aid organisation going to tell the Africans not to use an African company. And they always submit a low price.'

'Then push the price up as they go along. Hit problems during construction – suppliers late with deliveries, the weather.'

'You've got it. And the tender boards are not going to query it because they know what's going on. In any case, they want to keep their jobs.' We swung into Poto-Poto.

'We had a case recently with the head office of a new bank. Everything went out to international tender. At the tender meeting we decided the pricing was too technical for us to decide so we appointed a firm of international accountants to analyse the bids and recommend one. To keep everything straight we went to a firm from a country which had not submitted any tender.'

'A British firm.'

'Right,' he laughed, 'because the British never try to get contracts in French Africa.' We accepted the auditor's recommendation, and made our recommendation to the board. The board ignored our suggestion and gave the contract to an African country at a much higher price ... because the chairman's wife was a director and they all agreed they should encourage local companies. If they don't, local companies will never get the expertise and be able to compete.'

'So what other tricks are there?'

'Oh I heard a wonderful story the other day,' he said. 'A few years ago President Mobutu decided he wanted to improve his English. Somebody at the presidence rang up the American embassy and asked if anybody was interested in giving English lessons; nobody was, so they told them to ring the Peace Corps. The girl who answered at the Peace Corps said she wouldn't mind. When she turned up at the presidence she was taken into Mobutu.'

'You mean when they rang the embassy they didn't say the lessons were for Mobutu?'

'No. All hell broke loose when the embassy found out, but it was too late. Mobutu was happy with the girl.'

'Hilarious.'

'Oh, it gets better. Apparently Mobutu was in his office having his English lesson when some big US oil company turned up to sign contracts for more oil concessions. He told them to make out the contract to the girl, and he would give the concessions to her instead. So the girl gets a slice of all the oil.'

'Never.'

'This is Africa, you know.'

Who's to say what's right or wrong? Are such things surprising in a country where senior government officials earn less than £10 a month and have to walk to and from the office two hours every day? And even in straight-up-and-down places like Yorkshire you can't do a deal without adding something on top 'for luck'.

That's money. What about other forms of corruption? I came across a case once where a lawyer was actually suing a company of which he was a director. I was visiting a big company in Côte d'Ivoire. The president asked me if I would like to sit in on a meeting with their lawyer – the best in the country, he said. They were owed a lot of money by one of their distributors; friendly persuasion had achieved nothing, now they were going to throw the book at them. The lawyer I had met briefly a number of times. He was in his early thirties, very dashing, very professional. Everybody said he would be a minister one day.

When the name of the company they wanted to sue came out I couldn't help pointing out what to me was an obvious conflict of interest. This came as a surprise to the company director. 'But I am a lawyer,' he replied with all the dignity of the French nation. 'My duty is to my client.'

'But you have clients on both sides,' I gasped. 'How can you be objective?'

'I am only interested in justice,' he said stiffly.

'But if you're on both sides, you will only be interested in compromise,' I couldn't help replying.

The president intervened, asking the lawyer if what I said was true. He then asked him if he felt in all honesty it was possible for him to continue to represent the company. The lawyer said, without doubt, it was. There were two sides to every argument. Just because he was involved with both sides did not mean that he was not interested in the search for justice. In fact, he was even more interested. Normally he was concerned with winning a legal argument; this time the issue was justice. He made it seem that to comment, let alone question him further, would have been an affront to his dignity and France's as well. The president simply nodded.

Later I heard that the case had come to court, the company had won the legal argument but their distributor was not ordered to pay. Next time I saw the president I asked why he kept the lawyer on. 'Look, old chap,' he said, 'you had a perfectly valid point. No way could he represent our case impartially. But if I had replaced him he would have lost face, and would have been against me forever. And don't forget one day he could be a minister. All the other lawyers would have been against me too. They wouldn't say so, but they would have made excuses: too busy, out of town. The court would have been against me. I would most certainly have lost.'

'You didn't get your money back even so.'

'I know, but I can still live and do business in this country. There are some things, you know, more important than justice.'

I had had a typical Congolese day. I had been to a meeting about South Africa in Nelson Mandela Road. I had looked in at an exhibition of Cuban art in the Chamber of Commerce building. Outside I'd been stopped by some Americans asking me where downtown was. I had had a long discussion with a local doctor who was writing an article for *The Lancet*, the prestigious British medical journal, who believed AIDS was started by natives in the Great Lakes area who began injecting themselves with monkey blood as an aphrodisiac.

I had seen Dr Pierre Pelé, secretary general of the Congolais National Committee who wasn't worried where it began. He had launched a competition to discover the best poem, song or slogan against the disease and was trying to drum up publicity. And I had called in on the Congolese Authors' Association where everybody was talking about Zao – zero-admis-omniprésent – Congo's favourite pop singer whose first big hit was 'Ancien Combattant' and who had just been praising the counterfeiters and pirates for making him so successful.

I was staying at the Meridien Hotel, which was now practically empty; half the dining room closed off, the bar deserted, which suited me. I just wanted a couple of drinks, a quick meal and then call it a day. I'd just picked up my glass and started filling in a form the barman had given me which said in English, 'In the name of God, please may we have your comments,' when an American came up to me.

'Got a letter from the minister,' he said fumbling through his jacket pockets. 'Appointed me his personal investment adviser for the project. Because of my contacts.' He emptied his briefcase all over the bar. 'Signed by him. Personally. It's here somewhere. You don't get that very often. Known him a long time. Go back to the days when he was a clerk in their embassy in Yaounde. It's here somewhere. Gives me 5 percent finder's fee. To be shared, of course,' he said, winking and digging me in the ribs.

'So how is it going? Have you got any investors yet?' I asked innocently.

'Just playing them on the line,' he replied. 'Two big ones. One American. Real beauty. Never been outside the States before. They'll take it, no problem.'

'And the other?' Pause. 'You said you had two big ones.'

'Yes. Yes, of course, from Taiwan. Plenty of money. No

worries. Just got to sign on the dotted line.' Then came the long wait. He shuffled about, then lent forward and whispered, 'Of course if you know somebody better. I mean, a friend of yours, somebody who can move fast. I'd be prepared to do a deal.' A wink. A tap on the knee. One of those long handshakes. 'Because we're friends, of course. I feel as though I've known you a long time. When did we meet?'

'Yesterday in the minister's office,' I said.

'Yes. But it feels a long time,' he replied quickly. 'My brother.'

'My brother,' I repeated having gone through the same routine at least a thousand times in francophone Africa.

'Maybe we should go into business together,' said he. 'We could make a lot of money. My contacts here, your contacts in Europe. A unique combination.' A look over the shoulder. 'Of course, we'd have to look after you-know-who,' in a whisper, 'but I'll take care of that.'

'You must know him very well.'

'Like brothers.' A pause. 'Closer than brothers. He's got so many brothers he can't remember them all, but he remembers me.'

'That's why he gave you the letter?'

'Naturally. He knows I can help him.'

What he didn't know was that the minister has been handing out letters like that to everyone who has been into his office since he was appointed, and probably a couple of hundred more to people he has met on the flight to Paris or just hanging around hotel lobbies. And in many cases the letters don't even come from him. Often they are written and signed in his name by ambitious directors and junior clerks or even secretaries, all looking for the big deal that will enable them to live in luxury for the rest of their lives. I met an Austrian once who used to write his own letters from a minister. He would wait until lunchtime then go back to the minister's office, take some official letterheadings, stamp them with every official stamp he could find on the desk and write the most glowing letters to himself. When he first told me about it I didn't believe him, so he took me with him once, and it was true.

The hotel porter came to tell me I was wanted on the phone.

It was one of the ministers I had seen the previous day at the presidence. 'Come and have a drink,' he said. 'I'll send a car in about ten minutes.'

I had met the minister in Paris and London as well as in Brazzaville. An invitation to drinks was always welcome, but this was the first time I had been invited to his home. The car, a Suzuki, was punctual, and we drove through long, well-kept leafy streets overlooking the city, then downhill alongside a big brick wall that looked like the boundary of either a stately home or a prison. The Suzuki swung off the road to a big pair of iron gates. The driver hooted and the gates swung open. It was like the entrance to a prison. There were no trees or garden, everything was concrete from the gates up to the house, a single-storey building like a giant army hut. All around were men leaning against walls, sleeping on benches, playing cards or maybe just guarding the place. Everything was relaxed and dreamy. The iron gates slammed shut; the chauffeur motioned me to sit still. I thought to myself, I thought. Then I thought, What a crazy idea. I sat there for about twenty minutes. Nobody spoke to me. None of the soldiers – oops, I mean gardeners. It was as if they had either been told not to or had an excessive regard for protocol; the latter, I hoped.

The back door of the house opened and out came the minister dressed in what I was certain were pyjamas with a baby in his arms. Maybe, I thought, nobody had spoken to me because they had been so embarrassed that the minister had invited me round and promptly gone to bed. I was greeted like a long lost brother.

'I hate this place,' said the minister waving his free arm. 'And these walls. Give me London any day.' I was surprised. 'There are no walls in London. I like London very much. In Paris, there are walls. Everywhere there are walls, except in London.'

'Security?'

'No, not security,' he said, smiling. 'It's my duty to my country. What we have to do.' Two waiters came out with glasses and a bottle of Mouton-Rothschild '78. We toasted each other. It made a change from champagne. But I felt guilty.

'I'm so tired,' he sighed. 'But I can't sleep.'

I remembered that the last time we had met in London he

had spent all his time in the hotel. When he wasn't attending meetings he was in his room obviously trying to catch up on his sleep. 'Somebody told me it was something to do with the mosquitoes,' he continued. 'They wear you down. London has no mosquitoes.'

He asked me what could be done to stop people pirating cassettes. In spite of what Zao said it was a big problem. Recording companies were refusing to invest in the country. I explained my ideas for a stamp tax on all cassettes sold in the country. Unless a cassette had a special official government cassette stamp on it the dealer could be liable to a heavy fine. It could regulate the market as well as raise revenue for the government.

As I climbed back into the Suzuki I noticed an old lady sitting on a broken-down chair by the gate. She was slowly turning the pages of an old copy of *Country Life* studying the advertisements for grand country estates up for sale. Just as we began to pull away the minister ran up with an advertisement from *The Times* for Church's Old England shoes and asked me to bring a pair for him on my next visit.

The following day I saw him in the new PLM Hotel deep in conversation with two American businessmen who I later discovered were in the toxic waste business. They had already dumped over one million tons of solvents and chemical waste in the country. Now they wanted to dump a further million tons.

On my next trip I went to see the minister with a pair of size 8 Church's Old England shoes. But the toxic waste deal had blown up and he had just been sacked. The OAU had banned all imports of toxic waste into the continent.

The EC were tightening up their dumping rules. The Italian and German governments were buying back waste dumped in their name in different parts of Africa. Wole Soyinka was having 'apocalyptic visions' of 'poisons seeping into the blood-stream of our earth' making us 'slowly deteriorate as functional beings.' West African states at their annual meeting in Togo, after a quick flip through the newspapers and on the basis of a couple of unconfirmed reports from Agence France Press and Reuters, promptly slapped on their own ban. 'But how can you do that?' I asked one of the delegates. 'Surely you ought to check the facts, analyse the situation, see whether it's possible to –'

'Politics,' he said. 'How can we refuse to follow suit when everybody is saying this toxic waste is going to destroy the lives of our children? It's impossible. We must ban this evil trade in death.' With that he headed back to the bar to smoke another ten cigarettes and down another half-bottle of whisky.

Much later I saw the ex-minister by chance in Paris, when both our flights had been delayed. 'So what happened?' I said as we queued for our free meal tickets.

'Politics,' he said. 'After all the fuss, somebody had to go.'

'Did they ever prove that the waste was dangerous?'

'Of course not. How could they? They didn't even try.'

'And is it dangerous?'

'Sure, some of it is bound to be. The stuff they found in Koko in Nigeria looked pretty bad; it was leaking all over the place, the fumes were dreadful, it was obviously contaminating the soil. But the nuclear waste the French started to dump in Benin was a different matter. It was an official agreement between the two countries. It was properly packaged. Even the US environmental protection agency said it was all right. But the Nigerians made them break the agreement.'

'Even though Benin needed the money. Why?'

'Politics. Once Babangida started talking about crimes against Africa, mortgaging the future of our children, nobody could say no. It's simple,' he continued, as we headed for the restaurant. 'Waste is a big problem in Europe, in the States, and it's getting worse. We have the wide open spaces. We take the waste and dump it in the middle of nowhere. What could be more sensible than building an enormous dump in the middle of the Sahara and filling it with all the waste from everywhere?'

'How would you get it there?'

'By train. We could build a line from the coast right into the middle of the desert.'

'That would cost a fortune.'

'It would be worth it. Look at how much money there is in waste disposal at present. It now costs you about US $500–600 a ton to dispose of your waste in Europe or the US. I was being offered US $45 a ton. The costs are not high, the margins enormous. Think of what you could do with regular big consignments.'

'You could easily build a railway.'

'And push up the prices. I reckon I could get at least $100 a ton.'

'You'd easily get finance. Anybody would back that kind of project.'

'And it would be good for Africa. When you think there is something like US $600 million worth of waste to be disposed of over the next few years, it's crazy we don't do something about it.'

During the foie gras and a delicious caneton tour d'argent, washed down with a fabulous Haut Brion '53, he outlined his plans for a giant waste disposal site with fast trains and OAU-sponsored experts to ensure that everything was clean and above board. By the time we reached the camembert even tiny little Guinea-Bissau had balanced its budget and was turning away foreign investment.

'We would be rich,' he said as the wine waiter poured us two large 1948 Hines. Just as I was about to propose a toast to the waste of Europe, he suddenly remembered he should have called his wife and fled the restaurant. I finished my cognac, called the waiter and presented our meal tickets.

'But that only entitles you to the menu rapide,' he said, 'not the menu du luxe.'

'But it doesn't say so here,' I protested. 'It says, select the meal of your choice. Then present the voucher. With the compliments of . . .'

'That's the rules. Monsieur,' he said giving me a frozen smile.

In the end the discussion cost me US $273.50. Funny, he hasn't been in touch since . . .

COTE D'IVOIRE

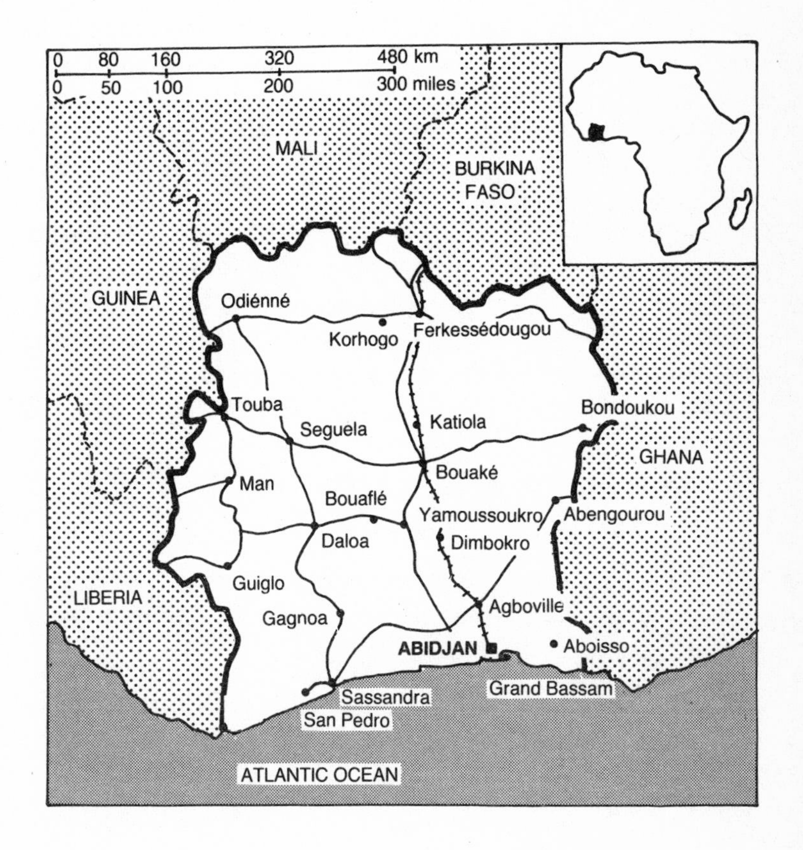

Out there was the oil rig, flames burning in the sky. I was standing on the beach with Komlan Aboua, his wife Kone, who had great patches of white skin on her face, arms and feet, and I don't know how many children. He called them all his children and they probably were.

We were about forty kilometres from the capital, Abidjan, just outside Grand Bassam which is today full of charming old colonial buildings gently falling apart. In *Heart of Darkness*, Joseph Conrad said it 'seemed to belong to some sordid farce acted in front of a sinister back-cloth.' But I reckon he was a bit too preoccupied with Mr Kurtz to appreciate it properly. At one time it was the capital and business centre of the country handling almost two-thirds of its exports. But disaster struck in 1899 with an outbreak of yellow fever and its golden age was over. The capital was transferred first to Bingerville, then in 1934 to Abidjan.

Today, in spite of brave attempts to renovate the town and various small shopkeepers and traders moving into the dilapidated buildings, it is still seedy and dusty and dirty and full of memories of le temps colonial perdu.

I first visited Grand Bassam with Vincent, who showed me where his great-grandfather used to live. Many French families have, of course, lived and worked in Africa for generations. A lot of them have been born in Africa, especially Algeria. But they have all been French first and African second. They have been brought up in that all-embracing French environment; they've attended French schools in either Africa or France; they've absorbed French culture. Many of them have also learnt African languages, studied African culture and truly learnt to love Africa and the Africans. But they have been outsiders looking in. Vincent was different.

His father was in the French civil service and posted to Côte d'Ivoire before the last war. It was the first time he had left France. He immediately fell in love with Africa, and spent all his spare time out in the country. He learnt Dioula, Baoule and even some Yacouba and Senoufo. He married a girl from Grand Bassam. He insisted Vincent should be brought up as an African first and a Frenchman second, and gave the boy to his mother's family.

'It was an amazing experience. I was African, in an African village. I learnt to fetch water. I carried everything on my head. I learnt to hunt and fish. I was one of them. I didn't learn French until I was thirteen,' he says. 'My father used to come out to the village. I didn't know who he was. We were all brought up as a family. Everybody shared everything – or nothing. We shared food, clothing, what we had – and disease.'

Today Vincent is a courier, taking tourists to visit the real Africa, the Africa he knows probably better than anybody and ironically the Africa he above all does not want destroyed by hotels, safari parks and all the paraphernalia of mass tourism.

'I can't remember when I first discovered who my real father was. It was a long time before I realised that I was white. I'd seen the difference, but I had not realised what it meant, what the implications were. We had mission doctors and teachers, but it took me a long time before I actually identified with them, before I realised I was on their side. No, *from* their side,' he told me as we drove out of Abidjan and passed the chateau overlooking the lagoon which used to be home for Bokassa after he went into exile and where, on Sunday afternoons, you could look through the gates and see him walking his dog.

'I had been very ill. This man came to see me. I thought he was a man from the mission, but it was my father. He said he was going to help me get better. I went back with him. But I got worse. He sent me back to France, where I learnt French, and learnt who my father was.'

'Was it a traumatic experience?'

'I don't think so. In Africa everybody lives as one big family. There are no really close ties; everybody is close. In France, in

Europe the family counts. It is a small group, it locks itself up from the others, has its own rules. Somehow living in France, with a family, it seemed natural that I should be part of that small unit.'

'And do you feel African or French?'

'I feel both. I know that's the simple answer, but it's true. With the Africans, I am African; with the French, I am French. It's no more unusual than having a French mother and an English father.'

'But do you think African or French?'

He replied slowly. 'If I'm in an African environment, in a village or out in the bush, I think African. I'm certain I see things the African way, or rather I see African things the African way. But if I'm in a European atmosphere, in the middle of Abidjan with all the skyscrapers I think European. I'm all right so long as the two worlds don't suddenly get mixed up. I was in a cocktail bar once in Abidjan, all dressed up, with a group of businessmen from Europe. Somebody suddenly shouted out the native word for danger. I threw myself on the floor. I just didn't think. It took some explaining afterwards.'

Komlan Aboua was one of the boys he grew up with in the village. We sat in his tiny reed hut on the beach which seemed a home. He had rolled out a thin mat on the sand on which we all sat cross-legged. The food was highly spiced, and we had literally hundreds of oysters. Not because they were squandering their oil on luxuries; the families living on the beach had seen little of the benefit of oil. Here, oysters were commonplace. Outside every house were mountains of empty shells. Komlan was leader of the village. He not only organised everything, he had even started his own religion for them.

At the last count, Côte d'Ivoire had over 200 different religious sects. While the Senegalese proliferate political parties, the Ivoirians prefer new religions. They range from the Muslim-based Wahabisme and Mouvement Hamalliste to the Protestant Christianisme Celeste and the Harristes to the more individual Mission Convergente des Croyances, the Nucleus Section Ivoirienne and the Association Sukyo Mahikare de Côte d'Ivoire. Then there is the Kimbanguist Church, one of the largest independent churches in Africa. It is Christian – in an African sense. One of their eighteenth-century saints, Kimbaveta or Donna Beatrice, claimed that the apostles were not Jews at all but Africans; that Christ did not forbid polygamy and that any African woman could have a virgin birth. When she tried to put this particular theory into practice, the Portuguese had her put to death at the stake, holding her son. Simon Kimbangu himself, who was in gaol from 1921 to 1951, today has over four million followers.

About 150 of these churches are broadly speaking Protestant. Over 100 have been investigated by the authorities, but forty-two have refused to reveal their secrets. Like inflation, growth came in the 1980s. From 1958 there had only been – only! – around thirty different religions in the country. By 1988 this had grown to forty-two. The following year twenty-five more were started. Since then they have multiplied non-stop. Komlan's religion, however, was probably too small to get into the statistics.

The whole village would gather in a hut whenever he decided to hold a service. Conscious of the competition, he would usually wait until everybody had been to mass. People would sing and talk, then he would give his sermon, which the day I was there consisted of rambling stories about his life coupled with injunctions not to smoke or drink and to look after your children and parents. He was more the village elder, but he insisted it was his church.

'I am the leader. I am the chief. These are my people. I am here to look after them. They are my children,' he said. His wife gave him the look wives give their husbands when they think they are speaking out of the backs of their necks but don't wish to say so, then retired into what Evelyn Waugh would describe as 'decent unobtrusiveness'.

'There are many things they must learn. I am their teacher. They must follow me,' he said.

And I must admit everybody seemed more than happy to follow their teacher. Perhaps they genuinely respected him; perhaps they listened because he told them to. Or perhaps they had nothing to do and he was the best show in town. I couldn't tell. Either way, when in full blast he had everybody eating out of his hand. When he threatened them with unspeakable evils, they quietened. When he laughed, they laughed uproariously. And when he started singing his strange combination of old French army songs and traditional African chants, they seemed to worship him even more.

I tried to ask him what it meant but I didn't get very far.

'I am with my ancestors. They tell me things. I have to tell my people what they say. I am an instrument.'

'Do you believe in being kind to people? Is it wrong to kill?'

'These questions are not important. It is the spirit that is important. The big things in life not the small details.'

'You mean it is all right to kill?'

'Killing or not killing is not important. It is important how we live. Sometimes it is right to kill. If somebody is harming my brother, I will kill. It is wrong when you do it to help yourself. It is not wrong to do it to help other people, your family, your friends. For you, I would kill.'

Fetishers or marabouts or magicians or prophets or just kindly, dotty old men like Komlan can be a problem in a modern society. I remembered an Ivoirian minister, Mr Matthew Ekra, once warning a conference of young civil servants to beware of fetishers, whose job was to spread fear and create divisions between people. 'Young people must play a determining role,' he said, 'rather than let themselves be hindered by fear and by relying on the older generation who, although still solid, are in decline.' Komlan wasn't exactly wearing a bone through his nose, but I could see what the minister was getting at.

Africa, like the US, has always been susceptible to quirky prophets and founders of new religions. One of the quirkiest prophets in Côte d'Ivoire was William Wade Harris, known as Latagbo to his followers. A Protestant preacher born in 1865 just over the border in Liberia, he was first a sailor, then a mason and finally a teacher before turning to religion full time. It was while he was in jail for causing a riot that the Archangel Gabriel came to him in a vision.

'I woke abruptly from my sleep and saw the angel in concrete shape, above my head. He struck the tip of my head three times and said: "I am asking you to sacrifice your wife; she will die but I will give you others to help you in the task you must undertake. Your wife will give you six shillings before her death; that will be your fortune and you will never need anything else ... I shall accompany you and reveal your mission, for which you have been destined by God, the master of the universe, whom men no longer respect."

'Shortly afterwards my wife died, following a vision of the angel; but before her death she predicted the difficulties I would encounter before succeeding in my mission.'

He decked himself out in a white dress, a black leather belt and a turban and he was off. For nearly twenty years he toured Côte d'Ivoire on foot followed by a group of women whom he referred to as his disciples, although others suggested something else. At the height of his popularity he was attracting thousands in huge ceremonies and putting the fear of God into the French colonial administration who feared such gatherings could easily turn their attention to more worldly affairs, and might even harbour such ungodly ideas as independence. Harris was summoned to the governor-general Angoulvant but, like Pontius Pilate, he could find no wrong in the man. He wasn't taking money from anybody; he wasn't even anti-French. He was more concerned about the destruction of fetishes than the destruction of the colonists. The governor-general let him go. Eventually, however, Harris was expelled. The French discovered that although he preached against adultery he practised polygamy.

I asked Komlan if everybody in his church agreed with him.

'If they did not agree with me they would not come.'

'Where do they come from?'

'From the village; from the houses on the road. Some people come from the town; but it's a long way for them to walk.'

I couldn't help thinking of the basilica of Our Lady of Peace built by Côte d'Ivoire's President Felix Houphouet-Boigny in gold and ivory and marble at Yamoussoukro, his home village in the centre of the country, at a cost of US $280 million, about half the national budget deficit. Some say he is building it with his own personal fortune; others that the money came from the sale of 16,000 state-owned flats and houses to civil servants. Either way, it is almost an exact replica of St Peter's in Rome and will accommodate over 300,000 people, although at the last count Yamoussoukro, now the official capital, could only muster 50,000 people.

Which is why Yamoussoukro must be one of the modern wonders of the third world. In the middle of nowhere, 170 miles north-east of Abidjan, it is one of the grandest, most luxurious capitals ever seen – like Versailles, Brasilia and Las Vegas rolled into one. There are eight-lane highways, golf courses, luxury palaces, artificial lagoons, panoramic restaurants, an airport capable of handling Concordes, a 2,500-seat conference centre, and sacred crocodiles fed with live chickens every evening. The basilica with its dome, the biggest in the world, and its stained-glass windows, larger than those in Chartres, dominates everything.

To some it's a sheer waste of resources; to others it's a valuable way of using public money to stimulate the economy; to others it's creating a national identity and pride, intangible but vitally important factors in the development of any nation. To Komlan, it was just another church, like his own.

'I want people to come to my church if they agree with me. I am happy talking to my brothers, my village. It is the people I think of, not myself.' He was saying all the right things and obviously meant every word. All his children were gathered round us, listening. They seemed to have a natural politeness and respect. One boy – he must have been four or five – sat on my knee and started whispering to me in Dioula. He took my hand. We were obviously great friends. The other children were playing quietly, or just staring at us. They were worlds apart from European children who would have been creating hell by now.

'I am a fisherman. We are all fishermen. We must go out and fish. It is our vocation. It is our duty to our families,' Komlan was saying.

His wife joined us on the beach, an old woolly cardigan around her shoulders, a Christmas gift from an Abidjan charity. We walked towards Grand Bassam. I had enjoyed my day. Everybody had made me very welcome. I was a million miles from Abidjan's skyscrapers. This, I felt, was the real Africa. Part of me would have been happy staying there. I got to my car and I could see the villagers lighting candles and oil lamps outside their homes. Night was coming in. As I climbed in, Komlan's wife bundled the boy who had been holding my hand into the back seat. 'You take him. He will have a much better life with you in Abidjan,' she said. 'You are friends. He wants to come with you. Take him. It is good for him and good for you.'

What could I say? This had never happened to me before although I discovered afterwards it was not unusual. Lots of people living in the bush or on the beaches would give their children away on the spur of the moment; partly because they knew they couldn't look after them properly, partly because they wanted their children to go to proper schools and live in the town. And partly, it must be said, out of courtesy and hospitality. It was the greatest gift they could offer. Sometimes children would be adopted for a few weeks, sometimes for good. Some would go back to their families for holidays, others would never go back. I looked at the boy and wondered what on earth I could say.

Glass and steel. Fantastic modern buildings. A city of ships, towers, domes, theatres and temples all bright and glistening in the smokeless air. The Cathedral of St Paul is the most exciting and futuristic church I've ever seen. Abidjan is amazing; a surprise – and a disappointment. A surprise because you don't expect to see such a modern city. A disappointment because you don't want to see such a modern city. It's not like Africa. You could be at home, or anywhere.

The sun flashes and sparkles on the towers and offices which seem to swoop and curve towards the sky, practically all with impressive marble entrances. There are doors with giant elephant tusks as handles. Not for nothing is this the Ivory Coast – ooops, Côte d'Ivoire. The government, after years of living with both names, recently decided that English was out. At night, the city is full of twinkling lights.

To me Abidjan is a mini-Manhattan. In the thirties, Geoffrey Gorer said it was 'a very new town, well designed and pretty'. I didn't get the same first impression; I felt cheated. This wasn't Africa. It looked like the States but had the atmosphere of France.

'Abidjan is fantastic,' I was told again and again by the French. 'It's so convenient for doing business in Africa.' 'If I'm covering problems in Africa, I always prefer to do it from Abidjan,' one so-called on-the-spot news reporter told me, sinking another delicious fanico in the bar at the Abidjan Hilton.

Everywhere there are French restaurants and pâtisseries and pink tablecloths and bone china and heavy silverware. The shops are full of French cheeses and pâtés and wines. The supermarkets are also full of Italian veal, Greek fruit, Belgian endives, New Zealand kiwi-fruit and – did I spot a jar of Colman's Mustard? No, nothing from the UK.

The Ivoirians will tell you Abidjan is run by the French, Zaire by the Greeks, Ghana by the Lebanese and Liberia by Citibank. I've drunk Beaujolais Nouveau in Abidjan before it's been released in France. You can even buy your French dogfood flown in from Paris. The stores and boutiques are full of Cartier, Yves St Laurent, Givenchy, Charles Jourdan – if it's not French it's not in Abidjan. But don't think they are prejudiced. Abidjan also has Chinese, Vietnamese, Moroccan, and Lebanese restaurants. They even have a Russian restaurant. Its the rive gauche in a heatwave.

In a population of two million there are only 30,000 French citizens in Abidjan – about one tenth the number of Lebanese – give or take the odd 900 French paratroopers, the 43rd Marine Battalion, permanently stationed near the airport. I know they are permanent because they are listed in the Abidjan telephone directory.

'So why are there so many French paratroopers here?' I once asked a French businessman.

'The French look after their own. That's why the Africans like them better than the British. They know we are here and won't turn our backs on them. That's very reassuring if you're running a country and you don't know from one minute to the next whether you're going to survive. With the French they know all they've got to do is pick up the phone and within minutes they're safe.'

'And even if you're criticised and attacked you'll still help them?'

'Why not? The French always think long term. The British are only interested in what is going to happen tomorrow, or maybe next week. The French are working for the future. We have a destiny. We are trying to rebuild an empire. You might not like us today – that's tactics, that's for the press. We know deep down you love us, you want to be French and we are prepared to help you.'

The French have been helping Côte d'Ivoire to be French since 1886 when they re-took the forts they had left in 1871. From these they controlled by means of treaties with local chiefs the whole coast from Liberia to Ghana. They then occupied Conakry and extended their control between Sierra Leone and Guinea. In 1893 they made Côte d'Ivoire and Guinea their colonies. Today Côte d'Ivoire has favourite nation status. Houphouet-Boigny is seen as one of the French family, wooed by presidents and ministers. Under Mitterrand this close relationship has got closer still thanks, in part, to Mitterrand fils, Jean Christophe, the former Agence France Press correspondent, who is now the official presidential adviser on African affairs. Continually on the move, glad-handing African presidents, Jean-Christophe is known in African diplomatic circles as Monsieur Papa-m'a-dit. But everyone is glad they have such a key adviser so close to the top.

'But we are also prepared to help Africa because we know Africa can help us,' continued my French insider.

'Trade. A big export market for French goods. Investment . . .'

'Not at all,' he dismissed the mere thought of anything so commercial. 'Contacts. That's what we get from Africa. In Africa we have access to everybody.'

'How? I don't understand.'

'How many Lebanese are there here in Abidjan?'

'Around 300,000.'

'Good. You know something about Côte d'Ivoire. Now, are these poor or rich Lebanese?'

'Mostly rich, I would guess.'

'Correct. Now we had a problem with Lebanon; they were holding French hostages in Beirut. So where did we come to talk to the Lebanese?' Light dawned. 'The Lebanese here know how to get into these hostage groups. Why wander around Beirut? They don't know anything. They're just the boys!'

'You mean the big bosses are here?'

He smiled. 'You remember the last French elections, how Chirac managed to get the French hostages released. Our Minister for the Interior, did all the negotiating here in Abidjan.'

'Out of sight of the press. In secret. Talking direct to the people who count.'

'Safer than in Paris.'

'And Paris probably wouldn't allow in some of the Lebanese you can talk to so easily here.' People like Sheikh Abdul Monen Zein, spiritual leader of the 200,000 Shias in Abidjan, who is secretly credited with delivering two French hostages to Beirut's Summerland Hotel.

'Which is why you don't mind thinking long-term, helping presidents – how *can* you get a president out in minutes?' I asked.

'Easy. Presidents in francophone Africa always live just a few minutes from an airport or landing strip. Every president says he likes to spend his time in his home village; there's always an airport nearby – maybe just a landing strip, but it works. They will tell you it's part of their plan to open up the interior, to attract tourists out of the capital or away from the beaches. It's there because it's their life assurance.'

'But that must cost a lot of money. How can they justify it?'

'The World Bank pays, the EC pays. It's tourist development; stimulating the economy; unlocking natural resources. The French will always find a reason. We'll even find the money if we have to. We are happier, of course, if somebody else does. It doesn't make any difference, French companies will get the job. France strengthens its ties with the president. It's a good deal.'

'But how can the French get a president out so quickly?'

'They are good at it. Every president lives near an airport, and round the back is a military airport. Why do you think they don't let people take photographs at airports? In the military airports there are always French advisers, some of whom are there to lift their man out if they get the telephone call.'

Wasn't it embarrassing for the Africans, I asked, to have so many French soldiers around?

'They've thought of that. The last thing an African country wants is people saying they are dependent on France. They don't mind people thinking it because if that's the price of security, it's a small price. But they don't want people saying it. So the French put their soldiers into the uniform of the African country. Voilà. They've avoided embarrassment and have boosted the strength and capability of the African army. Everybody's happy. It's the perfect French solution.'

'But who do they take their orders from?'

'From Paris, of course. Once a Frenchman always a Frenchman.'

'And the Africans accept it?'

'Of course they do. It's good insurance. So who's worried?'

'During the Falklands crisis Mrs Thatcher asked President Mitterrand for an assurance that France would not help Argentina against the British. Mitterrand said France would not help Argentina. Are you saying that France had people in Argentina wearing Argentine uniforms?'

'What do you think?'

'So Mrs Thatcher was asking the wrong question. She should have said, Will you assure me that no French advisers wearing French or Argentine uniforms will help Argentina?'

'Of course.'

'And if she had asked that question she might have got a different answer?'

'What do you think?'

It was a point that had never occurred to me before. I bet it had never occurred to Mrs Thatcher either. But the French are nothing if not subtle. 'The French would still have said no,' I replied. 'They would have read an additional meaning into the question and answered that question without asking for clarification.'

'Now you are beginning to understand the French,' he said. 'But it will take you another 1,000 years.'

On a later visit I met a policeman from Martinique on duty outside the French embassy, who explained he could only get promotion by serving some time in another French-speaking country.

The French are much more conscious of their community or

commonwealth spirit than the British. Everybody is made to feel part of the same glorious French family. It is not centred on Paris; it seems to be a determination to promote France and the world of Frenchness. And not just among policemen. I've come across customs officers, water board officials, lawyers, of course, and teachers. Everybody seems to be part of the French commonwealth.

I once met a soldier in Côte d'Ivoire from Alsace, recently transferred from Tahiti where he had been attached to the French nuclear testing programme. 'It was superb,' he said. 'Three days work, four days on the beach. For me the nuclear bomb is fantastic.'

We were wandering around the central Plateau area of the city. 'What's happened to the parking meters?' I asked him. The heads had all been removed. 'Thank the television for that,' he said.

The previous evening they had revealed that all money from the meters in Abidjan was going to the president's wife. The president promptly had the meters removed. Apparently, his wife had returned from a trip to Paris, decided that Abidjan needed parking meters, and had them installed. The city had thought they were the responsibility of the ministry of transport. The ministry thought they were the responsibility of the presidence. The presidence thought they were the responsibility of the city. And all the time the money was going straight to the president's wife.

We stopped to buy newspapers. 'The French never abandon a friend in need' said *Le Monde*, which sums up the French attitude to la francophonie, as they say, and explains why today francophone Africa is as united behind – oops, I mean with – la France as the Commonwealth is as united with – oops, I mean against – Britain. Sure it's politics, aid, trade, a measure of defence – but it's much more. It's as if they have been meant for each other. They might argue, they might disagree, but it's all very civilised; entre nous.

And if the French are successful in Africa, they deserve it. When Britain lost its empire we swung all our attention across to the US. When France lost their colonies they swung all their attention back to their colonies. As a result, today there are probably ten times as many Frenchmen in francophone Africa as there were twenty years ago. Most are working with the Africans in government and private enterprise. Many are running their own businesses, others managing subsidiaries for foreign companies. A few are leading the good life. And a few more are secret service and undercover men.

Most of their trade goes through France. Telephone calls and telexes until very recently all went via Paris, but then calls from anglophone Africa always used to go through London. Airlines are routed through Paris. And, of course, most of the countries are members of the CFA franc zone which at the end of the jour is run by the French. Some say this is colonialism by another name, but to the francophones it is a genuine two-way relationship based on mutual respect and assistance. More than half French aid money goes to Africa. On top of that they seem to be prepared to reschedule, recycle or just plain write off debts, at the drop of a chapeau.

The francophone countries may be Marxists or right-wingers, rich or poor; above all, they are French. They have their own cultures and traditions, but these co-exist with their Frenchness. They even boast of their French heritage. They are proud of their statues of French colonial heroes killed fighting in Africa. In Ndjamena, Chad, there still stands a monument to Commandant Lamy slain conquering the country at the turn of the century. 'He died,' the inscription says, 'for France and for civilisation.' How long would such a statue have survived in anglophone Africa, where they were pulling down pictures of Queen Victoria on the stroke of independence? To somebody brought up with English Africa, this depth of feeling between France and Africa is vraiment amazing.

But if la francophonie gives France their world role and guarantees their seat on the UN Security Council, France deserves it. When the British were ramming English history down the throats of the anglophones, the French were making the francophones French and distributing Louis Seize desks to every minister. When the British were building polo clubs as oases of the old country in 'these damned tropics', the French were sipping champagne with Africans in every bar in town. When the British were sending out catalogues to Africa – in

English – the French were setting up trading companies, writing the national specifications and making friends. Today they have a trade surplus with Africa of around US $3.4 billion a year, whereas the British are in retreat. In some countries, like Gabon, they have as much as 60 percent of the market. In others, like Cameroon, 40 percent.

When the British were keeping their children at school in Blighty, the French were building lycées all over Africa for black and white children and sending the brightest back to France. Senegal's former President Leopold Senghor went to the same schools in Africa and France as Pompidou. When the British were working late in the office the French were marrying Africans. No end of senior officials in francophone Africa have French wives.

Perhaps most significant of all, when Britain was gaoling Nkrumah and Kenyatta as dangerous nationalist firebrands, France was welcoming Houphouet-Boigny and Leopold Senghor, not only as members of the National Assembly in Paris along with Mamadu Konte from Mali and Gabriel d'Arboussier from Senegal, but also as ministers in the French cabinet.

As a result they did not start by having to fight for their independence; they were prepared to work within the system. At first they succeeded in abolishing forced labour in French colonies and some other excesses of French rule. They increased the rights of French citizenship. And so they were prepared to continue if some French settlers had not started opposing even such minor gains. New French politicians supported the settlers and before long the Africans had lost everything they had fought for within the system. One backlash always provokes another. The Africans now started demanding independence instead of requesting it.

Basically, the British believed in making the Africans independent while the French believed in making them French. To some people, this meant the Africans could never be free, but in practice the French system has a lot to commend it. At least today's francophones think so.

France continues to provide massive aid to Africa although, it is estimated, around 80 percent comes back in salaries, orders and profits. The CFA franc zone means that fifteen francophone countries have all the benefits of a hard currency. Admittedly in the past, because member countries had to keep around 30 percent of their deposits interest-free with the Banque de France, the deal yielded a small profit. But no longer. Hence the recent rumours that France will devalue, and counter-rumours that France, especially under Mitterand, will never devalue. Instead they will be forced by the EC to realign their currency when the European monetary union is introduced.

There will be problems whatever happens. France can't go on running the CFA franc zone. First, because it is costing them money. In public they dispute this, citing their faith in Africa, their refusal to walk away when times are hard. Second, because they can't take the CFA zone with them into a single European monetary union. Some EC officials say they will just run the zone alongside the new EC system. Others say no way because that will mean Europe, in effect, supporting the francophone countries.

Their finance officials say devaluation would resolve nothing. For francophone Africa it would increase the cost of imports of spare parts and machinery as well as of champagne. It would dampen demand, and increase unemployment and social tensions. It would increase their already enormous debt burdens, only a tiny proportion of which are denominated in CFAs. It would create huge exchange-rate losses for businessmen. It would increase their banks' debts to overseas financial institutions. It would make the region less attractive to investors.

Already France is suggesting the compromise: run the CFA franc zone alongside the EC monetary zone but let the French manage the whole show. To which, naturally, the rest of Europe is saying, Forget it. That way we get the problems and France gets the gloire.

President Bongo of Gabon suggested that if the EC was going to link the CFA franc zone with their new monetary union why didn't they logically extend the zone to all sixty-six African, Caribbean and Pacific countries in the Lomé Convention. 'About as logical as putting a nuclear power station in

Libreville,' one EC official told me, still reeling at the idea.

Clearly France is torn every which way. She sees her destiny in Europe yet doesn't want to let go of her destiny in Africa. Yet if she links the CFA franc zone to the new European monetary system she risks letting the rest of Europe into what has been her chasse garde for years, losing all that trade, influence, and prestige, and maybe her role as a world power.

Francophone Africa is torn in two. They can see the advantages of being linked to an EC monetary zone which would immediately plug them in to the deutschmark and sterling. But they don't want to risk France losing interest in them. All the same there is a minority in francophone Africa who feel that it would do them no harm to break away.

'We're linked to the French franc which means we can't devalue. Other countries have devalued; they have increased their competitiveness and restored the balance between imports and exports. But we can't,' one US-trained Senegalese economist told me.

'Why not leave the CFA zone then devalue on your own?'

'We couldn't do it. People wouldn't believe us. It would shake the zone to its foundations and,' he paused, 'I doubt whether the French would let us.'

'You mean they could stop you? But how?'

'They have their ways,' he said darkly. Which brings us back to the military aspect.

It is said there are nearly 50,000 troops in the Forces d'Action Rapide in France and another 15,000 Foreign Legionnaires in bases all over Africa just waiting for the phone call. In the case of Senegal the call came recently and the French promptly dispatched 2,000 troops to help President Diouf fight locusts. Who knows what the reason might be next time. What would the British have done? Nothing. Somehow the British don't seem to get on with Africans as well as the French. Take the British approach to doing business in Africa and the French approach. The British businessman meets a francophone minister for the first time. 'Now, Mr Minister, first things first. We're very blunt in my part of the world, we like to get straight to the point.'

'And so do we. I would like to thank you, therefore, on

behalf of our president for agreeing to see our delegation and sparing so much of your valuable time to meet us. I feel sure ...'

'Yes, thank you, very kind. Now we've checked with ECGD and quite frankly we have problems.'

'And, on behalf of our government, I would like to say we feel sure we will benefit by this meeting and discussing our proposals. Our Five Year Development Plan, you see, states that all our peoples must have freedom of movement. And freedom of movement means an integrated transport policy.'

'Quite so. Very important, but first we must talk about how you are going to pay for it. Quite frankly I don't see how you can find the wherewithal. We've been talking to the ODA and ECGD –'

'Our proposals at this stage show an integrated system linking villages, towns and city, facilities for freight and for passengers; special priority given to high category sectors. It is important, for example, when the president –'

'Yes, quite right. But your president is a fine man. I am sure he would be the first to agree that before we can discuss –'

'... Has to travel, he must be given priority. Attention must also be given to the defence of our country. And to the young, to the sick ...'

'But how much is all this going to cost? Quite frankly the sensible thing would be to consider a single link ...'

'A single link is not possible. Our development plan expressly states an integrated transport system ...'

And, you guessed it, the whole meeting disintegrates. The British suggest discussing the whole thing further over lunch which ends up with them virtually ignoring the African delegation and downing gin and tonics and talking among themselves.

French businessmen, by contrast, instead of going for the nitty-gritty, spend hours on generalities and philosophy and good intentions. 'Mon cher ami, monsieur le ministre, I am not here on behalf of the French government to ask you to do anything. That is the last thing I would ever consider and the last thing the French government would envisage. I am here to see how we can co-operate; how you can maintain your integrity and identity and authenticity, how we can mould and adapt our own integrity, our own personality to work together for the future.'

Guess who gets the contracts?

In anglophone Africa, the Englishmen – and there are still plenty – have all the good jobs and big cars and large houses. In francophone Africa you see Frenchmen who are butchers, bakers, candlestick makers. Whether it's repairing cars or oiling the wheels of state or commerce, the French work at it.

Ministers, presidential advisers, former ambassadors, retired businessmen seem to spend their lives touring francophone Africa as special envoys of the president, as representatives of some federation, or just as personal copains comme cochons of ministers. Hardly a day goes by without a newspaper sporting front page photograph and article about a French minister presenting 'un message des autorités française au chef d'état'. And that message, whatever it says, makes the big news of the day.

The British might send one junior minister to Abidjan for half a day who will spend so long having lunch with local British businessmen that he has no time to meet the minister of commerce let alone the press.

Joint French-African conferences, seminars, jours de réflexion take place all the time. Businessmen are all over the place. Teachers, doctors and nurses are on exchange programmes. Students are building latrines in the villages or looking after babies in leper hospitals. Pop into your local centre cultural français one evening (they are all over francophone Africa – they are even creeping into anglophone Africa), and there's bound to be maybe two or three events to interest you. How about a lecture on 'Les maladies transmisées par le sang'. No? What about a video on the 'Bicentenaire 1788', or 'L'Homme-Femme,' une comédie camerounaise, or a discussion about 'L'influence secrete de la musique'?

Me? I would certainly have a look at the exhibition about 'La revolution française sous les tropiques,' oeuvres des jeunes artistes haitiens, senegalais, français et togolais (note the order!), before drowning my anglophone sorrows at the 'Soirée théatrale: Bidiwaria ou La beauté du mal' par la troupe Ezalighi.

The francophone summit meetings include French-speaking countries from all over the world, as well as French-speaking provinces such as Quebec and New Brunswick, regions such as Wallonia and even communities such as Louisiana, New England and Val d'Aosta. Give or take the occasional row with Canada over fishing rights off Newfoundland, they are models of French gloire and decorum compared to the usual Commonwealth summit. President Mitterrand, who sees them simply as an opportunity for France to gather her children around her, opens the conference with his usual grand 'vive la francophonie' discours. Delegates then start on a round of tête-à-têtes, lunches and grand dinners. The 1989 meeting in Dakar was a little different, largely because Senegal was practically at war with its neighbour Mauritania. Armoured troops were marching to and from the border. Instead of staying in the centre of town everyone was dispatched to the nearby club Mediterranée for fear of, would you believe, air raids. But la gloire remained undiminished.

'But surely you should institutionalise the meeting much more?' I once asked a French official. 'Set up a secretariat, as we did with the Commonwealth.'

'Sans blague,' he said. 'And have all your problems?'

Some people not in la famille say that unless the francophone summits have a more definite objective they will fall apart. Insiders maintain that so long as they create enough gloire and provide enough champagne they will survive. 'Ecoute. Most francophone countries need us,' another French official whispered to me. 'They come to these meetings to make certain we're not going to leave them. Why give them more power and influence? Leave things as they are. Trouble with you British, you don't understand Africa.'

An elegant French patron climbed into his waiting Peugeot. A matronly dame d'une certaine age led her immaculately groomed poodle past a group of secretaries, pouring giggling out of the office opposite. The newspaper was full of the search for 'une vraie Miss africaine ... une pileuse en vêtement traditionnel, pas en bikini!'

Then between the feet of the secretaries and the poodle, outside the giant skyscrapers, between the Peugeots and Mercedes, you see them: lying like heaps of bones on the pavement, sleeping in the gutters, or just staring, hands outstretched – the poor, the old, the crippled; some of Africa's poorest people living and dying in the middle of one of Africa's richest cities. A boy with an old man's face, his legs twisted under him, pushed himself along the edge of the road on a board with wheels. An old man with stumps for legs was dragging himself along the pavement. Another man, his limbs knotted in unbelievable positions, was banging his tin at you.

'La "Miss" doit être une vraie femme africaine; c'est à dire, avoir un bassin type africain, une poitrine et un postérieur bien fournis mais sans exagération,' waxed lyrical the editorial.

A blind man in a filthy boiler suit stares fixedly ahead waiting for maybe the difference between life and death. A mother as thin as matchsticks bathes her two even thinner children with a rag and what looks like muddy water out of a baked bean tin.

Wandering down the road is an Arab with a horrible twisted face which looks as though his teeth are growing through his top lip.

'Le visage doit être charmant, harmonieux, avec une belle dentition, un nez pas trop épaté et un sourire éclatant.'

At first you are baffled. It's nothing like Calcutta – nor like below the arches at Charing Cross. At first, you try and give something to everyone, but it costs you a fortune. What's worse you are pursued by every half-able beggar in West Africa, demanding to know why you ignored him and gave to somebody who has only just arrived in Abidjan. Gradually you limit yourself: something to the first person you see leaving the hotel; to whoever opens the office door; maybe to the boy lying outside the restaurant and, of course, something to that gang of youths who always surround your car at traffic lights.

Abidjan, like all rich cities, has its poor; from the villages, from the countryside, from Burkina Faso, from Guinea – even from as far away as Mali, Niger and Senegal. After all if you are poor there is no point trying to beg, steal or borrow from people like yourself.

The Plateau has more people begging and living on its

pavements than any other city in francophone Africa. When you stop your car at the lights you're surrounded by people trying to sell anything from matches to Omega watches. Outside the banks and airline offices cripples will struggle to open the doors for you. Along the pavements blind men sit for hours hoping somebody will take something out of their tray and pay them handsomely.

'It is part of our culture,' the Muslims will tell you. 'We believe we have a duty to help our brothers. We feel it is enriching to give; to give is an honour.'

'Does everybody give?'

'Unfortunately no. There are exceptions, of course. But generally, no.'

Christians are more hardnosed. Within a week, they tell you, you will be ignoring the beggars, stepping over them without a second thought; you won't even see them as you fall out of the luxury restaurants. Maybe you'll be giving something to one beggar outside the hotel, trying to convince yourself that you do more good giving a lot to one instead of a little to everybody. And, of course, you'll still be giving something to the gang at the traffic lights because you're terrified they'll smash the windows.

If you're rich, of course, you'll live in Cocody in the shadow of the Ivoire Hotel so you won't have to bother about the poor. If you're middle-class you'll live in Marcory with an uneasy conscience. If, however, you're a worker you'll live with them across the lagoon in Treichville – or Trashville as cynical expats call it – in concrete houses, stucco bungalows and tin shacks.

On Twenty-first Street a Catholic church used to provide food and lodging for the poor. For nothing, you could sleep on the floor. For one dollar you had a bunk, the thin foam mattress caked with sweat. It was full of Ivoirians, Burkinabe, Malians, Senegalese, Guineans, Nigerians, people from all over West Africa, lured by Abidjan's bright lights and the tales of work. But all the jobs for clerks and secretaries were taken by Ivoirians; other jobs by thousands like themselves who got there first. So they waited and hoped and prayed.

In the mornings they would drink coffee at the café next door; during the day they would roam the Plateau, maybe trying to get a job, maybe trying a little begging. One man I met, a Malian, did well looking for money people had dropped outside the expensive shops and restaurants. Invariably he had enough for lunch, a bowl of rice or more coffee, which was more than most of the others.

In the evenings, they would wander around Treichville, its thousands of street stalls lit by flickering candles. At seven the shelter would open and everybody would hope they could get inside and then, if they had been lucky during the day, get a bunk rather than spend another night on the floor. Not that they wanted to sleep. Everybody seemed to want a bed so that they could entertain their friends; sitting on top of each other, hanging over the side, drinking coffee, or very occasionally beer or homemade gin; and talking and talking and talking.

Outside, by night, Treichville – Trech, to we vieux noctambules – is un autre pays. Cars and taxis are cruising les boulevards du crime, from the Boule Noire to the Black and White, the Treich can-can. Some recommend the Café des Arts, others swear by La Cabane Bambou. All, I'm told, full of terribly mondaine young ladies. The venturous just plunge into the rue Douze and live dangerously.

Trouble is in the last few years Abidjan has become more dangerous. The number of petty thefts has jumped alarmingly. Mugging has become more commonplace. Drivers and passengers have been dragged from cars and attacked. Outside Abidjan, cars have been held up and passengers robbed and beaten up. Abidjan also seems to have discovered drugs. A tonne of cannabis was found in a stack of timber at the airport waiting to be flown to the UK. People have been arrested for smuggling marijuana and heroin in snail shells, in omelettes, even in chips.

I decided I couldn't face the search for 'une vraie Miss africaine', so I returned to the Ivoire. Which, however, was far from a haven of peace. That morning the water had been cut off. In other African countries when that happens you just open a bottle of Perrier or whisky and wait for the water to come on again. In the Ivoire, where this kind of thing never happens, they went berserk. The staff were running into all the rooms checking if the taps were working. When the water came back on there was pandemonium. They had left the taps turned on and water was seeping under the doors, along the corridors and down the stairs. I almost went back to the rue Douze for some peace.

These are not the best of times for Côte d'Ivoire's dynamic businessmen, politicians and government officials. For he is not as mobile as he used to be. A bit frail, leans on his stick a lot, although he speaks as calmly as ever. Still wears that black homburg and those three-piece suits and still doesn't smoke or drink. But he is over eighty – some say over ninety. And the tradition is that when a chief dies, his best men are buried alongside him.

Felix Houphouet-Boigny, The No. 1 Peasant, le Vieux, le Sage, has been president of the Côte d'Ivoire for nearly thirty years. He became president three months after the country gained independence in 1960. He is also very much the father of francophone Africa and still the voice of moderation and reasonableness, although to some Africans he is more French than the French. But Houphouet was once arch-enemy of France. Shortly after the last war the French were determined to crush him and his Democratic Party; in 1949 they even sent Pechoux, a tough, no-nonsense administrator, to be the new governor with instructions to crush him. Dozens of party members and officials were killed, hundreds imprisoned. But history was against Pechoux.

Educated at the William Ponty School on the infamous slave island of Gorée and the Medical School in Dakar, Houphouet worked for the Medical Assistance Service until his brother died and he became chief of his village in 1940. Thanks to land left to him by his uncle, he returned to Côte d'Ivoire a rich man.

He became a successful coffee planter, but quickly realised that owning land was nothing if you could not get a decent price for your crops. Local farmers asked him to help set up the syndicat agricole africain. In 1944 he established Africa's first agricultural union, the African Democratic Rally, and began demanding minimum prices for coffee and cocoa, a fight which he has waged ever since.

And for over forty years he became ever richer until today he must be one of the richest men in the world. Years ago when faced with yet another allegation of corruption he explained how he did it. Whenever he sold coffee or cocoa, he said, he bought gold in Mali.

Houphouet was elected, like Senghor, to the French Assembly in Paris and went on to become a minister in Guy Mollet's government from 1957 to 1958, even pushing through legislation banning forced labour throughout the French colonies. But that was his last radical act. After that caution set in. He became so moderate that at first he was against the Côte d'Ivoire being granted independence because he feared the French would make them support the poorer francophone countries. He wanted a fudgy sort of self-government within a type of federation. But when he saw it was inevitable he moved quickly, put himself at the head of all the factions wanting freedom from France and has been there ever since, being elected again and again with virtually 100 percent of the vote.

Today he is the doyen of French ministers – he was also a minister under de Gaulle – honoured and respected throughout France. French prime ministers fly to Abidjan by Concorde to dine with him. There are even special clubs in his honour, such as le Club des Amis du Président Felix Houphouet-Boigny which tours francophone Africa preaching his ideals and beliefs.

Although he looks – and is – so conventional, to me Houphouet-Boigny is the true revolutionary. For while other francophone leaders were preaching Marxist-Leninism or flirting with Kim Il Sung, he alone stood against the tide and insisted that the only way to develop was with French aid, French money, French people. And in one of the poorest regions of the world Houphouet-Boigny has turned a backwater (it was even ignored by the slave traders because it lacked a natural harbour and was wracked by storms and impossible underwater currents) into one of the most modern countries in Africa with a staggering average income of over US $1,000 per capita. An amazing 20 percent of its budget is devoted to education with literacy at 60 percent, double the average for Africa. He has forbidden tribal tattoos and ritual scars. Filing teeth he has made an assault. He has also stopped the old tribal custom of paying for brides.

Abidjan is a thriving city. The countryside has vast pineapple, sugar, palm oil, coffee and cocoa plantations. The villages have electricity, running water and even telephones. Overall they have achieved the fastest and most consistent growth rate of any country in Africa. They are one of maybe four African countries to have achieved economic progress and political stability since independence.

While Houphouet-Boigny runs a tight ship – his Partie Democratique is the sole party – he tends to take an enlightened view of any opposition by trying to draw them into the family rather than attacking them head on. In 1966 he released three ministers who had plotted against him and even reappointed one of them to a government job. In 1973 he commuted death sentences against seven military officers found guilty of planning to overthrow him. Others are allowed back from exile, given a good talking to – some say also a case of champagne – and allowed to carry on pretty much regardless, providing, one assumes, they don't upset the family too much.

Other countries concentrated on prestige projects, but Houphouet never forgot his days as a coffee planter. He concentrated on planting coffee and cocoa. Before long he was rivalling Brazil as the world's number one coffee producer. Then came palm oil, pineapples, bananas and cotton. Côte d'Ivoire was not only self-sufficient, it had a solid agricultural base generating hard currency, improving the standard of living of its population and generating enough income to help it develop its own industrial base and build its own prestige projects. While other countries were struggling to feed themselves, Côte d'Ivoire was notching up staggering growth rates of 6 and 7 percent a year.

Such rapid development has a price. Today, for example, the Ivory Coast has very little ivory. Forty years ago there were hundreds of thousands of elephants in the country; now there are less than 1,000. Even twenty years ago the country boasted one of the richest varieties of wild life in Africa, but no longer. Up until 1973 when a ban on hunting was introduced, poachers virtually wiped out the wild life providing massive supplies of exotic foods such as the red duiker, the little brown bongo with white stripes along its back and the yellow-backed duiker, all now endangered species, to people unable to pay the high shop price for meat. At the same time farmers were cutting down trees, burning the undergrowth and planting cash crops in the thin forest soil to supply food to Abidjan and the other towns.

Forestry, their third largest export earner, is growing – or rather, exports are growing; the trees are not. Twenty years ago there were 15 million hectares of forests in the country; today there are around one million, with replantings covering a mere 5,000 hectares a year. Côte d'Ivoire aims to produce around four million cubic metres of timber every year, which is down on their peak years in the early 1970s when they were shipping out as much as five million cubic metres a year. The irony is that around 180,000 tons a year are shipped back to France in the form of charcoal to be used for barbecues by people enjoying the natural environment.

Rubber production is growing and on target to take 5 percent of the world market by 1990. Cotton is expanding rapidly. So is sugar. Palm oil is booming. In less than twenty years they have come from nowhere to be one of Africa's leading natural oil and fats producers. Overall, agriculture accounts for nearly 30 percent of GDP and over 70 percent of all exports.

But coffee and cocoa together account for over 40 percent of their overseas earnings. Côte d'Ivoire is the world's largest producer and exporter of cocoa and the UK's third largest supplier after Nigeria and Ghana. It is the world's third largest producer of Robusta coffee and Africa's leading exporter. But today cocoa is also the biggest problem, because they produce so much. Year after year, as the consumption of coffee and cocoa declines and the price with it – it halved in four years – Ivoirian production increases. The result: Houphouet, as he did over forty years ago, is damning 'speculators' who he claims cost the country over CFA 600 billion in lost revenue, and is stockpiling supplies in a bid to halt falling prices and force them back up again. With 60 percent of revenues coming from cocoa and coffee you don't need many coffee spoons to work out the impact this has on the economy. In 1988, as in the early 1980s, it knocked them sideways. Debt soared. Repayments were suspended, a previously unheard of thing for the World Bank's erstwhile best pupil. The World Bank was called in. A humbling moment for Africa's showpiece of free market liberalism.

'It's simple,' a ministry of agriculture official told me. 'The world price for cocoa is now around CFA 450 a kilo. But we have to pay our farmers CFA 400. Add to that CFA 200–300 for transport, administration, etc. and you see why the price must go up. We must get CFA 700 a kilo.'

'And can you cut the price you pay producers?'

'No way can we cut by the amount we would have to to meet the market prices. That would mean cuts of 50 percent.'

But what can they do? Stockpiling can only be a short term solution since it tends to stabilise falling prices rather than force them back up. Force people to drink more coffee?

'I have no idea,' an economist with Gill and Duffus, the London-based coffee dealers, told me. 'Production is still outstripping consumption. They can't go on stockpiling for ever. The International Cocoa Organisation is fighting for buffer stocks and minimum prices, but they are going to find that impossible to hold.'

'But isn't Ivoirian cocoa in big demand from Western confectionery manufacturers?'

'Sure, but at a price. There's plenty of Malaysian cocoa around, and it's cheap. Admittedly it's a bit more acidic than Ivoirian cocoa, but are you telling me the manufacturers can't get over that problem?'

Diversify? Economists say it is wrong for any country to be heavily dependent on a single crop, especially one subject to dramatic price changes. They should go into electronics and turn their illiterate peasants overnight into computer experts. Which to a non-economist doesn't sound too hopeful. My own solution is simply for the world to drink three cups of coffee a day instead of two and eat all the Chococam and Chocodi they can.

Le Vieux, I'm told, has other ideas. I was in Abidjan early in 1989 during the height of the crisis. I had a meeting with one of the country's top businessmen. When I went into his office he was in the middle of one of those African conversations that go round in circles.

'You will send it? ... It is important ... Yes I will tell you when it arrives ... It's important.'

'Must be important,' I said.

'Very important,' he said putting the phone down. 'You haven't heard? Last week le Vieux called us all into his office, about 200 of us, ministers, businessmen, bankers. The president said that because of the cocoa crisis the country was in serious economic difficulties. He wanted our help. We said we would do everything we could. The president then said ...' he took a deep breath, 'in that case he wanted us all to pay our back taxes.'

'I bet that shook you,' I laughed. 'Except you, of course. What did you say?'

'Some people said they would like to pay their taxes but times were hard. Then the president took out a pile of papers. These, he said, were all our bank accounts and deposit accounts from all over the world. He knew how much we were all worth, and how much tax we owed.'

'So what happened then?'

'Nothing. We all left.'

'So do you think everybody will pay up?'

'Sure.'

'The full amount?'

'Probably.'

'Of course,' I said, 'it could all be a bluff. Wouldn't that be fantastic? If the president got you all to pay up and you didn't have to.'

'Oh I don't think so,' he said slowly. 'The president has fabulous contacts.'

'And he has let you all get away with it for so long.'

'He's only got to pick up the phone and he gets all the information he wants.'

'So when have you all got to pay up?'

'Six months.'

The phone rang again, and I took my leave.

But it is not only in respect of the cocoa crisis that Houphouet has adopted his own approach, because obviously revenues somehow are flowing into the Treasury. Salaries are still being paid, so are social security and pensions. The government is still building roads. Everything is still working.

Le Vieux has also adopted his own approach to South Africa and Israel. There are no diplomatic relations, no trade ties, no exchange programmes. It's just that in Côte d'Ivoire, unlike in any other African country, you'll see South African Airways jets on the runways, South African tourists, South African businessmen. You'll see South African conferences and receptions taking place. You might even catch a glimpse of a South African minister – or president – on his way to see Houphouet himself. The South Africans are even supplying over 4,000 animals, to the president's national park at Yamoussoukro.

South African fruit, meat and dairy products sit happily on the supermarket shelves alongside French cheese. I'm told that South African wine has even appeared on the menus of Abidjan's leading hotels although I don't believe it. Not because it's South African, but because it's not French.

It's pretty commonplace nowadays, but after one of the first meetings between the two governments there was such an international storm that Houphouet sent his minister for information to South Africa to talk about the need for more interracial dialogue – and told him to take his attractive blonde French wife with him.

For negotiation and not confrontation is Houphouet's solution to South Africa as he never tires of saying. At the OAU he is the only head of state to say so. At international conferences Ivoirian delegates are the only Africans to talk about humanitarian solutions, not violent ones. He is against sanctions. He even banned coverage in the Ivoirian press of meetings in Dakar between white South Africans and the banned African National Congress.

'Make no mistake, the old man is against racialism,' an Ivoirian diplomat told me. 'But he is against Communism even more. He is prepared to be friends with Botha not because he believes in him but because he sees him as the last stand against Communism in South Africa.'

Le Vieux, of course, has seen it all before. He went through exactly the same over twenty-five years ago when he became the first head of state to make an official visit to Jerusalem to open an embassy there. 'Every African who has visited Israel has his heart full of love for Israel because African nations have suffered like the Jewish people in the past,' he said. Negotiation even then. And how many African countries today recognise Israel?

Et l'apres-Houphouet ...? Wherever you go that's what people want to discuss. Will he resign gracefully like Leopold Sedar Senghor, one-time president of Senegal? Nobody imagines for one minute it will be like Bourguiba, president of Tunisia for over thirty years, who at the age of eighty-four was one day unceremoniously sacked by the man he brought into government to protect him.

But every time anybody even whispers the question le Vieux appears in the media stating emphatically, 'Here in Côte d'Ivoire there is no number two or three or four. There is only a number one. And that's me. I will decide. And I don't share my decisions with anybody.'

The next question is, who? Some say George Ouagnie, the smooth, professional Afro-Lebanese who over the years has graduated from family doctor to head of protocol and le Vieux's righthand man. At airports he is first out of the plane, making certain everything is in place for the appearance of the great man. At conferences, he leads the way; guides le Sage to the place of honour, then afterwards escorts him to the most enthusiastic group of admirers for the benefit of the cameras. Crowds melt at his approach; he seems to induce a reverential distance around him that nobody dares invade, although I once heard him compared to 'an agitated eunuch nervous about the abolition of polygamy'. He is also superb on detail. The place of honour for le Patron must be the place of honour and not two millimetres down the table.

Antoine Cesareo is another name whispered over dinner tables. A tough, stocky Tunisian, he too has shown fierce loyalty to Houphouet. In 1977 he set up the Direction et Controle des Grands Travaux which has been responsible for over US $3 billion worth of government construction projects in the country, ensured they were completed on time and within budget and in the process saved the country over $2.5 billion.

He has also cleared up the public works sector and eliminated corruption.

Other people point to le grand favori, Dr Henri Konan Bedié, president of the National Assembly and the man next to le Vieux credited with Côte d'Ivoire's economic miracle. A fellow Baoule and a close confidant of the president, he would be the safest pair of hands from the point of view of the party, the Assembly, and one would guess the president himself.

My own view is that le Vieux will never die. Any man who spends CFA 40 billion building the world's largest basilica in his back garden must have some kind of influence.

We were in a big, rambling modern house in Cocody overlooking the lagoon. On a shelf in the living room were the first three volumes of the legendary Raymond Borremans' *Grande Dictionnaire Encyclopédique de la Côte d'Ivoire*, which has taken him a lifetime to write. It was the first time I had met anybody who had a copy.

We were about to sit down for dinner. The telephone rang. 'We'll have another glass,' said the minister as he finished his conversation. 'I've invited Monsieur da Porto to join us.'

There were five of us. The brother of the minister, a schoolteacher, was describing the daily struggle to teach children to read and write without enough pens and paper.

The minister, however, kept asking him about the secondary schoolteachers' union which has had various brushes with authority although everybody now seems to have been not only forgiven but paid all the back pay they have been owed since they were suspended. A cousin was a tailor and doing very well making suits for the government and diplomatic corps. The fifth member was a former minister, eager to maintain contacts in case the odd ambassadorship might come his way. We discussed the effectiveness of aid programmes, toxic waste being dumped in Africa, and South Africa. I am always amazed when South Africa is discussed in francophone Africa. They are certainly interested in it as a political issue, but they never seem as involved as the anglophones. It's almost as if it's a regional issue that one day will solve itself. Then our Italian bustled in, shaking hands and kissing everybody. 'If I may ask a favour, monsieur le ministre,' he said, 'my wife is outside in the car. May I bring her in? And my secretary?' The minister ordered two more places for dinner.

Signora da Porto was about fifty, fat and forbidding. The secretary was as thin as a rake, sallow, tiny little glasses and oozing a kind of icy stillness. We shook hands in silence and the minister led us into dinner.

If I said conversation was slow I would be exaggerating. We barely said a word throughout the first course. Both wife and secretary refused practically everything: they didn't want any bread; the foie gras they didn't like the look of; the fish they turned away. It was a struggle to get them to take some mineral water. While the table was being prepared for lobster, I asked the Italian if he was enjoying his holiday.

'I am not on holiday,' he said.

'He is working,' said his secretary, staring straight ahead.

'He is always working,' added the wife in a tone I've heard all over the world.

I continued to chip away at the block of ice forming over the table. This didn't look as though it was going to be the vrai repas gai we normally had. More like a tableau mort. 'Working? You must be an opera singer – or an icecream man.'

'He is a sculptor,' said the minister.

'The best sculptor in Italy,' added the secretary quickly.

'What kind of sculpture?' I asked, sensing breakthrough.

'Sculptures for national memorials,' he said solemnly. 'For historic occasions.' He spent his life persuading presidents to commission statues of themselves in dramatic poses; ministers to order off-the-shelf designs to recall independence days and national holidays, or even hangers-on to pay for fountains or memorial gardens in a bid to curry favour. For him a coup or a downfall of a president was good news; old statues had to be replaced. In the Côte d'Ivoire he had hit the jackpot; Houphouet made the Medicis look like pennypinching tradesmen. Judging by what he told us, he virtually had the field to himself. His only serious competitors were the North Koreans and the Chinese. Not because of their skill – they make everybody look Korean or Chinese – but because they do it for nothing.

'I could have a statue of myself tomorrow,' said the minister. 'But they would make me look like Mao Tse Tung.'

The ice was breaking. 'What are you doing now for example?' I asked.

'A big sculpture for a hotel. They want something outside the entrance to show their commitment to the country, how they share its aspirations.'

'Whose idea was that? Yours or theirs?'

'Mine. They are commercial. They can't think of art.'

'But that's great,' I said. 'You just go along with the idea and they buy it. You're in business.' We all laughed at Michelangelo's expense. Except his wife and secretary.

'What about something outside the World Bank office,' the tailor chipped in. Which provoked more laughter. 'It would have to be in gold,' he added.

A typical Baoule, I thought. Baoule, like all the tribes along the Coast, are hooked on gold. But as far as I can gather they are the only ones who value gold dust more than nuggets, ingots or whatever. They even developed their own elaborate system of weighing the dust with special scales they balanced on their fingers and different weights for different transactions. Female weights were used for buying or lending money; Male weights, which were a little heavier, for selling or repaying a loan. The difference between the two weights was, of course, the profit or interest on a loan. Then they had 'royal weights' which were heavier still. Here the difference was, in effect, a tax levied by the chief on the tribe.

The weights were based on animals or fish and each had a different meaning depending on who was using it. A weight shaped like a cock meant 'He might look proud, but he has still started life as an egg.' This was generally used by moneylenders as a reminder to clients that they still owed them money which might well have some connection with the Mafia's habit of stuffing their victims' mouths with baby chicks. An elephant weight meant, 'Follow in the footsteps of the elephant and you won't get soaked by the dew.' In other words, I suppose, stick with the boss and he will look after you. A crocodile weight meant, 'If you're in the middle of a river you don't insult the crocodile.' Two crocodiles, however, meant 'Every man can swallow but we only have one stomach,' which sounds like a nice way of saying don't rock the boat or you're going to get eaten.

Once the dust had been carefully measured, weighed with the appropriate animal, it was kept in tiny brass boxes decorated with serpents or figures or exquisite carvings. What happened if somebody dropped the box, or sneezed halfway through the weighing ceremony, I don't know.

I asked an assistant in the IFAN museum in Abidjan why the Baoules kept their gold as dust and didn't melt it down into ingots or coins like other tribes. He thought about it for a time, which probably meant it had never occurred to him before, then gave me two reasons. First, so many people had a vested interest in keeping the gold as dust, the weight makers, the box makers, the dealers, even the chiefs, that there would have been an enormous resistance to change. Second, he added, because the weights had different meanings the system was not only a means of exchange, it was part of their culture and, again, would have been difficult to change. 'You had your books,' he said. 'We had our weights.'

I asked the sculptor how he sold his sculptures, gold or otherwise. 'Do you write letters? Do you ring up presidents and say, Hey I've got a good idea?'

'I know people. They tell me what to do.'

'You mean agents?'

'I have no agents. I always deal directly with my clients.'

'You mean they come to you by recommendation?'

'He does samples,' said the former minister. 'In soap.' And laughed into his handkerchief.

Then it occurred to me. 'Hey, wait a minute,' I said. 'I know how you get your business. You're an Italian. You're a Mason. You're all in P2.' I said it just to get him going. I thought, of course he'll deny it. But he didn't.

'Of course I'm a Mason,' he said. 'You have to be a Mason to get business.'

I remembered my brief career as a go-between, ordering regalia from London for francophone Masons, and pretended to give the Masons' handshake. We all started shaking each others' hands and talking about our mothers' ages. Except for the wife and secretary. Signor da Porto joined in and actually showed us the real Masons' handshake.

'This,' he said, 'is how you shake hands with a Master.' He pressed one finger against my wrist. 'This is a Grand Master.' He pressed two fingers against my wrist. 'And for an Imperial Master, this.' Three fingers.

'So who is an Imperial Master?' I asked.

'Why Houphouet-Boigny, of course,' he said as if the whole world knew it.

'Houphouet,' whispered the minister.

'Of course,' he said. 'For Africa. He is also one of the senior Masons in France, of course.'

'That's why everybody shakes hands with everybody in francophone Africa,' I said. 'They're all trying to find out who the Imperial Master is.' And we all burst out laughing and shaking hands again. Except, of course, the wife and secretary.

The Italian started to give us a history of the Masons; how they had fought during the French Revolution; Garibaldi, Winston Churchill, Prince Philip.

'So why don't you make us all Masons?' I said.

'You want to be Masons?' roared the Italian, 'I'll make you all Masons.' He stood up. 'To the new Masons' Lodge,' he cried. 'We'll call it P3.'

It was time to go. What had started out as a disaster had turned into a marvellous evening.

'I didn't know you were a Mason,' I heard the secretary saying to the Master of our new lodge as they left.

'Never tells me anything either,' mumbled his wife.

I had arranged to have dinner with an Ivoirian businessman, but when I arrived at his office his secretary told me he was throwing a party at the Hotel Ivoire, and had left word for me to join him.

'A party? What for?' I said.

'To celebrate having stolen a million dollars from the French,' she said.

Houphouet-Boigny is said to be realistic about corruption. It's wrong and he does everything he can to stamp it out. He calls it 'This economic and commercial plague'. Apparently he insists that if a government official is on the take, he keep the money in Côte d'Ivoire. Swiss banks are out. The money must be used to benefit the country. Which is logical in an African sort of way. In Switzerland, it creates jobs for Swiss bankers. In the Côte d'Ivoire it can be used to create jobs for Ivoirians.

I didn't have the courage to gatecrash at the Ivoire. Instead I wandered into the casino. I never play, but it's always interesting to see the unofficial economy at work: locals who are not supposed to play getting rid of foreign currency; Chinese and North Koreans recycling their profits; and the usual mish-mash of foreign businessmen (always lots of Lebanese) and tourists.

The place was about half full. A fat American with one of those loud-check convention jackets was puffing cigar smoke all over the roulette table and shouting and screaming like an all-night stand in Las Vegas. Not at all like the decorum of Monte Carlo. But he looked as though he was losing so nobody took any notice. A group of Chinese occupied about the same square footage at the other end of the table. They seemed to have a system, which also seemed to work. Three of the card tables were empty. The croupiers sat staring into space.

'Quiet tonight,' I said.

'Always the same on a Wednesday,' said the manager. He was from Romford just outside London, had been trained by Ladbrokes and couldn't get a job in England. 'We're cheap,' he said. 'Much cheaper than the French.'

'And they can trust us,' said the girl, also from London, spinning the wheel. 'Worse luck,' they added together.

The casino was run by a Lebanese group, all the senior executives were Lebanese, but the staff working the tables were English.

'So how much do people lose?' I asked.

'Not much. There are limits on the betting. About $1000–$2000 a night.' Which is still big money, in a country where the annual per capita income is about the same.

'And how much do they win?'

'About the same.'

'What's the most anybody has won?'

'About $10,000,' said the manager. 'We're very small.'

I wandered back into the bar. A group of local journalists were sitting in the corner sipping Perrier and fruit juice.

'Any news?' I asked.

'You're all trying to poison us,' said one, 'by sending us radioactive milk powder.'

'Where did you get that from?'

'From the EC. It's in all the papers. You're giving milk powder to Africa because it's been contaminated by Chernobyl and you don't want anything to do with it.'

'Do you believe it?' I asked.

'No. I don't believe you would do it deliberately. But it's a good story.'

The local Japanese journalist came in from the casino. Japan now gives over US $3.5 billion a year to developing countries. It seems as though the more they give, the more journalists they send to check how the money is being spent. He was with another Japanese. We introduced ourselves and I called the waiter across. The Japanese both ordered 'Wannie Porker Wack Rabel Warge Woms'. I didn't mind. They were helping our balance of payments.

Three German sailors came in, whom I had met a couple of times in Lomé. They were on their way from the Far East to the States, delivering more Japanese, Taiwanese and Korean products for the booming American market. They were in Abidjan for repairs. They were all old Africa hands; the captain, the bursar and the mate. Between them they said they ran the ship, one of those sophisticated, purpose-built ones.

'So life is easy,' I said. 'No problems, just press a button.'

They fell about. 'Mein Gott,' they said. 'Never had more problems. More danger. You forget the crew.'

'What's wrong with the crew?'

'They know nothing,' said the captain.

'Who are the crew?'

'Africans.'

'Aren't they trained?'

'Sure they are trained,' said the captain. 'In African training schools.'

'So what's wrong?' I said.

The captain shuffled his chair. 'I will tell you,' he said. 'We are lucky to be here. It is terrifying. We picked up a big load in Japan. An 800-ton reactor for America. Straightforward. Done it hundreds of times. Sophisticated ship. As you say, a piece of gâteau. I ask the second mate to use the sextant. Has no idea. I ask the third mate. Useless. And they are both trained.'

'You'll never believe this,' said the bosun. 'The duty engineer makes a mistake. He takes the main valve off the fuel-oil tanks. Floods the whole engineroom. Could have easily caused a fire. Could have sunk the whole ship.'

'Well, everybody makes mistakes,' I said. 'I can remember . . .'

'Then we tried our emergency procedures,' said the mate. 'We thought if the crew are as bad as this we had better be ready. Nobody knew what to do. They just wandered around.'

'On German boats everybody knows what to do. They are trained,' said the captain. 'In German training schools.'

'And maintenance,' said the mate. 'Disaster.'

'There was no maintenance on that ship at all,' said the captain. 'There was grease on the runners. It was a disgrace.'

'And when we come in to the port here, what happens?' said the bosun. I was frightened to ask. 'The pilot hits the berth and damages the bridge.' He sinks his head in his hands. 'I ask you. Even the pilots cannot get it right.'

'The crew couldn't even offload,' said the captain. 'We had to operate all the controls, had to do everything otherwise we'd still be there.'

'African training schools,' they sighed together.

'But don't you complain?' I asked. 'If things are as bad as you say, something should be done, otherwise there is going to be a big accident.'

They all laughed. 'Mein Herr,' said the captain, leaning towards me, 'who shall we complain to?'

'The owners of the ship.'

'Not interested. If the cargo is delivered they're not worried. The voyage has been a success.'

'The shipping companies.'

'Not interested. So one ship has problems, they'll charter another one.'

'What about the training schools?' I said, solving the

problem. 'Surely they're interested in raising their standards?' I'd never seen Germans laugh so much. The mate had to go outside to get his breath back. 'What have I said?'

'You want me to tell African training schools they are not doing their job properly,' said the captain. 'I thought you knew Africa. Do you think any African is going to believe me if I tell them that their schools are not turning out qualified graduates? And me a European? As far as they are concerned their graduates are better than ours. The fact is even the teachers don't know as much as our students. But they have their colleges, their diplomas, their big cars. That's all that counts.'

'And if we complained,' said the bosun, 'what do you think would happen to us? Where would we get another job?'

'So what's going to happen?'

'I don't care,' he shrugged. 'I've had enough. I'm going to retire at the end of this trip.'

'Me too,' said the captain. There was still no sign of the mate who seemed to have quit already.

The Japanese journalist asked me to join them. As I sat down they were ordering yet another round of Ronnie Jalkers. The second Japanese turned out to be a professor at Kyoto University. Was he over here studying the impact of Japanese aid on the economy, I asked him.

'No,' he said taking his glasses off and wiping them with his handkerchief.

'The impact of Japanese cars on the rural community, perhaps?'

'No.' He polished his lenses with his tie.

'The market for Walkmen?'

'No.'

I was about to ask if he was a professor of communication studies when the journalist told me he was a specialist on anthropological studies, Japan's leading expert on tribal speech patterns. He was a very important man, an adviser to the Japanese Ministry of Foreign Affairs and a consultant to the prime minister.

'The professor has published books on speech patterns,' said the journalist. 'He has a big library of recordings he has collected from tribes all over Africa.'

'I have over 3,000 hours of recordings, n'est-ce pas,' added the professor, who sounded as if he kept Sony in business.

'How do you study speech patterns?' I asked him.

'I listen to their conversations, n'est-ce-pas. I prefer the conversations around the campfires.'

'So how do you get them?'

'I go out in the countryside, n'est-ce pas.'

'Just wander into a village and sit down with them round the campfire?'

'N'est-ce pas.'

The expert on speech patterns couldn't stop himself saying 'N'est-ce pas.' I looked at the journalist in desperation. 'So what does the professor do when he has collected all these conversations?' I asked him.

'He analyses them.'

The idea of a Japanese professor wandering into African villages, pulling up his Walkman to the campfire, recording the casual remarks of a group of bushmen and then analysing every phrase, syllable and grunt was too much for me. I wanted to know exactly how he analysed their conversations.

'I study the word patterns first. Then the words themselves. That is very important. Some words are used more than others. That gives you a clue to their thought processes,' he said leaning forward and obviously warming to his own speech pattern. 'Then I study the silences. Silence is very important. It puts the words into context, n'est-ce pas.'

'What about the silence when people have nothing to say?'

'That is a negative silence,' he said firmly.

'So what's the difference between a negative and a positive silence?'

'The intensity,' he said intensely, 'n'est-ce pas.'

I suddenly thought the whole thing was some kind of Japanese joke. The more the professor said, the less I understood. Damn it, I couldn't even understand his silences.

'Well, how can you tell the intensity?' I asked, completely baffled.

'We measure it on a scale of 1 to 1,000 intensities.'

'How?'

'By experience, n'est-ce pas.'

'So you're sitting by the campfire,' I said. 'Everybody is talking about shoes and ships and sealing wax and –'

'And women,' said the professor. 'The way men talk about women is the key to discovering their speech patterns and thought processes. It is the vital factor on all human understanding.' I looked to see if there was a horse standing by the bar. But there wasn't. I took un vache de coup de Lonny Forker.

'Well what do African men say about women?' I asked as seriously as I could.

'So far I have analysed over 300 different speech patterns,' he replied, 'but there are many more – maybe 2,000 more. They must be studied. Everything is on computer.'

By now the African journalists had joined us and were on the edge of their seats staring hard at the professor. I would have given anything to analyse their silences.

'And what do you do with the computer?'

'I search for the most common speech patterns. These we study in order to improve our communications with the African people.'

'The professor advises the prime minister,' repeated the Japanese journalist, completely misinterpreting my speech pattern.

'You mean before the prime minister has a meeting with an African president he studies your reports?'

'My work is at the service of my country,' said the professor. 'N'est-ce pas.'

'He is very famous,' said the journalist.

'I'm not surprised,' I replied. 'He deserves to be.'

At this the professor jumped up. For a moment I thought he was going to hit me. Instead he shook my hand fiercely. 'You are very understanding,' he said. 'You understand the importance of my work.'

'N'est-ce pas,' I stuttered, trying to free my hand.

'Now we drink,' he said shouting at the waiter to bring three bottles of Wakkle Rabble. The waiter jumped out of his skin. Probably nobody had ever ordered three bottles in one go. The local journalists fled without a word. The Japanese journalist pulled his chair closer to the table. We were in for an evening of interesting speech patterns.

The following afternoon when I came to the papers were full of stories about the EC sending radioactive milk to Africa. *Fraternité Matin* also reported a reception given by the minister at the Ivoire, but wasn't too specific about the reason for the gathering.

MALI

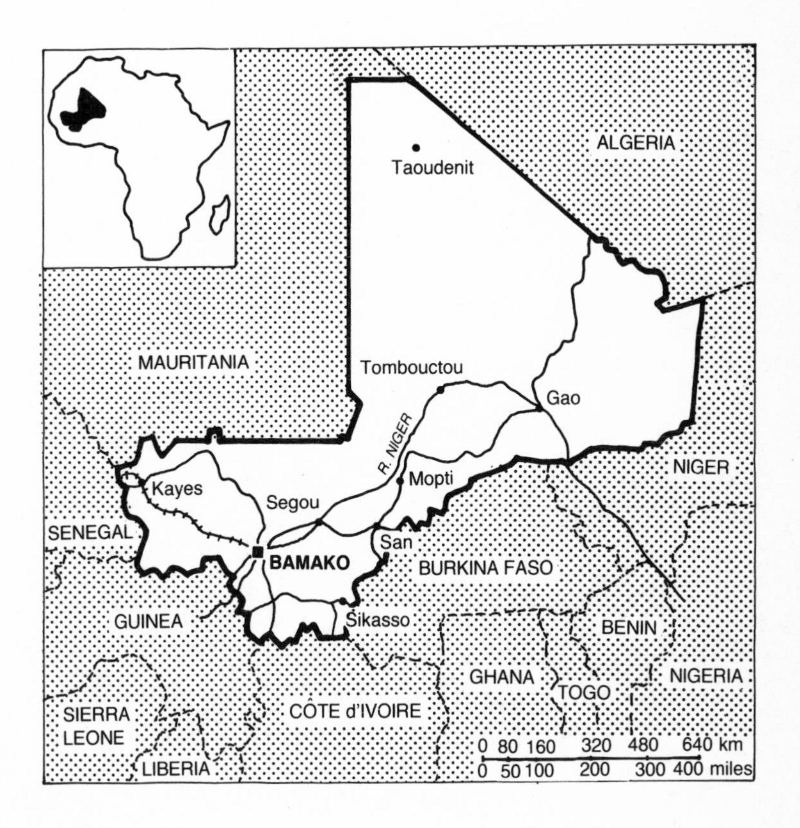
ALGERIA
Taoudenit
MAURITANIA
Tombouctou
Gao
R. NIGER
NIGER
Mopti
Kayes
Segou
SENEGAL
San
BAMAKO
BURKINA FASO
GUINEA
Sikasso
BENIN
GHANA
TOGO
NIGERIA
SIERRA
LEONE
CÔTE d'IVOIRE
LIBERIA
0 80 160 320 480 640 km
0 50 100 200 300 400 miles

Suddenly there were streaks of red and pink. It was very cold, very quiet. Then slowly the light began to spread across the sky. Dawn is always exciting, but especially in the desert. In the middle of the Sahara it's like the beginning of the world. Après another nuit à la belle étoile I threw off my blanket, tried to shake the sand off my sweater and jeans, gave up, pulled on my boots and shuffled off to relight the fire.

Then from nowhere there was a speck on the horizon. Maybe a mile, maybe a hundred miles away. Slowly, slowly it came closer. After I don't know how long I could make out a camel and rider. Maybe a lone desert policeman. Maybe a bandit.

By now the desert was wide awake, the light intense, the air crisp and fresh. The temperature was beginning to climb. It was going to be another étouffement de l'enfer. The speck, I could now see, was swathed in blue and swaying from side to side on his camel. He was alone. Slowly, slowly he plodded up to me. The camel swayed to a halt. The ancient desert visitor bowed down towards me and said in a voice that 'drew itself up from a deep chime of silence', 'Well hallo, ole chap. Spiffing weather. How's Blighty?' Vintage prewar RAF slang rang round the emptiness. My dreams were shattered. Out of nowhere had appeared an Arab who had worked for the British in the war, and taken the accents and mannerisms of the British back to the desert. He was straight out of a time machine.

We talked dans un discours émotionnel: about the desert; about the war; about the British. We drank tea, talked some more. Then he climbed on board his camel, turned back to the desert and shouted over his shoulder, 'Must be going. Toodle pip.'

Forget Air Afrique flights from Paris or even the train from Senegal. The only way to enter Mali is on camel, across thousands of miles of desert. If you can't go by camel, go by Land Rover.

I first went to Mali by Land Rover, from Paris. I left de très bonne heure in the morning; had Beaujolais nouveau to wake myself up just before we hit the route nationale; breakfast at Beaune; lunch at Lyons, and dinner at Le Pigonnet in Aix-en-Provence. Around midnight I checked into the Astoria Hotel in Marseilles, très timide of le premier cru sleaze not to mention la pègre. We had driven 510 miles, used up hundreds of litres of petrol and put on thousands of calories. The following day was easier. I was up just before dawn, took the boat to Tunis and headed straight for Nefta where I was forced to down mountains of couscous and gallons of spicy vegetable sauce followed by hot, sweet tea in thick, dirty green glasses with branches of fresh mint. Instead of After Eights, we were offered honeyed locusts.

With locusts repeating on me like cucumber, we began preparing for Mali. Gallons of fuel were strapped to the top of the Land Rover, cases of Johnnie Walker Black Label packed inside, not to mention the odd tin of baked beans, boxes of biscuits and two goatskins for water which I strapped to the bumpers. Just for photographing. No way was I going to ruin the Johnnie Walker with water stored in a goatskin. We were now ready for the great desert crossing. Immediately we suffered the greatest trial every desert traveller has suffered since time immemorial: we went through an Algerian customs post.

Evelyn Waugh said that for the real travel-snob, recurrent clashes with authority at customs houses and police stations were half the fun of travelling. He never went to Algeria.

'Why haven't you got any papers?' said the customs officer.

'I gave them to you.'

'But you should have them. It is against the law to give them to somebody else.'

'But you asked me for them.'

'It is forbidden to argue with a customs officer. Wait outside.'

'But –'

'Tomorrow. I am too busy now. You must come back tomorrow.'

I lifted up my eyes to the hills. But no help came. So we camped overnight in no-man's-land between the Tunisian and the Algerian customs posts. At first we were hopping mad. All the documentation had been agreed with the Algerian ambassadors in London and Paris. Everybody had been notified in advance. It was a complete waste of time. We were also freezing cold. But the more Johnnie Walker we sampled, the more we relaxed. The following morning after a fascinating glimpse into the nuances of Algerian customs and a few bottles of Johnnie Walker which they kept telling us were extrêmement rare dans les pays mussulmans we were through the customs post in two shakes of an Algerian policeman's wallet and on our way to El Oued, the famous city of 1,000 cupolas, then to Ghardaia and on to the holy city of Beni Isguen. At first it was boring. Instead of sand we were driving through mile after mile of stones and shingle. Gradually the dull grey grit turned to black sand, then to rolling plains, deep valleys and those steep volcanic mountains of sand. We were getting into the desert.

Ghardaia was a maze of tiny narrow streets packed with shops. At one stall I bought an 'imma, a traditional Arab scarf, for protection against the heat, humidity and sand. At another I bought a djellabah, a woollen robe. The days were warm but not hot, like a typical English summer's day. The nights, however, were freezing. Before I left people kept saying the nights would feel cold because the days were so hot. Not so. This was real, below-freezing cold. The djellabah, I was hoping, would keep out the cold until we were way into Mali.

From Ghardaia to El Golea, nearly 250 kilometres away, the sand disappeared and the Sahara looked like an enormous coal tip. As we started to cross the plateau of Tademait we were entertained to lunch and glasses of chachumba, which tasted like raw spirit, with shepherds who were feeding their flocks from broken oil drums. Into the Ain-el-Hadjadj valley and the coal tip suddenly turned into a spectacular sweeping plain carved out of red sand with camels, goats and even donkeys grazing.

After another freezing night in the open we arrived in In

Salah, a marvellous compact desert town carved out of the sand which twenty years ago was threatened with destruction by the dunes. It has been saved, worse luck. I had no sooner arrived than I was arrested for driving the wrong way up a one-way street.

'But there was no sign,' I protested to the head of the secret police at their very public headquarters.

'That is no excuse.'

'But I've only just arrived. This is the first –'

'Did you ask anyone?'

'How do I know I should ask somebody if it is a one-way street if I don't know it's a one-way street?'

'Wait here.'

I waited and waited, and eventually after un long pourparler with the police chief into the early hours and another lesson, this time in the nuances of the Algerian police force, plus the assistance of a few more bottles of Johnnie Walker, I was released.

It was now very early in the morning. Instead of risking another traffic offence I walked through the town and stumbled on the local butcher slaughtering camels for market before the sun came up.

'Salaam 'alaykum. How's business?' I asked him.

'Salaam 'alaykum. Not so good,' he replied, peeling back the skin over the hump of a camel which had been slaughtered while sitting hobbled in the sand. People are only interested in male camels not females,' he said lifting the two great lumps of fat which compose the hump onto the sand.

'So what can you do about it?' I ventured.

'No problem,' he grinned. 'I just hang the testicles in front of the female meat. They buy for good price.'

He picked up a sheep's head, swung his axe above it and brought it down with a thud neatly splitting the skull and everything inside it into two equal parts. 'But it's getting worse,' he grunted. 'They are building a new market. That means modern facilities and modern facilities mean more competition.' He split open another sheep's head. 'In the old days we bought camels, donkeys and sheep, slaughtered them outside town before the sun came up and brought the meat into town to sell it. The new market will have refrigerators.'

'Surely that is better for you? You can keep the meat longer and –'

'No. It's worse. If I don't sell my meat today it goes rotten, right?'

'Yes.'

'With refrigerators it will keep. Which means that tomorrow there will be two days' meat on the market.'

'C'est vrai.'

'And two days' meat means cheaper prices,' he sighed. 'I want to be able to select animals, slaughter them and sell the meat all the same day. How can I do that if you refrigerate the meat? C'est fou.' It was a point that had not occurred to me.

'And they are building the market in the centre of town. Nobody goes there. I sell my meat at the crossroads, by the buses and the park, where the people are. How can I sell my meat if there are no people?'

Just north of Arak we drove through fech-fech for the first time. Fech-fech is very fine, loosely packed sand which billows up into enormous clouds if you as much as look at it. To cross the fech-fech I had to close my eyes, slam my foot on the accelerator and hope for the best. I could see nothing through the windscreen. Whether I went slow or fast, the sand would billow around us. My theory was therefore that the quicker we got past the moment of danger the better. In any case the odds of hitting a Land Rover coming in the opposite direction were pretty minimal, although maybe next time the odds will be shorter.

Now we were in the tropics. For 400 kilometres we drove along the worst road in the world – un chemin difficile, said the guide – full of giant potholes. The whole journey took twenty-nine hours. It was the most exhausting, bonewracking and exciting journey of my life. Around 2 am we drove into Tamanrasset, the centre of the Sahara, along, would you believe it, a dual carriage way complete with lampposts. Tamanrasset, the ancient city of the Tuareg, was like Milton Keynes with more character. But there weren't any camels in town. Another vieux rêve shattered. The only consolation was to drink their palm wine, which was amazingly sticky, and eat their local bread which was full of weevils. Live weevils.

Now the real adventure was about to begin. The Sahara is the cruellest desert in the world and we were about to cross the worst part. An ancient, gruff Tuareg in the marketplace where we were stocking up on supplies told me, 'Tighten your belt. There is no comfort in the desert. If you miss a waterhole you are dead.' He seemed to know what he was talking about and he didn't ask for an arm and a leg, so I asked if he would be our khabirr, our desert guide. He agreed and two days later we headed south. Twenty minutes out of Tamanrasset we turned off the road on to the sand. This was the start of the Sahara proper. For days we drove across sand, sand and still more sand. And we drove fast; swinging, sliding, skidding, hour after hour at 80–100 kph. It was exhilarating, like a cross between a power boat and a snow plough. The air seemed so pure. The sunlight saturated everything. The colours kept changing, from red to gold to orange to purple and back to yellow and red and gold again. The heat was écrasant.

Now things really turned tough. The Tanezrouft is a long plain with enormous hills of sand and crystalline mountains over 800 metres high. You might see a solitary tree surrounded by nothing. The roots, the guide told me, could go down for sixty feet in search of moisture. Or the occasional skeletons of camels burnt white by the sand. The only living creature we saw all day was a fennec, a desert fox, a tiny catlike creature with great big ears, found all over the Sahara as well as in the Sinai and Arabian deserts. This was the unluckiest fennec ever. In the middle of the vast Sahara it was hit by one of the Land Rovers.

'Oh no! Poor little thing,' screamed all the English members of the expedition as they leapt out to give it the kiss of life.

'Oh great,' shouted all the French. 'Now we can have meat for lunch.'

And before the British could shed a tear, let alone call the RSPCA, it was skinned and cooked and served as fennec au Johnnie Walker sauce. I chose the tiniest portion. I have eaten many things in Africa but the thought of hitting a desert fox and then having it for lunch was a bit much. Normally they don't come out in daytime, but stick to their burrows which can run for hundreds of metres under the sand. This one had to break the habits of a million years of evolution just when a

Land Rover full of Frenchmen came along.

The fennec was light and stringy; not much meat on it, obviously, but quite delicate. Better than rat or python; not as good as alligator or antelope. And certainly nothing like porcupine. In Italy I eat spaghetti, in Japan I eat sushi, and in the US I eat junk food. In Africa, therefore, I always try to eat the local food even though at times I feel I shouldn't.

Most English people I know visit Africa frightened to eat or drink anything. Of course African food is different, but it's not all designed to make you throw up. Fish is never a problem, although they tend to be bigger and meatier than the little fish you get in Europe. My favourite is capitaine. I knew one African ambassador in London who would get up early one morning a week and go to Billingsgate fish market to search for capitaine. The lobsters, of course, are enormous, chunky and full of flavour.

With vegetables, things start getting different. Maize and manioc, especially with gari, are quite fun. Corn or millet paste and maybe grilled plantain and even fermented cornflour are more exciting. But my first prize goes to gombi. It looks like spinach, but boil it and it becomes a thick, gluey, green slime. It is truly dégueulasse. It sticks to the plate; dip your fork into it and it sticks like mad, like elasticated sticky green spaghetti. Try to cut it and your knife becomes entwined. It's like trying to eat shredded . . . slime. After years of trying and a fortune spent on drycleaning, I discovered the best way to eat it is to swill it around the dish – the faster, the less sticky it seems to be. Then, with a flick of the fork, spin it straight into your mouth. But be warned: one second too fast, one fraction of a millimetre too high or too low, you'll end up with green slime all down your trousers. And nobody will believe you when you try and tell them it was gombi. Take my word for it.

'Not as good as tortoise,' growled a big beefy Frenchman.

'Lizard, that's my favourite. Especially the big multicoloured ones,' interrupted an academic type. 'They're very tender. But only the white meat. Never touch the blackish meat. It tastes like mouse droppings.' He sounded like an expert. I wondered if he was an explorer. 'Not at all,' he shrugged. 'I'm a chef. I feed the workers building pipelines across the desert.'

I had settled down dans l'hospitalité bonhomme with the guide to try my hand at Woaley-Woaley, a traditional African game a bit like chess and backgammon combined. L'hospitalité bonhomme was all on my side; the guide hardly said a word. I smoothed over a patch of sand, scooped out two rows of six holes and put four pebbles into each hole.

'Antelope, now that is fantastic,' said the beefy Frenchman.

I picked the pebbles from a hole on my side and dropped one in the next hole, one in the one after it, one in the next and one in the next. The guide did the same on his side.

'Elephant, that's the best,' said the chef. 'We used to kill elephants in the bush. The natives would go mad to get elephant. Especially the tip of the tongue. They would kill for it.'

Again I picked up four pebbles and dropped them into adjoining holes. The guide did the same, staring all the time at the sand. Some holes were now empty, others had only one or two pebbles in them.

'I prefer antelope. I . . .'

'Zebra fillets –'

'They're much too fatty. I like –'

The guide was clearing the board, picking up the two pebbles in holes and dropping them into adjoining holes; picking up some more in the next; distributing them along the board. I could see I was going to lose yet again. But still he didn't say a word.

'Isn't hippopotamus very sweet?'

'Sure. You can eat it raw. A bit like giraffe. I like giraffe, marinated in wild strawberries.'

'Somebody said it looks like a baby's nappy left overnight on a radiator.'

The pebbles were disappearing before my eyes. I was well and truly beaten. 'Another game?' I said. The guide nodded. Not even the slightest smile to acknowledge victory. I smoothed out another patch of sand and scooped out more holes.

'I once had flamingo,' said the beefy man. Which must have been a long time ago since it is now a protected species. He also said he had eaten heron, stork and even ostrich. 'But you've eaten sheep's heads, antelope trotters and lizard haven't you,' he went on.

'Never,' I replied.

'What do you mean?' said the chef. 'You've never had a curry in an African restaurant?'

'Sans blague,' I exclaimed. 'They all say that. You're just trying to scare me.'

'No, serious,' he said. 'They don't have health inspectors here – a couple of lizards thrown in is neither here nor there. That way they make more money. What would you do?'

By now I was losing again. I blamed all the talk about food. It was difficult to concentrate, I said. The guide just looked at me.

The beefy man stood up sharply. 'Anybody got any Coca-Cola?' he asked. 'After all that talk about food I think I've got the trots. Coke always cures it fast.' He headed into the night avec un grand determination.

That night was bitterly cold even with the djellabah, two sweaters and my boots on; even though we kept the fires burning and were full of Johnnie Walker. We were after all at 4,000 feet.

The following morning in the broiling heat, as Robert Byron would say, we drove through Tim Missao with its solitary hut for travellers. I saw the Southern Cross for the first time. We stopped to celebrate and finished our Black Label. We also had a decision to take. We were low on fuel and had almost used up our wood; food supplies were lower than we had thought. Should we stick to the official route to Tesalit and Mali, lined every few hundred kilometres with oil drums, or should we take the shortest and most difficult route across the desert?

'The official route,' the guide grunted.

We decided to cut across country. He mumbled something about a franj, which I'm sure is something to do with foreigners. We turned off the official route and headed for Mali.

Three hours later, we wished we hadn't. Suddenly the sky turned a thick brown. We were surrounded by a gooey fog. Visibility was nil. We were in the middle of our first sandstorm. From nowhere the wind roared down on us and lashed and buffeted the Land Rovers. Sand streamed through every cranny. Desperately we tried to block up the windows, the air vents. Impossible. Within seconds there was as much sand inside the Land Rover as outside. People say it is possible to suffocate in a sand storm; I could see how. In Europe you can't imagine it. In the middle of it you can see how sand and disease can be carried along by such enormous winds. I wrapped my scarf tighter around my face, but still the sand cut through it. My eyes were streaming.

'Allez-y,' shouted the guide. 'Vite. Vite!' Our instinct was to stop until it had blown over. But he said if we did that we risked being buried alive. It was better to keep going. At times I couldn't even see the bonnet. But we kept on the move, inch by inch, fighting the wind and the sand, wiping the sand out of our eyes, spitting it out of our mouths. Just trying to breathe was a problem.

Then suddenly it had gone. There was no wind. The sky was blue. Everything was still. 'Alhamdulellah,' muttered the guide.

It was when we climbed out of the Land Rovers we realised how bad the storm had been. We were all covered from head to toe in sand. My scarf, jacket, shirt, trousers, boots – everything was caked. We had to strip out the Land Rovers; inside books and notebooks, inside sealed containers, was sand. Inside the tubes and pipes and fittings was more sand. I looked up and saw on the horizon a camel train. 'Barashoot,' said the guide, 'smugglers. Gold smugglers heading for Guinea.'

Poor chaps, I thought. Dashed long way from Blighty.

The guide said we were entering the graveyard. This was Mark Thatcher country – abandoned vehicles: Peugeots, Land Rovers, even the occasional Mercedes container lorry. From here to Bordj-Moktar, an old army fort close to the Mali border, is the most dangerous part of the Sahara.

Ibn Battuta, one of the world's greatest travellers and a famous Islamic scholar, describes how in 1352 'We met a caravan on our way, and they told us that some men had become separated from them. We found one of them dead, with his clothes on him and a whip in his hand, under a little tree of the kind that grows in the sand. There was water a mile or so away from him.'

A week before we arrived four people had lost their way, run out of petrol, abandoned their car and started walking. Never seen again. We came across a French driver whose lorry had broken down, our first outside contact for nearly a week. Instead of walking he had stayed with the truck, enduring eleven burning days and freezing nights until we came along. He was virtually out of water and infested with fleas. He was one of the lucky ones.

That night we arrived at Tesalit. We were in Mali – the second largest country in West Africa and, with a per capita income of US $200, one of the three poorest countries in the world. The sky was sharp and vivid. The stars looked like real stars not like the plastic ones at home. Saint Exupéry said he used to see shooting stars as he lay in the desert waiting for day break. Moorhouse kept on about the moon being 'the colour of a Gloucester cheese'. We filled ourselves on mechaoui, lamb lightly roasted while the carcass is still warm. The hyenas were howling. The French were still talking about food. And the guide was praying. Five times a day he made his raka just to beat me at Woaley-Woaley.

I'm still slightly taken back by the frankness of the Muslims. I'm afraid I'm very much of the school that believes in going 'into thy inner room and shutting the door upon thyself and so praying in secret'. Not so the Muslims; praying is as much part of life as eating and sleeping. I've seen ministers in their offices with the Koran open on their desk reading their prayers, or lounging in the back of their Mercedes ploughing through Job.

And, of course, African Muslims are Muslims at home and abroad, not like Arabs. I knew one Arab businessman who was a very strict muslim but drank like a fish. When I had known him a number of years I said that I thought Muslims were not allowed to drink.

'You must read your Koran,' he said. 'It says you must not let a drop of alcohol pass your lips. That's why whenever I have a drink, I flick a drop on the table. That way I am not letting a drop pass my lips.'

The Africans, however, honour the spirit of the law. For them, the ideal way to finish a day is not sinking a bottle of whisky or Dom Perignon, but sipping a Perrier and retiring early to say their prayers.

From Tesalit, the Sahara played another of its tricks and turned into grey-black slate. We drove across it – there were no roads – until, oh so slowly, it began to turn green. First, the occasional tuft of grass; then the occasional bush; from time to time a tiny, shrivelled, forlorn-looking tree. The Sahara was giving way to the Sahel, the Arabic for edge or shore, the no-man's-land between desert and savanna. Between 1968 and 1973, the years of the great drought, the Sahel claimed somewhere between 50,000 and 250,000 lives and probably millions of cattle and other animals. The soil is virtually nonexistent. Deforestation is appalling. If the tiniest patch of ground can be grazed it has been over-grazed a million times. Some experts say it comes in cycles – periods of drought, followed by periods of non-drought. Other experts claim that the rainy season throughout the Sahel has been declining for 200 years and will go on declining. A few even say the Sahel is the result of the greenhouse effect, caused by increased levels of carbon dioxide in the atmosphere.

One leading metereologist, Derek Winstanley, at the US National Oceanic and Atmospheric Administration, is convinced the weather is changing dramatically. He can prove there has been a steady decline in the rainfall between June and September over the last 200 years. The World Met Office and the University of Reading disagree. Admittedly the rivers are not as high as they used to be; admittedly the Akosombo dam which provides electricity to Togo and Ghana is only inches above its minimum level; admittedly Lake Chad is now one-third of its size and one-quarter of its volume compared with twenty years ago; admittedly the Egyptians are terrified in case the low levels of the Aswan dam are a sign of seven years' drought, but the figures, they say, are not conclusive. They put it all down to 'a natural fluctuation' in the weather pattern.

Natural fluctuation or not, twenty-five years ago the Sahel was not only self-sufficient in basic foodstuffs, they were actually exporting cereals. Today that is a dream. And the reason: progress. In the last thirty years there have been such advances in medical technology that more people are living longer. There has been corresponding progress in veterinary science. More people mean more cattle. The fragile environment couldn't cope. Over-grazing, deforestation, intensive cultivation – plus the unlicensed use of sprays and insecticides which have actually resulted in desertification, described by Lloyd Timberlake in his book, *Africa in Crisis*, as 'a rash which breaks out in patches wherever the planet's skin is mistreated.'

We drove into a tiny village in the middle of nowhere. There are one or two houses, the rest are huts; no roads, no amenities, just sand. Eventually one or two people appear, as if they have been asleep for eternity and we have woken them up. They drift towards us. Not interested in seeing us, not even uninterested. It is as if the sand has sent them to sleep. One man offers to kill a sheep for us. More mechaoui. We accept gladly. They are all ragged and filthy, their plain, full-length Arab shirts look as if they have been worn day and night for fifty years. Their faces are wrinkled and grizzled. The Tuaregs are the kings of the desert, the men in blue.

To many Malians, however, they are simply baggara, the nomads, a wandering stateless people who live outside governments and national boundaries, and break all the rules. The Tuaregs on the other hand say they ask nothing of anybody or any government. Many Malians say they are bandits and a law unto themselves. The Tuaregs say all they ask is the roughest of grazing for their goats, cows and camels and some water. Malians say they destroy what pastures there are and ruin the wells for other people. Their harshest critics are the aid officials and development fund advisers who cannot cope with an entire nation commuting at irregular intervals between six Sahelian countries.

The head man now appears, claps his hands and shouts. Straw mats are spread out on the sand. We are invited to tea. Tea to the Tuareg is nothing as common as a drink. It is his greatest luxury, the highest honour he can bestow; drinking tea is more a religion than a social occasion.

First the venue. In front of the tent – or maybe a little to the right. On the other hand there is a nice spot over by that solitary tree in a million miles of emptiness. Perhaps just by your car is suitable. But there is a convenient dip in the sand over there …

Then there is the spreading of the mats. I used grandly to grab a couple and scatter them around ready for a picnic. Never in a million years. The right mats have to be selected for the right people. A large mat, all clean and bright, and you're the tops. A dirty, chewed-up mat and you're nobody.

Arranging the mats is the next problem. Your host has to have the place of honour; everybody takes the lead from him. As a guest, you wait your turn. On a first invitation, you will probably sit halfway between top and bottom, which shows your host is being courteous without going overboard. If you pass the test, you graduate to his right on the top mat.

You must then wait to be invited to sit or kneel or squat or a mixture of all three depending on how used you are to Tuareg tea parties. The headman will usually stand by his mat with his hands crossed in front of him. He will bow slightly. You bow in return, a little like the Japanese. He will then gather his robes in front of him and stand there. The uninitiated take this as a signal that the party is about to begin and flop to the ground, which marks you out as an infidel forever. The head man will gaze at his guests, perhaps say a word to the person on his right, maybe throw you a weak smile and then settle down on his mat. Once he is firmly installed you can also sit down, but not without another bow and another weak smile.

Now the tea ceremony proper begins. The headman will motion either to pour the tea himself or that somebody worthier than himself should have the honour. Either way, there will be long pauses and much delicate gesturing before the matter is decided. If you are thirsty, forget it. There is no such thing as an instant cuppa. You may be asked a question: Do you like their country? How long are you staying? Where are you from? Somebody may be asked to ask you. Or you may be ignored altogether.

If the headman speaks to you, you will find yourself replying in the same slow, over-elaborate style. 'Mes frères tell me that we are very honoured to have in our company such an experienced traveller who knows so well the ways and traditions of our country.'

'It is a great honour to be visiting your country again and meeting and talking to your people once more. I would like to express my heartfelt appreciation for this invitation and for this opportunity of being received by you and your family.' For the first time in your life you understand why American ambassadors talk to the Queen about 'elements of refurbishment' instead of saying furniture.

The headman offers you tea. The glass is about the size of an egg cup, very thick and sticky. You wonder how many other honoured guests have drunk from it, then banish the thought forever. The tea is hot and very sweet, like glue mixed with treacle. Everybody watches as you lift it to your lips. You sip it slowly, smile quietly trying to assume the dignity of the desert, and bow to your host. There is another pause and you wonder whether you did the right thing.

'Mes frères say you know our country well and have visited us often.'

'Pas du tout. Je suis touriste,' you say avec le flegme anglais. 'Your friends are correct, I have visited your country many times. I like the desert. It is so quiet, so beautiful, so empty.'

The headman looks at me, pours me another glass of tea. I am beginning to think I've made a mistake. 'I don't understand everything you say. You come from a different world,' he says, looking at everybody for support. 'But I feel you are our brother.'

The ice est frappé. Now we chatter and laugh and gossip. They tell stories about hunting and expeditions and visits to the towns. They describe other visitors. Even our ever silent guide joins in, and tells me he once worked in Paris and lived in dingy hostels. But he preferred the desert. Which was easy to understand.

Tea over, we take our leave, promising to send postcards and drop in next time we happen to be passing. More miles of desert. Now and then a bit of scrub, the occasional tree. Years ago the development agencies didn't bother about trees; now they are as important as food crops. They provide fruit, nuts, leaves, building poles, tool handles, bark for cord and medicine, thorn branches for fencing, green manure and, of course, firewood. A World Bank economist once told me that the present crops and livestock in the Sahel could support almost four million people, but the trees could only provide enough fuel for 400,000.

'So why don't they grow more trees?' I asked him.

'They don't think it's important,' he said.

'But how are they going to get the fuel?'

'They don't think it's a problem, because it's up to the women to find the fuel. The men don't care how difficult it is.'

We turned into another collection of huts, and children came rushing up. One minute you're alone, the next you're the centre of a gently seething mass of smiling faces and outstretched hands. But in Mali the children, anything from three to maybe sixteen-years-old, are not asking for money, but pens. 'Bic. I need a Bic. Please monsieur, let me have a Bic.'

You're frightened to set foot outside the door in Algeria or parts of Tunisia because you'll be hounded by thousands of children. It's not so bad in Abidjan, although every office block or hotel has its complement of down-and-outs and beggars. In Togo, Benin and Burkina Faso you might get the occasional child asking for a 'cadeau' but they seem to be doing it more because they think you expect it than from conviction, let alone hunger. Mali, however, is different. The children want pens. Then out come the exercise books. They might not have pens but they can certainly write.

'Please, see my book, I am studying French and history,' one young boy told me. 'Here's my book. Please look at it.' I sat in the sand with him and read his book. It was a revelation. In spite of poor pens, lack of books, practically nothing to write on, this boy seemed to be getting a far better education than many children in Europe. And he was enjoying it. He was thrilled with the idea of learning as well as by everything he was learning.

Other children brought me their books to read. They were only ten or eleven but they were writing about France and French history – not much about Africa. They wrote little essays in flowing, elaborate French. I asked them about England and they told me all about the Queen and the royal family. One boy told me about Mrs Thatcher, La Dame de Fer, as she is known throughout francophone Africa. 'Can a man be prime minister?' he asked me.

Another boy, a tiny, spindly little thing, told me he had read Charles Dickens. He was a great writer, I said. 'Could he do joined-up writing?' Mrs Thatcher's friend butted in.

The pity is that schools and teachers are in desperately short supply, as well as basic materials. It is probably the only country in the world where students pass examinations to university without ever having books or Bics of their own.

The local schoolteacher told me he had never read a book until he went to Paris on a scholarship. 'We do not have them. We have nothing. But we want to learn. One day we will be an educated country. The problem is the government gives all its money to the police. A policeman earns more than a teacher.' But then I suppose a British policeman earns more than a British schoolteacher.

'We think we are very badly off as schoolteachers, but at least we have a job. I feel sorry for our students because we are educating them for nothing. No way will they ever get a job in Mali. Even where there are jobs, the government wants to get rid of them. Their advisers keep telling them to reduce the number of jobs in the state sector. In France or anywhere else they will always have to take second place. I don't know what's going to happen to them. They can't even become policemen. We already have more than we need.'

Mali is probably the only country in the world which once believed in higher education and now doesn't. Instead of creating an enlightened and civilised society they found it created nothing but problems. Graduates felt that they deserved important jobs, but there were very few. The government was forced to guarantee all graduates a job. As a result there were so many in the ministries and state enterprises that there was nothing for them to do. On top of that there was no money. The government couldn't print more money, so they simply divided the existing budget between more and more employees, until the over-educated employees were getting practically nothing to live on. And in Africa, when you are getting nothing to live on you have to start looking for favours, presents, contributions towards expenses, and so on.

The government also found that in a country of philosophers there were no plumbers. Nobody wanted to do the menial jobs. People had to wait longer for simple jobs to be done; the longer they had to wait, the more the country's fragile infrastructure cracked. And the longer they had to wait the more it cost to get the job done. The World Bank had to run almost an anti-education programme before the country ground to a standstill.

Many educated Africans will never be able to use their learning. Education is spreading rapidly in West Africa, but the computer is spreading faster. As one man is qualified, two jobs are lost to the computer or increased efficiency. Again and again you come across clerks and secretaries who have studied in their own countries, have degrees from the Sorbonne or Montreal or London, speak three, maybe four languages, but are unable to find a job to match their qualifications and abilities.

Koffi is a clerk in a pharmacy in Lomé. He should be in a bank or working in the finance department of a big trading company. Tikum is in a bank in Douala, in charge of foreign transfers. He qualified as a doctor, but had to come home to look after his family. Antoine is secretary to the chef du cabinet in the Ministry of Information in Cotonou, Benin. He speaks French, English, German and a little Russian and is studying Italian in the evenings. But he spends all day typing letters with up to six carbons on a battered old Remington. Somehow you can't see them being able to break out. If only the computer could have passed them by at least they would have had some hope.

As I climbed back into the Land Rover a boy rushed up to me. He must have been ten or eleven although he looked much younger.

'Ça va?' he said.

'Ça va,' I replied.

He handed me a small piece of paper torn from some official form. 'Write to me,' he said. 'Please. I want a friend. Everybody says they are going to write. But they never write.'

As we drove away the sun was strafing down. The sweat was running off me. I saw a slight breath of wind on the sand. Then without warning we were in the middle of another stretch of fech-fech. The sand billowed up and engulfed us. Instinctively I wanted to brake. I couldn't see where I was going – it was like an old-time London smog. Instead I held my hands rigid on the wheel, kept my foot on the accelerator, glued my eyes to the speedometer and made certain that I maintained my 80–85 kph. Madness. But I was driving in convoy. If I slowed down or swerved I risked hitting the others. We had to maintain that straight line, the same speed, or else ... After maybe four, five minutes the fog disappeared, daylight returned. Blood flowed back into my hands, my heart started beating again. We pulled into Anefis as it was getting dark. We had covered 300 kms since morning. It was getting bitterly cold.

The following morning I woke up frozen to the ground. 'There has been a disaster!' I heard the big Frenchman shouting. 'We must go back! I've lost all my money. It's all gone.'

'What do you mean? It's been stolen?'

'No, it's lost. We must go back.'

'So how did you lose it?'

'It was hidden in my underpants,' he said, suddenly looking less like the great explorer. 'And last night when I got the trots and I went to the toilet, it all fell out.'

Everybody collapsed in laughter. 'And you expect us to go back and try to find it ...' Even the guide started laughing.

Here in the Sahel, like William Lithgow, a slightly jaundiced seventeenth-century adventurer, we found 'the best inhabitants halfe ded, the Vulgars naked, the Countrey void of villages, rivers or culterage' although from place to place 'the Soyle was rich in Bestiall, abounding in sheep, goats, camels, dromidores and passing good horses.' But not wanting to follow his example after 'seven daies' trying to 'finde people and tents to relieve us with Victuales and informe us of the Countrey,' being forced to 'relye upon Tobacco and to drinke our own wayning pisse,' we headed for the first oasis on the map.

We stopped at a well surrounded by livestock. Two men were drawing up water in rawhide buckets and shouting at each other. I spoke to one of them, who tried to sell me a camel for £150. It was a magnificent white bull camel, but in the end I turned him down. Which seemed to upset him – the camel, that is. At first he gave a bit of a gurgle. Then the gurgle turned into a roar. Then he spat sticky green slime. I was about to change my mind when the owner raised the price to £200. Which struck me as a novel way of bargaining, but I was grateful; I could leave with a good conscience.

Now the Sahara became glorious sand again. We drove for

hour after hour, nothing in sight, kicking up vast, billowing clouds of sand. We were heading towards the Sahel proper and les criquets pelerins, the pilgrim crickets; it sounds better in French than plain locusts. It's impossible to imagine the damage locusts have caused in Mali. Chinese experts have told me they have seen single swarms covering entire towns, and regions stretching up to 100 miles wide and 25 miles deep. I've never seen anything like that, thank goodness. But I've seen enormous dark-pinky clouds of locusts in the distance swooping silently over herds of cattle; turning and engulfing entire villages then swinging like a cloud of glass blotting out the sun and descending en masse upon miles of healthy crops. Everybody ran after them, trying to swot them with sticks, doing everything they could to protect their crops. But in vain.

Worse still, I've seen the results. In Mali, in Niger, in Burkina Faso, I've seen acres stripped clean in seconds. Crops to feed whole towns for a year can be destroyed in hours. Yet the means exist to control if not destroy them. The problem is, as ever, cost and deciding the right approach.

Some aid organisations will tell you: 'Dieldrin. That'll do it. Always has.' Others, especially Americans, will say, 'Never. Use fenitrothian backed up by satellite reconnaissance and improved ground surveillance.' The problem is that half the world says dieldrin can get into the food chain where it can be dangerous for humans. It is also lethal for birds. The US banned it in 1974, the EC followed in 1981.

'Dieldrin has protected Africa from locusts for 30 years,' one aid officer in Bamako, Mali's capital, told me. 'It's crazy not to use it. Okay it kills birds, it can kill if it gets into the food supply, but only in temperate, northern climates, not in Africa. In Europe it will last for months, here it only lasts a few weeks. The heat and light destroy it, so the risk to birds or animals is minimal. In any case, it causes nothing like the damage a plague of locusts can cause.' Which seems fair to me.

The other half say, at one extreme, 'Nothing's been proved,' and at the other, 'The potential risks far outweigh the devastation caused by not using it.' Even the Food and Agriculture Organisation has said that locusts can be checked 'only by controlled and supervised use of the pesticide dieldrin'. Most

French and African experts I have spoken to agree. During the last locust plague in Africa, from 1949 to 1963, long stretches of vegetation several miles apart were sprayed with dieldrin at the rate of just two ounces an acre. At each stretch the locusts picked up more spray. With each dose lasting up to six weeks they eventually poisoned themselves. It was easier and cheaper to spray the ground than the locusts. It was easy to anticipate each stage of the locusts' journey. Locusts always follow the prevailing winds, which inevitably lead to rain, which in turn provides their food and gives them good egg-laying conditions. But today the argument is against dieldrin.

And in the meantime those simple grasshoppers, suddenly given the right conditions, are changing and multiplying maybe as much as 500 percent in a month. Their wings are getting bigger, their back legs shorter. They are changing colour from brown to yellow. And they are becoming more and more dangerous killers.

'The Africans can't win,' said the aid officer. 'If it doesn't rain, they lose their crops. If it does rain, the locusts eat them. If you kill the locusts you get rats.'

After locusts swept through the Sahel in 1986, they were followed by millions of hungry rats, many of them large kangaroo rats. Locusts you can spray. The only way to kill rats is by baiting them with a poisonous mixture of sorghum and maize that has to be administered by hand at the rate of one kilogram per family. Per family of rats, that is.

We were now within striking distance of Gao. With luck we could make it by nightfall. Then in the distance I saw a road block. We were still driving on sand. We could easily have avoided it. But that would probably have created more problems.

'Your passport, please.' I've been stopped by policemen and soldiers all over French Africa, but this was the first time I had been asked for my passport.

'I think I've got it here,' I said fumbling in my pocket, my briefcase. 'I'm sorry, I can't find it.'

'You will come with me.'

I've heard all about African prisons; a hundred people packed into a cell the size of a hotel bedroom, no light, no air, no toilets. The floor hosed out once a day, stifling heat, and the only food what your family or friends bring in for you.

Some countries have a fairly good basic system of justice. I've visited courts and seen prisoners shuffling along manacled to each other, but at least they come to court. In other countries it's more primitive. Wives can claim husbands have run off with the housekeeping and have them locked up. Neighbours can report neighbours for too many Saturday night parties. And policemen can arrest anyone they fancy. And there they stay until the person making the complaint decides enough is enough, or until the prisoner or his family buys him out.

Mali was supposed to have a notorious prison at Taoudenni, in a military zone in the middle of the Sahara. Some Malians in Paris tell you it's kept just for political prisoners. Others tell you about friends arrested for petty theft and sent there for years. Then suddenly in 1989 it was closed down and all the prisoners pardoned in what the president called a gesture of 'political clemency, magnanimity, tolerance and humanism'. 'Nonsense,' say the Malians in Paris. 'Traore has discovered that the prison is sitting on enormous salt deposits. He wants to develop it into an industrial complex.'

I didn't exactly want to research Mali's prisons at first hand. I followed the policeman into the police station. It was pitch black, papers and rubbish everywhere. He went into an office and switched on a desk light. 'You will come in,' he said.

It was like offices all over francophone Africa: plaster walls, no paint on the woodwork, cupboards and files all around the walls, papers everywhere. An old man was fast asleep, his head sideways on a tabletop with his arms dangling on the floor. A tableau vivant to African bureaucracy.

'Sit down,' said the policeman, kicking his shoes off.

'Look, I can explain,' I said. 'About the passport. I'm sure it –'

'I don't want to talk about the passport,' he said. 'I want to have a serious talk with you.'

Serious, I thought. Oh no. Taoudenni here I come.

'Such as politics, the American election, what Mrs Thatcher is doing . . .' Was I hearing correctly? 'What France is doing in the Common Market. The Channel Tunnel. The World economy ...' He was smiling through his goldrimmed spectacles. 'I hope you don't mind,' he said.

He was a graduate; he had studied in Paris and Toronto, and visited London and Rome. At one time he had thought of becoming a priest. He had also visited New York and Moscow. His brother was a minister and had told him he had to come home and work for his country. He wanted to work in the ministry of foreign affairs, but first he had to do something else. He had decided to be a policeman because it gave him plenty of spare time to read and, because he was a graduate, he immediately became a captain. 'But the problem is, there is nobody to talk to. Everybody is afraid of you.'

'Haven't you got any friends?'

'How can I have friends? If I talk to somebody everybody thinks they are a criminal or an informer.' He pulled his feet up in front of him and picked his toes.

He was twenty-six, and had previously been based in the north where his family came from. There it was much better. 'I am a desert man,' he said. 'The open air. The desert. You can breathe.'

The old man stirred and looked up, then dropped his head back on the table. The captain went across and shook him and told him to get us coffee. The old man grunted and found a filthy black saucepan under some papers. He shuffled off with it, muttering and scratching his head.

'Now let's talk about America,' said the captain. 'Who do you think will win the election? I like Dukakis. He is young, strong, vigorous. Do you like him?'

'No. I prefer Bush.' I didn't, but if he wanted to talk I thought there was little point in agreeing with everything he said. 'I prefer old men.'

This stunned him. 'But you should have somebody like Kennedy. He was strong. A man of action –'

'And dangerous ... The Bay of Pigs. The missile crisis. Young men make war. Old men make peace.'

He looked up from his feet and burst out laughing. 'Quick, give me a pen. I will write that down. I will quote it to my friends.'

The old man now returned with two mugs of coffee. There

were more chips around the rim than rim. Probably had more social diseases on it per square millimetre than the centre of Lagos. But I drank it; it was safer than being thrown into gaol.

'Well, what about Madame Thatcher?' the policeman said. 'La Dame de Fer. She is changing things?'

'Ah, but she is not a politician, she is a revolution.'

'She is prime minister!'

'Madame Thatcher is a social revolution. She is changing the way we think, the way we do business, the way we make money. Our attitude to government. Our attitude to old people, young people, the family, government ... everything.'

'She is a very great lady,' he said seriously.

I walked across to the window. The old man was standing with his foot on a chair. He had rolled up his trouser leg and was picking scabs off his leg and flicking them all over the room. I rushed back to my coffee, just in case ...'

'Now tell me about Africa,' I said. 'Why is Africa in such a mess? Look at India – Japan – Korea; look at Indonesia, or Papua New Guinea. They all had nothing, but look at them today. If they can do it why can't Africa?'

'We have lost our way,' he said slowly. 'We must return to our roots, rebuild our structures based on traditional values, not on the values of the West. Africa has a long tradition, a great culture. Our peoples were civilised thousands of years before Britain.'

'Or the United States.'

'The United States is still not civilised,' he said laughing. 'They are all killing each other. That is not civilisation.' He almost spat the words out. 'We must return to our own culture.'

'Such as?' I asked nervously.

'The rule of the traditional chiefs; the Council of Wise Men, the village assembly. In the villages we work together. We get things done. There is no war, no argument. That's what we need. Then Africa will be strong.' In his village in the north, he said, everybody shared in running the village. He wanted the same system throughout Africa.

'But Africa is too big for that type of system,' I said.

'Not at all,' he said. 'The chiefs have sub-chiefs, sub-chiefs have village chiefs. Everyone works together.'

'But that takes too long.'

'It doesn't matter how long it takes as long as we reach the right decisions.'

'But it does. People are dying of starvation, unemployment is increasing, the population is increasing. You haven't got much time.'

'That is the fault of the West,' he said. 'The West told us to build power stations, bridges, factories, steel mills, phosphate mines. We built them because you said so, and the way you told us. But now they don't work you tell us we must pay for them with our money. That is not fair. You told us to build them, you should pay for them. We didn't want them.'

He walked over to where the old man was picking and flicking scabs. 'Look, I am a poor man, hungry. Does it make any difference to me if the fishermen have dug-out canoes like our people have had for generations or a big, shiny nuclear ship? Of course not. The important thing is that we have something to eat. What happens? The West comes along and says, your canoes are old-fashioned, you must have something modern. We don't know what to say because we are not the experts. You are. So we buy the ships with our money. You don't give them to us, you make us buy them.'

Flick. The old man is now flicking scabs towards me. I try and shuffle out of range.

'What happens? They don't work. We don't get any fish. It's your fault, but we still have to pay for them. If you left us alone we would still have fish to eat. Now we have to buy fish from you as well.' He slumped back in his chair. 'Under our traditional system the chiefs would have controlled the fishermen, the fishermen would have said no. We would have fish to eat and we would not be in debt.'

'But . . .'

'Look, under our traditional system we discuss everything. If we agree, we do something, if we don't agree we don't do it.'

'What happens if you disagree with your chief?'

'The chiefs vote and decide. If they decide they want a new chief, we have a new chief.'

'And the chief goes?'

'Of course. Our chiefs are not dictators. They don't go

around with bodyguards and policemen and soldiers like President Reagan or Madame Thatcher. They are men of peace. Why shouldn't they accept the decision of the village?'

'You should be a politician,' I said.

'No, I want to be a diplomat,' he replied, 'at the United Nations. I want to tell people what they have done to Africa.'

'You know the definition of a diplomat?' I asked him. 'He is a man who is sent abroad to lie for his country.'

He creased with laughter, slapping the table. 'You are a dangerous man,' he said, wiping his face with his hat.

'So if you want to be a diplomat,' I said, trying to get the conversation back on track in case he really thought I was dangerous and should be locked up, 'what would you do with the OAU?'

'I would make it the extension of the village. The village has its council of elders, so Africa should have its council of elders.'

'I thought that was what the OAU was already.'

'No. It is talking. We want action. We want it to be stronger.' He looked at me. The old man had dislodged a giant scab from behind his left ear. 'You want us to be weak.'

Splat. The scab landed right in the middle of the officer's hat, but he was too tied up with the OAU to notice. 'The weaker we are the stronger you are. Africa is becoming more dangerous; more coups d'état, more famines, more civil wars. That is good for you. If we are weak, you are in charge. But if we become strong we will tell you what to do, you will be frightened of us. You won't like that.' He was now deadly serious. I could see him at the UN, thumping the rostrum.

'But look at all the money we are giving Africa to build itself up.'

'Yes, but you are telling us how to spend it.'

'But we are doing it in co-operation with you.'

'You give us money. You tell us to build a power station. We don't want a power station. Then you take back the money and say that is the debt we owe you for building a power station we did not want. You call that co-operation? No, we must strengthen the OAU, make Africa strong again. Without your help.'

Something told me this was as far as I should go. 'Yes, maybe, you're right,' I said slowly. 'I hadn't thought of it like that before.' I waved away the flies that had settled on the scab on his hat. It was gradually getting lighter. 'Hey,' I said looking at my watch. 'Do you know what time it is?'

'We have had a good discussion,' he said. 'I enjoyed it.' He jumped up, grabbed his hat, spinning the giant scab and its coating of flies onto the desk. 'Come. I will take you back to the car.'

Outside we shook hands. He asked for my card and we promised to meet again. 'I'll see you at the United Nations,' I said.

He leant into the car and waved his stick at me. 'Next time you come here,' he said, being the policeman, 'make certain your lights are working otherwise I will arrest you. Then you will see what an African gaol is like. You are a dangerous man.'

'Oui, monsieur l'ambassadeur,' I shouted as we spun off the sand on the way to Gao.

Apologies to Quentin Crewe, one of our greatest writers for armchair travellers. He says Gao is dismal. To me it is fabulous.

It was the capital of one of the great Mali empires, the starting point for one of the great routes across the Sahara. And the people, tall, erect, calm and majestic in their bearing, look as if they still remember those days. Over 1,000 years ago they were trading with Algeria. They have dealt in gold, salt and slaves.There are dark rumours that Gao is still the centre of the slave trade, shipping young men and women and even children from outlying districts of the Sahel up north to Tuaregs in Algeria. I've seen camel trains moving slowly across the desert in 130 degrees of heat. I once spent a day with the camel train. But I've never seen any sign of slaves although the Peul, for example, who live near the border with Niger and Burkina Faso in the ancient kingdom of Liptako, still have Matiubes, or captives, who do the running around for the Babades at the top of the tree.

I checked into the Hotel Atlantide on the banks of the Niger, which Crewe says is 'hideous'. To me it's one of the best in the world. My room was enormous, a cross between a chapel and a Turkish bath. I gave practically all my clothes to the old man assigned to look after me. Everything was caked with sand and stained with sweat. By the time I had finished my shower he was back with everything washed and ironed. The shirts were folded, the collars and cuffs starched. I've never known such service. He was so anxious for more, I gave him two suits that had travelled across the Sahara rolled up in the bottom of a kitbag. I had been ashamed to give him them before. He beamed and blessed me in the name of Allah.

Sit in the courtyard under the palm trees sipping a beer and listen to every language under the sun: Babades speaking Peul; Fool Foold from Dioula; Hassanic Arabic; if you're lucky Tedega, spoken by the mysterious Muslim Teda who are supposed to be the best desert guides of all, not to mention boring old French and German. Hardly ever English unless there is a Japanese trade delegation in town.

Watch the people in the marketplace; a Moaga selling salt; a Mossi selling kola nuts; a Tuareg swaying past on his camel, or even a Derde in his big black cloak, chosen to rule his people not because he is the eldest son but because he is the best man for the job.

Wander along the banks of the River Niger. To me that above all is fabulous because in the middle of the desert the last thing I imagined seeing was a full, flowing, vibrant, colourful river. I'm not a river freak. I've no plans to do a Jonathan Raban down the Mississippi. But the Niger is different. Other rivers may be brown gods; this one is a rich, golden goddess. At Akka it opens out into Lake Debo, with its sandcastle houses and mosques and salesmen who swim out to sell you their wares. It's so big you cannot see the other side. Further north, it splits into a mass of streams with islands of pelicans and herons and kingfishers. Here the fishermen, the Bozo, are masters at handling their fragile boats in choppy waters. At dawn and dusk the river comes alive; the sun glows through the light mist, the water 'lapping with low sounds by the shore'. The fishermen propel themselves along with long poles.

I have tellement de choses à faire. First, the Land Rover. I ask the shirt man if he knows anybody who can service it. His son is an expert on cars; his nephew is a taxi driver. Within minutes I am in a taxi on my way to the ferry. We find his son hidden away in a tiny square. He and his family treat the Land Rover as his father looked after my shirts – immaculately. They haven't anything to jack it up with, so they dig a pit in the sand and look underneath.

'Is the engine all right?' I wondered, after the pounding it had been getting.

'If it is not good we put in another one,' they laughed. 'We won't let it die.' The previous week, they told me, they had had to service a Mercedes which had practically collapsed on the way across the desert.

'Have you got plenty of spare parts?' I asked.

'We have no money for spare parts,' they said. 'We took out the engine and put in one from a Datsun.' They grinned.

I didn't ask where the Datsun engine came from. I've known Africans work miracles with cars. Once we had broken a gasket in the middle of nowhere and an African used resin he drew from a tree to repair it. I left them to it and walked back along the banks of the Niger.

The palm trees were swaying in the light breeze. Strictly speaking, palm trees are not trees, but plants. And pretty poor ones at that. They produce only one bud in the whole of their existence, and devote their whole time to turning the bud into leaves. There are around 3000 different types of palm plant.

My favourite is the tall, elegant savanna palm because it produces palm wine. Unfortunately to get at the wine you have to break open the bud and that kills the tree. Should the savanna palm survive the drinkers, it can survive as a sugar refinery. Its fruit and nuts are full of sugar and a great favourite for birds, animals, and the occasional human.

The date palm is the all-purpose one. To me it looks untidy, a chunky trunk with its branches drooping all over the place. You can eat the fruit. Its leaves you can use for building your little Robinson Crusoe hut on the beach; its fibres for filling your mattress and the cushions scattered about your hut, and its trunk for building a grand house to retire to when Man Friday gets on your nerves.

After the date palm comes the coconut palm, the one you see on postcards and desert islands. There is nothing better than slicing the top off a coconut, pouring in a couple of slugs of

Bacardi and forgetting your problems. Then you can crush the shell for oil and cobra, dry the husks for cattle feed and turn its fibres into elegant floor coverings and shades.

The desert or doum palm dates back to antiquity. Excuse the pun. It's the one whose trunk splits into two or three thick branches with leaves on top of each. Finally there's the oil palm which either makes you or breaks you depending on whom you talk to. Half the world, including the National Heart Savers Association of the US, the Nigerian Cardiac Society and the worldwide soyabean industry, say both the oil from the fibrous part of the nut and the more vegetably oil from the nut itself are so high in edible fats that they raise cholesterol levels and cause heart attacks. The other half, including the producers and many doctors, claim the opposite. Palm oil, they say, is rich in imoleic acid, a polyunsaturated fat which prevents heart disease. It's the same with cassava, the basic diet for practically half of Africa. Now half the world is saying it contains a hydrogen cyanide compound which makes you blind while the other half says it is only in the skin so it doesn't. You pays your money and you takes your choice.

When I got back to the hotel the old man was still there. On the bed, immaculately clean, were my two suits, with the jackets folded and pressed. Like shirts. With razor-sharp creases. Down the sleeves. Across the cuffs. Through the middle of the jacket . . .

The Dogon I have always admired. Their week has only five days. Imagine a week without boring Mondays and agonising Fridays; going away for weekends from Thursday until Tuesday. Had it not been for the Dogons I would probably have stayed in Gao forever.

As the sun was rising we drove across the Niger, my golden goddess, all the more amazing for being surrounded by all that sand. Along the banks you could spot the Tamachek nomads and the Bambara peasants. The fabulous Peul shepherds were bringing their sheep down to drink. The Bozo fishermen were starting another day's work. One fisherman told me that at Fafa I could find the biggest capitaine I would ever see. 'They swim up to the water's edge. If you go swimming they can surround you and nip you all over,' he said. 'At worst,' he added, 'they could kill you.' At best, I suppose, you could kill them.

Ahead of us was Niamey, the capital of Niger and – a tarmac road. We cheered and cheered to be back on tarmac again, but the road ran out before our cheering. After three kilometres we were back on sand, except this time the sand had formed itself into solid ruts, like railway sleepers. We drove slowly at first, dropping down into each gap then climbing out again. But it was shaking us and the Land Rovers to pieces. We decided to drive as fast as we could so we would fly over the tops of the ruts and avoid the ups and downs. It was more risky because to work we had to drive at around 100 kph, and because we were in convoy we all had to keep up the same speed. But it was worth it. We flew all the way to the road to Sangha, the capital of the Dogon, where the calabash, or gourd, is the backbone of the local economy. They are made into plates, cups, bowls, even musical instruments.

Mopti, on the other hand, is the straw mat capital de la monde. On the banks of the Niger you will see every size and type of straw mat imaginable packed onto canoes and barges and stacked along the shore. They are used for everything from roofs to carpets, from pillows to prayer mats. Around the Komoguel mosque, a giant sandcastle, in the middle of a babble of Bambara, Malinke, Sarakole and Bozo, there is practically nothing but straw mats.

The Peul, with their traditional multicoloured conical hats, are carrying mats. A woman comes by dressed in pink with a headdress of calabashes, gold earrings like saucepans, the traditional noserings and masses of multicoloured beads and necklaces; what is she carrying? Straw mats.

Everybody keeps on about Timbuktu, the legendary city, which the French claim was discovered by René Caille, one of their greatest explorers. The British, however, maintain that an Englishman, Major Gordon Laing, was the first to reach Timbuktu – the local Tamachek for an old lady guarding an oasis – but died in the Sahara on his return. Caille, they say, stole his notebooks and claimed he was the first. Either way it's boring: dirty streets; fading, crumbling houses; Tuaregs pushing tourist junk. Gone are the days when it was a flourishing intellectual centre boasting two great universities, 180 schools and over 20,000 students. The Malians call it the pearl of the desert. If it is, it's been cast to the swine and pretty effectively hidden – by sand. For every year the Sahara advances another twenty miles. One day, in spite of all attempts to stem the tide, Timbuktu will disappear. Nothing in its life will become it like the leaving of it.

Sangha on market day is a million times better: a riot of colour. A million people fighting over the price of a calabash. And burning hot. It's Mali's answer to Harrods' sale.

At Koriome, I discovered the mysterious Ghimbala, who believe water spirits live in the waterfalls and rocks and cliffs of the delta. I had been visiting the market overflowing with leatherware and waterskins and belts and carpets and asking people if they had ever seen any spirits or gangis. One stall-holder, an old man in a blue and gold boubou who was probably only twenty-seven, told me he had never seen one but his father had. Much the same as the Irish with leprechauns. Anyway, he turned out to be an authority on water spirits. There were two kinds, he told me: from the upper level and from the lower level. All the time they were travelling from one level to another. If anyone interrupted or stopped them making their journey they became angry and anything could happen. They could bring you bad luck, make you sick or fall in the water and drown. The priest, or gaw, protected you from the spirits; stopped you from making them angry or helped you calm them down.

This was remarkably similar to another cult I had come across in Togo, where people living near the lagoon in Be worshipped a serpent with the head of a woman. I had seen their ceremonies and was eager to see the Ghimbala rites. Both were popular among fishermen and people living close to water. Both, apparently, relied on noise and music and whirling and dancing and hypnosis and trances.

The Ghimbala are one of the oldest fetishes in Mali, going back thousands of years. A modern version, a little like the New Testament, however, only goes back to the early 1800s when the first gaw was called in by the first Peul emperor to cure his daughter. He performed the kanji, an elaborate exorcism ceremony, and the girl was right as rain. After that priest and emperor became good friends, much to the annoyance of the other holy men. Today the cult has picked up heavy overtones of Islam.

The stallholder took me to a small house at the back of the market. We went into a tiny room full of people; five or six were dancing round and round, slowly and rhythmically, big white robes on their shoulders. In a corner, six men were playing homemade instruments all loosely based on the ubiquitous calabash. It was already hot and stuffy. More people came into the room, sat on the floor or started dancing. I could sense the music getting faster and louder. The dancers began to sway. One woman started jerking violently, another started murmuring, long and low. I had seen films of the howling dervishes; this, I thought, was the Sahara equivalent. The music was becoming stranger and more repetitive. One man with a sombe, Ghimbala's traditional instrument shaped like the beak of a pelican, was reeling on the floor. They seemed to be repeating the same piece over and over.

'Awa is coming. Watch,' whispered the stallkeeper. 'And then Moussa. Can you tell?'

'Who is Awa?' I asked.

'Awa is the god of water. Moussa is her brother. They are the most important spirits.'

An old man in a white robe sat in a corner, a big bowl of water in front of him with a calabash bobbing in it. From time to time people would go up and kneel before him. He would dip his hands in the water and place them over their heads. 'He is driving the evil spirits away so that the good spirits can come.'

The musicians were now in a trance, playing the same piece again and again so quickly you could sense it was becoming automatic. Sweat was pouring off their faces. It was a wonder they didn't collapse. Another old man drifted in front of them, humming, then waiting, then droning prayers to the spirits. The atmosphere was almost electric. You could sense a feeling in the air – maybe Awa herself. I wanted to ask the stallholder what was happening but I was frightened of breaking the spell.

The room was now a mass of whirling, dancing, singing,

droning disciples of Awa. I'd never experienced anything like it. You could imagine one word, one gesture and the whole mass could have turned in a second and done anything. But amazingly there was no leader; they had whipped themselves up into this frenzy. I was too scared to move; in case I struck the match that set the whole place alight, and in case I upset what was obviously a genuine spiritual occasion.

At last I sensed the music slowing down, the dancers beginning to relax. The priest seemed to sit back, not quite so intent on his blessings. One dancer, a boy, collapsed on the ground exhausted. Others sank slowly alongside him. You could feel the energy draining away. I realised that I was freezing cold. The temperature must have been in the 100s, but I was shivering. I clenched my teeth, and as I relaxed I could feel the cold draining away from me and the heat pouring in. Within seconds I was perspiring like mad. 'I've never felt like this before,' I whispered to the stallholder.

'It's the spirits,' he said. Or maybe a touch of malaria, I thought. It was a strange sensation, but the atmosphere was losing its charge, things were coming back to normal.

'The ceremony is over,' said my guide. 'Would you like a Johnnie Walker?'

'I thought you didn't drink?' I said, taken aback by the conventional end to an unconventional evening.

'I don't drink,' he said, 'because in the Koran it says that if you are a good Muslim you end up in heaven where the rivers are flowing with wine. I don't want to miss those rivers, but you can have one.'

'Thank you very much,' I said. 'Just so you can have the place to yourself.'

I looked up. The road ahead seemed blocked.

'They'll get out of the way. They always jump at the last minute.' I nodded and kept quiet. I am used to being put in my place by American experts on African affairs on their première visite en Afrique. We came rapidly closer. 'There is something wrong,' I said.

'They'll move. Don't worry.' We got within a couple of

hundred metres. The driver sounded his horn, but the crowd did not move. He slammed on his brakes; we swerved, skidded, then shot off the road onto the sand, bumped and thudded over rocks, scraped a couple of palm trees and came to a stop nose down in a ditch.

I was touring with a group of international journalists. We had been looking at aid projects and talking to businessmen, bankers and government officials. Or some of us had. Most of the French had been talking, drinking and improving their tan; the Americans complaining about the food, drinking Coke and trying to avoid getting a tan; the Italians grooming themselves; the British drinking; the Canadians telling everybody they were not Americans and the sole Swiss stealing food from the stores and hiding it in his luggage in case we crashed in the desert. 'Can't get out of the habit of hiding things in the mountain,' I said when his Gucci travel bag burst open revealing tins of foie gras and truffe. The rest of the world suddenly forgot his neutrality and wanted to lynch him.

We were on our way back to Bamako. It was getting on for midday, and it was getting hot. We had been inside Land Rovers for nearly three hours; not the most comfortable of vehicles, especially when they skid to a halt. Luckily nobody was seriously hurt, only a bit bruised and scratched and shaken up. I climbed out and immediately saw the reason for the crowd. There had been a terrible accident. A car had hit a jungle taxi and there were bodies everywhere, some looking pretty ghastly. One young man had a massive gash across his face; blood was oozing out like lumps of jelly over the road. An old woman, thin as a rake, was piled beside him like a heap of matchsticks. About five other bodies were sprawled around, one with a horribly twisted leg. Four or five more were sitting up, crying. An old man was sobbing for all his life was worth. It was the nearest I had been to a battlefield. I was dazed. All this so far from town, from medical help.

The second Land Rover pulled up and out jumped a German African specialist who wrote for the big newspapers and magazines. He went straight to the accident, knelt down by the serious-looking casualties, moved them gently, felt pulses and spoke to them quietly. He came back to the Land Rover, got out his battered leather holdall and took out a small first aid kit. 'Come. I need you,' he said to me.

We had had a drink together the previous evening, and he had told me he had left home when he finished university to become a big game hunter in South Africa. Since then he had divided his time between hunting and journalism.

'You go into town and get an ambulance,' he told the second driver. 'We need help fast.' The driver leapt into the Land Rover followed rapidement by all the others. Obviously nobody wanted to get involved. 'See you in L'Africana,' they shouted. It was one of the best bars in town.

I was left behind with the German hunter and un certain problème. He moved to the most serious-looking victim. By now the blood was thick and lumpy, flies were crawling around, great gashes of flesh were hanging loose.

'Can't do much,' he said. 'Very bad.' He took out a syringe, broke open a packet of needles, fitted and filled it and pumped it into the poor man.

'What's that?'

'Pain killer. Always carry it. You never know. This is Africa.'

'But you can only get that if you're a doctor.'

'I am a doctor,' he replied.

'But you said you were a big game hunter, then a journalist.'

'I qualified as a doctor first.' We mopped up the badly injured, shuffled broken limbs into improvised splints, swatted a million flies, bundled up a couple of corpses and waited.

After nearly an hour I spotted something coming along the road. I had been expecting an ambulance, but it was an old army truck, which was obviously why it took so long to reach us. It was big, so we could get everybody on board; on the other hand lifting the badly injured three feet up into a truck is not exactly good health care. But we did it. They sat on benches holding their wounds, weeping quietly or just staring straight ahead. It was uncanny; they were in pain and had had none of the care let alone medication that we would get at home. But it was as if they were used to it. Then we came to the dead.

'Put them in the truck with the others,' said the driver. 'But you can't,' I said. 'How are the rest of them going to feel sitting there looking at dead bodies?'

'This is Africa,' said the German. We lifted them up like carpets and just threw them on to the floor of the truck. There was nothing else we could do. There were no stretchers. The advantage was they were strangers. We were dispassionate about it, probably like ambulance crews the world over.

We clambered up in front. The driver pushed the engine into gear and it leapt forward at 100 mph. Then he turned round on a sixpence and rocketed back to town. We were thrown all over the cab. I looked behind, dreading what had happened to our poor victims. Miraculously they were all still there. The dead bodies, however, had unrolled and were spreadeagled over the floor, limbs tossed up on some of the passengers. 'Shouldn't we ...?' I murmured. The German shook his head and stared out of the window.

We got to town two hours later, having stopped twice. Once because the driver wanted to see his brother, and we hung around for nearly half an hour while they laughed and joked and smoked. The second time because he wanted to buy fish. The woman selling the fish threw themselves all over the lorry beseeching us to buy. They tugged at our patients and saw the bodies but didn't take any notice. We arrived in Bamako just as it was getting dark. Near the hospital we turned off on to a sandy track and drew up outside a large dirty building. 'The maison mortuaire,' the driver said.

'But we should have gone to the hospital first,' I said.

'You don't take dead people to the hospital.'

The German smiled. 'I know, but the others need treatment.'

'Come on. We're here,' said the driver. 'Might as well get them off.'

He was right. I volunteered to go for trolleys, and went inside. This wasn't my idea of a mortuary. It was decrepit and absolutely filthy. There was slime and grime everywhere. The place was deserted. The metal doors at the end of the reception area were closed. I could hear the engine revving outside – the driver was impatient for his fish. I couldn't find anyone let alone a trolley. I went back to report. As I opened the door the lorry roared off into the night. The German was standing on the path, bodies heaped on the sand around him. 'Can't find any trolleys,' I said.

We walked back into the entrance hall. 'We'll use the table,' he said. 'They're getting a bit strong to be lifting them around.' We soon had them inside and I was about to say, 'Well, what now?' when an old Peugeot 504 crept up the road and stopped. It was the mortuary director.

'I saw the lorry. I guessed there would be some business for me,' he said. He was an old man, lots of grey hair, very thin, practically gaunt; a cigarette in his mouth, a filthy yellowing coat. His shoes were falling apart. He opened the metal doors and switched on the light. It was worse than I expected: giant filing cabinets down one wall; in front, a series of marble slabs; all around dustbins and buckets and cans. The floor was greasy. We carried the table inside.

'How much do you want to spend?' the director asked me.

'Spend? I don't understand,' I replied.

'Money. How much money have you got?'

'Nothing,' I said. I'd left my jacket in the Land Rover. I'd forgotten all about it.

'Well you won't want the luxury accommodation,' he said.

'You charge for accommodation here?'

'Sure. If you want a room for your friends you'll have to pay. If not, they share.' Even in death, not all men are equal. 'Okay. They share.'

The director told us to put the table down facing one of the bigger filing cabinets. He opened the door. Inside were a pile of bodies. 'Nice and cosy in there,' he grunted. 'We'll put them to bed.' He pulled an enormous hook out of his pocket, jabbed it under the chin of one of the bodies and dragged it into the box.

'You can't do that!' I said.

'Why not, he's dead isn't he?'

'I know, but . . .' It just seemed wrong somehow. No dignity, no respect. Not something Flaubert's father would have done even though he put his cigar between the toes of the bodies he was examining. The same for the next – a jab under the chin, a quick pull, in it went. The third time it didn't seem so odd; just routine.

'I'll keep them there a couple of weeks in case anybody claims them,' said the director putting the hook back into his pocket. Didn't even bother to wipe it.

'And if not?'

'Then I'll sell them,' he said with a shrug.

'To whom?' I wondered how many medical schools there were in Bamako.

'To the gold smugglers. Last thing the police want to do is look inside a dead body for gold – even if they thought of it.' He grinned.

'Shall we wipe the table down?' I asked, not wanting to think about it either.

'Don't bother, they can sort it out in the morning,' said the director.

'Operated on worse things than that,' said the German. I wasn't going to argue any more.

'Come back and have something to eat,' said the director. 'You're probably hungry by now.' I didn't know what to say. Rather, I knew what to say but not how to say it.

'No thanks, must join the others,' said the German. 'At L'Africana. They'll be wondering what we've been up to.'

'Wouldn't worry,' replied the director. 'All the bars are closed for the whole of June. It's Ramadan. You might as well come back with me.'

'And now Mali's biggest export, le meilleur du monde,' said the economic adviser. I thought I was in for another visit to a cotton mill or groundnut plantation. Instead he punched a tape into the cassette player. 'Salif Keita,' he said.

Through the speakers came this soulful, wailing voice. Born in Djoiliba in 1949, he is an albino, a descendant of Sounjata Keita, one of Mali's great warrior kings. He has known hunger and destitution, but today he is one of the greats of African music. At least so everybody tells you.

We were driving through the outskirts of Bamako with its long avenues of tall trees, gardens cascading with bougainvillaeas, comfortable villas and splendid imperial buildings with marble floors. Not to mention lots of French restaurants. It is a languid, leisurely, imperial city on the banks of the Niger. And it is hot.

As we passed the splendid police building Salif Keita was singing about oppression and racism. In France.

'But I thought you were socialists, and against private enterprise,' I said.

'Not any more. Tout est changé.'

A few years ago it was quite common for even honest, respectable Africans to say businessmen should all be shot. Not any more. The government is now pro-business, even in Mali, which once boasted outrageously of its 'African socialism'.

The reason is probably threefold. First, those policies have obviously not worked. Populations in the Sahel have been growing at around 2.5 percent a year while growth in food production has, at best, been hovering around 0.5 percent. It is still cheaper to import rice from halfway around the world than produce it in the region. Second, attitudes are changing. If steel mills can be privatised, why not food production, marketing and distribution? Third, donors, the aid organisations, are rooting for the trader.

'As long as rice produced by Thai peasants and wheat produced by mid-Western farmers can arrive more cheaply than the cereals produced by Sahelian farmers can we seriously think that food self-sufficiency is possible?' is a question asked more than once in aid seminars and conferences around the region in recent years. The automatic African response, at least today, is straightforward. 'If you sleep on somebody else's mat, you can never sleep peacefully.' Self-sufficiency is vital, which is where the trader comes in. The more open the market, the more competition there is for local farmers' crops, the more money the farmer will receive and the more crops he will grow. That's the theory. But there are obstacles, like national diet. Thailand has been pouring rice into the Sahel for so long it has become their national dish. Nobody wants millet any more. And, of course, governments are making easy money slapping duties on imported rice.

We passed a building site; Salif Keita was now going on about alcohol and drugs. All over it people were buying and selling. Two boys were mending bicycles. An old man, with a baby's dummy in his mouth, was taking photographs with the most ancient of cameras. This was something new. 'Private enterprise?' I asked.

If Bamako is languid and leisurely, the street traders are not.

At least not the ones who live and work on the pavements, between the impressive buildings, on empty sites or in the fields at the edge of town. By day they are buying, selling, mending and fixing. By night they are collecting corrugated iron, cardboard, whatever they can find to turn a shanty hut into a home. Sometimes the police and the army come in the night and bulldoze them, but it doesn't seem to make any difference. The following morning they are back on the streets, repairing punctures, cutting hair, taking photographs and looking for more building materials.

Mali is suffering probably as badly as, if not worse than, any other francophone country. Trapped in the middle of the desert and subject to drought for fifteen of the last twenty years, it is virtually in a perpetual state of crisis. Cotton, its chief export, suffers again and again from the weather. Groundnuts, its second crop, also. One austere budget is followed by an even more austere budget. In one year alone they were forced to cut back by a staggering 25 percent, and each cut is accompanied by the same ritual. Bakary Karambe, leader of the only trade union in the country, L'Union Nationale des Travailleurs Maliens, attacks the government because firms 'have been closed down, the property of the Malian people has become dilapidated, the laws of the Republic are no longer respected, purchasing power of the people has plummeted, prices have soared, employment is no longer guaranteed and salaries not even paid on time.' And the Imam of Bamako appeals to Muslims to pray for rain.

In 1988 the government couldn't pay any salaries for months; with over 52,000 employees that created more problems and increased the numbers living on the streets. The unions staged token forty-eight-hour strikes. The Imam prayed again for rain but it made little impact. The government then started privatising as many of the fifty state enterprises as it could. It even passed laws against 'les crimes d'enrichissement illicite et la corruption' which would be used, they declared, 'sans acrimonie ou esprit de vengeance' to recoup 'les biens dont le peuple a été spolié.'

While in Bamako, I went to call on a Muslim banker, Mohamed Alhousseyni. He was sitting in his flowing, elegant robes.

There are great debates about Islamic banking in Africa. To many it means no interest payments; interest is usury, therefore no interest can be paid by an Islamic bank. I wondered if that was true. He disagreed immediately.

'The whole tradition of Islamic banking,' he said, 'is that the needy must not be abused.' It was the first time I had heard of such a tradition in banking. 'In other words,' he continued, 'if you come to me and say you want to marry off your daughter and you ask to borrow 100,000 francs and I give you 100,000 francs and I then say that after three months you must pay me back 150,000, that is abusing a person in need, because you have no choice. You have to marry off your daughter; you have to accept. But if I give you 100,000 and say you must pay me back 100,000 that is all right. You are my friend and I am helping you protéger vos intérêts.'

I understood the principle, but was that a practical banking policy? 'Why not? That is Islamic banking,' he said as if I came from another planet. 'We must help our friends.'

I was interested in the concept of need. 'What happens,' I asked him, 'if I borrow 100,000 francs and I'm worth one million. Will you still only want 100,000 back?'

'No. If you are not needy, you can pay me back with interest. And I can accept it,' he said triumphantly.

'But some Islamic banks don't charge any interest at all? They treat everybody alike.'

'Impossible,' he said. 'That is an abuse of Islam. Islamic law says everything must be decided according to the needs of the individual.'

'What about service charges?'

'An abuse of Islam,' he retorted. 'They shouldn't do it.' He tapped me on the arm. 'I'll tell you something else. Under Islamic law if you are my partner then we must share our profits and our losses.'

'So what happens if I invest in a bank and the bank invests in a number of projects?'

'Then you must share the profits and the losses.'

'I do,' I said, 'depending on the nature of my investment.'

'Then that is wrong. In the successful projects you must share in the profits. In the unsuccessful projects you must share in the losses.'

'But you can't do it on a project by project basis. You have to do it as a whole.'

'Then it is wrong. If the bank makes more profits than losses you must have more profits. It is abusing you to give you an average. And what's more,' he said, 'it is wrong to pay you dividends. Dividends are an anticipation of profits. Until the company makes profits they should not pay you profits otherwise you are abusing them.'

I could see his logic, but it would send shivers down the spine of any European banker. 'So what about the amount of profits paid out?'

'It should vary according to the needs of the individual.'

'You mean you'll pay me 5 percent but somebody else 50 percent?'

'Why not? If the other person needs it more than you, that is just.'

'But how can you work it all out, especially nowadays?'

'We have computers. It is easier today.'

'But is it practical?'

'It is the law.'

I told him how I had been in Egypt during the crisis that hit their Islamic banking sector and had met bank directors sitting with machine guns on their desks. 'They were making certain nobody abused them,' he said without batting an eyelid.

I asked him about the CFA franc zone. Launched in 1958, two years before Harold Macmillan's famous Wind of Change speech, which proves how far behind the anglophones were even then in appreciating Africa, it is based on the old French Community of Africa from which it derives its name. First various francophone West African States formed a West African Monetary Union with their own joint central bank, BCEAO. Guinea refused to join because Sekou Toure at that time was complaining about everything. A similar body, the Central African Monetary Union, with the same rules and benefits, was set up covering Congo, Central African Republique, Gabon, Cameroon, Chad and Zaire, although Zaire has dropped out. Mali is the only country that started off a member, quit in 1962 and rejoined in 1984.

'Why did you quit?'

'The government said we were too dependent on France. We thought we could control our fate by controlling our currency.'

'Could you?'

'No. We are dependent on France, there is no escaping it. Most of our imports are from France. Most of our investment and aid is from France. And the CFA zone means people can do business with us and be paid in a hard currency.'

In return, however, members have to keep 65 percent of their foreign exchange earnings in France. The French also ensure, through control over monetary policies by the central banks, that members don't run a deficit with them.

I drove with Mohamed Alhoussenyi to a meeting on the other side of Bamako. We parked and walked along the Boulevard du Peuple. Just as we turned into the Avenue du Reuve with its government offices and mosques he pulled me back. 'Watch out,' he said. 'A leper.' It took me by surprise. 'You still get lepers here?'

'Of course. They've got nowhere else to go. They come into town looking for money.' He was standing by the edge of the pavement obviously trying to catch motorists as they pulled up. He looked about thirty, scruffy and dirty. His face was blown up like a balloon and a bit reddish. One hand was just a stump.

'But isn't that dangerous?'

'Not really. It's not the worst form of leprosy. But it's best to be careful.'

It's difficult to believe that Mali was once a mighty empire with an administration, a system of revenue and taxation that rivalled China. Or that in the fourteenth century Mali could take Cairo by storm and in a few days because of their extravagance bring about a collapse in the price of Egyptian gold.

The man responsible was the Emperor Mansa Kankan Musa who arrived with 1,000 courtiers, all the gold they could carry and his wife Inari Konte, who complained all the way across the Sahara that she couldn't have a bath.

'The man flooded Cairo with his benefactors,' wrote a Syrian, Ibn Fadl al-Umari, who collected the gossip from the emperor's chief of staff. 'He left no courtier nor holder of a royal office without the gift of a load of gold.'

So what happened? The shopkeepers immediately upped their prices. Common old shirts were marked up from one dinar to five. Then, being traders, instead of locking up the gold safe and sound the Egyptians started trading everything they had been given. As a result prices crashed. 'They exchanged gold until they depressed its value and caused the price to fall,' said Ibn.

The following morning I got to the airport early. I was booked on an Air Mali flight to Mopti. The plane was their standard Russian Antonov turboprop with two Ivchenko Seriiny engines, six bald tyres and safety instructions in Russian. At least they usually manage to take off on time. This time, however, the engine refused to start. The batteries were flat. They tried to jump start it from a car battery. Nothing happened. Then with the airport's only fire engine. Nothing.

Somebody suggested calling the Russians; after all it was their plane. Trouble was they were hundreds of miles away in a secret camp in the desert. Then somebody remembered seeing some Russians in the market that morning. Eventually they were apparently found sampling les saveurs et tentations of the desert in a room at the back of the US embassy. With two very un-Malian mondaine young ladies.

Within seconds the Russians connected up the aircraft's cables to a series of truck batteries. The pilot switched on the ignition. There was a cough and a splutter. The propellers started turning. More coughing. Some sparks. Wild cheers. 'Many thanks,' I said to one of the Russians. 'Obviously if you're an aircraft engineer you know all about these things.'

'I'm not an aircraft engineer,' he said. 'I'm the cook at the army camp. But everybody knows how to get these old engines started. I have to or I'd never get the kitchens working. Don't worry,' he added, registering my blank stare, 'it's the same in Russia.'

NIGER

LIBYA
ALGERIA
AIR
MOUNTAINS
MALI
R. NIGER
Agadez
CHAD
Tahoua
Birni Nkonni
NIAMEY
L. CHAD
Zinder
Maradi
Dosso
BURKINA
FASO
BENIN
NIGERIA
TOGO
R. NIGER
CAMEROON
GHANA
0 80 160 320 km
0 50 100 200 miles

Dans le grand soleil it was around 100 degrees. We had just driven into Arlit in the Air Mountains, the first town you reach in Niger after crossing the Sahara. There were shops and bars, Coca-Cola and beer and lots of people. And uranium. For Arlit is the centre of Niger's once-booming uranium industry.

In the old days the mines worked three shifts a day nonstop. More than 500 men at a time would be lowered in creaking, rusty cages from the heat of the desert 250 metres down into the dank caves glistening with seams of yellow cake, a uranium oxide concentrate. At one time, Niger, the world's seventh largest producer, was mining over 4,500 tonnes a year. More than 80 percent of their revenue was coming from below ground. They were gearing themselves up for a gigantic dash for growth and modernisation – then came Chernobyl. Demand fell to less than 3,000 tonnes. Sales accounted for just 12 percent of revenues. The mines cut back to two shifts. Prices fell. Wages halved. But the number of miners grew. The more prices fell, the more the red goatskin tents around the town multiplied; the more miners were prepared to work longer hours – some up to twenty-eight hours at a time – for less and less. For the mines were their only hope.

We had camped overnight at Labezanga on the border with Mali. The guards kept us waiting for nearly five hours arguing about passports and visas. We had reached an impasse. I had run out of whisky so there was no point trying to discuss the matter. In desperation I challenged the guide to another game of Woaley-Woaley.

We smoothed out a patch of sand, made little pockets and

deposited our stones. At first I was losing hand over fist, then suddenly my luck changed. I started to win – at first by the skin of my teeth, then by a margin as big as the Sahara. The guide began muttering, no doubt pulling down a rain of curses on me, my so-called father and my entire Allah-forsaken existence. Once more I beat him into the sand. He said he had to say his prayers and stalked off in the direction of Mecca kicking sand. Telle camaraderie, I thought.

I collected up my lucky stones and pulled out a book. Forget Proust, Gide, Saint Exupéry, even Agatha Christie. The best books to read in francophone Africa hanging around airports, waiting for taxis and especially sleeping under Land Rovers waiting for customs posts to open are Surtees' everyday stories of fox-hunting folk in Victorian England. If anything is calculated to ease the blood pressure and wash away those hours of frustration it is reading about the misadventures of that wealthy cockney grocer, John Jorrocks: ''Unting is all that's worth living for. All time is lost wot is not spent in 'unting – it is like the hair we breathe – if we have it not we die – it's the sport of kings, the image of war without its guilt, and only five and twenty per cent of its danger.' Or following Facey Romford as he charges across 'frightful fences, yawning ditches and bottomless brooks' in the mad pursuit of the uneatable.

I was into *Mr Sponge's Sporting Tour* for the umpteenth time (it was that kind of trip), when a customs man came over. I stood up to smile, wish him bon soir and thank him for delaying us. He picked up the book, studied the cover, flicked through the pages and put it down. 'It's not Shakespeare,' he said sharply.

'No. I'm sorry.' I racked my brains in case there was a new import tax on bringing non-Shakespeare books into Niger.

'Good.' he said. 'I don't like Shakespeare. Shakespeare is bad for Africa.'

'But I thought everybody liked Shakespeare,' I said defensively.

'Not me. It is wrong for Africans to read Shakespeare. Africans should read African authors. We have many famous African authors, better than Shakespeare.'

'But Shakespeare belongs to the world,' I said hesitantly.

Defending Shakespeare is not something I am used to. Usually I am desperately trying to defend Surtees. 'His message is universal.'

'Are you another of those salesmen?' The last thing I was trying to do was sell books, even Shakespeare. I was just surprised anybody should be so anti-Shakespeare. After all there were many more things to be anti, given the environment we were in.

'What about Chinweizu, Soyinka, Senghor, Achebe? They are all important writers. And they are African. They are about today, not ancient Rome or Venice or Scotland. That is what people should be reading, not old-fashioned poetry they don't understand.'

It turned out he used to be an inspector of education in Agadez where the government were trying to persuade the Tuaregs to settle down in council flats and send their children to school. But it was taking longer than the government planned to change a society which had remained unchanged for a thousand years. They were not interested in the moyen et long terme. They closed the school down. The only job he could get was as a customs officer. Yet another educational drop-out.

Shakespeare, he told me, he had studied at school. But he didn't like his poetry or plays, apart from *Julius Caesar.* 'I like the scene in the forum. The beggar says to Julius Caesar, cowards die many times before their death. That's very true,' he said wagging his finger. 'Beggars always have something interesting to say. Shakespeare taught me that.'

His favourite novel was Thomas Hardy's *The Mayor of Casterbridge.* 'I like the scene where he sells his wife,' he chuckled. 'A good idea. Very clever man. Especially if you have only one wife. In Africa we have many wives, but nobody to sell them to.'

He said his son was reading it now, in English. But the best book of all, he told me, was *The Growth and Foundations of the British Empire* by Williamson – 'A wonderful book'. His other favourites were Charles Dickens's *Hard Times*, 'Grim Grin's' *The Honorary Consul*, Raymond Chandler's *Adieu Ma Jolie*, as well as James Baldwin, Arthur Miller, Hemingway and Chekhov.

'So what have you got against Shakespeare?'

'Nothing. He is a great author. The greatest. I've read them all. *Macbeth*, *Henry VIII*, *School for Scandal*,' I didn't even blink. 'But it is a question of priorities. In Africa we haven't enough money for exercise books. Those who bring paper and pens we can teach. Those who can't ...' He shrugged. 'We should spend what money we have on African authors. Why should we teach a foreign culture, especially when the foreign culture denies us paper and pens for our schools?'

Well, I admitted, he had a point. African children should study their own culture, although Africa was such a big place a Nigerian author probably had as much in common with a Zairean poet as Chekhov's lady with her little dog.

'Which African writers have you heard of?' he asked.

'Soyinka,' I said immediately, but had to admit that I hadn't read his books, though I had read plenty of articles by him. I also had to admit I couldn't name any other African writers.

'Grace Agot? Hesino Vinoko Akpalu? They write in English. Agot is Kenyan, Akpalu was Ghanaian; both famous. What about Bernard Dadie, Cheik Hamidou Kane and Sembene Ousmarie? They write in French. And Sony Labou Tans and Tchicaya U Tam 'Si? They're Congolese. They write in French. Breyten Breytenbach, André Brink; South African. You don't know our writers. Why should we learn about yours? But we do. You only know your literature. We know your literature and our literature, so we must be better.' He smiled broadly. I couldn't tell whether he was being mischievous or malicious; either way he was winning the argument. And he was still a customs officer who could keep me waiting indefinitely. I nodded wisely.

'Literature is not the only point,' he added. 'All our children know where Great Britain is. Every African baby can tell you about France. But how many European children can point to Niger on the map? I went to school in Devon. I was a teacher at Exeter. People asked where I came from; I said Niger. The headmaster said, That's somewhere near Cuba or the Virgin Isles isn't it?' He paused. 'How ignorant can you be? And that's the headmaster. What about you?' he snapped. 'What do you know about my country?'

There I had him. I reeled off the president, how long he had been in power, members of the government, the gross national product, annual uranium production figure, and the telephone number of the Takoubakoye, the best club in Niamey. I threw in everything I could remember about the Hausa down in Zinder, the Djerma-Songlais, the Peul and Fulani, the farmers; the Kanvsi and Beri-Beris, who live along the Niger and, of course, the Tuaregs.

'I am sorry,' he said. 'You are a friend of Africa.' He shook my hand. 'You are my brother.' He went back to his office. I thought he was so pleased he was going to bring back my passport and let me through. Instead he came back with a book; maybe he was going to detain me for not knowing the works of Tchicaya U Tam 'Si.

'You are my brother,' he said, 'and I would like to present you with a book of African poetry in token of our friendship.' He scribbled his name inside the front cover and solemnly presented it to me. I felt guilty, but I accepted gracefully. It was *African Poetry for Schools.*

'African poetry,' he said. 'Better than Shakespeare.'

'Yes,' I agreed, 'of course.'

He put his hand in his pocket and pulled out my passport.

'Yes, much, much better,' I said. 'Much, much, much better. Much, much . . .'

It seemed like a good idea at the time. In Paris I buy champagne; in Rome, spaghetti; and when I go to Blackpool I still treat myself to a stick of rock. Having crossed the Sahara it seemed the natural thing to do. After all, Niger boasts one of the largest camel populations in the world as well as the two largest camel markets in Africa. So I bought a real live camel. With a hump, an outrageous haughty expression, dirty teeth and bad breath. And when it spits, it really spits.

Museli, a dealer in the marketplace at Ayorou just across the border from Mali, put me up to it. He had been in camels all his life. He buys, sells and breeds them. He washes in their urine for warmth then mixes it with charcoal to make ink. He uses their dung as fuel. He drinks their milk. In desperation, he told me, he once drank the fluid from their stomachs because his water supplies had run out. And, of course, he eats them. So do most of the guests in the hotels, I bet. He uses their hide for water bags, belts and sandals and their wool to weave clothes and tents. The ultimate moteur économique.

In return, all the camel wants is leaves, sharp-thorned acacias, some prickly pears, which they consider a delicacy, ground plants and, of course, water, although he can go up to five days without if he has to. Dirty water will do; impurities do not affect them. Neither do sudden changes in temperature. They can lower their body temperature by as much as 6° celsius and survive sharp changes in blood plasma levels that would kill humans. They can also survive the most terrible sandstorms by sitting down and shutting their eyes and nostrils.

In Dubai, the world centre for camel racing, they are fed the best Canadian oats and alfalfa, given cows' milk kept specially for the purpose and looked after by vets and consultants flown in from abroad. The biggest camel owners such as the Crown Prince, have even built swimming pools to keep their camels happy. Which is not surprising, as some spectacular camels change hands for as much as US $10 million.

But Niger is not Dubai. It is where the desert comes to town. It is the Sahara – over 480,000 square miles of it – with less than 0.007 people to the square mile. It's where the Arabs meet black Africa. After the desert, it's the Sahel, where the thorn bushes come alive. It's mosquitoes. It's the Hamathan which bites into you from November to January when it blows in from the desert. It's also drought and famine. It is the land of desertification with Niamey and Lake Chad, bottom left and bottom right, and an average life expectancy of forty-three years.

It is also, of course, the River Niger. All respect to Mungo Park, the young Scottish surgeon who in 1796 discovered that it flowed from west to east, but in no way does it remind me of the Thames at Westminster. 'The numerous canoes upon the river. The crowded population. And the cultivated state of the surrounding country formed altogether a prospect of civilisation and magnificence which I little expected to find in the bosom of Africa,' he wrote. What a shock to him then to discover that the king wasn't the slightest bit interested and didn't want to see him. He sent Park 5,000 shells and virtually told him to clear off. Park could only see the good in him. 'He argued probably as my guide argued,' he wrote, 'who when he was told that I had come from a great distance and through many dangers to behold the river, naturally inquired if there were no rivers in my own country, and whether one river was not like another.'

Before the rainy season, the river is calm and flat. Cattle graze on the edge, their reflections in a mirror. After the rains, it's deeper and wider, the little islands have disappeared, strong currents have suddenly appeared. A million times better than the Thames. But the amazing thing is that there is hardly any vegetation either side of it. Flying over Egypt, I saw a thick, definite green line all the way down the Nile. Alongside the Niger, hardly anything. I have driven all along the banks into Niamey and you see little sign of people using the river, harnessing its tremendous energy, though many were obviously going hungry.

Niger shares not only its name but a fair proportion of its people with Nigeria next door. The majority of Nigerians are in fact Hausa. Don't breathe a word of this in Côte d'Ivoire but this is one reason why Niger and Houphouet-Boigny don't get on as well as other francophone countries. During the Biafran civil war in the late 1960s Houphouet recognised the breakaway province, but Niger's president, M. Diori, aware of the number of Hausa in his country, did not; he argued for a negotiated settlement through the OAU.

Northern Niger, Gaddafi has said several times, is on his hit list after Chad. He has claimed 200 square miles as Libyan territory, most of it rich in uranium. He has rolled out the red carpet for Nigerians, from Niger not Nigeria, to work in Libya. He has also paid for mosques, hospitals and roads to be built in Niger; but so far without making much impact on the government.

And no impact whatsoever on the people of Ayorou which for six days a week is a dusty, sleepy village on the east bank of the Niger. On Sunday, however, it explodes into life. From Mali, from Burkina Faso, from as far away as Nigeria but not from Libya, and from all over Niger on foot, on donkey, on camel as well as by bus, car and even canoe the world pours in for one of the largest, liveliest and most colourful markets in the Sahel.

The village square was packed with camels and cattle, goats and donkeys, chickens, fruits, vegetables and every kind of spice. There were textiles and tinned food, leathergoods and cans of milk. Everything was covered with a thick cloud of dust kicked up by thousands of shuffling feet. And it was at least 120° à l'ombre. Women were selling eggs and bread, rice, groundnuts and melon seeds and neat piles of dried fish. Chickens were tied to boxes and pieces of wood stuck in the sand. Breathe deeply and you breathe in spices and smoke, coffee and sweat, dung and urine.

As we wandered round Museli told me an old Arab saying: 'The camel is God's greatest gift to man. Without the camel, there would be no food, no tents, no clothes, nothing – and no men. Only the camel is great!' Naturally, I agreed, and from then on I was in the running for a camel. If the camel was God's greatest gift, how could I survive without one?

We inspected camels as they came in, languid, bored and terribly superior, sniffing the morning. They were tied head to tail. As they reached the well in the centre they circled it accompanied by their owners dressed in long, ragged, filthy shirts and headcloths, most of them barefooted, every one majestic. As the camels came to a halt they tugged at their ropes to make them sit down, then hobbled them with a loop of rope tied around their knees and a peg the other end hammered into the ground. Most flopped down with relief. One old bull camel refused to budge. He roared, he belched, he gargled, he spat slime. Then suddenly, pleased with the commotion he had created, he too just flopped down and contented himself with flicking sand over everybody with his tail.

We started inspecting the different types. There were brown camels from Mauritania; big and old and very mangy. Some had bones sticking out of their shoulders and rumps. They looked as though they had had a rough, tough life. One gave out an awful smell. Museli reckoned it was so old and exhausted it had begun to rot inside. I preferred the Tuareg ones; they were whiter, woollier and altogether more handsome.

They can average 30 mph fully loaded and cover up to 100 miles a day. Now it was just a matter of time.

Museli warned me that Tuareg camels are built for speed and must be ridden at nothing less than a gallop. In Mali the border police still use them for patrolling the frontier and tracking down smugglers and illegal immigrants. They tried horses, which were stronger but did not have the stamina, then motor vehicles. But nothing measured up to the camel. He asked me if I had ever been to a camel race.

On our way to Ayorou, I told him, we had pulled up at what looked a perfect site for the night. It was getting dark and cold. The desert was soft, halfway between the sands of unruliness and the sands of submission. Thorn bushes were dotted around. We were surrounded by dunes.

The following morning we discovered we were in the middle of an abattoir, much bigger than the one-man effort in Mali. All around us were the town's butchers slaughtering and cutting up camels. They brought in the old and diseased camels as well as those, I'm sure, who were just galled, sorefooted and perhaps a bit refractory before dawn, and were eager to get the meat into town and sold before the sun was too high. I have seen cattle slaughtered in England. I have even killed my own poultry. But this was my first chance to study the techniques of slaughtering camels.

First, they were made to sit, which they did without the slightest problem. No hissing or spitting. Maybe they knew this was the end of the line. The butcher then plunged a knife into the main neck artery, sending a spurt of blood over the sand. A thick spurt and everybody would cheer; a dribble and most seemed to feel guilty. Perhaps it was ungentlemanly to kill something weaker than yourself. Then the butcher turned the knife and made a quick, clean cut. The camels remained upright. Within seconds they were skinned. The humps looked like two thick lumps of fat stuck on the animal's back. The bones were expertly cut away and divided into thin strips for roasting. Within minutes the meat was in one pile, the skin rolled up in another. Everything else had been buried.

One butcher told me they constantly move their slaughter-house. There was a limit to the number of carcasses they could bury in one place. They also liked the change of scenery. He gave me some useful advice. 'If you are outside a town, never camp inside the dunes. That's where we like to slaughter the animals. We're protected from the winds and nobody can see us.' Like all good advice, too late.

They took me to a camel race. I had imagined a grand spectacle, but it was about as exciting as a sack race when you don't know the competitors. The camels paraded and lined up. Somebody gave the off and they all headed straight into the desert. Within seconds they were out of sight. They had ten to fifteen miles to cover, so we waited. Suddenly they were on top of us racing to the finishing line – which, I must admit, was exciting – then it was all over.

Museli and I walked over to the best-looking camel; he had une belle tête, une belle allure et il se déplace bien. Museli pulled its tail hard. The camel took no notice, which apparently means it has a pleasant temperament. If it hadn't we probably wouldn't have lived to tell the tale. Next he looked at its toenails. Some camels have long toenails like claws. This one had stumps, flush with the pad; you would have no problems with stones in the desert. The soles of its feet were smooth, no cuts or bumps, another good sign. Museli swung his big camel stick against its forelegs and gave them a sharp crack. The camel hardly blinked, then meekly sat down. It was also obedient.

He proceeded to punch the hump – which is not where the camel keeps his water supplies. They store water – up to 150 litres – in the walls of their stomachs. The hump is simply a block of fat, but a strong hump means a camel can carry heavy loads – up to 1,600 lbs for up to three days at a time. He then felt its ribs. They were strong. He examined its face. The eyes and nostrils were in order, for coping with sandstorms. There was a ring in its right nostril which showed it was a lead camel. Not only did it have a good temper, it was fast and obedient as well. Next Museli examined its teeth; they were filthy, but they were all there. At the back of its neck was a small bald patch, another tell-tale sign; the bigger the patch, the more the camel has been ridden.

Museli reckoned it was about five years old which, he said,

was a good age for a camel. They are not weaned until they are two and you cannot ride them until they are four. I could keep this one for four or five years and then kill it. Camels are always killed when they are nine or ten, the end of their working life. There are no homes for old camels in the Sahara.

It was time for a test drive. The camel had a light, Mali saddle on, more like the mitred Tuareg saddles than the cumbersome Mauritanian saddles with butterfly wings and back piece. This had no sides, just a slim piece of wood in front with a high back, which is fine for high speeds but is more difficult to mount. With other saddles you clamber on any way you like. In this case, I had to pull the camel's head by its lower lip, throw one leg over then rest my legs on its neck. I was in the driving seat.

Sitting on a camel when it stands up is something I shall never get used to. First, you're flung violently backwards. The camel is now on its knees. Then you're flung sharply forwards. The camel is now on its hind legs. Then just as sharply you're flung backwards once again. The camel is standing up.

Museli gave me a long riding stick and my instructions. Tap the right side of its neck if you want to turn left and the left side to turn right. To make it trot, hit it on the rump or dig your heels into its neck, or both. To stop, pull the headrope. And to make it sit down tap it on the back of the head and hiss at it hard.

We walked calmly around the marketplace with that marvellous, gentle rocking motion. Once on the street, I plucked up courage and hit it sharply on the rump. Immediately it broke into a trot. I was now a professional. I was sold.

Back we came to the market. I pulled the headrope and it stopped at once. We were made for each other. A gentle tap on its head and the camel sat down. How could I refuse?

Some camels are apparently so irritable they bite their owners. A bad-tempered camel can suddenly turn its head, grab the rider with its teeth, pull him to the ground and trample on him. Museli showed me the special liquid he carries in case he is ever bitten by a camel, though he never had been in over fifty years. But a camel bite, he said, was very dangerous. It was not worth the risk. But I knew my camel would never bite me.

He was not a moyen de transport. He was going to be mon bon pot.

Quickly we agreed the price. Museli wanted one cow or fifteen goats. I didn't have any with me, so we compromised. I gave him £150, a good price, as camels are fetching between £1,000 and £2,000 in Niamey. And that included the saddle and some of Museli's special ointment – in case someone else's camel ever bit me.

I now had to get my camel branded. While we were waiting our turn for the camel-brander a fellow Tuareg told me I had paid too much. There was now a plague of camels in the north of Senegal. The government were slaughtering thousands every month. He was on his way to help them. With the camel-brander, I agreed the brand, a mixture of two of his designs. I made the camel sit down and we put a rope around its jaw and pulled its head to its side. The man then quickly burnt the brand on its neck. The camel gave out a piercing roar, spat a great slug of slime at me and struggled to its feet. There was grey smoke coming from its hide and the acrid fumes of burning wool. The camel grunted and stared straight through me. I felt that things would never be the same again.

Museli walked back with me to the hotel. He promised to look after the camel until my next visit. Maybe it will have forgotten the branding by then.

When it comes to African agriculture, the statistics are terrifying:

1. The more Africa invests in cash crops the more food production per capita declines.
2. Per capita food production in Africa is lower than it was ten years ago.
3. Yields per hectare, in spite of enormous scientific and technological advances, have collapsed by over fifty percent in fifty years.
4. Countries that were major food exporters are now importing more than half their food.
5. Africa's entire urban population is fed on imported grain.

And so on. As far as I'm concerned, African farming suffers from thin soils, too much water, long fingernails, and not enough credit.

Most African soils, especially in Niger, are thin and infertile. Too much emphasis on cash crops has created enormous problems of soil erosion, and too many irrigation projects have washed away what good top soil they had, cut underground supplies, increased saturity in the soil and reduced crop yields. Just enough, or drip or trickle supplies, often create mini-catchment areas, hold back erosion and boost yields. And, of course, are much cheaper than enormous dams and irrigation systems.

Mounkeila Gournandakaye, Niger's forestry director, also believes there is too much water in the country. Excessive use of water, he maintains, creates as many problems as too little. Year after year in the north of the country they sank boreholes. During the dry season everybody flocked to the boreholes with their animals. The land became overstocked, erosion set in, desertification began. The boreholes had created the very problems they were meant to remedy. Now against all the odds, and enormous opposition, M. Gournandakaye has started rationing water: stock levels in the north have adjusted to the water available, the grass has started to grow back and the desert has been stopped in its tracks.

But even too much water would be manageable if it wasn't for the long fingernail, especially on the little finger of the right hand. For many young African farmers and especially farm managers let this nail grow as a sign that they are not really farmers but administrators, intellectuals.

I visited a 1,200-hectare farm in the Sahel financed by an aid organisation one boiling July day. I met the director in his air-conditioned office. We had a glass of champagne, in the middle of a drought. I asked how the farm was doing. 'Not very well. We're having problems with the cereals. Yields are down. There is a lot of disease. The animals are also very bad,' he said.

I know a bit about farming. Many's the time I've pulled a calf out, cleared the afterbirth off and stuck it on its mother, or sat up all night when it took a turn for the worse. Similarly with pigs and sheep. Coffee and cocoa and pineapple plantations I know inside out, even plantations growing rubber plants to be sold in Marks & Spencer. I asked if I could have a look. He agreed, pressed a buzzer for his farm manager. I immediately noticed the fingernail. As we walked round, I asked how he ran the farm.

'I have too much to do,' he said. 'If I want to know how the crops are doing, I send a boy down to the fields to have a look. I have to do the same with the cattle. I haven't got time any more. The director always wants reports. I'm stuck behind my desk all day long. I have to rely on others.'

The more I look at aid projects, the more I wonder whether we've got it right. Half of me says we shouldn't give aid at all. The World Bank never pumped a penny into the Wild West. In Europe it took us 500 years to build roads, develop trade links, stimulate the economy, build our infrastructure, create jobs and so on. Aid programmes are trying to force countries to do in twenty or thirty years what we took centuries to achieve. The other half of me says aid money is vital. It is wrong to see our fellow human beings trying to scratch a living in the face of famine and poverty. Natural justice says we should help.

The problem is deciding what kind of aid. Most aid is provided not because it is what the Africans want but because it's what the donor wants to give: we'll give them a grant providing they buy our tractors. They can't handle tractors; they're not mechanics, they don't understand them. Or tractors are not right for the job; instead of improving the land and the crops they will ruin them.

I was in Zaire once, on a run-down farm, walking along a dirt track. Suddenly the director of the plantation, elegant in his Mobutu suit and long fingernails, shouted out, 'Watch out. Here comes –' I looked down the track. A battered old blue tractor was chugging its way towards us.

'So what's the problem?' I asked. 'It's only a tractor.'

'But it is driven by le vieux Dondo. He's only got one eye.'

'What difference does that make?' I asked, slightly puzzled.

'It means he can only turn right. He's frightened to turn left because he can't see. That's why he's here in the middle of nowhere. If he could turn left he would have been back at the farm hours ago.'

'But that's crazy,' I said. 'It must cost a fortune for him to drive all this way. How can you afford it?'

'We can't. The aid organisations pay,' he laughed. 'They see all the kilometres on the clock and think he is using the tractor on farms all over the area. They are even talking of giving him a big new tractor. He is one of their success stories. They want to make a film about him.'

The other problem is the size of the grants. Most governments and aid organisations now say their administration costs are so high they can't afford to give small items of aid any more. Big projects are all they are interested in. 'We've just carried out a major resources study of the whole sub-region. Our computer projections show that it is perfectly viable to increase the out-take by stepping up the in-puts and introducing critical path techniques.'

In other words, let's dump this traditional African farming. Forget the fact that for generations villagers have grown their own food and survived. A few uneven patches of ground a few yards from the village; one small crop here, another there. All very disorganised and labour-intensive, but it worked. Instead let's turn the whole area into a huge European or US-style farm. Let's go for big-scale single-crop farming; that way you get economies of scale. You can introduce your beloved tractors and giant harvesting machines. And, of course, you get increased production. They have studies, produce reports, make films supporting their case. And to underline their confidence and, they say, to prove they are only interested in helping villagers to feed themselves, they slap more aid money on the table.

Governments don't know what to do. 'We were in a very difficult position,' one official in the Sahel told me. 'We wanted more food. We knew it was better to grow our own. Everything looked impressive – the reports, the films. They took us around the world to see how well this system had worked elsewhere. In the end, we said yes. They were the experts.'

The project went ahead. Enormous tractors tore up all the little vegetable patches and established regular 100–150 hectare fields. They brought in the seeds and big machines. Everything was set for the biggest advance in agriculture since Moses found manna in the desert.

It was a disaster. The weather failed and they lost the entire crop. Which was why the villagers always planted two or three different crops. They – and their fathers and grandfathers before them – knew that if they planted three crops and one failed, they would still have two left.

'The trouble was we forgot to ask the villagers,' say the government officials. 'We didn't think they knew anything. We had the latest technology, we thought we could help them. But we couldn't.' Nobody ever asks the Africans, not even Bob Geldof. When he was buying grain for emergency relief he bought it from the US, which was great for the poor American farmer. He did not ask farmers in Malawi or elsewhere in Africa if they could supply probably better rice at a better price. It never occurred to him.

Then there is what's known as the lorry syndrome. 'It means you can't push people too far, too fast. They will break up. Or worse, they will change in a way completely different than you planned,' another government official told me also in the Sahel.

'But why the lorry syndrome?'

'There's a famous story in aid circles about plans to distribute lorries to villagers in the bush. They would be given lorries so they could get their crops to market in time and get a good price for them. They would then have enough money to feed their families and buy seed and fertiliser for next year. But as soon as they got their lorries they realised there was no point working all year round to produce crops to sell in the town when all they had to do was jump on the lorry and go and buy everything they wanted from other farmers. So they stopped growing their own crops and bought them from other people. Which was fine the first year, but come the second year they didn't have enough money to buy what they wanted. In any case prices had increased because there was now a shortage of food. Then the lorry started breaking down. The whole thing was a mess. When they wanted to start growing their own food again they didn't have any money; they couldn't get into town for seed and fertiliser because they didn't have a lorry.' He shook his head. 'The lorries set them back maybe five years.'

At the other end of the scale is the Indian approach. They work directly with individual Africans, on a small scale. Once a small project works they will go on to a medium-sized project, or maybe introduce lots more of the same small projects. One of the best development schemes I have ever seen would bring joy to the heart of Norman Tebbit; it's the Indian 'on-yer-bike' project. They choose a bush village miles from any town. There they select one keen young man and teach him all about bicycles. If he picks it up, they give him three or four bicycles and show him how to rent them to other villagers, how to charge, how to check bicycles on their return, and how to use the money to buy more bicycles.

For me, it's perfect. It's helping people to help themselves – at their own pace and in their own way. It suits the villagers; it's completely under their control. Once they have acquired the basic skills they can do what they want – they can stay the same, or they can grow. And it does not dramatically upset the patterns of the community.

I asked one of the Indians on the bicycle project what was his solution to Africa's agricultural problem. 'In India 30 percent of the land is cultivated. In Africa it is less than 5 percent,' he told me.

'But isn't that because you have better soils, better weather and maybe better management?'

'Not really,' he replied. 'Much of sub-Sahara has red laterite soils. So do we. But our soil is better looked after. It has more nutrients. It retains water better. In Africa it is sandier.'

'So what are the best crops for that type of soil?'

'Sorghum and cassava.'

'So why are they growing wheat, maize, rice . . .?'

'I don't know,' he said bluntly. 'Dry, hot weather can kill off maize before it gets a chance to start growing. Hybrids do better. But there is all the difference in the world between growing wheat and maize and rice on a massive commercial scale and growing it in small patches outside the village.'

'So what's your solution?'

'Do everything small,' he said, 'until you know it's going to work. Then increase the size of the project. But slow.'

That's what I told him some farmers in Burkina Faso decided to do. They were not making any money out of maize, sorghum or rice so they decided to plant cotton. In good years, they make money. In bad years, they starve. Because although they have the money to buy food, farmers in other less fertile parts of the country have not been able to produce the maize, sorghum and rice for them to buy.

'Africa is Africa,' he said. He told me about a big rice project nearby, however, which was doing this, and suggested I look at it.

The scenery as we arrived the following morning was interesting but not exciting, a little like the New Forest on a rainy day, but the farm was fascinating. The rice fields themselves were remarkably uninteresting, but the techniques and troubles and triumphs were riveting. 'If I can't do it, I don't ask our workers to do it,' the Canadian manager kept telling me. He said he was an agronomist although he looked more like a hippie who had lost his way. But he was the farmer, the labourer, the engineer, the tractor driver, the computer operator, the manager and the guide. He also made his own coffee. 'You've got to lead by example. Once the African knows you know what you are talking about, he will respect you. If not, he ignores you.'

We finished our coffee and climbed into his battered Land Cruiser. 'Better than Land Rovers. Cheaper. Doesn't break down so much. No problems with spare parts. You have to go slower on really rough ground, but how often do I go on rough ground? Land Rovers are not worth the money. In any case there is a seven-month waiting list. This I got in a week,' he said.

We drove across flat open country. I had expected to see miles of paddy fields, similar to a big coffee or cocoa plantation; straight paths and driveways, everything at right angles. Instead, there was a patchwork of different shaped fields, some maybe the size of a football pitch, most half that size, one or two about the size of the penalty area. Running between them were irrigation channels. Now and then we saw enormous valves controlling the flow of water.

'I'm surprised. I thought it was going to be much more organised, more regimented,' I said.

'It should be but we didn't have the money. We thought it better to operate at, say, 60 percent efficiency and do it today than operate at 80–90 percent and wait five years to get everything shipshape,' he replied.

There were children everywhere, running up and down waving handkerchiefs or meandering around looking sad and listless. A few had given up and were fast asleep under rough shelters.

'They're our scarecrows,' he said. 'We tried everything. Automatic guns were too expensive, coloured strips of paper were useless. We couldn't even get them in place. I even put special humming wires up, but they didn't work. Nor did scarecrows. So I thought I'd use the children. They're good, and very cheap. Costs me a few cents a day. They're happy, their parents are happy, and I'm happy.'

I wondered whether he had problems finding workers. 'Not now. They're from the local villages. But I had big problems to start with. Nobody wanted to come. I think it was because it was something different. I find that Africans, even the children, are very traditional. If they've done something one way they always want to do it that way. They don't seem interested in experimenting to find a better way.'

'But all farmers are traditional the world over.'

'Yes, but this applies to everybody; government ministers, businessmen. I've met some very rich Africans, running enormous companies, who still run the company like a village shop.'

'So what happens when you bring in all the new machinery?' He raised his eyes to the heavens, smiled weakly and thumped the steering wheel in exhaustion. It was obviously a sore point.

'Do you know the biggest problem I have trying to run this place?' he said. 'It's getting the African to feel for the machine. I can get them to sit on the tractor. I can get them to drive up and down all day. I can even get them to park it in the shed at night and switch the engine off. But they don't seem to have a feel for what they are doing. Look,' he pointed to an old reconditioned Indian tractor that looked remarkably like an old Massey Ferguson. 'I can sit on that tractor for five minutes and tell you whether the engine is ticking over correctly, whether the overdrive is properly set, if the steering needs adjusting. I might even be able to tell if the tyres need pumping up. An African doesn't know a thing. To him, it's a machine. He switches on the engine. It works. He doesn't care if it doesn't work *properly.*'

'Yes, but he doesn't have the experience. It's not in his culture. We had an industrial revolution, we grew up with machines. The Africans didn't. You can hardly blame them for that.'

'I know. But it's very difficult living with the problem.'

We stopped by a pumping station, obviously the nerve centre of the operation. An African was working on a tractor engine. 'He knows tractors,' I said.

'He's my only success to date,' said the Canadian pushing his baseball cap back and wiping his face with an oily rag. 'When I first came here he had just left school. Didn't know a thing, didn't even seem interested in learning. I tried him as a porter. Useless. I tried him as a chauffeur. Couldn't drive in a straight line. He wasn't interested in anything, but I kept on, I don't know why. He hardly said a word. He certainly wasn't a pleasant or a friendly lad. Then one day a tractor driver didn't turn up. A funeral or something. The boy asked whether he could take the tractor out. I didn't even know he could manage a tractor. It takes some getting used to. I said yes, and, do you know, he was born to it. He made it sing. Apparently he'd been taking lessons from the drivers, helping them whenever he could.'

He was obviously his pride and joy. 'We taught him maintenance. I even got on to the French and they sent him to a tractor school in France. This boy knows everything. All he's got to do is sit on a tractor and he can tell you if there's a nut loose. And that's before he turns the engine on.'

'That must give you enormous satisfaction?'

'That's what it's all about. Growing rice is important, but it's much more important to make sure the people can run this place on their own. After all I'm not going to stay forever.'

'Do you get many like him?'

'He's the best. He'll work through his lunch – work all night if he has to. The others are beginning to learn, but it's a struggle. They don't have our concept of work – or our concept of time or getting a job done.'

'You mean African time?'

'It's not that they turn up late, quite often that they don't turn up at all. We lost about 25 percent of our crop last year. The weather was bad and we had to pick on a Saturday. I told everybody, we must work over the weekend otherwise we'll lose the harvest. They didn't come in. I was devastated. All this time we'd been working for nothing.'

'But why didn't they come in?'

'They said they don't work on Saturday; the harvest could wait until Monday.'

'But farming's not like that.'

'I know that, you know that, but they don't know that. They've never seen farms like this. They think it's like their village farms – they harvested when they wanted to. They didn't see why I was making so much fuss.'

Nor is harvesting the biggest problem. When African farms manage to harvest their biggest problem is getting their crops to market, or even to store. Some experts claim that if they could stop the crops from rotting while awaiting collection that alone would solve the problem of famine. If the roads are good, the trucks break down. If the roads are bad the trucks can't get through. If they get through the crops are not ready, or the sacks have not arrived or the boxes are broken. If they don't get through the crops rot by the roadside.

We drove to the bagging plant, in one corner of a dilapidated barn. One end was fenced off. It was their stores, with everything neatly laid out and counted; a model of organisation. They seemed to have everything.

'I know what you're thinking,' he said. 'We have to keep at least two years' supplies of spares.'

'Two years. That's expensive.'

'It's more expensive not to. Here, everything takes time, plus there are problems getting authorisation; problems with shipping and transport. And,' he drew a deep breath, 'it must be said trouble getting the stuff from Europe or wherever. We can't afford the delays.'

The fencing looked pretty strong. 'Do you have problems with security?' I asked.

'Not stealing, probably because nobody wants this kind of thing. But we have problems with poaching.'

'How do you mean? Stealing the crops?'

'That's a big problem for us now. At first they didn't know if we were worth stealing from. Now they do.'

'How much do you lose?'

'At one time, it was as much as 25 percent of the crop. They even took the seeds.'

'To plant or to eat?'

'To eat. If they had been taking them to plant, I'd have given them as much as they wanted. We mounted guards all round the plantation, but they were helping people to take even more crops and, of course, helping themselves. It was crazy. Then it hit me. They were taking the crops because they need the food. So why not save all the time and money and give them the food? I also thought, if I tell them how to grow crops themselves they won't want mine.'

'You've got to think like an African.'

'Sure. So I invited all the local farmers here, showed them everything we were doing, then showed them how they could do the same on a smaller scale.'

'Did it work?'

'It's working. These people are slow, they're conservative. The average size of a farm is only around 6,000 square metres, most run by maybe the father and two sons.'

'And the crops?'

'From October to February, wheat and barley; April to June, corn, tomatoes, onions, herbs; July to September, corn again.'

'All for their own consumption?'

'Depends on the crop. The surplus usually goes on camel to the towns. Some goes across the border, especially to Nigeria.'

'Are they good farmers? Can you help them?'

'Over the last few months, some have said they would like to try. Or they send their children to ask me; that way, if they fail they say the children got it all wrong.'

'Do you visit them to see how they are doing?'

'I try to, but there's not much time. We could do with two or three people here doing just that, but it's not possible.'

'And how about the cost? Do you charge them?'

'I try not to, but sometimes I must. The government are planning a special credit union for farmers. That should help them.'

The man they should talk to, I thought, is Dogbeda Aggrey who has set up no less than 16 credit unions for farmers in Togo with over 700 members. When I met him he had left Lomé and moved into Badou, the centre of the Litime region, famous for its enormous cocoa plantations, the spell-binding Akposso marriage dances and the health-giving waters of the Akrowa waterfall. In five years he had become a credit to the region: over £3,000 of credit. In a country where the average wage is £27 a month that is big money. His members pay anything between 20p and £20 to join, and whatever they can afford each month. In return they can borrow between two and three times what they have deposited to pay for anything from seeds, fertilisers and equipment to part-time labour or their children's schooling.

As a result credit unions have become big business in Togo, the first French-speaking country in West and Central Africa to have them, and they are helping to stimulate the economy to a dramatic extent. In 1980 only 2.4 percent of the total credit available in the country was lent for agricultural purposes – an average of £3 per individual employed in agriculture. During the last three years credit unions have increased this figure to £40. For over 30 percent of all loans by credit unions are for agricultural purposes and of those between 25 and 55 percent are for hiring extra labour during the coffee and cocoa harvest. The same thing could happen in Niger.

Mr Komlan Bellow, who runs CONAUDEC, the national Togolese credit union organisation, told me, 'We are helping people to help themselves; small farmers, low-income earners and young people. We are helping to increase the amount of crops the farmers produce, and this helps the economy.' In the last two years membership of credit unions has increased 30 percent, savings 47 percent and loans by 57 percent. In the next five years, Mr Bellow estimates membership will grow from 6,800 to 14,500, savings from £380,000 to £1.4 million and loans from £180,000 to £860,000.

CONAUDEC estimate that at least 25 percent of local society members are women and in 22 percent of societies women are vice presidents. Thirty percent of loans to women are for productive investment in small and medium-size trading activities, which illustrates the increasing role of women in private sector activity.

The sooner Niger's farmers get their own credit union the better.

The Canadian's home was like a retirement bungalow in Eastbourne – very neat and English. His wife was American, but not at all relaxed or casual like most Americans I've met. At first I thought this was because she didn't fancy living in Africa. But not at all, she was thoroughly enjoying herself. She'd organised the local women and formed community groups; she was teaching child care and health care – even how to slit open a vein with a razor blade to take a blood sample. She'd organised a school and was teaching the children. She was doing great things for the district.

We had a traditional African meal – real American hamburgers from the deep freeze. 'We have the biggest deep freeze in the country,' she told me. 'I love Africa but I can't stand the food. I must have good old American food or I leave. That was the deal. So Joe built me the biggest deep freeze you've ever seen. Come on, I'll show you.'

The deep freeze was built of whitewashed concrete blocks. I opened the door to reveal hamburgers by the thousand and french fries by the million. On one shelf were dozens of giant tins. 'Milk shakes,' she said. On another were packs of meat. 'All-American steak.' On top of them was a big plastic sack. 'What are they – potatoes?' I asked.

'Oh no,' she said. 'That's one of the village children. She died a couple of days ago. We want to do a post mortem so we are keeping her here until we next go into town. We also act as the local mortuary.'

She was right; I'd never seen a deep freeze like it. And I'd never met a couple so ready and happy to battle against the odds.

The plane was late. I was on my way back from Agadez, Henri Barth's happy town on the way to everywhere, which I always think is a barometer town. If Agadez is happy, Niger is happy. If Agadez is crying so is the rest of the country. Agadez was smiling quietly.

Founded in the fifteenth century by the Tuaregs it stands on the junction of four main trading routes: to the north, Tamanrasset, Tuat and Tripoli; to the east, Bilma, Tibesti and Kufra; to the south, Zinder and Kano and to the west, Gao and Timbuktu. In the sixteenth century it was the centre of the gold trade, with a population of no less than 30,000. It was one of the richest cities in Africa. When the Moroccans marched in that was the end of the gold business. Agadez then turned to salt. They had extensive pastures so they could feed enormous numbers of camels for the convoys which could be made up of as many as 20,000 stretching for 50 kilometres. From the mines at Bilma, 610 kilometres to the east in the middle of the harsh Tenere desert, they would collect salt and take it to Kano to exchange for goods from the Hausa.

In the middle of the nineteenth century, when Barth arrived, business was bad. There were fewer caravans, and many of them were travelling via Iferouane 300 kilometres to the north. The population was down to 3,000. 'The streets and the market-place were still empty when we went through them, which left upon me the impression of a deserted place of bygone times; for even in the most important and central quarters of the town most of the dwelling houses were in ruins. Some meat was lying ready for sale, and a bullock was tied to the stake, while a number of large vultures ... were sitting on the pinnacles of the crumbling walls, ready to pounce upon any kind of offal ... Agadez is in no respect a place of resort for wealthy merchants, not even Arabs, while with regard to Europe its importance consists in its lying on the most direct road to Sokoto and that part of Sudan. But the town revealed many striking examples of good humour and happiness.'

Today Agadez was not perhaps as busy as other times, but it was busy. Climb the minaret of the Great Mosque which was built in 1515 but looks like a grand hotel and you'll see the place humming with activity. In the central market the silversmiths are pumping out their special Agadez crosses, the Tuaregs have no trouble selling their leatherwork, the Bouza are buying and selling everything. Everywhere in the sandy streets and dusty shops and houses there are Hausas and Fulani and occasionally even Kanouri all the way from Lake Chad.

Trucks laden with waterskins or jerrycans plough through the sand. Container lorries commuting between Algeria and Nigeria litter the streets. Lorries and Land Rovers shuttle between the old colonial préfet and the sultanate.

Agadez is the uranium capital of Niger, although the mines are at Arlit. In 1980 uranium accounted for 75 percent of their exports and was scheduled to rise to 90 percent by 1990, until everybody started having second thoughts about nuclear energy. Listen to the reasoned liberal arguments in Europe, then see the reaction in Agadez and you appreciate the problem. Today their two national companies, Somair and Cominak, are working at 50 percent capacity. Export earnings have fallen to 12 percent of export revenue. President Saibou has been appealing for help from the EC, their largest customer. They have had to cut back all investment plans including critical self-sufficiency programmes. But they are surviving.

Ali Saibou, compared to his predecessor, Seyni Kountche, is a jolly man who seems to enjoy the glad-handing and back-slapping of francophone politics. At conferences and summit meetings he is very much one of the boys. If anybody can persuade the EC to come across he can. Kountche, who died in 1988, was stiff and austere, a stickler for the books and discipline. Very much the rough, tough, bluff military man. He had ruled the country with a steady hand since coming to power in April 1974 in classic Frederick Forsyth style.

Niger had been given its independence in 1960. But there had been problems from the start with Sawaba, a strong leftwing organisation led by Djibo Bakary and supported by the Hausa majority. More pro-Nigerian than pro-French, they had failed to win power in the first independent elections because, they claimed, the vote had been rigged against them. There were severe economic and social problems caused by drought.

A defence agreement had just been signed with Libya. Members of the armed forces were unhappy about it. Pompidou had just died and France was without a president. The commander of the French troops in Niamey was away on a hunting trip. And Jacques Foccart, the sinister minister responsible for Africa who had no love for the previous president because he was pro-Niger instead of pro-France was still in office. Some say there were lots of nods and winks. Some say poor President Diori couldn't control the situation. Some say France was scared in case the uranium fell into other hands. The answer is obviously buried somewhere in Foccart's secret files, which took seven lorries to shift when he left the Elyśee in 1974.

Either way Kountche – some say he was a member of the French secret service in Africa, a strict Muslim who lived in a tiny house with just one wife and four children, ran the country in spite of three fairly serious coup attempts for nearly fifteen years on strict, hard-working, pro-French terms. Saibou, a cousin of the old president and like him a Djerma, is following suit, although with perhaps a lighter touch. Former opponents, including ex-president Diori and Djibo Bakary, have been released from house arrest. There is talk of a Niger form of democracy. Good relations have been established with Nigeria, and the Hausas have been virtually told they can get on with business and smuggling and wheeler-dealing if they leave politics to the minority Djerma. But the big problem remains: food.

Niger suffered enormously during the drought of 1968–74 and again between 1981–85. In 1974 it was producing less than half of what it was doing six years before. Almost half its cattle had died. People were starving to death. While drought was the cause many people claimed the government's policies made matters worse because instead of producing lots of different crops on a small-scale they tried to concentrate on growing a single crop on a large scale – the administrator's dream. But it was not practical politics – or farming. Politically, it meant putting all your eggs in one basket. Agriculturally, it meant forcing farmers to grow crops they were not familiar with and driving cattle farmers off their traditional grazing areas and concentrating them on smaller areas which meant less feed, poorer cattle, over-grazing and the quick downhill slope to desertification. When the drought hit, food stocks were low; alternatives were non-existent and cattle were few.

Between 1981 and 1985 they were almost hammered into the ground. Their livestock were practically wiped out. Crops almost disappeared. In spite, or maybe because of all the help that has poured in they still face enormous problems. In 1984, for example, during the drought farmers were selling millet for CFA 18,000 per sack. Today they get CFA 4,000. 'Under such circumstances how can farmers be expected to invest in crop intensification?' a former minister of agriculture once asked me.

I went to the camel market to find out what the farmers thought. You can always tell when you're coming to a market or an oasis. From miles away you see a billowing cloud of dust kicked up by the camels and cattle. About a mile away you hear a slight hum; the closer you get, the louder the noise. Then suddenly you're in the middle of Piccadilly Circus on New Year's Eve; animals stomping and bellowing and barging. An old man was kneeling in the middle of the confusion, bowing, obviously praying for a good price. Around the edge were houses made of grass, thrown together like amateur haystacks. They seemed to stand; in any case they would only be lived in for a few weeks before everybody moved on.

Niger, with its poor, impossible land, inescapable heat and desperate conditions, may be the last place you would expect to find cattle, but the Nigerians are famous herdsmen. I've met them in Burkina Faso, in the north of Togo, even along the grass verges outside Abidjan's international airport desperately trying to put a few more kilos on their cattle before taking them to the slaughterhouses.

But farming is not the reason for Agadez's success. It is uranium – and the drought. The drought forced thousands of nomads to seek food and shelter in the towns, and many have stayed. The drought also attracted aid organisations and advisers and suppliers.

In the Hotel de l'Air in the centre of Agadez, which looks like a mosque converted into a cathedral – it is the only hotel I know which will let you sleep on the roof, officially – I met one group planning to reclaim nearly 30,000 hectares of desert by planting millions of trees at a cost of US $35 million. 'Keita will be green again,' the project director Mainassara Issifou told me.

If it is it will be thanks to the women. Hundreds of women from all over the region are clearing the land and digging trenches to collect rainwater because there are no men to do the work. After the big drought in 1984 over 30,000 left. They could only look after their families by getting a job in Abidjan or Paris and sending the money home. With babies strapped to their backs, the women have so far saved eleven villages from extinction and their crops from dying.

The trenches catch up to 80 percent of the rainwater which would otherwise be wasted. 'And when you only get 300 or 400 millimetres a year you can't afford to waste a drop,' added Mr Issifou.

Once the desert has been cleared by the women, tractors prepare the ground for planting. Most is for trees, but outside every village land is set aside for the villagers. There the women grow their millet, rice or sorghum. Some I saw were growing potatoes, carrots and onions as well. 'Once they can see that all their hard work means food – especially fresh, green vegetables – they don't mind working. They can see it is helping them and their children,' said the proud project leader.

And you could see what he meant. Each family had been given three hectares and they were all neat and tidy; sharp little irrigation channels, the soil moist and fertile, plants in straight rows. 'If people don't look after their plot, we take it away from them,' he added. 'But do you know we haven't had to do that once? What we want now are livestock; then veterinary care. Then the men will start returning home. Then I suppose,' he said with a sigh, 'we'll have to find money for midwives and clinics and looking after children . . .'

It's a far cry from the plans drawn up immediately after the drought to create huge industrial plantations utilising all the latest equipment and covering thousands of hectares. Trees provide up to 90 percent of a country's energy requirements but less than 1 percent of national budgets are devoted to forestry, ran the argument. Therefore, we must think big. But yields per hectare in the big plantations were not that much different from yields in smaller plantations. Productivity differences were also marginal. It was not worth the effort. Today, like Mr Issifou's scheme, the emphasis is on self-help village projects, planting woods and copses around the edges of fields.

I went with Mr Issifou to see the local préfet. When we went into his office he was reading *Le Sahel.* Upside down. 'Can't he read?' I asked the director afterwards. He shook his head. 'So how does he get on as préfet?'

'Oh easy,' he replied. 'He starts every meeting by looking through the documents very quickly, then asks me to summarise the main points before we decide what to do.'

'And nobody notices?'

'Of course everybody notices, but we don't say anything. That way we can do what we want to do. It's much more efficient.'

'And the préfet?'

'He doesn't mind. He's a big success. We're the only town doing things. He'll be a minister one day.'

Why couldn't the president put him in charge of agriculture, I thought as I settled down for another long wait at the airport on my way back to Niamey. Around three o'clock in the morning the plane arrived and everyone rushed on board. I drank a good deal of cognac and tried to sleep, but woke suddenly as the plane rocked sharply and dropped a few thousand feet.

'We are in an area of turbulence. Please return to your seats, tighten your seatbelts and extinguish all cigarettes,' said the pilot.

'Will you drink this? I can't finish it,' said a snotty little kid next to me – snotty kids always sit next to me on planes – thrusting a greasy glass of spit and orange at me.

'He's a good guy,' I said ignoring him – if I argue with them I always lose – and turning to the passenger on the other side. 'Obviously worries about his passengers.'

'Oh, you can't blame him. He's doing his best,' he said casually. Obviously another million-miles a year man. 'These new DC10s are so light to fly. The slightest thing triggers them off. In the old days you had to practically fight with the controls, and it takes a long time to get out of the habit. That's why so many planes take off at 90 degrees. The pilots haven't got the hang of it yet.'

'But don't they train them on the new planes?'

'Can't afford it.'

I gulped. 'I suppose they must be better to fly?'

'Sure, they're safer to actually fly.' He paused. 'But up here over the Sahara it's more dangerous. There are planes flying east-west-east and north-south-north, not to mention all the unknown military fighters and the Libyans playing games whenever they feel like it.'

'So what do they do?' I asked him.

'The pilot switches on automatic and sits back,' he said. 'There haven't been any problems. But there have been plenty of near misses.'

'Don't air traffic control tell the pilots everything?'

He looked me straight in the eye. 'There is no air traffic control.'

'What do you mean? There is air traffic control everywhere. There must be.'

'Not in West Africa there isn't. They can get him up and down all right, it's the bit in the middle that's the problem. In between Abidjan and Accra, there's nothing. In between Bamako and Niamey and Lomé there's nothing. First, they can't afford it. Second, one half is French, the other half English. They can't link the two.'

'But that's crazy.'

'Of course, but there haven't been any real problems so far. Why worry?'

I had travelled all over Africa in every sort of plane. Not once had it occurred to me that we were flying blind. A thought occurred to me: 'Wait a minute, how do you know there's no air traffic control?'

'I'm taking over this thing in Niamey,' he said. 'I'm the next pilot.' I had another cognac.

We were going to explore the emptiest of all the empty quarters of Niger. I had seen dinosaur fossils at Gadoujaoma, which had amazed me. It had never occurred to me there had been dinosaurs in the Sahara, and to look at the desert now you would never imagine there had once been enough vegetation to support a donkey let alone dinosaurs. The fossils stretched for over 60 miles, continually being covered and then uncovered by the sand. One of the drivers, a tiny Frenchman who had lived in Africa all his life, told us there were dinosaurs all over Niger.

'Many, many types can be found here,' he said waving his arm across a thousand miles of sand. 'There are even fossil crocodiles, some even ten metres long. C'est l'oeuvre de Dieu.'

We left the fossils to another million years of solitude and made for Bilma, the old salt capital of Niger. For generations caravans of up to 1,000 camels made the 1,000 kilometre journey in the blistering heat between Bilma and Agadez. Today they are no more. There is no grazing, only the occasional acacia tree, a pathetic reminder of what were the would you believe? forests of the Sahara, and fewer and fewer waterholes. But even if there were unlimited grazing and water, the caravans would still not run for today it is cheaper to produce sea-salt, and the consumption of salt is declining.

Trading – especially salt and slave trading – made some of these tiny kingdoms along the banks of the Niger incredibly rich. In 1826 for example, the King of Warri gave his daughter in marriage to the ruler of Bonny. To show his appreciation he 'loaded canoe after canoe with rare and most valuable treasures: English, French, Spanish and Portuguese merchandise extracted from his warehouses – gold and silver plate, costly silks and fine clothes, embroidered laces and other articles too numerous to mention.' And then on the wedding day itself he actually told a visiting European: 'I give wine, brandy, plenty puncheon – pass twenty. I give for my people and Warri's. All Bonny glad too much. Every man, every woman, for my town, I give cloth – pass one thousand piece I give that day. Pass twenty barrel powder I fire that day.'

After Bilma we came to Fachi, a tiny beautifully green village surrounded by salt pans. There we stepped into the past and saw blocks of salt being made. The salt was dug out of the earth and dissolved in pans scattered between the palm trees. Slowly the water evaporates leaving the crystals behind. This is repeated until the salt is pure, then it is poured into moulds carved from the trunks of palm trees.

Just outside the village was an eerie hill of skulls. Years ago – nobody could tell me when – all the men had been massacred. According to Muslim law the women could not give them a proper burial, so they heaped up the bodies at the end of their gardens and left them to rot.

One evening during our long trek along the Djabo plateau I got talking to a Frenchman who turned out to be an expert on African architecture. He had come to Niger to see the Yaama mosque in Tahona which had just won the Aga Khan's Award for Architecture. Until then I had never thought much about African architecture except that whatever building I had been in, whether a reed hut in Côte d'Ivoire, or the smallest tata in Benin, everything seemed to have a purpose. Families seem to live in their homes as a family, not like in Europe or the US where everybody wants their own virtually self-contained unit.

The French architect said that even today Africans, rich or poor, will insist on designing their own homes whether they are good at it or not simply because they know what they want. Once they have decided on the basic size and shape they will call in the village workmen or, in the case of the rich, the surveyors, designers, carpenters, and master craftsmen to sort out the detail.

Many Africans also build their homes and even entire villages not only in honour of their gods but in the shape of their gods. One building represents the head, another the feet, a whole group of houses the body, and so on. Similarly their temples and mosques. In North Africa and throughout the Middle East mosques follow a general pattern. In black Africa each one is different, reflecting local attitudes as well as local crafts and skills.

Later as we edged our way gently into Azaouak, west of Agadez, I saw the infamous Iridel, a dreaded three-legged striped hyena which the Tuaregs told us later had been terrorising sheep and goats in the region. 'Stop, stop,' the French all whispered.

'No! You're not going to eat him as well,' I protested. 'On-y-va.' But it was too late. The prospect of food comes before everything for the French. The Land Rovers pulled up on what looked like a snake-infested hill, which was just as well. Nobody had a recipe for snake au vin so we all climbed back on board and carried on talking about architecture.

'So what about modern African architecture?'

'What architecture?' he said. 'It's all international. Look at the buildings. You could be anywhere.'

This took me aback because I am continually impressed by the originality and, in many cases, the African flavour of the architecture. Pierre Gondjuby, a Senegalese architect, designs buildings full of symbolism and meaning. His design for the headquarters of the ECOWAS Fund in Lomé was brilliant. The Fund links all anglophone and francophone countries in West Africa in one community. What was his design? Two towers symbolising the anglophone and the francophone linked by a bridge. And the conference hall? A circular building with a circular table. Fantastic. Komlavi Apety and Adoh Grunitzky are recognised for their designs for the BIAO Bank, also in Lomé. Then there is Ble Gnangia in Côte d'Ivoire; Copo Chichi and Kelli Gbenon in Benin and Lacoh Donou, who designed the ministry of foreign affairs building in Niamey.

There is plenty of competition from outside as well, usually from Mr Comianos Agapitos, probably the most famous foreign architect practising in francophone Africa. Greek-born, brought up in Egypt, now working from Paris, he has been responsible for many of the sweeping new buildings that have appeared in the region in recent years.

'Africans love beautiful things. If they see beautiful buildings they are happy,' he told me once. 'That is why I try to create a beautiful environment rather than an hotel or an office. Africa is unique for the architect. We are starting at the beginning, creating the future. But we must not make mistakes.'

Mr Apey, a Togolese architect, agrees. 'In Europe there is a conflict between ideas and regulations. In Africa there are fewer regulations so we have more freedom. That enables us to use the environment, to develop our ideas,' he told me.

Mr Paul Ahyi, a professor at l'Ecole Africaine et Mauricienne d'Architecture et d'Urbanisme, and one of Africa's leading sculptors, goes a stage further. He believes that African architects have such a good reputation for innovation because they don't just think of the outside of the building but the inside as well. 'It is no longer enough to design a building and leave it at that. One has to think of the furniture, the doors, the wall coverings, even the uniforms of the staff. It's the total environment that counts.'

And nothing helps create and maintain that environment

better than using local materials. 'Africa is full of interesting materials: marble, stone, clay, bricks. Whenever I can I use local materials. It's more economic than bringing in materials, and it helps create the feeling that the building is a natural extension of its surroundings,' said Mr Agapitos.

But if architects in Africa have the freedom they want, they also have intense competition. 'More and more big projects are being decided by special competitions, and it's getting tougher all the time,' says Mr Apey. The competition to design the new ECOWAS Fund headquarters, for example, attracted more than sixty entries from all over West Africa.

'Competitions are very hard,' said Mr Agapitos, who told me he spends around $35,000 preparing for each one. 'You have to devote a lot of time and expertise submitting your proposals. And it is all an investment. You don't know the judges' criteria. But I can't complain, I have won many international competitions in Africa.'

The French architect waved all my examples aside.

'Out of all the buildings since independence, it's not much is it?'

I changed tack. 'How many buildings are put up using local materials?'

'Inside or outside?'

'Outside.'

'Not many. For big prestige buildings, governments want only the best; marble, special claddings, anything but local materials. They feel that if it's local it must be cheap and inferior. They want the best in the world. For smaller projects the problem is always cost. The materials are available but it usually costs too much to use them.'

'But why?'

'Because they have to be made by hand, which takes a long time. It's all right if you are building your own little house, but for a hotel or a ministry ...' he waved his hands, 'pas possible. The cost of making everything, the cost of transport – it's horrible. It's much cheaper to bring everything in.'

'But that's ruining the environment, preventing local industries from developing, killing off local craftsmen –'

'Je sais, vous avez raison. Tell the World Bank, don't tell me.'

'So what do the African architects say?'

He laughed. 'The last thing they want to use is local material. They are only interested in big prestige projects, and prestige means imported materials.'

'Well what about the inside of the buildings?'

He waved his arms about again. 'Pictures, tapestries, wood carvings and more wood carvings. That's all. Who wants to go into a hotel and collapse on a wooden bed made by a local carpenter? Nobody. Not even the Africans – especially the Africans,' he said with feeling. 'They want the best. And the best doesn't come from Africa, unfortunately.'

'So what's going to happen?'

'Everything is going to become like one vast impersonal Novotel. Everything will be international.' He shrugged. 'It won't be African, it'll be a desert.'

When we popped in for tea with local Tuaregs they told us more about the three-legged Iridel. He had killed hundreds of their animals. They kept setting traps for him but he kept escaping, although once one of his paws was caught. He'd eaten through his own leg and left the paw in the trap. I'd heard similar stories in Ireland, but this time I'd actually seen the three-pawed hyena. Later that night I was sleeping under the Land Rover when I saw my one and only desert cat, about the size of an ordinary cat but heavier built, yellow eyes and a long tail. It sniffed around the food left over from supper then strolled off into the desert.

We had been driving across the plateau now for three or four days. We had turned around close to the border and were making our way along the foot of the Adrar mountains back to Agadez when we came across more fossils of animals and of prehistoric stone tools and weapons – thousands of them. I am no expert but it was a marvellous experience picking through them. Probably the first person to do so in a million years. I picked up one fossil which seemed different from the others and looked at it more closely; it looked just like a fish. But a fish in the middle of the Sahara Desert? 'Take it to the National Museum in Niamey,' the French fossil expert told me. 'They'll tell you what it is.' I packed it away carefully.

For three days we explored the Kaouar mountains, the

empty quarter close to the Libyan border. 'The Libyans are crazy. They send planes up all the time to patrol their border, though there is nothing here,' the drivers told us.

Sure enough, at least twice a day planes would fly overhead which everybody said were Libyan. 'Why do they do this? We don't fly over their house. Why do they fly over our house?'

'Don't you like Gaddafi?'

'He is a bad man. Our president says he wants to take our land away from us.'

Discussing politics in Africa is fascinating. They are rarely cynical about politics or politicians, whom they don't see as the power-hungry, double-dealing schemers that we tend to. They respect their leaders, call them Father or Leader or Guide. On the other hand they enjoy gossip about Reagan and Mitterrand or Mrs Thatcher.

When it comes to global issues, Africans simplify them, almost always in family terms.

'There is a big debate in Europe about whether we should accept Gorbachev's zero-zero option,' I begin.

'If someone is outside your home and he says, If you destroy my home and my family I will destroy yours, you must sit down and discuss the matter,' they reply. 'You then say, all right I won't destroy your house so you mustn't destroy mine. And once you've said that you might as well say, If we're not going to destroy each other's houses we might as well be friends and throw away our weapons. That is what Mr Gorbachev is saying. It is very sensible.'

I once asked an African diplomat why we never heard Africans criticising their leaders. 'In Africa we are all one family,' he said. 'And like families we criticise each other, but inside the family; not even among friends. When we have had our arguments and discussions, we agree. Then we speak as a family. That's the way to do it.'

Or take regional development. Why do the Africans, who spent so much time fighting for independence, now spend so much time trying to form federations and regional groups? Surely independence is independence? 'Of course it is,' a foreign minister told me, 'but we mustn't forget our neighbours. You can't live in a village and see your nextdoor neighbour starving. You must help him. He is your brother. It is the same for African countries; we are independent, but we must help one another. Helping your neighbour also means you can help yourself. If your neighbour's house catches fire you can't ignore it.'

This type of family reasoning is part of the African heritage; but they are also French and there is a strong element of French thinking in everything they do and say. They are quite at home, for example, discussing logic and philosophy. To us, it's something effete and to be avoided, at least in public. We believe in the practical realities of life. Not so the francophone. On one occasion, an African minister was planning a visit to London. I had arranged meetings at the foreign office, discussions with ministers and press interviews. I asked if there was anybody else he would like to see.

'I would like to meet some British intellectuals to discuss their philosophy of world development,' he said. No British minister would make such a request, but Africans like to intellectualise everything. Many is the time I've been told, 'We are Cartesian. We are logical. We are not emotional.'

One minister in Niamey told me, 'We are Cartesian. Unless we can see the solution, we are not interested.'

'As a Cartesian then you start with the solution?'

'Yes, of course.'

'But surely you have to start with the problem?'

'That is the mistake the Anglo Saxons always make. You must start with the solution.'

'And work back to the problem and therefore understand it?'

'Exactly. That is Cartesian.'

'But how do you know you are working back to the problem correctly and not making a mistake?'

'Because you can't. If you are being logical you will always work back to the problem. Don't you see there is a direct line between problem and solution?'

'But surely a problem can have lots of solutions.'

'Agreed.' I thought I was at last making a dent in his Cartesian logic, but he added quickly, 'But only one correct solution. Logic will give you the correct solution.' I had lost. He had put Descartes before the horse – and won.

We were now visiting caves deep in the mountains and saw marvellous prehistoric paintings – sharp, bright, vivid; obviously Cartesian in concept and design. It made you think. So many years ago and in such conditions.

Later I took my fossil fish to the National Museum. When I first went in, I was very proud of it. But as I wandered around and saw their fossil crocodile ten metres long I began to feel less enthusiastic. I left.

SENEGAL

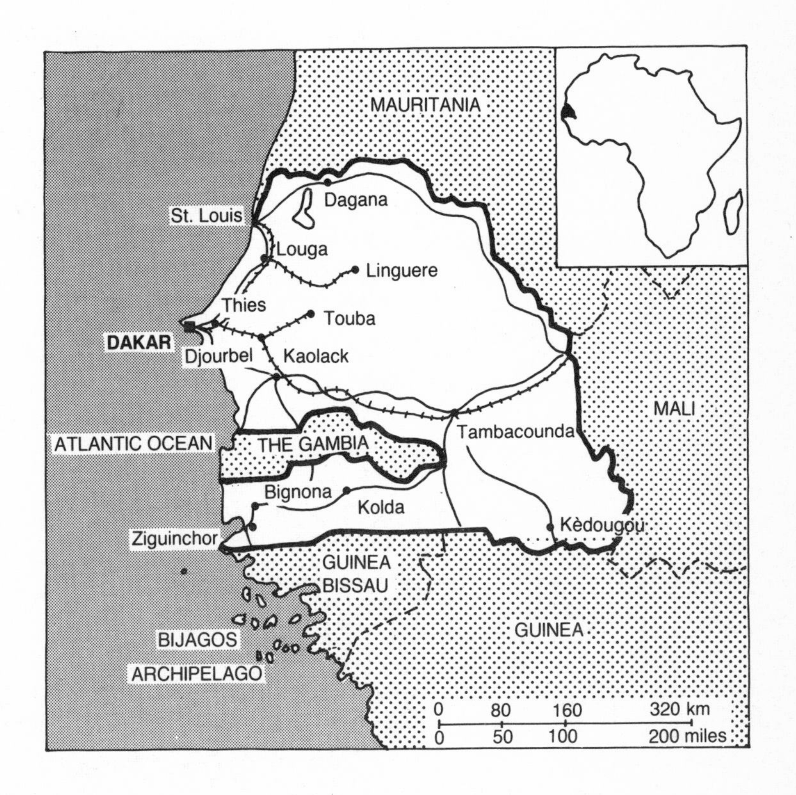
MAURITANIA
Dagana
St. Louis
Louga
Linguere
Thies
Touba
DAKAR
Djourbel
Kaolack
MALI
Tambacounda
ATLANTIC OCEAN
THE GAMBIA
Bignona
Kolda
Ziguinchor
Kèdougou
GUINEA
BISSAU
GUINEA
BIJAGOS
ARCHIPELAGO
0
80
160
320 km
0
50
100
200 miles

Outside the hotels; on every street corner; lurking behind the pillars in the Place de l'Indépendance; even inside the cathedral; Senegalese street traders, les banas-banas, are the best – or the worst – in the world.

Relax with a copy of *Le Soleil* waiting to see a government official and they burst through the door with three dozen pantalons under one arm and a box of réproductions plastifées de la vie du Christ under the other. Open the drinks cabinet in your hotel room and three traders selling Seiko watches, cassettes of a Band Aid concert or a cheap pair of Indian sandals will jump out on top of you.

The Senegalese street trader is a deadly disease for which there is no known cure. Ignore him and he'll follow you into the Pharmacie Guigon. Tell him you haven't any money and he'll still escort you round the Body Shop, because they know it's not true. Break down in tears at his feet in front of the high altar in the cathedral during mass and he will still follow you to heaven and back trying to persuade you to buy a portrait of les lieux saints de l'Islam.

Businessmen in a hurry will buy whatever they're offered just to get through them. Tourists, exhausted by haggling, will buy every wooden mask, ivory bracelet and brass warrior that's forced upon them only to leave them behind in their hotels to be thrust at the next wave of tourists. I've seen traders selling pirated feather dusters from South Korea and the collected works of William Shakespeare in French not only follow gentle old ladies into a salon du thé but join them for a meal as well. You think you know a way to fight them off? I've tried everything.

I once actually spoke to an old man whose teeth were as black and yellow as an old carthorse's for over an hour and a half in a desperate bid to exhaust him. I ended up buying two dreadful sand paintings which I later gave to a beggar outside Harry's Club. But he gave them back to me. I've tried saying I'm Chinese and speaking gibberish; they call their friends over to introduce them to the first Chinaman to come to Dakar. Walk fast and they'll walk faster. Even the ones on crutches. I've tried the short, sharp, American approach; 'Look fellas, I bought something off you yesterday. Now push off and have a nice day.' No way. Every street trader in Dakar seems to think that to sell to an American twice in one week is some kind of virility symbol.

Senegalese street traders are all over francophone Africa; exchanging money on the border between Togo and Ghana, selling ivory on the beach in Grand Bassam, pushing shirts through your car window in Cotonou, waving watches at you in Bamako. They are breaking out in Paris. I've even seen a rash of them selling ivory bracelets and cheap sunglasses on the steps of the leaning tower of Pisa. At best they are part of the scene, an integral part of the noise and hassle of Africa. At worst, they are a pain in the neck. In Dakar they are the commercial equivalent of a maladie exotique.

The shame is, they consume so much of Senegal's national energy that there is none left for the rest of the country. Not that the rest of the Senegalese are lazy; but in the Novotel in Dakar, for example, I've seen Senegalese workmen paint round the spare toilet roll on top of the cistern rather than move it.

The only advice I can give you is to wait until just after lunch, when everybody rolls down their mats and turns to Mecca. On my calculations, you've then got exactly seven-and-a-half minutes to do the town and get back to the security of your hotel. It could be worth it, but I can't promise.

First things first. Senegal is Leopold Sedar Senghor, the poet statesman who, having created France in 1946 – he was a leading member of the committee that drew up the new French constitution – went on to create modern Senegal and lead it as president for the first twenty years of its independence. Ask any Senegalese what is significant about 1945 and they will tell you first, it's the year Senghor wrote *Chants d'Ombre.* Second, it's the year he was elected to parliament. He was francophone Africa's first great modern poet as well as their first great modern politician.

Not for him protest marches, violence and wars of independence. He simply sat down between verses with General de Gaulle for a civilised conversation. Senegal was independent.

An African married to a white Frenchwoman, a Catholic in a Muslim nation, an outstanding poet in a country where more than 50 percent of the population were illiterate, and for many years a contender for the Nobel Prize, Senghor called himself a socialist, ruled like a conservative and behaved like a liberal. He allowed his opponents to challenge him in elections. He even stepped down voluntarily as president in 1980 at the age of seventy-four and handed over to his almost shy prime minister of ten years' standing, Abdou Diouf.

Senghor is also very much part of France and French culture. There are even special 'Senghors', like Oscars, presented every year to outstanding blacks resident in France. The super Senghor, a black statuette of an African woman, was presented by Senghor himself to Wole Soyinka a few years ago, though how Soyinka came to be eligible is yet another tribute to French diplomacy.

As a result, Senegal 'the most French of all francophone countries' occupies a special position in the French commonwealth. It is liked and trusted. It has a free press, active trade unions, regular elections. It is still the only democratic multiparty state in francophone Africa. In many ways Dakar, the capital, once the unhealthiest town in West Africa, is today with its elegant shops and cafés very much Paris in the sunshine. And yet in many ways it is also the most Arabic of all francophone countries.

Senegal is a country which walks tall, and so do its inhabitants. They all seem to be around six-foot-six. They claim to have discovered America before Christopher Columbus. One of their kings in the fourteenth century equipped over 400 ships with men, food, water and abundant supplies of gold and told them, 'Do not return until you reach the end of the ocean or your food and water runs out.' Only one ship returned, whose captain reported that all the others had disappeared in 'what seemed a river with a powerful current' in the open sea.

The king, fascinated, ordered another 2,000 ships to be built: 1,000 for himself and his men, the others for provisions. He then sailed off to discover the New World for himself. Neither he nor any of his ships returned, but talk to any Senegalese, especially late at night over a pastis, and they will hold your hand and tell you Christopher Columbus was a Johnny-come-lately. But don't worry, they're not serious. About holding your hand, I mean.

Everybody holds hands in francophone Africa, but the Senegalese seem to do it for longer than anybody else. Grahame Greene noticed it when he was in Dakar: 'On the quay ... the men walked hand-in-hand, laughing sleepily together under the blinding vertical glare. Sometimes they put their arms round each other's necks; they seemed to like to touch each other, as if it made them feel good to know the other man was there. It wasn't love; it didn't mean anything we could understand.'

They are still there, still holding hands. Outside le présidence, like an elegant chateau; outside the National Assembly, a modern, imposing building with an entrance rising through fountains and waterfalls; outside the Chamber of Commerce which looks more like a chapel for a cloistered order of nuns than a temple of Mammon; outside the cathedral which might have been carved out of icing sugar; all over the Place de l'Indépendance which, with its four lanes of traffic on either side and its tall office blocks, looks a little worn around the edges. Probably like the country itself after the bruising it has taken in the last few years of structural readjustment. And throughout the suburbs which are a cross between manicured French suburbia and the back streets of Marseilles.

But the place to see francophone Africa holding hands with anglophone Africa is at the annual meeting of the Banque Africaine de Developpement – the African Development Bank to les roast beefs. It's the only place I've ever been where if you don't hold hands with someone people look at you as if you're odd.

'Don't be fooled,' a big Nigerian general winked at me. 'They're not just holding our hands, they're leading us in their direction. Their grip gets tighter every time.'

An annual meeting of the ADB is a wonderful place to see francophone talking to anglophone, as well as Japanese talking to Arabs talking to Finns talking to South Koreans talking to British. The anglophones will tell you it has a very strong francophone flavour today, but the ADB was founded, in 1964, largely thanks to the efforts of an americaphone, Dr Romeo Horton, a Liberian banker, and a group of African intellectuals championing pan-African development. Its objective: to use the financial and technical resources at its disposal for the promotion of economic and social progress in its member countries.

The ADB's origin could not have been humbler. The institution which today has assets of US $30 billion started in three rooms without enough money to pay the staff; directors and employees had to be paid direct by their own national governments. Money for the bank was, therefore, the big problem. Then in 1973 the leap in oil prices meant Nigeria was suddenly awash with money. For years they had preached economic co-operation. Now they could do something about it. They gave the bank US $80 million to establish the Nigerian Trust Fund. The ADB was in business.

In 1978 came the breakthrough: the bank decided to allow in non-African shareholders – hence all the Japanese, Arabs, Finns, South Koreans and British. Whereas before they were hampered by lack of funds, a dwindling number of projects and loss of credibility on international capital markets, now, in spite of objections from Nigeria, Algeria and Libya, they were able to expand into the force they are today. With 50 African and 25 non-African shareholders their capital base has soared to heights undreamt of by Mr Horton.

The ADB has probably done more for Africa than any other organisation, yet it is overlooked by many Africans. Finance ministers will tell you about the IMF and the Paris Club; government officials will talk about the World Bank, the FAO, the WHO and a thousand other initials, but nobody ever mentions the ADB. I've even heard the finance minister of the Côte d'Ivoire, speaking in the ADB's headquarters in Abidjan and in front of senior ADB staff, praise the World Bank and the IMF for their assistance – but not a word about the ADB, which has given Côte d'Ivoire far more money over a longer period.

The bank's president, a Senegalese who learnt his English in Eastbourne, Babacar N'Diaye, fifty-two, is the man who has made the bank what it is today. Highly qualified, very experienced, a non-stop traveller and an unfailingly effective diplomatist, he joined the bank in 1965. In 1985 he was elected president, since when the ADB's activities have soared.

From a simple solar energy plant in Bamako to massive regional energy projects; from railway projects in Cameroon to bridges in Côte d'Ivoire, and from irrigation projects in the Sahel to health centres practically everywhere, there is not a country in Africa that has not benefited from the work of the ADB. Guinea worm and river blindness have disappeared from many regions thanks to ADB sewage systems. Roads have been improved as well as built. Railways have been rehabilitated. New airports have sprung up, massive oil palm plantations have been resuscitated, sugar processing industries established.

Altogether the ADB has financed over 1,000 loans totalling over US $10 billion since it started, with the lion's share going to agriculture, then public utilities, transport and telecommunications. Of course Africa still has enormous problems, but the ADB has stuck admirably to its brief.

Having a literary president and a free press has made Senegal virtually the literary centre of francophone Africa, at least when it comes to journalism. I reckon there are well over fifty different newspapers, magazines and broadsheets published throughout the country, which must make it the biggest newspaper reading nation in Africa.

At the very pinnacle is *La Présence Africaine*, first a literary magazine, then a publishing company, now the literary and intellectual Rome, Mecca and Jerusalem of the black intelligentsia the world over. The first issue appeared in 1947, published by Alioune Diop. Its sponsors included Sartre, Camus and, of course, Leopold Senghor as both poet and politician. André Gide wrote the preface, in which he said the magazine would welcome 'everybody identified with the Black cause and all the voices of Black people everywhere that deserve to be heard'. Diop stressed, however, that the magazine would owe 'no allegiance to any philosophical or political ideology'. It was a sensation, giving black intellectuals not only a literary but also a political platform. *PA* soon developed into an intellectual powerhouse of anti-colonialism; fighting on the streets was one thing, but fighting for intellectual superiority in its pages was far more important.

With the intellectual argument won and French colonialism defeated, in 1960 Diop turned his attention to the States, Portugal and South Africa. He founded the society for African Culture to bring together black writers and artists in the States with their counterparts in Africa. He organised international congresses. In 1966 he organised the first world festival of arts nègres in Dakar. By 1980, when he died, *PA* had inevitably lost some of its fire. The battles in the US had arguably been won, certainly on the intellectual side; Portugal had been driven out of Africa; only South Africa remained, but that had broken stronger men than Diop.

Go into *PA* today, meet Madame Alioune Diop, and it's like visiting a literary Sistine Chapel, the Reading Room at the British Museum and an ordinary bookshop all rolled or bound into one. All Dakar bookshops are splendid – for example the Librairie Clairafrique, like the Charing Cross Road in the old days, crammed with books on anything that stands still. French books, of course, by the million, but the occasional English book – translated into French, of course.

On the more commercial, popular side comes the state and national daily *Le Soleil*, which has reporters in practically every town and a nationwide circulation of over 30,000. Privately owned publications range from party newspapers and Muslim magazines to *Fippu*, produced by Yewi Yewi, a women's group, against 'the patriarchal society which alienates women, confirms them in secondary roles and prevents them from expressing their creativity'.

The scurrilous press comes as a shock and a delight, especially *Le Cafard Libéré*, the liberated cockroach, a wonderful imitation of France's *Le Canard Enchaîné.* You want to know all the gossip and scandal and rumours in Africa; pick up a copy: how much money has Houphouet-Boigny stashed away in Switzerland? What was Doe trying to hide this week? How did Jawara buy that big house in England? All stories that would not be tolerated in other parts of Africa.

The francophone press as a whole doesn't have quite the same news values as we have. In Abidjan, for example, local television reported the opening of the Berlin Wall in November 1989 after coverage of a Club des Managers meeting in the capital and reports of two football matches in France. Some say this is because the press is owned or controlled by governments, with the notable exception of Senegal. Partly, I think, this is true. But partly not.

'Our newspapers are different because they represent our society and our values, not yours,' a Malian journalist once told me. Many people forget this when they criticise African newspapers for being the mouthpiece of government. Besides, nobody wants to invest in newspapers here because they never sell enough copies even to cover costs.

'We have limited resources. Our people are living in poverty. We are trying to repay our debts. Companies are trying to survive on spare parts. Our machines are old-fashioned. There is very little to argue about, we are all agreed on the objectives. It would be wrong, therefore, to criticise the government for the sake of criticising, or to please Western liberals,' another journalist, a Nigerian, told me.

'We print what the president says. We report everything the government does,' said a reporter in Burkina Faso. '*The Times* of London always said it was a newspaper of record. Why shouldn't we be a newspaper of record?' Why not indeed? If you are struggling to feed your people, if you have limited resources, which means limited supplies of newsprint, it is difficult to argue that you should devote page after page to criticism, knocking copy or so-called investigative journalism.

Senegal, which launches publications about as fast as it forms political parties, is the exception. *Le Soleil,* which is 60 percent owned by a loss-making government holding company and 40 percent by various French publishers, reports all the activities of the opposition and even violently anti-government criticism. *Ande Soppi*, a monthly with a circulation of around 10,000, is as Marxist as you can get. *Jaay Doole Bi-le Proletaire*, a bi-weekly, is virtually Maoist.

Don't be misled by circulation figures, however. On the one hand there is a thriving trade in secondhand newspapers. Leave your newspaper on a seat outside your hotel and it will instantly disappear. Those little boys who don't look as though they've had a good meal for a fortnight can sell the same newspaper three or four times in a morning. On the other hand, every publisher likes to claim a bigger circulation than anybody else; especially if he is Senegalese and in opposition to the government.

In recent months, three things have struck me about francophone newspapers. First, they are becoming more professional. They are printing more colour, layouts and design are improving. Picture quality is still not perfect, but then I often see double when I read some British popular newspapers. Second, from the point of view of the advertiser, they are becoming more flexible. In the old days it was virtually impossible to get a rate-card; now you can get a rate card, and even book certain positions and publication dates. Third, the quality is improving. The editorial is becoming much more newsy and readable. Of course, you still get the official government news, but foreign news coverage has improved dramatically.

The other major breakthrough has been the advent of the special supplement, which modesty forbids me from mentioning since it was my idea. Readers of Togo's *Nouvelle Marche* will have noticed a twelve-page supplement on Britain which attracted wide advertising support from UK companies and featured the country's first-ever full colour advertisement, and an eight-page prospectus for a local share issue which helped raise nearly $1 million from local investors for a newly privatised steel mill. If you can raise that kind of money by advertising in one of the poorest countries in francophone Africa at this time who can possibly doubt the effectiveness of the African news media? Providing you have the right adviser, of course.

But if *La Nouvelle Marche* gets my *Financial Times* award for francophone Africa, other publications deserve similar honours. My *Independent* award for layout, style and sheer professionalism would go to Côte d'Ivoire's *Fraternité Matin*; my *Time* magazine award for a news magazine to Benin's new *Eco* magazine; my technical magazine award to *Construire Afrique*, and, of course, my *Private Eye* award for scandalous gossip to *Le Cafard Libéré*.

The pan-African francophone press circulating either regionally or throughout the continent is another matter. Here *Jeune Afrique*, a weekly news magazine published out of Paris, can stand alongside any in the world. Similarly, *Africa*, published in Senegal by a Belgian, Joel Decupper, although it is perhaps more *Newsweek* to *Jeune Afrique*'s *Time* magazine. The monthly *Jeune Afrique Economie*, run by a Cameroonian, Blaise-Pascal Talla, which is virtually the *Economist* published by the *Sunday Times* colour magazine, is formidable. And *Afrique Elite* is pure class.

Francophone newspapers are full of histoires drôles, strip cartoons and sayings of the president, partly because in countries bouncing along the bottom they cannot afford the staff to fill the space. Most newspapers operate out of almost derelict buildings; only one or two have computers; most have barely enough pencils to go round. To solve this problem, and to counteract what African governments said was the distorted reporting of the big five international news agencies, the Pan-African News Agency was established in Dakar in 1983. Unfortunately it didn't quite work out. PANA has almost empty offices, a demoralised staff and quantities of unused material.

They lack the resources to field their own journalists and have to rely on government statements and official press releases, which is not the basis of a crusading, objective news service. Then they have problems transmitting the information. News is news, but when it is sent by a single short-wave transmitter hired from SONATEL, the national telecoms company in Senegal, it is not likely to be printed extensively. Especially if that transmitter only has a range of 1,500 kilometres.

Maybe things will change. Their new director-general, a Congolese, Auguste Mpassi-Muba, who took over in 1988, quickly negotiated a deal for direct access to one of the Soviet Union's big Stasionar 4 communication satellites with ground stations in Khartoum, Kinshasa, Lusaka, Lagos and Tripoli. The price: a mere US $12,500 a year. He has also persuaded UNESCO to cough up US $2 million to fund further development and the Italians to computerise their editorial operations, and is trying to sell special African news services to embassies and companies worldwide. He has even tried to interest Reuters, Agence-France Presse, United Press International, Tass and Associated Press – the previously despised big five – to buy their African news coverage from him instead of doing it themselves. Which they probably thought was another histoire drôle.

When it comes to books, francophone countries have both the best and the worst records in Africa. Guinea doesn't have one bookshop. Togo has more bookshops per head than any other African country, and one library for every 140,000 people, an almost unbelievable record followed closely by Senegal. Guinea has one library for every 2 million people.

Mickey Mouse, James Bond, Clint Eastwood et al. are as well known as anywhere in the world. Most towns have their local cinema, major cities have two or three. Most cinemas seem to be owned by Lebanese who gradually build snack bars, restaurants, even casinos and hotels around them. A few more adventurous businessmen have started sending mobile cinemas into the villages.

'So what about videos?' I asked a Lebanese cinema owner in Lomé.

'Videos are for the rich. Cinemas are for the poor. And there are always more poor people in a country than rich people,' he replied in that disarming way of theirs.

Every country, of course, has its radio station although I often wonder whether it is there as a symbol of office – 'I control the radio station, therefore I control the country' – more than as a source of news and entertainment. In francophone

Africa everybody listens to the radio, but few to local radio.

'Why should I? You can't trust what they say,' I've been told a thousand times.

'So which station do you listen to?' I ask.

'The BBC. They are always the first to tell you if there has been a coup.'

I was in Lomé when Babangida took over in Nigeria. Everybody heard it first on the BBC. Those who heard it later did not believe it until they heard it repeated on the BBC. Similarly with the coup in Burkina Faso and the attempted coups in Gabon and Ghana in 1989; nobody believes it until they hear it on the BBC.

'But why not French radio?' I nervously asked a minister in Brazzaville. 'Because you can trust the BBC,' he replied. 'With French radio you never know if the government is involved. It could be a trick.'

Television in French-speaking Africa is pretty uninspiring, although *Dynasty* and all the other US soaps take on a new dimension when seen sitting on an oil drum outside a tiny sandstone compound in Mopti on the edge of the Sahara on a freezing November evening. You also see all the French soaps, not to mention a neverending stream of what look like 1930 B-movies about Louis XIV. Occasionally you see the joint US-French productions that were meant to set the world alight.

Most television and radio stations have been built with French assistance. Most of the staffs have been trained in Paris, and many have worked for the overseas French radio service. But most equipment is Japanese; certainly all the new equipment going in nowadays is. 'The French tell me their equipment is the best, but I tell them Japanese is better,' one minister of information told me. 'If something else is better and cheaper then I will buy it. Japanese equipment doesn't break down either.'

What they do with the French advice and Japanese equipment is, unfortunately, very little. Most television stations only operate in the evenings from, say, 7 pm to 11 pm during the week and maybe from midday at weekends. Of that only one hour, maybe two, will be produced locally: the news, of course, and simple quiz games such as Scrabble played by contestants sitting at desks in front of a single, stationary camera.

In Zaire they are a little more daring. There they run general knowledge competitions in front of a wall plastered with posters saying 'What do you want to be when you grow up?', a picture of Mobutu, two cameras and an audience of teachers and old soldiers. Occasionally a jeune artiste de la chanson will be filmed standing in front of the local oil refinery making her première attempt to become une étoile. At weekends there is football; local football, French football, even English football.

In Benin you can only watch television on Thursday, Saturday and Sunday and then only for a few hours. Founded in 1972, 'La Voix de la Revolution Populaise' snubbed the French and chose West Germany's system. The Germans gave them the equipment and nothing else. For eleven years the station failed to transmit a single programme until Benin and France made it up and Mitterrand gave Kerekou the television equipment he had refused to buy so that they could cover his state visit. Benin still has only one transmitter which can just about reach the whole of Cotonou. Television sets are few. But it did, according to the Beninois, boast the best newsreader in the world: General Mattias Kerekou, the former president, who often insisted on reading the news, especially if it was of national importance. Benin is still one of my favourite television stations in francophone Africa. They refuse to transmit *Dynasty* because, according to the minister of culture, all Western television is 'vulgar and obscene' and 'could tarnish the image of the Beninese revolution'.

At the other extreme is Cameroon with its massive US $20 million purpose-built 13-storey white marble-and-glass television station on the edge of the posh Bastos area of Yaounde, the largest single investment project ever undertaken by the government. It has eight ultramodern studios, one of which can accommodate 500 people. The power it requires to operate would support a town of several hundred thousand people. Yet it is still not providing a full service. It only operates Wednesday, Thursday, Friday evenings and eight hours at weekends. Only 22 of the 32 transmitters are working, and they are still debating the split between locally produced and imported programmes. On my last visit it was running at around 7:3 in favour of Cameroon, including some pretty impressive concerts from Yaounde's Congress Hall. At least the audience seemed to be enjoying themselves, unlike the zombie-like audiences you see on so much francophone television. But the best programmes are the sports programmes. Normally I find football matches deeply unexciting, but in Cameroon they're fantastic – because in officially bilingual Cameroon the commentary switches from English to French and back again so much you don't know whether to rire or cry.

But to me the benchmark of a television station is the news: the contents and how well it is presented. One evening I got back to my Abidjan hotel after a hectic day and switched on the news. In the first item, housewives were urged to cut down on the use of aerosol hairsprays because of the damage to the ozone layer. Then there was a report from the Middle East which I missed because the telephone rang. When I got back they were running a report about Niger looking for foreign investors. Then in about three minutes we took in reports from China, Israeli soldiers beating up protesters on the West Bank, and the Ayatollah, all supplied by a French television news agency. An item about Chad and Libya was beginning when someone knocked on my door. It was a Senegalese selling ivory tusks, sunglasses and leather belts.

By the time I got back with my new sunglasses and three belts the sports news was on: reports of two local football matches, a major French tournament and some tennis match in San Francisco. Then there was another knock on the door. The Senegalese said I hadn't paid him enough money. If I gave him what I owed him he would give me another belt. As I dashed back to the television the newsreader was saying, '. . . Explosion in the Soviet Union. A nuclear cloud is drifting slowly across Europe. Mesdames, messieurs, bon soir.'

Beneath all its freedom of speech Senegal is still a trifle crispé. Since Diouf, who like most Senegalese is over 6′6″ and thin as a beanpole, came to power in 1981 he has had to struggle to establish his own identity with Senghor still rumbling away in the background. A bit like Eden taking over from Churchill. A lawyer and financial administrator, he was first known rather contemptuously as le grand commis, because of his ability to shuffle the paperwork. Then he had to put his own imprint on the party, which again was not easy given the volatile nature of the political environment and the Senegalese eagerness to debate everything. Finally, he had to trump the opposition parties and devise and push through policies for coping with problems never even imagined by Senghor. Overall he has succeeded admirably. In 1985 he became chairman of the OAU. He made a forceful impression at the UN. He has spoken out strongly on African debt and other major issues affecting the continent. To many world leaders he is Africa's senior statesman, certainly far more intellectual and international than Houphouet-Boigny, a friend and regular visitor to his home town, Louga, and his nearest rival for the title.

At home he seems deliberately to play everything low key. Some presidents will only travel in the middle of the day which means barricading every main street, switching half the country's police force from normal duties and guaranteeing a crowd. Diouf prefers to slink in and out of town when nobody's looking. The last time I saw him leave town, early in the morning, the only people present were myself and a road sweeper.

And yet, talk to any Senegalese and they wave their hands, look up in the air and mutter and moan. 'So what's the problem with Senegal?' I asked a journalist on *Le Cafard Libéré* as we sat outside his house one evening.

'We're probably too intellectual,' he said in that rapid-fire Senegalese accent that sounds like a machine gun swallowing a chicken. 'We want to argue and rationalise; we're philosophers, not politicians. We're more interested in concepts than in reality.'

'But you can't get things done if you're not practical.'

'That's the problem, we don't like decisions, we like discussion.' He poured another pastis. 'There's only one person in the country who likes taking decisions.'

'You mean Diouf?'

'No, Madame Diouf.' He laughed uproariously. 'She's the real tough politician. One day she is organising chess tournaments, the next signing construction contracts.'

'So what about Diouf?'

'He's too intellectual, like the rest of us. He goes off worrying about the world economic situation, making speeches. What is he doing here? Prices are increasing all the time, wages are not. He goes on about moins d'état, mieux d'état. What is he doing about our bloated bureaucracy?'

'But didn't he sack the old guard, promote younger people, bring non-party members into the government, increase the role of women . . .'

'His wife's influence, again!'

'Didn't he even try and crack down on corruption? Bring in more democracy? Even cut electricity prices?'

'But to what effect? Ministers can't even read out a message from the president at a pop concert without being shouted down.'

'So what's going to happen?'

He shrugged. 'Maybe we have too much freedom. If we had only one party we wouldn't have to worry about taking the right decision, it would all be done for us. Although some people say democracy is our biggest foreign exchange earner. If we weren't so democratic maybe we wouldn't have been able to reschedule our debts eight times in eight years.'

Even the opposition parties agree that there are too many parties. The principal opposition party is the Partie Démocratique Senegalais (PDS); next is the Marxist Ligue Démocratique-Mouvement pour le Partie du Travail (LD-MPT), then there are the Mouvement Démocratique Populaire, the Rassemblement National Démocratique, the real intellectuals' party which is openly pro-Muslim, campaigning for national languages to be given priority over French, the Partie de l'Indépendance et du Travail; the Partie Africaine de l'Indépendance, the country's oldest Marxist party, the Partie pour la Liberation du Peuple, and up to ten other smaller parties.

'Wherever two or three people in other parts of francophone Africa gather together,' he said, 'they start planning a coup. In Senegal we start forming another political party.'

The PDS is probably more liberal than socialist. They disagree with Diouf's moins d'état, mieux d'état, and say it should be less of state socialism, more of state intervention. The

LD-MPT however is for nationalising everything. But only Diouf's Partie Socialiste and the PDS are represented in the National Assembly, Diouf with 103 seats and the PDS with 17.

'Do you think you'll ever reduce the number of parties?' I asked. 'Maybe restrict them to three like under Senghor?'

'You mean forcibly?'

'No, by agreement.'

'I doubt it. We can never agree on anything, I told you.'

'But Diouf threw the opposition leader, Wade, in jail after the last election.'

'And his two assistants. And the leader of the PIT, Amath Dantsoho, and Dr Bathily of the LD-MPT.'

'So why did he do that?'

'First, to stabilise the situation. As soon as the election was over there was an outcry about ballot-rigging and so on – riots, police, everything. The state of emergency calmed the situation down. Don't forget we've had states of emergency before – in '68 when Senghor had problems with students, and in '69 with a general strike. And Diouf didn't want to make Wade a martyr. If he had only arrested Wade, we would have had Free Wade marches and concerts. It was a shrewd move. And it saved us from those awful concerts.'

'So if all these parties are a problem why did Diouf agree to them in the first place?'

'He realised he could never have the same grip on the country as Senghor, and the Senegalese were demanding more say. By allowing an unlimited number of parties to be established and by forbidding alliances and coalitions he forced the opposition out into the open and split the opposition vote. Of course, he disguised it all very well; he wanted a national consensus, everybody to work together to rebuild a better Senegal. Very clever.'

He has also had to push through one of the most comprehensive and certainly the longest-term structural adjustment programme in Africa. Civil servants had to be dismissed. State enterprises began shedding employees. Potholes started appearing in the Route du Front de Terre, once one of Dakar's more impressive suburban streets. And the poor peasants who make up 75 percent of the population became poorer still.

Social services were out. Guaranteed prices were eliminated if the government were buying but increased if the peasants were buying. And food prices soared almost as high as Diouf's nose.

Overall, it looks as if it is going to work. Real capital growth has been achieved three years in a row. The current account deficit is shrinking. Savings are up. Domestic credit is under control. Inflation has dropped dramatically. But I still wouldn't risk the Route du Front de Terre on a rainy day, and everything could still be knocked sideways by either too little or too much rain, by locusts, or by the price of groundnuts.

In the last few years the groundnut harvest has been at record levels. But the world price has been at record low levels. The processed oil has sold for barely half of what it cost to produce.

'What would Wade have done?' I asked as we finished another pastis.

'Probably the same. There's really no choice, except that he would have sacked Jean Collin.' Depending on whom you talk to, Collin, a lifelong friend of the president, is either his fixer, the man who gets things done, or a latter day Rasputin.

Most francophone presidents seem to have a Jean Collin. In Benin, President Kerekou's right hand man was Mohamed Amadou Cisse, a marabout or holy man, who previously worked for Zaire's President Mobutu. A Malian, he was first minister of security, then minister with special responsibilities for security and relations with other Islamic countries.

But he is small beer compared to Oumarou Amadou, another marabout, who managed to work at the same time for Niger and Côte d'Ivoire before he fell from grace. In Niger, he was special adviser to the president, chief of police and head of the secret service although he could read neither Arabic nor French. In Côte d'Ivoire, he was a consultant to their transport minister. When it all came to an end, he did what every African does when he loses his job, he went back to work on the land. Except in his case he had by then acquired a number of big farms in Niger as well as extensive properties in France.

M'babanin Cissoko is another marabout with strong links throughout French Africa, particularly in Gabon, where he has amassed a fortune. In a country where a secondhand bicycle is a luxury, he has a fleet of cars at his disposal and has even built a landing strip for his private jet in his village in Mali.

President Diouf relies enormously on his marabout, Djily M'Baye, said by many to be the most powerful man in the country. Chief of the Mouride Brotherhood in Diouf's home town, he is a multi-millionaire who deals mainly in commodities, and is involved in prospecting for oil with the Senegalese government as well as privatising a number of state enterprises.

But not all marabouts work for presidents; another Senegalese marabout was recently arrested in France and sentenced to six months for fraud. He was advertising in newspapers offering 'all forms of magic expected of a marabout'. For CFA 150,000 he would bring home runaway husbands. For another CFS 50,000 he would stop you from being sacked. You could pay him in jewellery, television sets, even video recorders. Surely he wasn't a genuine marabout, the magistrate asked him before sentencing him. But he was, he protested. It was written in his passport.

Jean Collin, however, a 'marabout blanc', is in a class of his own. A mysterious, sinister French civil servant who shortly after independence became a Senegalese citizen, he has since then been the link man between Senegal and Paris, loyal to both. His break came in February 1964 when Senghor appointed him minister of justice. Today he is the general secretary to the presidency. If there are tough problems to be sorted out, Collin takes care of them.

Take the police, for example. When I first went to Senegal you thought twice before asking a policeman the time, because some at least were the roughest in francophone Africa, especially the riot police who caused more damage than the riots they were trying to break up. They went on strike in 1987 not because seven of them had been jailed for torturing a Muslim prisoner to death in a police station five years earlier but because the station superintendent was not jailed with them. Collin was sent to the ministry of the interior by Diouf to sort them out. He fired about one third of the force, and completely reorganised the rest. Today they are unnervingly friendly. They are even, I am told, refusing to accept bribes from motorists stopped for minor offences.

'So will Diouf become another Senghor?' I asked.

'Maybe. Maybe not.' He went to pour another pastis, but the bottle was empty. 'Come on,' he said. 'Let's go to the Novotel. Le Beaujolais Nouveau est arrivé. Everyone will be there – politicians, diplomats, businessmen, civil servants. You can ask them.'

That year I drank Beaujolais Nouveau before they were drinking it in Paris. But I didn't get a chance to hold hands with Jean Collin. Maybe la prochaine fois.

Guediwaye, about ten kilometres outside Dakar, is probably the world capital of glass painting. Once highly developed and practised in ancient China, Persia and throughout the Middle East, today glass painting is only really practised in Senegal, by Monsieur Gora Mbengue in particular. Scenes of everyday life, historical themes, delicate birds and butterflies, even paintings in a distinct Muslim style of terrified young ladies racing down a mountain on what look like diamond-encrusted skis: they are all subjects for M. Mbengue, one of francophone Africa's leading artists. Others such as Togo's Paul Ayhi, who is responsible for many major outdoor sculptures and giant murals, and Zaire's Tamba Ndembe, who produces table-top bronze sculptures, I'd already met. This was my chance to see M. Mbengue.

After the sometimes primitive and aggressive art of most of francophone Africa – the statuettes of Mali, the masks of Yamassoukro, even the paintings of the Nouvelle Generation of Kinshasa or of l'Ecole de Lumbumbashi in Zaire – Senegal seems to be at the more refined end of the market.

Their tapestries I find fascinating. They will often reject hundreds of designs until they find just the right one. Their colouring and attention to detail are superb. An average tapestry will have, perhaps, twenty colours; the best, as many as a hundred. They take anything from three months to a year to weave. Their sand paintings, too, can take months to complete.

Unfortunately, I wasn't able to meet M. Mbengue. Instead, my travelling companions – the driver, and four of his friends we had picked up on the way – insisted that I be introduced to 'their brother'. They took me to a small dusty house. Inside it was white, modern, beautifully furnished, air-conditioned. Their brother, Abdul Aziz, was sitting on a white leather sofa wearing a flowing blue robe, white slippers and twisting an expensive Omega Constellation around his wrist. He said he had just got back from Touba, the holy city of the Mourides, probably the most influential and certainly the most numerous and hardworking of the increasingly important Islamic brotherhoods in Senegal.

Founded in the late nineteenth century by Amadou Bamba, they are a branch of the Qadiriyya, themselves part of the Sufi branch of Islam and believe, like the Benedictines, in Dem Ien Ligeey, work as well as prayer. Although nowhere near as violent and dangerous as, say, the Mahdi in Sudan, Bamba caused so many problems for the French that he was twice exiled for a total of twelve years. Today the Mourides, with three million members out of a population of five million, and virtual control of the groundnut industry, are the dominant force in Senegalese society.

Touba, about three hours' drive from Dakar, is to them Mecca; some Mourides claim that a pilgrimage to Touba is as good as if not better than a pilgrimage to Mecca, although to the orthodox this is heretical. The city is dominated by a huge mosque with a minaret almost 300 feet high, probably the tallest in Africa. Alongside they are building a new Islamic university, a library which will eventually house over one million books and a palace for the Khalife-General, the direct successor of Bamba. Luckily for Diouf, the Mourides are among his strongest supporters even though he is a member of the minority Tidiane Brotherhood which can only muster 1.25 million members. Some say the Khalife-General supports him because he says Bamba would have wished it. Others say it's because when his father died, Diouf gave his mother to the Khalife-General and it's difficult for even a descendant of Bamba to ignore a president who gives you such a present even though Wade, the leader of the opposition, is a Mouride.

'Pilgrimage?' I asked. I had read about the Great Magal, the most important event in the Mourides' year, when abattoirs are hired and thousands of sheep sacrificed.

'Business,' he smiled. Touba is also the centre of Senegal's booming smuggling industry and the Mourides run one of the biggest smuggling operations in West Africa. Which is perhaps another reason for their growing influence; for smuggling has become a vital sector of the Senegalese economy. It generates trade, creates jobs, stimulates all kinds of services, oils wheels and pumps revenue into the economy.

Every francophone country has its smuggling operations. In Zaire, it's a way of life. Everybody is dealing in cooking oil, corn meal and soap. The big operators charter planes to Angola and Zambia. A few years ago the big money was in pharmaceuticals; today it's spare parts, cotton, cigarettes and whisky. The really big boys stick to gold and diamonds. In Cameroon it's usually cars and spare parts from Nigeria. In the other direction, it's whatever you can carry. Nigeria is desperate for everything. So is Niger. Some days Niamey airport looks like an international trade centre. Togo has almost legitimised its smuggling operations; they export $150 million in gold and nearly $50 million in diamonds every year, yet none of it comes from there. It is all smuggled in.

Abdul Aziz was, of course, at the respectable end of the business, knew everybody, lunched with ministers, mingled with bankers and traded with everybody.

'But isn't it wrong?' I asked him. 'Especially for a religious organisation. Isn't it breaking the law?'

'If it was wrong, I wouldn't be here,' he said, 'I would be arrested.'

Yes, well, I thought. 'But maybe that's what's wrong with Africa?' I replied. 'Nobody takes any notice of the rules.'

'If it wasn't for us,' he said, 'the system would break down. We're the safety valve; we preserve the peace and the status quo.'

'Which is why the politicians don't touch you.'

'Exactement. If it wasn't for smuggling you would have uproar in Africa. People would be rioting, governments crashing. We are the means of giving people what they want. The poor man wants soap – that's not much to ask, but the government can't give it to him. So he buys it on the black market. He is happy, the traders are happy. If he couldn't get soap he'd go mad, tear the place apart. Now the rich man; he works hard, he has problems. He goes home at night, he wants a whisky – but you can't buy whisky in the shops, or if you can it's too expensive. He gets whisky on the black market. He's happy, the trader is happy. So what's wrong with that?'

'Nothing, I suppose. But . . .'

'I agree the government doesn't get its money from the customs. But if they did the World Bank would say, you've got enough money, we're not going to help you.' He laughed. 'What good is that to Africa?'

'D'accord,' I said. 'You're doing a grand job. But tell me why is it the Muslims who always seem to be behind these smuggling operations?'

'Une bonne question,' he said. 'I've often thought about it. Muslims are international. Nos frères sont partout. In business terms that means I have contacts; brothers I know I can trust. All our business is informal – no computers issuing orders and printing delivery instructions. Most of our transactions are in cash. We use banks of course, but the actual trading all along the line is in cash. If you are doing that you must do business with people you can trust.'

'I was told that if anybody was caught stealing, you poured paraffin over their hands and set light to them,' I smiled gently.

'Jamais. Stories,' he exclaimed. 'Look, we're a brotherhood. It is our culture to help our brothers. If I go to the mosque and there is not a poor man I can help I feel guilty. Why would anybody want to steal? No. Jamais.' I asked him about the big deals: gold, diamonds, foreign currencies, but as I wasn't in the brotherhood, he said he couldn't tell me. But he told me how he had started by working for a small trader who smuggled cans of beer. As his boss got older he found it more difficult carrying the cans from the lorries to his shop, so one evening he asked Abdul Aziz to do it. He had never looked back. Was he the president directeur-general, I asked him.

'I am a businessman,' he smiled. He then told me about the Mourides' system of charitable donation. From what he told me about how much he gave every time he went to the mosque, or to Touba, and based on the three million membership, I worked out that the brotherhood must be given US $100 million a year.

This, he said, was currently being used for the new Islamic buildings in Touba.

As well as money, the faithful will give their time, even their lives, to the Khalife-General. They will work for years on end for a pittance on the brotherhood's farms with little to eat and the barest of essentials; they do it willingly, for the Koran promises that when they die they will be repaid one hundred fold.

Some day surely Senegal would become the Islamic Republic of Senegal, I asked him, because it's more or less that already, in its culture, its politics, its attitudes.

'Vous avez raison,' he said. 'But I don't think it will. If we become an Islamic republic it will be an encouragement to the extremists. The government doesn't want extremists, and neither do we.'

'Bad for business,' I said.

He laughed. We had been chatting so freely I thought I'd slip in the story about Diouf's mother.

'So how many wives does the Khalife-General have?'

'Thirty.'

I was taken aback. I was expecting maybe five.

'He is a rich man. In our country anybody can have four or five wives. All big men have lots of wives.'

'What about Diouf giving his mother to the Khalife-General. Is it true?'

'Why not? It is a great honour if the president gives you his mother, and it's good politics. When a president gives you his mother you can hardly refuse –'

'Not even if you're the Khalife-General?'

'Not even if you're the Khalife-General. And if your son-in-law is president you can hardly tell people not to vote for him.'

'Even if he belongs to another brotherhood.'

'Exactement.'

'And people do as the Khalife-General says?'

'Exactement.'

During the First World War, the French had problems finding enough soldiers to fight in France, so they asked the then Khalife-General for help. 'All who believe in me and Allah will enlist,' he said. And off to France went every single man of military age in the country frightened they would lose their right to heaven if they did not obey the marabout's call. So voting for the Khalife-General's son-in-law was peanuts. Senegalese, of course.

I was coming through Dakar airport when I saw this Air Afrique captain lying on the floor in front of this Mauritanian. 'Get up,' I said. 'I can't,' he said. 'He is my master.'

'How do you mean master? I thought all that was abolished years ago.'

It was, except in Mauritania. There are still slaves there. They're a million years behind the rest of the world, but it's gradually changing.

'You mean they've changed the law?' I asked him later.

'No. They changed the law in 1980,' he said.

'They had slaves in Mauritania until 1980?'

'Sure.'

'So why are things changing now?'

'Education.'

'You mean education is spreading throughout the country?'

'No. Only among the slaves.'

'I don't understand. I'd have thought if the upper classes became more –'

'Mauritania is divided into two: the Beydane, the white Moors, the masters; and the Harratine, the black Moors, the slaves. Throughout history the Beydane lorded it over the Harratine. They never lifted a finger. The slaves looked after the camels, then they looked after the cars and the trucks. They are still doing everything for the Beydane, except today they are flying the private planes, operating the computers –'

'So the slaves are now the educated elite and the Beydane are at their mercy.'

'Exactement, but the social structure is still there, the master-slave relationship. But it won't be long before that goes as well.'

Christian Diop, who runs one of the small internal Senegalese airlines, started by telling me over lunch about the Falklands crisis: how the British used Dakar airport as a staging post, as they did during the last world war, because of its strategic position: how one evening he had counted sixty-two British planes on the runway and a solitary Argentinian plane, also using the airport as its staging post to Europe.

'You mean to France?' I wondered.

'And all the crews were staying at the same hotel.'

'But what could the Argentines have been doing with the French?'

'All in the same bar. You'd never have thought there was a war going on.'

'The French gave a categorical assurance that –'

'The best of friends ...'

'Never ...'

'Of course not ...'

Then suddenly he changed the subject and we were talking about Mauritania, Senegal's northern neighbour, and le climat de belligérance that existed between them.

'So why aren't you good neighbours?' I asked.

'Because we have so much in common,' he said.

Both countries share virtually the same culture and the same religion. Both have highly structured societies although the structures are breaking down quicker in Senegal. Both have a strong trading mentality, both are fanatical about education – for themselves and their own class, not for others.

In May 1989 an insignificant dispute about grazing rights along their common border suddenly became a major international incident with hundreds of deaths, rioting and looting, massive repatriations and a thousand rumours. The Senegalese said the Harratines were killing people on their masters' instructions, using the incident as an excuse. The Mauritanians said the Senegalese were trying to make political capital out of the incident; they wanted to murder the Mauritanians because they were jealous they had captured so much of the small-time commerce. In any case President Diouf had not apologised officially, so he was probably orchestrating everything. And so on.

'Why can't you agree?'

'Because the people who have the power don't have the money; the people who have the money are not educated; the people who are educated are not the traders; the people who are trading don't have the power.'

Lunch was taking ages. The hotel was full of advance teams preparing for the Paris-Dakar rally – French engineers from Peugeot, hundreds of Japanese from Yamaha and Mitsubishi. At the next table was a doctor from Europ Assistance trying to set up emergency facilities along the route which in 1988 claimed two deaths, two quadriplegics and dozens of broken limbs. 'What can I do?' he said. 'Nobody is interested. They only want to kill themselves.'

After all the talk about slaves, I thought I'd visit the infamous slave island just off Dakar. I know Ouidah, the slave port in Benin, very well. But this was my first visit to the Ile de Gorée which, from around 1500 to 1848 when Napoleon abolished slavery, shipped out over three million slaves from all over West Africa. I was going to Gorée to remember, just as I did at Ouidah, where every red mud brick and every eerie little shack creeps with the memory of the appalling suffering that must have taken place there. But somehow the atmosphere wasn't right. Instead of being mean and desolate, Gorée turned out to be a pretty little island splashed with pink-roofed houses, lots of greenery, cascades of bougainvillaea, and a neat little beach. It was like a Mediterranean hideaway for the rich. The people, many of whose families have lived on the island for generations, were open, friendly, matter-of-fact; nothing like Ouidah, where you can feel their eyes burning into your back.

As soon as I stepped off the boat I met my guide. At least he told me he was. 'I am your guide. Very good guide. I explain you everything. My name is Papa Sow. But you can call me Papa. We start at this restaurant. Restaurant Kolingba.'

'But I want to visit the island.'

'Very good restaurant. Run by my uncle.'

It took some persuading him, but we set out to explore the island which is a speck on the ocean, only some 900 metres by 300 metres, not large enough for bicycles let alone cars. The rest of the boat lunched in his uncle's restaurant and lay on the beach. We walked between two rows of dilapidated houses and stopped in front of a pair of wooden doors.

'This is the Maison des Slaves, built by the Dutch in 1582. I explain you everything. Inside the first room is the weighing room. You had to be 60 kilos to be a good slave. If you are not 60 kilos they put you in another room. Feed you like a pig until you are 60 kilos. Then they sell you,' said Mr Sow. 'There is no doctor in the slaves' house. If you are sick they throw you in the sea. The slaves then pull you back and eat you. They are very hungry. The guardians have young girls. When they are pregnant they sell them. They sell everyone. Everybody crying. I explain you everything.'

But nothing like the way Conrad explained it: 'They walked erect and slow ... and the clink kept time with their footsteps ... I could see every rib, the joints of their limbs were like knots in a rope; each had an iron collar on his neck and all were connected together with a chain whose bights swung between them, rhythmically clinking.'

On the way to the top of the island, Mr Sow explains that his sister is Aminata Sow Fall, one of the most famous women novelists in francophone Africa. I tell him I've read her first novel, *Le Revenant.* He is so pleased he insists we return to his uncle's restaurant to celebrate, but with respect to Madame Fall I insist we continue.

We turn into a tiny house which is full of glass paintings by Gora Mbengue. The little gallery is run by his daughter who tells me that her father had just died and they are transferring everything from Guadiwaye to Gorée. I buy two paintings and leave. On the way to the church Mr Sow explains me that he has just shown George Schultz, the American Secretary of State, around the island. 'Very big man. He wants the best guide. I explain him everything.'

The church is like a giant shoebox, everything square, angular, the beams running in straight lines. Just the kind of church that would be built by the Dutch. 'The slaves come in here, all chains. The guards stand behind with their guns. I explain you. Afterwards they go back to the cells. The church is the same church, only they change the roof every ten years.'

I wanted to know how many slaves were shipped out over the years; their average lifespan; where they went; how the system ended. But Mr Sow had to explain one other thing. 'Mr Schultz. At the end of the tour he is so happy with me he gives me so much money.'

'How much?'

'I explain you. But you don't believe me.'

'How much?'

'US $500.'

'I don't believe you.'

For a one-hour tour Mr Sow had to go to the American embassy in Dakar with a bit of paper signed by Mr Schultz and pick up his $500. He was going to have a shock when I gave him my bit of paper.

Now we were standing on a little pillbox near the top of the island. 'This is exclusive girls' school,' Mr Sow was explaining to a neat cluster of red roofs gathered around a couple of mobile netball racks. 'Mariama Ma, the famous writer. Very good school. Every day for one hour they learn about history of slavery. I explain you everything.'

But there was not much left to explain. We inspected a poston tree whose sap the slaves used to treat everything from scratches to vicious amputations; we clambered over a rusty gun emplacement built by the French in 1907; and we stood on the cliff used at the start of *The Guns of Navarone* – because it looked more Greek than the Greek cliffs. Then we walked back towards the little port.

Soon we were in the marketplace, the centre of Gorée's slave trade. Here the governor and all the big dealers stood on an elegant decorated platform; around them the slaves, as near to 60 kilos as their jailers could get them. But it didn't have any memories. Stalls were selling postcards, T-shirts, biscuits, Hawaiian-style shorts.

'It was here,' said Mr Sow, 'they sold the Yorubas from Nigeria and Benin. They were the strong men. That is why the black American athletes are the best in the world – they come from the slaves who were sold here. I explain you everything.'

'So explain me the role of the Wolofs,' I said.

As far as I'm concerned you can't talk about Senegal without talking about the Wolofs. Senegal comes from the Wolof 'sunu gaal' meaning 'our boat'. They are probably one of the oldest peoples in Africa. Some researchers have traced them back to Ancient Egypt and even identified similarities between the languages. Others have gone further back to India. Either way the Wolofs come from Waalo, a dry, fertile area on the banks of the Senegal River. Their society was organised on strict hierarchical terms: at the top were the aristocrats of pure Wolof blood; then the peasants – free, not slaves – but of inferior blood; next the craftsmen, organised according to their trade and finally the slaves. Each group was further sub-divided into smaller groups, all based on the purity of their blood.

When the French landed at what is now St Louis at the mouth of the Senegal River in 1659 the Wolof aristocrats agreed to sell them their slaves for goods and armaments. They even developed their own form of consumer credit, borrowing from the French traders and paying them back in slaves. When they ran out of their own slaves they started raiding surrounding villages to pay off their debts.

But Mr Sow couldn't explain me anything about them. Instead he took me to see a small statue just off the square, a memorial to the French doctors and nurses who came to Gorée in 1878 to care for the slaves in the middle of a plague epidemic and died in the process. It looked as if it had been neglected since 1879. We walked out on to the port and I saw a tiny fort surrounded by a dried-up moat.

'Just been bought by American businessmen for US $1 million. They have given it to the government. They want to make it historic museum of Gorée.'

'What kind of businessmen?'

'They are musicians. The New Brass Band from New Orleans. See, I explain you everything.'

At the restaurant, people were talking about everything but Gorée.

'I'm hot. Let's move in the shade.'

'Deux Fantas.'

'The fish round here is fantastic. Got a blue marlin last week. Three-hundred kilos.'

'Don't go in those toilets if you can help it.'

'Thirty minutes I'm hanging on, then this girl on the switchboard comes on. Are you calling abroad, she says. No, I said, I'm calling my wife.'

If you want to be horrified by the barbarism and brutality of slavery, don't go to Gorée. Go to Dakar airport. I have explained you.

*

I was being driven around the suburbs of Dakar by probably the worst taxi driver ever. He had failed to find the West African Central Bank, where I had had an appointment with the governor. It was pouring with rain and the taxi windows didn't work, so I was soaking wet. He was now failing to find my hotel. I caught sight of a sign – Société d'Exploitation des Resources Animales de Senegal – and asked him to stop. It was an abattoir, bien sûr, but it was also a vast market selling every type of cage bird under the soleil; one of the biggest animal markets in the world supplying pets to shops in Britain, France, Germany, the States, Japan.

I saw one cage full of parrots. 'How much are they?' I asked.

'CFA 80,000 each.' About £150. And there were probably hundreds in the cage.

In another cage I saw thousands of tiny birds with pink beaks and blue bodies sitting on a perch on top of one another. In another cage was a pile of what looked like orange boxes wrapped round with fine-mesh wire. Inside were little birds with red faces and red dots on their tails.

'How much are these?' I asked.

'Already sold.'

'Who to?'

'Germany.'

'The lot?'

'The lot.'

'How many do you sell in a week?'

'Thousands and thousands. I don't know, you must ask le patron.'

Le patron turned out to be Diallo Peet. Peet is the Arabic for bird. He virtually controls Senegal's booming trade in wild birds. He has over 1,000 agents throughout the country supplying him with wild birds. All the canaries and budgies in Britain probably come from Senegal.

'How do you catch them?' I asked one of Diallo Peet's assistants.

'You get a live bird, tie it to the ground, give it food and water. The other birds come. You catch them. It's easy.'

'You export them?'

'All over the world.'

'How many? Hundreds? Thousands?'

'Millions,' he laughed.

'Can anybody catch birds and send them to you?'

'No. You must have a licence.'

'And if I get a licence how many can I catch?'

'As many as you like. Some people catch 500. Some catch 1,000. Some catch 5,000 a year.'

'So how do you export them?'

'By air – Lufthansa, Air France, Sabena.'

'Are they all right going by air?'

'You send us day-old chicks for our chicken farms by air.'

'True,' I said. 'But what about health problems, guarantees, that kind of thing?'

'Health inspection is very strict,' he said.

How strict I don't know. The management of the société said the birds were healthy when they left Senegal. That was their duty. But they were not responsible for health regulations in the rest of the world.

On the way back to the hotel the taxi ran out of petrol. It began to rain again.

It's my last day. I've only been caught by traders twice; one selling spanners, the other, bottles of champagne with dirty rags stuffed down the neck. Which is not bad for the course.

I get a car to the airport. Normal check-in is three hours before departure. I arrive four hours before departure. That way I reckon I can avoid the traders who will be pestering the life out of passengers queuing to check in. There is nobody in sight, not even airline staff, but I'm not going to give up now. I go down to the staffroom of Air Afrique and persuade a girl I will be violently ill unless I can get through customs into the departure hall. She is suspicious, but it works. I check in the old black Delsey that travels with me everywhere and a brand new leather Louis Vuitton travelling companion full of the cassettes, towels, spectacles, weighing machines, textiles, wooden masks, bronze ornaments, T-shirts and miscellaneous junk I was forced to buy from my 15,000 friendly street traders in Dakar. It had to be a Vuitton because that was all the nice French lady in the Avenue Lamine Gueye had left.

I go through customs. The policeman thinks I'm crazy because I don't want to spend my last evening in Dakar. Finally I'm in the departure hall. Safe. No more traders. I bury myself in my book. The plane is called and I get on board. In the seat next to mine is an enormous woman – at least thirty stone. I ask for another seat. The plane is full. I clamber over her and squeeze into the three inches left between her and the outer skin of the plane. Eventually all the other, remarkably thin, passengers are on board. The door closes, the engines rev and we are airborne.

I breathe the best sigh of relief I can in the cramped space available. At last I am free from Senegalese street traders. Then I feel the person behind me tapping my shoulder. 'My friend. My friend,' a voice is saying. 'You are my friend ...'

TOGO

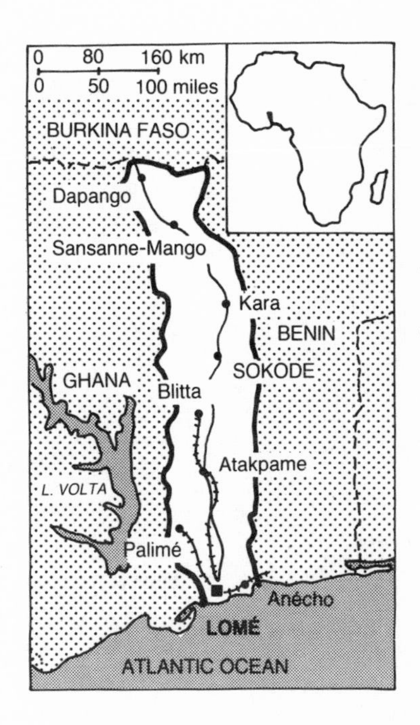

0 80 160 km
0 50 100 miles
BURKINA FASO
Dapango
Sansanne-Mango
Kara
BENIN
GHANA
SOKODE
Blitta
Atakpame
L. VOLTA
Palimé
Anécho
LOMÉ
ATLANTIC OCEAN

I couldn't believe it. Out of the corner of my eye, I thought I saw row after row of cats' heads lined up on the counter for sale. I looked again, and there they were. About forty cats' heads – and worse, forty pairs of eyes staring straight at me.

Less than 100 yards away were the fabulous five-star luxury hotels of Togo's capital with Olympic-size swimming pools, cocktail bars and restaurants serving vintage champagnes and premier clarets.

Grégoire (he had just given me his visiting card) was sitting on an oil drum. He got up and extended his hand. 'Bonjour, monsieur. Comment allez-vous?' he said.

'Bonjour, monsieur,' I said for all the world as if I was entering Yves St Laurent's salon. This was not, however, a Parisian haute-couture house but one of the biggest black magic markets in the world – or rather white magic, for Grégoire and his fellow shopkeepers in the market of Be, in Lomé, only dealt in herbs, powders, skulls, bones and feathers which did good to people, not harm.

Next to the cats' heads was a pile of lizard skins. On another stall were dead birds. Another was piled high with bones; the man in charge told me some were children's bones.

And sitting all around were the witchdoctors or féticheurs with their little bags containing their equivalent of a rosary and a collection of shells, skulls and bones. From time to time people would go up to them and whisper in their ears. The witchdoctor would give them a grigris, a type of armband to protect them from evil spirits. Occasionally you would also see girls and women all dressed in white. These are the féticheuses.

'What can I interest you in today?' Grégoire continued.

'No thank you. Just looking,' I said dismissively, quickly turning away from the ants and flies crawling out of a monkey carcass on the table.

Grégoire told me that voodoo was still very strong in parts of Togo. There were over forty ethnic groups in the country, most of whom had their own special form of voodoo. They had to bring in supplies from Niger and Mali to keep up with demand. Throughout the southern part of the country, the different groups have their own animal gods and taboos. Some worship lions, others pythons or crocodiles. In Be they worship the pigeon which is supposed to have saved their ancestors by covering up their footprints while they were trying to escape from a neighbouring tribe.

The Lamba worship Seon, a python, as well as the baobab and kapok trees. The Kabye believe their capital of Sahoude, or Kara as it is called today, was the home of the first men on earth. But be warned. In Togoville you're supposed to place an offering at the feet of their fetish before taking photographs otherwise they won't come out.

As we walked round the market, Grégoire showed me statuettes used by the Ewes to worship twins. Eight days after twins have been born the parents, and all the other twins in the area, go out into the bush and gather branches of certain plants with the left hand only. They put them in a jar containing seven days' supply of drinking and bathing water for the twins as an offering for the gods. Later on they repeat the ceremony, adding four roosters or four hens or two roosters and two hens depending on the sex of the twins and bury them in a hut in special pots under a mound of clay. From then on the hut is sacred to the twin gods. However, the Bassaris, he said, believed twins were a curse. If it was a boy and a girl, they would keep the boy. If the same, only the stronger would be allowed to survive. If the mother gave birth to twins again both would be killed.

Grégoire introduced me to some of his fellow stallholders. One man was selling ga-kokwes, a small bell used to summon a fetish. Another had a collection of cattle bells used by the Ewes, Minas and Watyis to create ghosts. And another seemed to be a witchdoctor doctor, if you see what I mean. He had a collection of healing herbs and potions. For ulcers, he recommended banana seeds, for anything from a scratch to an open wound, pepper leaves; and for sleeping sickness, he suggested boiling mango leaves and drinking the juice. We then got on to poisons. One old, old man told me he mixed cayman bile, crocodile scales, the dried heads of poisonous snakes and scorpion tails in a thick stew and threw in plant juices, bits of flesh and bones of rotten animal carcasses for good measure. Put that on the tip of your arrow, he said, and the slightest scratch will kill your victim.

The stallholder I really liked was Koffi, a big, fat, jolly man, always laughing and wiping his face with his great big hands. He showed me what he said was the best selling item in the market – a fetish telephone.

'How much?' I asked.

'Two and a half million francs,' he replied, or at least that's what it sounded like.

'E-hoh-gin-toh,' I gasped. He collapsed in laughter.

I'm no good at languages, but I always try to learn the basic phrases. Some are hard – I once spent two whole days trying to learn the Kabye for bonjour madame – but it's fun, if you don't go as far as a Gentleman of Experience writing in 1890 in *A Guide to the Native Languages of Africa*: 'In the matter of language it is always best to go to a little more trouble and learn the exact equivalent if possible. "I am an Englishman and require instant attention to the damage done to my solar topee" is far better than any equivocation that may be meant well but will gain little respect.'

I prefer the equivocation. Neither do I agree with a Gentleman of Quality who wrote four years later: 'Why is there no marmalade available?' is better understood in the form "Quelle marmalade non?" "Bring marmalade" may be simply rendered as "Marmalade demandez", always remembering that the z is silent as in "demanday". The little English joke about jam may be easily translated if one wishes to amuse the proprietor: "Hier, marmalade; demain, marmalade; mais jamais marmalade de jour." Such little pleasantries are often appreciated.'

I'm halfway between experience and quality. My Lingala, for

example, is not very good, but it improves once I get into the villages in Zaire or Congo. I can say the odd word in Arabic, enough to get invited to the local mosque. But my best language is Mina, which is spoken along the coast in Togo and across the border into Benin, almost up to the Nigerian border. But it's difficult because not only do you have to remember the words, but you must memorise the intonation.

I was with an Italian priest once in Anécho, a pretty little town on the coast. We were sitting outside the church watching the dangerous surf.

The waves are so strong and the current along the coast so vicious that they are sweeping away the land. They have already destroyed coastal roads and swallowed up one or two smaller villages. Now they are threatening some of the small towns and holiday hotels. The current, which in a year can sweep away over 1.5 million tons of sand and soil, is one of the strongest in the world.

Talk to a thousand experts and you get two thousand explanations, but most theories blame the construction of the Akosombo dam along the coast in Ghana in 1961 which upset the flow of the River Niger. This would not have been so bad if the Togolese had not then built their international deep-sea port in Lomé, plus a 1,300-metre breakwater. Suddenly the currents had nowhere to go. The currents on the west dumped their sand from Ghana and turned back on themselves. The currents from the east headed for the coast.

'Unless something is done we will have no coast,' one of the villagers in Kpeme had told me. 'Ten years ago the water was there,' he pointed to an area twenty metres away. 'Today it is here. They must do something.'

At first the authorities thought a bank of sandstone unearthed by the current itself would do the trick. But within weeks that too had been conquered. They then thought it would be cheaper to build a new hotel set above a new village than to protect the coastline. And at £2 million for just one kilometre that's what they were planning to do until I suppose the EC and others stepped in with a loan.

The priest and I were talking about African languages and showing off to each other. He, of course, knew much more than I did.

'I must tell you,' he said, 'I've been learning the mass in Mina. It's taken me ages, but I found a book with the mass in Mina written by an old missionary,' he leant across and whispered, 'and today I'm going to surprise everybody. They'll be so happy. Some of the local priests say mass in their own language, but this will be the first time one of us has done it.'

'Must be like learning Chinese,' I said.

'You must remember the music, forget the words, that's the secret,' the good father said, tapping his ear. 'It will give me a chance to get my own back. When I first came I gave sermons in French and asked the boys to interpret. Trouble is I would say, You mustn't do that; that's forbidden. And the boys would say the opposite. I wondered why the congregations were getting bigger every Sunday.'

Soon it was time for mass. I walked into the church and sat at the back, checking which side the men were sitting. In some countries men and women split up. Once I ended up surrounded by women smiling much more than usual. The priest entered and the church exploded with a hymn. The singing in African churches is really singing, not like our self-conscious murmurings. I even joined in myself. The priest reached the steps at the foot of the altar, the singing stopped and the priest intoned in a deep, solemn voice, 'Maw-wenge fey-oh'.

Everybody looked at each other. A group of children kneeling in front of me started laughing. A fat lady walking up the aisle buried her face in her shawl. 'Lay fee oh-chum,' continued the priest. The smiles now turned to laughter. Children were rolling all over the benches, the women slapping each other with their handkerchiefs. A big man was laughing and mopping his brow like Satchmo.

'Lay dee poh.' The church exploded. The old man next to me flopped down on the bench, burying his head in his hands.

'Tohsh ma-voh. Heyey ma-voh. Amen.' People were now clutching their sides and running out of the church. I joined them and practically got drowned in the tears. Outside I spotted someone I knew. 'What's going on?' I asked.

'He was speaking our language,' he said.

'What's wrong with that?'

'The intonation,' he said, dabbing his eyes. 'What does the priest say at the beginning of mass? He prays to God the Father, Who art in heaven.'

'So what did the priest say?'

'He said, The great big monkey, who lives all the time in the trees, is going to stay there for ever and ever and ever.' And he collapsed laughing all over again.

Eventually, in spite or perhaps because of my intonation, Koffi's price collapsed to around CFA 1,000, which still wasn't bad as the fetish telephone was just a piece of painted wood with a hole drilled in the centre and attached to it a peg with a piece of string. To use the telephone, Koffi told me, you take the peg out of the hole, make your wish to the telephone then trap it inside by putting the peg back as quickly as possible. Trouble is, it only works early in the morning before you've had anything to eat. It seemed cheap at the price. In any case, I thought, it would probably work as well as the phone in my office.

The first wish I would make with it, I told Koffi, was that somebody bought the other phones for two and a half million francs, each. That did it. We immediately became the best of friends and he showed me the whole voodoo world of Lomé; fetish convents, fetish hospitals, fetish temples.

'And now,' said Koffi, 'we must visit the witchdoctor.' We drove out of Lomé on the coast road to Anécho and Benin. About 40 kilometres out we turned left and headed towards Agbadrafo and the Hotel du Lac. There we jumped into a precarious shallow dug-out canoe and paddled across Lake Togo. It took about fifteen minutes. It was nearly 100 degrees, and getting hotter. Togoville is the home of the descendants of King Nlapa who in 1884 signed a treaty with Germany giving them control of the area and virtually creating modern Togo. Today, it is a voodoo stronghold, where men and women devote their lives to the god Vodoun. They shave their heads, wear white and remain shut off from everyday life.

We were met by the children. Although Togoville is by no means cut off, few people manage to make the trip, so visitors attract attention. The village is carved out of red sand. The houses, many of which have stood for generations, are small and squat. Outside each is a small enclosure and by each doorway are the small mounds of earth which serve as altars to their gods.

The Ewes believe the world was created by Lissa and Mahou. They have well over 600 gods, such as Ebiosso, the god of thunder, and Sakpata, the god of smallpox. In Glidji they start their New Year in September with four days and nights of spectacular singing and dancing to the god Egou, during which time they consult their oracles. If the oracles produce a white stone it means they are in for a good year. A black stone means a year of hardship.

As the oracles had forecast a good year, we had been told that the witchdoctor in Togoville sometimes agreed to see visitors. Koffi told the children we would like to pay him our respects – in Togoville the witchdoctor still rules like a king – and a young man called Koffi Koffi offered to help us. He took us further into the village which seemed deserted although we knew people were watching us. It was difficult to walk along the steep, narrow paths since over the years the rains had carved out deep channels in the clay and rock. If we were going to see the witchdoctor, Koffi Koffi told us, we would have to change into traditional dress. So I exchanged my pinstripes for a dark green cloth tied around my waist.

After a wait in a courtyard dotted with small altars and bones and skulls burnt white by the sun, Koffi Koffi told us we could go in. The house was about twelve foot square, dark and surprisingly cool. Sitting facing us was the witchdoctor; he was very old, very lined and looked very weak. He wore a black robe thrown over one shoulder like a toga and a hat or, I suppose, crown made of basketwork like an upside-down cake stand. In front of him were two long rush mats. Koffi Koffi told us to kneel on the mats and pay our respects by bowing very low and clapping. After that we were allowed to sit on the floor.

I started in French to thank the witchdoctor, but Koffi Koffi said we had to give him our questions and he would interpret. I thanked the witchdoctor for seeing us and said we had wanted to visit him for some time. I asked how old he was. No reply. I asked him about Togoville. He said he was the head man and had four people to help him.

He showed us an old bag made of alligator skin; inside were shells, teeth and old bones. He also showed us a faded photograph of his father in full regalia taken around the turn of the century, surrounded by German officers.

People were coming in and out, paying their respects then sitting listening to what we were saying. Koffi Koffi considered our questions carefully before translating, and the witchdoctor was slow with his replies. These were usually only one or two words, sometimes a grunt, but Koffi Koffi always gave us a long and elaborate translation in impeccable French.

When we had been there nearly thirty minutes, the witchdoctor suddenly clapped his hands and two men appeared carrying a coconut shell and an old bottle. He had decided to offer us da-ha, or palm wine. He poured some into the shell and passed it around. First, the men closest to him had a drink, next Koffi, then the others sitting along the wall. Finalement it was my turn. All eyes were turned on me. I took a deep breath – and a tiny sip. If it was not raw alcohol, it couldn't have been far off. I wanted fresh air. I turned to Koffi, and forgetting where I was I said in English, 'Ask him if we can take his picture then we'll go.'

At this a man in a blue robe sitting next to the witchdoctor said to me, also in English, 'You are English?'

Taken aback, I asked where he had learnt English.

'In London,' he said, to my astonishment. 'I used to work for Guinness in Park Royal. I lived in Paddington for years.'

After that we were the toast of the village. They brought us more da-ha, then skewered meat and banana fritters and coconuts. And more da-ha. The man who spoke English turned out to be the witchdoctor's son. He had studied at the local school and gone on to colleges and universities in Cameroon, Montreal and Paris. He had worked for Guinness in London and Dublin, but as his father was old he had decided to exchange his house in Paddington for a red sand hut in Togoville and had returned home with his wife who was from the same village and his two children.

*

To me Togo is the Dom Perignon of French Africa; exciting, refreshing, exquisite and very bubbly. It is a country on its toes. It gets up early, it starts work early and it gets things done. It's bright and crisp and efficient. The streets are swept every day. Pick up the telephone and you can dial anywhere in the world. Ask for ice with your drink and you get ice. Tell the driver to collect you at eight o'clock and he is there. And everybody is friendly and polite and willing to help. Walk along the beach or stroll along the backstreets of Lomé and people will smile and whisper bonjour. Try that in parts of anglophone Africa and you'll be lucky to come back alive. Drop into a roadside bar for a drink and you'll be given a drink. No hassling. Try that in other parts of Africa and you'll be lucky to get away with your wallet. Or go into one of their fabulous luxury restaurants and order the best caviar, lobsters the size of tennis rackets and Chateau Margaux 1959 or even 1961 and without a bat of an eyelid it will be on your table in minutes, impeccably prepared, exquisitely cooked and beautifully served. C'est une terre bénie des dieux.

If you drive across West Africa with your eyes closed, you can tell immediately you hit Togo. The car stops hurtling you back and forth. Your stomach leaves your mouth and returns to its rightful place. You are on straight, smooth roads. Togolese, or should I say Lomans, believe in good roads.

The supermarkets are packed with the necessities of life: foie gras, snails, truffles, cheeses, clarets, champagnes. Le Grand Marché, the traditional market in the centre of Lomé and all the little markets all over the country are bursting with food. A far cry from the appalling conditions next door in Ghana. I've been in supermarkets in Accra which were empty except for one shelf of custard powder, costing £5 a tin. So it's no surprise to see Ghanaian border guards and customs officers shopping in Lomé, the very thing they are supposed to stop their fellow countrymen from doing.

Pop your head round one of the battered doors along any street in Lomé that say Lotosport, the national lottery, and you won't see dirty benches and dirtier raffle tickets as you do practically all over Africa, but electronic gambling machines with a range of microcomputer-based games. Press a button and you can win US $6,000.

The Togolese are genuinely friendly and organised, in no way snarling or suspicious or waiting for the opportunity to trick you. They immediately make you feel as though you've been there for years. In other parts of francophone Africa, the street signs say boldly, 'Interdit d'uriner ici'. In Togo they say, 'Pour raison d'hygiène il est formellement interdit d'uriner tout de long de ce mur. Merci beaucoup.' Maybe it's something to do with being a small country; its coastline is barely 50 kilometres long and it covers just 55,000 square kilometres, so it retains a family feeling. Perhaps it's something to do with its present state of development.

'The policies of nearly all African governments favour the urban elite by keeping food prices low, or by seeing to it that profits from major cash-cropping schemes go to urban-based companies and industries,' writes Lloyd Timberlake in his angry book, *Africa in Crisis.* 'Governments see little economic motive for investing in the rural hinterland. One of Africa's many vicious cycles is at work here: government policies degrade the rural resource base; degraded farmland produces little of economic value.'

He should come to Togo, the exception that proves the rule. For in spite of its luxury hotels and thriving port and profitable steel mill, it's still very much a rural community. The emphasis is on agriculture, the need to be self-sufficient. It is still very tribal; respect for the family and village elders still marked, even among young people.

Togo supplies most of the administrators and officials to Africa's international organisations; most of the teachers in West Africa; most of the chefs and hotel staff all over Africa. A Togolese, Kofi Yamgnane, was the first African to be elected mayor of a French town, Saint-Coulitz, in 1989. Another Togolese, Tete Michel Kpomasoie, was not only the first black African ever to visit the Arctic but virtually became an eskimo; he learnt their language, adopted their customs and absorbed their lifestyle. And as a black he made the same impact as the white explorers did when they first arrived in Africa. He became a legend; people came out of their houses to stare, children mobbed him in the street, touching his hair to see if it was real. 'They called me Michel the Giant. They couldn't believe I was real. At first they were afraid, then curious,' he says.

Somehow the Togolese make things work. It is sans doute la meilleure entrée anybody could possibly have to les splendeurs de l'Afrique francophone. But this was not always the case. From 1914 for nearly forty years the country stagnated. Exports were the same in 1949 as in 1914. The breakthrough came in the 1970s. The price of phosphate, Togo's biggest export earner – they are the second largest supplier in the world – increased fourfold. With virtually no infrastructure, no investments and no foreign earnings the government, backed by the World Bank and every aid organisation under the sun, decided to make a dash for growth, to use the income from phosphate to provide the basics as well as to turn themselves into a country which could attract additional foreign investment. They enlarged their phosphate works at Kpeme, built an oil refinery, a steel works, textile plants and enlarged their port. To attract foreign spenders they built modern hotels and a giant 35-storey international convention centre, which has since hosted the famous Lomé Convention. Then in 1975–76 the price of phosphate collapsed from US $68 a tonne to just US $14. Togo's bid for economic freedom was in shreds.

The bankers and advisers who had urged Togo to spend, spend, spend now insisted on cut, cut, cut. Government expenditure was cut back by almost 20 percent. A 'national solidarity tax' was introduced. Living standards fell by around 20 percent. The IMF stepped in. Then, still reeling from the cuts, Togo was hit by one of its worst droughts for centuries.

But, again, Togo pulled through and is today restructuring. It has privatised over eighteen state enterprises, closed down sixteen, liquidated eight and in the process cut government expenditure, eliminated state subsidies, strengthened its economy, introduced a local investment code, a balanced development policy and completely revitalised its private sector. It is a big World Bank and IMF success story.

It is still one of the poorest countries in the world. Per capita income is less than US $250 a year, way below the World Bank's definition of poverty of US $400 a year. Yet Togo means business. In agriculture, a disaster area for most developing countries, it is the only country in sub-Sahara Africa to be self-sufficient in basic foodstuffs, and they even send aid to surrounding countries, including the once oil-rich Nigeria.

Lomé is the major banking and financial centre in West Africa. With the recent opening of ECOBank, the private sector development bank sponsored by the Economic Community of West African States, Lomé now boasts twelve national and international banks – more than 50 percent of all banks in West Africa – employing more than 1,300 people, over 90 percent of them Togolese, making banking a major sector of the economy. With more international banks eager to follow suit not only because of the financial infrastrucure of the country and its liberal tax and foreign exchange regulations, but also because of its first-class telecommunications services and living conditions, the government and banking community have drawn up combined in-depth plans for its continued expansion as a financial centre.

A Centre de Formation Bancaire has just been established capable of training 300 banking students at three different degree levels including a special Togolese banking diploma. Staffed by nine professors, two lawyers and eighteen practical bankers, the Centre is also open in the evenings for students to study after work. They organise courses and seminars in Atakpame, Kara and other towns. Plans are also in hand to establish correspondence courses.

Under the director, Mr Kokou Tingue, students – 10 percent are women – study mathematics, accountancy, statistics, computers as well as banking. There are plans to add English to the curriculum. Pass rates are high, and the Centre is attracting students from other parts of Africa. A similar banking training centre has also just been opened by the Union Togolaise de Banque, one of the country's biggest banking groups.

On the technical side, Togo has CENETI, its information technology and computer centre. With more main-frame computers installed in government offices than in any other country in the region, they are again determined to have trained technical staff as the need arises. They are even planning to launch a special course at Lomé's Benin University on computer maintenance. Under director Ayaovi Figah, they not only analyse government ministries and banks and assess their computer requirements, they have developed a growing list of outside commercial clients requiring consultancy and advice.

Finally, Togo has been playing a leading role in developing and co-ordinating banking policies for the region. They are investigating ways of harmonising all banking documentation as well as trying to establish a bilingual training centre for bank staff from all over the region.

In management and training Togo has an enviable reputation for administration and efficiency. Their Ecole Nationale d'Administration is francophone Africa's equivalent of the top French grandes écoles. 'Our standards are very high. We can only accept the best. There are a great many students to choose from, and there are limited opportunities in our government service,' Professor Nakom K. Baba, one of the directors of study at the school told me.

When I first met him students were preparing to take the entry examinations – harder than similar examinations in France. Many were already at schools and universities with perhaps two degrees. They spoke French and English. Others, already in government service with additional professional qualifications, wanted further experience. Last year over 300 people passed the entry examination, but only fifty could be accepted. Students who are not accepted have to take the examinations again to be reconsidered; if they are still not accepted that is their last chance.

Run by a professor of law, Mr Nessan Acoutey, who studied and taught in France, the school only has five permanent staff. All the lecturers are ministers or officials working full-time in the Togolese civil service. Overall, the school has 170 lecturers who know the theory as well as the practice of government administration. 'The emphasis is on practical knowledge. We want our students to know what happens in government,' says Professor Baba.

And in presentation and ceremonial. If anybody can turn a boring political event into a spectacular occasion it is the Togolese. Conferences can bore one to distraction, but people flock to them when they are held in Togo, thanks to les Animateurs, the thousands of singing and dancing young people who grace every official event, like a showbusiness Household Cavalry or the Beefeaters designed and managed by Walt Disney. They are a million times better at it than the Americans.

The pot was now quite a pot. Assana Hougbegnou had hollowed out the inside and was smoothing the surface. In a few minutes she had transformed a lump of red clay into a pot, using nothing but water, skill and backbreaking effort.

'Do you like making pots? You're very good at it,' I said.

'That is my work.'

'But you must like it?'

'I like it,' she said without committing herself.

'Who taught you?'

'My mother taught me everything. She could make pots and jugs and dishes. She was very good. I can't make jugs and dishes. They are too difficult.'

'How many pots do you make in a day?'

'Sometimes six, sometimes seven. It depends on the clay. If the clay is good I can make maybe eight. If the clay is bad I can make two.'

'Where does the clay come from?'

'From the village.'

'Is there lots of it? Will you ever run out?'

'Lots and lots,' she laughed. 'Enough for millions of pots.'

The thought of making millions of pots would have terrified me, but it obviously appealed to her even though her potter's wheel was not a wheel but a platform. And instead of the platform moving, Assana moved round and round the platform, which was just inches off the ground, moulding her giant waterpots.

According to the Society for International Development in Rome, 80 percent of agricultural energy in Africa is provided by women and 84 percent of arable land is tilled by hand – women's hands. What machinery there is, is used by men. Most farmers and food growers are women: 85 percent of rural women work in agriculture and 80 percent of the food consumed by the family is produced, processed and stored by women. Women manage all aspects of the food system; they plant and tend the crops, they harvest, process, store and prepare the grains, do the cooking and make the cooking pots.

I asked if she was tired. The Society says that women work twice as hard as men. They spend twenty hours a week looking for and carrying water and firewood. And in their spare time they care for the home, bear children and provide the social security systems of their communities – they care for the young, the sick, the old, and shelter the homeless.

'No, I'm not tired. I have work to do,' she said giving the clay a splash of water.

'Do you do this every day?'

'If I don't we don't eat.'

'What about weekends: Saturday and Sunday?'

'We must eat Saturday and Sunday as well.'

It was around 100 degrees. She had been working for over five hours, and she had a baby strapped around her. She had another four hours' work in front of her, then had to walk four miles for water, prepare and cook the meal for the family which included untold numbers of in-laws, cousins, aunts and uncles. Then if she was lucky a few hours' sleep before starting all over again.

'Why don't you make the pots where the clay is? Surely bringing it here gives you extra work?'

'But here I am with my family. If they want me I am here.'

Of course. Why do I ask such silly questions?

I had left Fazao, about 600 kilometres north of Lomé, in the early morning, driving through two wildlife reserves, Koue covering 40,000 hectares and Kamassi covering 17,000 hectares, famous for their wide range of monkeys, including cynocephali, better known as dog-faced baboons because of their long faces and their bark. There are also green monkeys and the impressive black-haired quadrumana chimpanzees with their projecting jaws, wide ears and long front legs.

Fazao, which is about the centre of Togo, is becoming more and more popular as a safari centre with the opening of the luxurious Hotel Fazao, although the villagers' habit of welcoming each guest by tearing the head off a chicken and dripping the blood over the bonnet of their car does not exactly encourage people to come back.

Now I was about 250 kilometres further south in a little

village just outside Atakpame, Togo's crossroads city. Not only is it on the main north-south highway, it stands on the main Lomé-Blita railway line and in addition provides access east-west through Togo and on into Ghana. It has been occupied by the Ewe, the Ana and later the Akposso. While Togo was a German colony, Atakpame was the favourite town of the German administrators. Slightly east, in Kamina, was the radio station they installed in 1914 with direct access to Berlin. It was blown up on August 26 1914 prior to the local German army surrendering to the French and British.

The area is famous for two things: first the cemetery at Chakpeli, where one half is reserved for 'good' people, who are buried in elaborate L-shaped tombs, the other half for 'bad' people, buried in an ordinary ditch. Second the local dance, the chebe, performed on stilts five metres high, which is quite terrifying even when you are standing on the ground watching.

When I first arrived in Atakpame I noticed the old German warehouse had been completely revamped to become the headquarters of a unique, thriving, work-for-food scheme, involving over 8,000 people who were being resettled as a result of the construction of a $140 million dam further east at Nangbeto. Designed to provide electricity to Togo and Benin, it covers 180 square kilometres including a giant manmade lake.

With previous projects of this scale in other parts of the world little attention was paid to the social and humanitarian aspects of resettling large numbers of people, but Togo has insisted on a positive resettlement programme. They wanted the people affected to feel they were involved, so they called in the World Food Programme, and with Mr Richard Dalrymple, their Togo representative, worked out a special US $1 million programme in which everybody is encouraged to build their new village themselves – not for money, but for food.

Assana's husband, Koffi, told me he gets 200 gms of corn, 200 gms of flour, 30 gms of vegetable oil, 20 gms of meat and 20 gms of dried peas a day for helping to build not only a new house for his family but the new village of Adigo as well. He has also been bringing home two sacks of flour, one sack of rice, fifty cans of sardines, four cans of cooking oil and one-tenth of a sack of dried peas a month.

'A construction company could have done the work, but the people had always built their own houses. The government didn't want to upset their culture. They wanted something that was in keeping with the environment,' Mr Dalrymple told me. 'They wanted to compensate them for the work, but not with money.'

A year before they would have to move, teams visited all the affected villages and explained the situation to them, many of whom did not even know the dam was being built. They told them that they would have to be rehoused away from the flood waters. Areas had been selected, but they could choose where they wanted to live. The government provided skilled masons and carpenters and offered to provide transport every day to take people from their present homes to the site of their new village and return them in the evening. 'The villagers liked the idea. They needed the work. Skilled people do the skilled work, they help and do the labouring,' Mr Dalrymple said.

The villagers who were moving home only would be paid for the nine months it was estimated it would take to build their new villages. Farmers and others who were living off the land that was to be flooded would be paid for an additional nine months because they needed the extra time to prepare their new land, and plant and harvest their crops.

With everything donated by other countries – meat from Finland, fish from Italy, Japan and Norway, cereals from the US, which also supplied vegetable oil together with Holland and Sweden, and peas from Canada – the programme very quickly became known as 'Vive PAM' throughout the region. The old German warehouse was taken over as the central distribution point. From there every two to three weeks the resettlement teams visit the villages. They stack all the food in the centre of the village and call everybody to the distribution: those who are not working as well as those who are. For distributing food in such a public way is meant not only to reward the good guys, but to chide the bad guys. All the villagers are called out by name. The workers are then invited to take their rice and cornflour, each being greeted by a hearty handshake and a cheer. The names of those who are not working are followed by silence.

Assana thought it was a good idea. It made the young people work, although it was harder for the older men and women.

'How old are you?' I asked her.

'Tuitième,' she replied.

'How old is tuitième?'

'It's what they say in town. Instead of saying dix-huitième, vingt-huitième or trente-huitième, you say tuitième. It's nicer.' She laughed.

'So how long have you been married?' I asked passant du coq a l'âne.

'A long time.'

'Is that your first baby?' I asked, nodding towards the lump tied around her back.

'No, he is my fourth,' she said. 'Two died.'

'Do you like children?'

'Of course. I am a mother. Mothers like children.'

Of course they do. Why was I asking such questions? Well, it was hot and she didn't seem to mind talking.

'Why did the babies die?'

'They just died.'

'Were they sick?'

'They were sick.'

'Do you take them to hospital?'

'There is no hospital here, just a clinic. The hospital is in the town. The first baby who died, I didn't take him. He just died. The second baby I took to the clinic. They gave him medicine.'

'What kind of medicine?'

'Just medicine.'

'What was wrong with him?'

'He was just sick. He died.'

Sounded like another case of a baby dying of diarrhoea because their mothers don't give them a lump of sugar. The same thing happened to Anna Alipui, another hardworking lady. She started selling cigarettes when she was nine years old, and built up quite a business. Then she bought a fish-smoking unit and started selling produce in the marketplace. When I met her just after her baby died she was planning to buy more smokers and start exporting to neighbouring countries, with the aid of Women's World Banking, a women-only development bank started ten years ago which operates extensively throughout Africa and the world.

'We help women who would normally not qualify for bank loans: small-scale women farmers, women working in the marketplace, women cooking fish and selling it by the side of the road,' one of the bank's directors, retired Ghanaian judge Annie Jiagge, told me once. 'These are people below the poverty line that rural banks are not interested in. Even our indigenous promotion of capital, the susu system – similar to a credit union – is woefully inadequate for this requirement. We give them some money, then as their business expands we take them to the commercial banks and provide the security for them to borrow more.'

Woman's World Banking also organises business management courses to help the women operate more efficiently and profitably. The whole operation, unique in the developing world, is low-key and very small-scale. Loans to buy special Chokor smokers for fish, for example, are as little as $10–$15. But it is that vital first step. With most women able to earn some $6 a day selling fish, the loan is secure and easily repayable. 'The women always pay back their loans faithfully, they are very responsible,' Mrs Jiagge said. 'They can make a lot of money once we help them get started, and often it's not long before the women are earning more than their husbands. First you see them putting a tin roof on their houses, then they buy bricks and build a wall inside the mud wall. When they have enough bricks they take down the mud wall.

'National planning fails to recognise the role of women in development,' Mrs Jiagge said. 'Women are by-passed by international technical and financial assistance, although they are the main producers of food and are engaged in marketing. About 60 percent of all retail trade is in the hands of women.'

The biggest business hurdles facing women like Assana and Anna are lack of capital, which Women's World Banking is beginning to remedy, and lack of education. 'Women welcome new skills and equipment to minimise waste of energy and time,' Mrs Jiagge said. 'But the majority of women in Africa are illiterate. The choice of technology must be based on what is acceptable to women; it must be related to what is already familiar to them. This is why upgrading traditional technology is important to increase productivity and provide purchasing power at poverty level. It is an area of development that deserves international assistance.'

The Chokor smoker had enabled hundreds of African women to escape from poverty and to become successful, independent businesswomen. An improvement on the traditional smoker, it revolutionised the fish smoking industry in parts of Africa and proved so successful that UNICEF and the UN Food and Agriculture Organisation have introduced it to other parts of Africa.

Another example of adapting technology for women was the donkey plough. 'If most food crops are produced by women it's absurd to give farms bullock ploughs,' Mrs Jiagge said. 'Donkey ploughs are far easier for women to manage.'

With the right technology and financial assistance from Women's World Banking, she saw an increasingly important role for women in development. 'It is not enough merely to give women the vote or create equal opportunities in education,' she said. 'What's necessary is a bold progressive policy in favour of the advancement of women if the untapped reservoir of women's energy and talent is to be unleashed for national development. It's like running a race on a circular track. An athlete near the inner circle has a shorter distance to run than one on the outer circle, so the athlete on the inside is given a handicap. There must be bias in favour of women in education and job opportunities to give them a fair chance to win the race.'

Assana's pot was almost finished. It was about three foot high and bulged out to about two foot across. It was smooth and moist. Now she was giving it a neat circular design around the neck, running around it with her hand on the neck to ensure an even design. If I hadn't seen the original lump of clay I would never have believed it possible to produce a waterpot using nothing but your hands and occasional splashes of water.

'What do the other members of your family do?'

'They are working as well.'

'And your mother? Your father?'

'He can't work. He has problems with his foot. He can't walk. I work for him.'

'Can't he help you?' I asked, in as neutral a tone as I could.

'He can't walk. He can't work.'

'What does he do?'

'He is in our house.'

'Does he look after the children?'

'Looking after the children is my work. There is nothing he can do. I must look after him. It is my duty. If not he will leave us. Where would he go? What would he do?'

Assana was making pots to help look after her father. At Lomé's impressive international airport one Friday evening I met two girls doing the same thing, although in a completely different line of business. I was watching lots of heavy, anonymous-looking boxes being wheeled out to a waiting KLM plane and wondering whether anything fishy was going on. There seemed to be a lot of activity around the boxes but nobody doing anything in particular. I asked a friendly policeman. 'It's for the gold. We call it the Friday gold rush,' he said.

'But how can you export gold when you don't produce it?' I said.

'That's easy,' he said. 'Smuggling.'

'But that's dangerous.'

'Of course it's dangerous. It's against the law. We're very strict about it.'

'Where does it come from?'

'Ghana.'

'Who smuggles it in?'

'Plenty try, not many succeed. The best smugglers are girls.' He spoke as one professional about another. 'If you want to talk to smugglers, talk to those girls over there.' He nodded to two Ghanaians standing by the security barriers – well dressed, in their twenties. 'They always come here to say goodbye to their gold. We know them well. They're very nice.' Un bénéfice énorme.

'Why don't you arrest them?'

'Smuggling gold is only an offence in Ghana. You're not allowed to take gold out of the country. But there is nothing to stop you bringing gold into Togo, it's not an offence here. It's good for the country.'

The girls told me they were sisters, born just inside the Togo border but brought up in Ghana. When they were young there was no work in Togo so the family had moved across the border. Their father had been a taxi driver in Accra, their mother worked as a nurse at the British High Commission. They lived well, but not luxuriously. Today, however, they were in luxury. They had a house in Accra and two houses in Lomé although they preferred to rent a suite at the Hotel 2 Fevrier. Their father had now retired. They had bought him a house just outside Accra.

The policeman walked back into the airport for a drink and I asked the sisters how much money they made.

'Lots and lots,' they giggled.

'And you don't pay any tax?' I said. They laughed even more.

'But isn't it dangerous?' I said. 'Aren't you frightened of going to gaol?'

The taller girl with big purple earrings replied. 'We won't be caught,' she said. 'We're careful. We're professional. There are lots of people trying to smuggle gold out of Ghana. Lots get caught – they're not careful.'

'So how are you careful?'

'It's easy. First, we know the police,' she said. 'They are our friends. We know they have to arrest people so we help them. If we know somebody else is trying to smuggle gold we tell the police. It helps them. And,' they laughed, 'it helps us.'

'But that's unfair,' I said.

'It's business,' they said together.

'Where do you get the gold from?'

'We work with people in Accra and Obuasi who give it to us and we take it across the border.'

'But where do these people get the gold from?'

'From the galamseyers, the small-scale goldminers.'

In an attempt to control illegal smuggling, keep the money in the country and bolster their economy, the Ghanaians had just legalised small-scale mining. As a result it was now de rigueur to be a small-scale miner among truanting children, farmers, drop-outs and, of course, the miners themselves.

'The miners are always taking gold out of the mines. For them it's simple,' the younger girl put in. 'I met somebody who worked in the mines in South Africa. He said it was impossible to take anything out, security was very, very strict. It's not like that in Ghana.'

Purple earrings continued. 'And people win gold by playing cards, or hide it away and keep it until they are desperate for money. And today in Ghana lots of people are desperate for money, so we get lots of gold.'

They made it sound like a game, but Ghana loses millions of dollars through theft and smuggling. The State Gold Mining Corporation and Ashanti Gold Corporation together reckon they lose 20 percent of their production, around US $25 million every year; Ghana Consolidated Diamonds claim as much as 70 percent goes the same way.

But wasn't it dangerous, I insisted, taking the gold across the border? 'If we have time it's not dangerous at all. We just wait for the best time then cross the border. It is dangerous when you must get the gold across by a certain time and that's the time the police have a special drive on to catch smugglers. Or if the border is closed.'

'What do you do then?'

'If it's very strict at the border we'll go up country and walk across. We used to live there, we could do it with our eyes shut.'

The younger girl looked serious again. 'There was one time when it was dangerous. The border was closed so we went up country, but the area was full of soldiers. We had to get the gold across, so we thumbed a lift all the way up to the border with Burkina Faso. It was a black Range Rover with the British High Commission in Accra.'

What would have happened, I thought, if the car had been stopped and the gold discovered by the police. Or maybe it wouldn't have been discovered, if you see what I mean.

'We then got in a lorry and went across the border. It took a long time, but we made our delivery on time.'

'How much gold can you carry at a time? Surely it's pretty heavy stuff?'

'We don't have to carry much. Sometimes we just hide it, sometimes we carry it. Once we hid a big load underneath the car and drove across the border.'

I told them what the policeman said about them saying goodbye to their gold.

'We always watch the plane taking off. Then we know we've finished the job,' they said.

We walked back to the bar. 'What will you have?' I asked. 'A beer? Une boisson douce?'

'Oh,' they giggled. 'We always drink champagne.' Sure enough two waiters were already heading towards us carrying Dom Perignon. Les fruits du travail. Outside I saw two policemen taking their hats off and smiling broadly, obviously hoping their daughters would take after them.

'What happens now?' I asked Assana.

'The pot dries in the sun. Then the man from town comes with his lorry and takes it away to sell.'

'Does he pay you a lot of money? I bet you're the richest lady in the country.'

She laughed. The idea obviously appealed to her. 'No,' she said, 'but I look after my family. He pays me CFA 100.'

'For one pot.'

'Sometimes, for a big one. He says they are difficult to sell. He is working hard for me.'

One hundred francs is about 10p which is shocking when they involve so much time and effort. But it helps to keep her and her family, and it's much more than many other people ever get.

'Spaghetti? You make spaghetti? Here? In Togo?' I was sitting at the bar in the five-star Sarakawa Hotel on the beach talking to a small, bustling man. He had even won awards for his spaghetti. From the Italians. He was Guido Savi de Tove. His father had lived in Italy, hence the name. Until ten years ago he had run the state textile factories. Today his factory at Agoenyive, ten kilometres from the centre of Lomé, was the first in West Africa producing spaghetti, vermicelli and tagliatelle.

'I can remember when I was a small boy I saw a Togolese chef who made his own spaghetti. All the time he used to say, Congo, Madagascar, macaroni. He said only rich people could buy it. It was a luxury product,' he told me. 'Ten years ago people only had maize or manioc. They had rice on special occasions. Now everybody eats rice. I thought I would do the same with macaroni. People want a better diet, even in the interior.'

For over twenty years Mr Savi de Tove had worked for other people. 'I always wanted to work for myself,' he said. 'But people in Togo don't like taking risks in business. They like trading because there is not so much risk and you get your money quicker. I like taking calculated risks.'

He asked if I would like to visit his factory. I accepted immediately. What struck me was how simple everything was. The spaghetti machine looked like the giant containers you see on the backs of lorries blocking the streets. The semolina and water you pour in one end and out of the other comes spaghetti. You want macaroni? Turn a switch on the container. Vermicelli? Turn the switch again. Staff were collecting the spaghetti and packing it into boxes. It was a marvellous operation.

With finance from the banks he had set up the $300,000 factory with materials and equipment from Italy. At first they were producing only 500 tons of macaroni a year. Now, working day and night five days a week, production is over 1,000 tons. Maximum capacity is 2,000 tons although with additional drying facilities they could push it to 2,500 tons. As they have become more experienced the work force has dropped from eighteen to fourteen.

But to Mr Savi de Tove production was only part of the operation. 'Our success is based on semolina, water and marketing. Marketing, that's what counts,' he said. And marketing is behind everything he does. First the name. 'We call our macaroni Ludo. Everybody plays Ludo. They remember the name. Small boys ask their mothers for Ludo. It's good for them. They buy macaroni,' he said.

Then the packaging. 'I don't like the cardboard boxes we sell it in. I'd like to use cellophane or plastic, it's cheaper. But that's not what the market wants. Some people can't afford to buy our macaroni at present so I'm going to introduce smaller boxes which will make it cheaper for them.' The price is pitched at the right level. At 25 cents for 250 grams it is a better buy than imported products and still manages to appeal to a market where the average monthly wage is $45.

His approach is paying dividends. When he started, all macaroni and spaghetti for Togo had to be imported. Now, he estimates, he has not only replaced the 500 tons of annual imports but more than doubled the market in four years. And it is still growing. Today he offers six different types of macaroni products, and has started exporting to Ghana, Benin, Burkina Faso, Niger, Nigeria, even Congo. But Mr Savi de Tove will not stop there. With the packaging in French and English he clearly sees the whole of West Africa as his potential market. 'In Togo we have a free market. We are able to make business, to expand. There are no problems like in other parts. Everybody wants to help you.'

Mr Savi de Tove dropped me off in the middle of Lomé. I walked along the rue du Commerce. I was going to have a drink in the Hotel du Golfe before visiting the Chamber of Commerce for a seminar on 'Stimulating new enterprises: How to encourage new entrepreneurs'. As I passed the Librairie Evangélique, the local bookshop, I spotted a book in the window, *115 Ways to Make Money.* I bought a copy.

It turned out to be the first how-to-be-a-millionaire book aimed at helping Africans make a fortune running their own business. I read it as I sipped my drink. I had never seen an African business book like this before. The author, Kokougan Senyo Apaloo, had obviously been inspired by American models. He started with his keys to success – motivation, professionalism, positive thinking, and so on, asked questions designed to test your business aptitude, then gave his thoughts on how time is money. Sleeping, for example, is time spent not working.

I suspected the seminar might turn out to be a waste of time too, but I went anyway. I wanted to know how they were going about creating their own enterprise society. My suspicions were proved correct. All the discussions were very academic, full of French concepts and modules.

I did meet one interesting delegate, however, over drinks. He must have been about fifty-five, specks of grey appearing in his hair, old-fashioned spectacles and one gold tooth at the front.

'Are you going to become another African millionaire?' I asked him.

He smiled. 'I'm a poor man,' he said softly. 'I'm not American.'

'They don't make money,' I said. 'They borrow it.'

He laughed and we started discussing the seminar. He thought there was too much theory, not enough hard, practical stuff about making money. I asked what kind of business he was in. He said he was a chicken farmer from Zaire. The bell sounded and we all trooped back in for the closing speeches. As I sat down, a local journalist came up to me. I asked him whom I had been speaking to. He said he was one of the richest men in the country. I was surprised. He didn't look the normal kind of African millionaire.

The closing speeches were even more boring and less relevant than the original papers. As I left, the chicken farmer offered me a lift back to the hotel.

'So how easy is it to make money in Africa?' I asked him.

'Very difficult.'

'If you know the right people,' I added.

'Then it's easy,' he laughed.

'But how much money? How many millionaires are there?'

'You mean businessmen or politicians?'

'Both.' We laughed.

'Can you go into business and make a lot of money, or is it all tied up?'

'How can it all be tied up?' He turned towards me. 'We have nothing. Everything has to be imported – soap, toilet paper, machinery, wine, even water. There are so many opportunities. The problem in Africa is how not to make money.'

'So why don't you have more businessmen?' I asked.

'Because we're not interested in business.'

'You mean everybody wants to work for the government?'

'Or become a teacher. Have a big office, a white shirt, a big car.'

He dropped me at the hotel and offered to collect me for dinner the following evening. I accepted. I called some friends to find out what I could about him. Everybody said he was worth a lot of money, but nobody knew how much, nor what he actually did to make his money.

I picked up Mr Apaloo's book, and read his list of 115 ways to make money. Among his ideas were setting up a company to look after domestic animals, starting a pottery or going into the carwash business. For fit people who like the outdoor life he suggested they opened a sports centre, become a bodyguard or gave yoga lessons. For the more sophisticated he proposed starting a photographic studio or a marriage bureau; for intellectuals, becoming an editor, translator or starting a press-clipping service. Page after page of ideas, but at idea number 54 I discovered I had to get some sleep, whatever Mr Apaloo thought about it. As a bookmark I used the card the hotel always gave me when I signed a bill in the restaurant, which on one side said, 'Afin d'éviter toute erreur, nous vous remercions d'avoir l'amabilité de bien vouloir signer votre commande,' and on the other, 'In order to avoid any mistakes would you be so kind as to sign your door knob.'

The following morning I pursued my researches into Togo's business community. In Africa, as in Europe and the US, everybody is doing everything they can to encourage small businessmen. Governments have established special funds for developing the private sector. Togo has launched the Société National d'Investissement; banks like the Caisse Nationale de Crédit Agricole, backed by the European Development Fund, have the resources to encourage small companies; even aid organisations are now trying to promote more African-owned and managed enterprises. In Togo, the Entente Fund, in association with the US Agency for International Development, has invested nearly $2 million with the Banque Togolaise de Developpement 'to provide financial and technical assistance to small and medium-sized Togolese entrepreneurs to encourage the development of a modern Togolese entrepreneurial class.'

But still there are problems. The banks complain of the lack of entrepreneurs and suitable projects, not enough business experience and, of course, not enough security. The entrepreneurs complain, like businessmen the world over, of the attitude of the banks; too many reports, too many questions. But when the right bank does find the right project, everybody is happy. For if any place needs entrepreneurs, especially manufacturers, it is Africa.

'There are plenty of successful businessmen in Africa, but usually in commerce. Africa wants more small industrial companies,' Mr Sylvain Dauban, director general of the Caisse Nationale de Credit Agricole once told me. 'Virtually everyone is a trader; it is the manufacturing skills we need more than anything, and import substitution activities.'

Togo is one of the few countries in the third world with a specific policy for developing small business. All banks are required to place 5 percent of their investments in the private sector. A preferential interest rate is offered on loans to small and medium-sized companies. Grants totalling $150,000 are available for importing manufacturing equipment rather than raw materials.

That day I met two successful Togolese entrepreneurs – Mr Komlan Apeke, who had just opened the first mirror-factory in West Africa, and Mr Kwame Abah, who makes soap. Mr Apeke, forty, left school at sixteen to become a painter. After a four-year apprenticeship he worked in Côte d'Ivoire for eighteen months as a painter, before working for a glass merchant for four years, ending up as manager. 'I learnt the business. I always wanted to work on my own, but I didn't have any capital. I knew I would have to start small,' he told me.

He came back to Lomé, took a small shop on the site of his present factory, and started as a painter and glass merchant. He had five staff. Ten years later, with thirty staff, he is one of the biggest glass merchants in the country. He runs a fitting service and still undertakes painting contracts.

'The potential for mirrors was obvious. All our mirrors are imported so I told the banks I wanted to build a factory to make them. They were very interested, but they ask too many questions. They wanted to know who owns the land. They wanted accounts from the year we started, they wanted reports,' he said.

Ever since Mr Apeke started, however, he has ploughed all profits back into his business. Unlike some successful businessmen, he still lives in the same house and drives a Honda Accord. As a result, he was able to put $10,000 of his own money into the project, otherwise his plans would have collapsed. The SNI put in $25,000 and the Banque Togolaise de Developpement put in the remaining $37,500.

So far production is on target. Mr Apeke next wants to start producing aluminium window frames, and gradually build up his own building materials group.

As well as mirrors, Togo has always had to import soap from Lever Brothers – from Ghana, Nigeria, or Europe. Mr Abah decided he would make his own. He started Société Industrielle Togolaise (Socito) with the help of a friend. Between them they raised just $1,500. He built an open factory of concrete blocks with few doors or windows, no wall coverings, no floor coverings and definitely no rubber plants in reception. He bought machinery from Italy and hired a staff of sixty-nine.

Mr Abah was ready for business. But very quickly, like most small businessmen, he hit two problems: production was harder than expected and he had to raise more money. It proved very difficult to produce soap anywhere near the quality of the imported brands. A consultant was hired from England, stayed two years and still could not solve the problem. In desperation Mr Abah hired the entire six-man production team from Lever Brothers' big margarine, detergent and soap factory outside Accra.

Today the factory works three shifts a day, the only one to do so in the country, production has soared and the quality is perfect. Made from local palm oil, the soap is a unique marketing exercise; it has no decoration, no wrapping and no brand name although everybody in Lomé calls it Amaman, the local word for naked, because it is smooth and unwrapped.

'Everything we produce, we sell. The market ladies literally fight to get the soap from us, it's so popular,' Mr Peter Detcher, the production manager, explained. 'And it's all cash. No cash, no soap.' Socito sell cartons containing 100 bars of soap at £13. In the markets, it sells for between 15–20p a bar, depending on whether there are other supplies of soap on sale.

Plans are now in hand to boost production of laundry soaps to 6,000 tonnes and toilet soaps to 3,000 tonnes a year in two stages at a cost of £850,000. This would mean work for a further 200 people. Under phase one the laundry soap line would produce a higher quality translucent soap, and bars would be stamped, wrapped and given brand names for the first time. Under phase two the toilet soap line would produce cosmetic grade toilet soap with the aid of a new fifty-ton silo for soap noodles installed on the laundry line. A new warehouse and laboratory would be built. They are also considering moving into the production of crude glycerine, a by-product of soap making, for the export market.

The poor chicken farmer came to fetch me for dinner in a brand-new Peugeot 505, but he didn't seem to have a chauffeur. In the back seat was a collection of newspapers and a bible with lots of coloured silk markers and bits of paper stuck inside. We drove to the luxury Hotel 2 Fevrier in the centre of town. 'Can't afford a house, too expensive,' he said. 'I have to stay here.'

Dinner, set in a private suite, was delicious and, of course included chicken. We talked business: how easy it was to start; how difficult to continue; how the banks made life impossible. Their terms were pretty onerous. Nothing was lent unless it was backed to the hilt. Interest payments were high, anything from 14 to 18 percent. Repayment was always short term. In spite of all their grants from funding organisations, local banks were operating more strictly than they would in Europe. This had the good effect of making businessmen cash conscious. Citoyen Bemba Saolona, a Zairean millionaire, once told me he funded everthing from his own internal resources – the biggest private airline operator in Africa paid even for his planes in cash. But it's no help for the man starting up in business.

'What's the best business to be in?' I asked my host.

'A cash business, nothing to do with the government, where you can sell direct to the public,' he said.

'Like chickens.'

He had one farm with 36,000 hens. He used to buy his baby chicks from France. 'The French would send us one-day-old chicks by plane,' he said. 'Can you imagine putting day-old chicks in a cargo plane? It's all right for dogs. Not chicks. We were getting 40–50 percent losses. Now we produce our own.'

For three or four months they produced nothing. Now they lay up to 30,000 eggs a day. After a year the hens are slaughtered and sold in the market. It sounded straightforward. I wondered how much equipment and staff he had. I had visited chicken farms all over Africa so I was something of a mini-expert.

'Machinery?' he said. 'Hardly any. Big wooden pens, wooden boxes for laying. Nothing much.'

'But don't you have them packed in big wire cages, eggs dropping onto conveyor belts, a girl at the end putting the eggs into boxes?'

'Much too expensive,' he said. 'Who needs machinery in Africa? Labour is cheap. In any case, machines always go wrong. How long will they take to repair, here?'

'How many people do you employ?'

'About fifty, one hundred, it doesn't make any difference.'

'Well, how much do they cost you?'

'A dollar a day, and that's generous. Plenty of people pay much less. You see, labour costs nothing – why buy expensive machinery?'

Now the crunch question. We seemed to have struck up a good rapport. 'So how much are you making?' I asked innocently as he poured a second bottle of Dom Perignon. He wriggled and dodged, but at last I got him to own up to making a quarter of a million dollars – a month.

'That's not bad business,' I said. 'I'll be your partner.' We laughed. 'So how many are there like you?'

'Lots.'

'But you all keep your heads down? Because its wrong to make money?'

'Because some people think it's wrong to make so much money.'

I was amazed he had told me how much he was making, and doubly amazed at the amount. 'So how about all these others?' I said. 'How much are they worth?'

'Much more.' I was staggered. 'Twenty times more. They have chateaux in Paris, apartments in London and New York, houses in Washington.' He paused and looked over his shoulder. 'You think I'm making a lot of money. Okay, but I work hard for it. There are plenty of people making money who don't work hard, who . . .' he leant towards me, 'who only sign their name on a piece of paper. Is that right?'

'Such as?' I asked, as innocently as I could.

He looked sideways. 'I'll tell you who. I was in Liberia last week. The government there is building a new telephone line. They're buying a microwave transmitter. Three million dollars. All they need is some new linking cable – $100,000, that's all. You tell me why they're spending three million?'

'You mean because –'

'Of course because –' He sounded quite angry. 'Because who wants commission on $100,000?' He pushed his plate aside. 'In Zaire food is rotting in packing cases because nobody wants to sign a piece of paper. We have supplies of spare parts rusting away because nobody will sign because they're not going to get enough commission.' He banged the table.

'You mean they're hanging on for more money? But that's shocking.'

'Of course it's shocking.' Another bang on the table. 'But that's Africa.'

'Why don't they just sign? Something's better than nothing.'

'Because they're greedy.'

I wanted to find out how people get their money out of the country.

'There are ways. We don't talk about it.'

'Because of the government?'

'Oh no,' he said. 'In Zaire the government think we are doing a good job, creating employment, building up the industrial structure. If it wasn't for us, they would have more problems. But they don't like admitting it.' He smiled and refilled my glass.

'So do you keep your money in the country, or get it out as quickly as possible?'

'You're asking lots of unusual questions,' he said.

'I'm sorry,' I replied. 'I mean other businessmen. What's their general policy?'

'Get it out as quickly as possible.'

'But surely that's wrong. Surely you should keep it there?'

'Would you keep your money there?' he asked seriously.

It was a difficult question. Of course, if I was a local businessman I would want to get my money out. But I would also want to keep some money in the country to see what I could do to help it develop.

'Ninety percent?' he asked. This was unfair, I thought. I wanted to ask the questions. In the end, I had to admit I would probably take half out and re-invest half locally. I then thought, didn't they have to pay taxes?

'Not really.'

'It depends who you know,' I said. 'So what about balance sheets, auditors' reports, accountants?' He smiled. 'No problems?' I said. 'But that's unfair.'

'Africa is unfair.'

'You mean you pay no tax whatsoever?' I queried.

'No tax whatever,' he repeated. 'Depending on whom you know in the tax department.'

I really wanted to know how much he persuaded his local tax people and how, but he wouldn't tell me. My guess is, a mixture of airline tickets to Brussels and cheques to Société Général.

We had had a wonderful meal, and much wonderful champagne – so much that I read no more of Mr Apaloo's book that night. The following morning I decided to visit the author in person and find out why he wrote the book. He turned out to be a career diplomat, a former ambassador to Canada, who had never been in business. 'You don't have to be a businessman to understand business,' he told me. 'In many ways you understand business much better by not being involved.'

So why did he write the book? For the money? 'No, to encourage more people to go into business,' he said. 'We have lots of intelligent, competent students, but they are going into the civil service and the public sector. They want to get diplomas, they don't want to go into business. We must change their attitude, encourage them to become traders and industrialists and entrepreneurs. Africa needs businessmen.'

Mr Apaloo, who took six months to write the book, confessed that even after writing it he had never been tempted to go into business. 'I am an author. I have reflected on my experience in Africa, Britain, Canada and the States. This experience I have now put at the disposal of my readers. It is for them to take advantage of the lessons I have learnt,' he said.

'So what about chicken farming?' I asked him. 'Could I make money at that?'

'Never,' he said looking up at the ceiling. 'Farmers are always poor people.'

The high court is a big open-air building. The judge sits on a high dais above an ancient wood carving. On the left is the dock, on the right sits the clerk of court in blue shirtsleeves. Before them are the lawyers in their elegant French costumes, trimmed with white. The remainder of the building is packed with wooden benches like a church. The fans swirl in the heat, outside is the noise of traffic. Small boys are selling matches, women are selling rice and sweetcorn. People come and go, looking for lawyers, waiting to see officials. A soldier comes up the steps with six young men handcuffed together, others come to watch. The judge enters. Everybody stands. The high court is in session.

Togo has a growing reputation for its administration of justice and its emphasis on human rights. Over the last few years, French law has been revised and replaced by Togolese law. To civil and criminal law have been added labour law and special labour courts. There are special courts dealing solely with children up to the age of sixteen. Togo has also developed its own form of local courts, still run by village chiefs according to their ancient traditions, but nowadays the chief is accompanied by a magistrate when giving judgement.

With one third of the population Muslim, Togo recognises polygamy which means the divorce laws have a slightly different approach to French or British law. They have also established an independent human rights commission, the only country in Africa to do so.

'We are very proud of our reputation and respect for the law,' Mr Nyaku Dantey, the procureur de la république, similar to the attorney general under the English system, told me. He also said at one time he worked as a schoolteacher in Essex. As procureur, Mr Dantey combines the role of government attorney with that of chief administrator for all courts from village courts up to the high court.

There are over twenty local courts in Togo serving a population of two million; most of their work is civil rather than criminal. In Lomé, with its population of 300,000, there were 2,770 civil cases last year compared to 1,152 criminal cases, of which only 102 were sent to the high court. The social court, which deals with family matters, handled 51 cases while the children's court had only 33 cases.

'We are a very peaceful country,' said Mr Dantey, who used to be a judge at Sokode, in the north. Most crimes are theft. Murders are rare. The last murder case involved a German and a Swiss who was sent to prison for twelve years. The one before that was a crime passionelle; a man had poisoned his wife's lover with a secret recipe of herbs. 'Both prosecution and defence wanted to know the formula, but the man wouldn't reveal it. He went to prison for twelve years,' said Mr Dantey.

The death penalty exists but is never used. It is now reserved for crimes against the state. Convicted murderers are sentenced to a maximum of twenty years' imprisonment. Manslaughter usually warrants five to ten years, but armed robbery is treated more severely, with sentences of between twelve and fifteen years.

There are appeal courts in Lomé and in Kara in the north. The high court is responsible for criminal and civil cases as well as social and industrial legislation. Togo has fifty judges, men and women aged between thirty-two and fifty-five, the official retiring age. Unlike in the English system, being a judge is a profession in its own right; people train to become judges as others train to become doctors or dentists. They study at a legal school in France for two years then spend two years visiting courts throughout France to gain practical experience.

One of Togo's youngest judges, Kodjo Bruce, was appointed when he was only twenty-five. But he recently resigned in order to become an advocat, or barrister. 'I did not like being a functionary,' he told me. 'I wanted to be able to work for myself.' Today, still only thirty-seven, he has one of the most successful practices in the country.

There are twenty-four other advocats in Lomé, and Maître Bruce told me that more were needed. As Togo develops and expands, more companies will be attracted to the country, which means more experts will be needed in commercial and labour law. Also there will be more traffic on the streets and more traffic offences, crashes and injuries.

Maître Bruce concentrates on civil and commercial law. 'There are a lot of land disputes and a lot of cases to do with inheritance. It is very complicated,' he says. He is currently involved in a case that rivals Jarndyce v. Jarndyce. It began over twenty years ago when two large families began disputing ownership of an enormous block of land facing the beach on the edge of Lomé, at that time a small, desperately poor town. Today the thriving city has expanded to cover the 200 hectares with houses, shops, petrol stations, offices. The beach is full of tourists.

To complicate matters further, the two families have grown. Many original members have died and under Togolese law, as in French law, have passed on their claims to their male descendants. Even some sons have died and their claims in turn have been sub-divided and passed on. Today, there are over 200 people involved in the dispute.

The Labour Court sits at the high court one morning a week under a judge with two assessors, one from the employers' organisation, and the other from the trade union federation, Le Confédération Nationale des Travailleurs du Togo; in fact he is its secretary general, Mr Mawulom Doevi-Tsibiaku.

'So how successful has the federation been?' I asked.

He listed their achievements: regular annual salary increases; 100 percent increases in family allowances; introduction of old age pensions; a hotel; a chain of cut-price shops; a publishing company and printing works; construction of 1,500 homes. Which shook me. Not many trade unions could boast so many successes in just ten years. Now they are planning to open health centres and retirement homes and build more low-cost accommodation. In addition, having already won tax concessions for small farmers, he wanted to integrate them more into the activities of the union and increase awareness of the importance of women in trade union activities.

Trade unions are not new in Africa; the first in Togo was founded in 1945. But their approach is different. 'We believe in working with people. You get far more results that way,' says Mr Doevi-Tsibiaku. The CNTT is today recognised as one of the most far-sighted and successful unions in Africa. Even

French trade unions use it as a standard.

They run seminars throughout the country training people to be good trade union members and spokesmen in industrial affairs. These have proved so successful that they attract people from other parts of Africa. 'Worker education is vital,' said Mr Doevi-Tsibiaku, 'to change the attitudes of the workforce. Training creates a higher level of awareness and that helps people to solve problems more quickly.'

But they also tackle day-to-day matters like their European counterparts. Thanks to the efforts of the CNTT, Togolese workers have been granted permission to attend training courses on full pay and leave of absence for social and medical reasons. They are also trying to boost the authority of the inspectorate responsible for working conditions; to improve transport facilities for workers in Lomé and introduce stricter controls on taxi fares.

Mr Doevi-Tsibiaku also wants to see the introduction of workers' councils in large companies. Their only success in this respect has been with the Caisse Nationale de Securité Sociale which has agreed joint management-employee committees to study certain issues. In banking and insurance, however, they have been able to negotiate salaries and conditions of employment for everyone from chauffeurs and caretakers to senior grades in Togo's fast-growing financial services industry.

Next I met Maître Yawo Agboyibor, the president of Togo's human rights commission. 'It is a national commission,' he told me, 'established by law, and composed of thirteen people drawn from all walks of life. It will not just denounce violations of human rights, it will receive complaints and, backed by the powers conferred upon it by the law, put a stop to them.'

Only three other African countries have human rights commissions, none of them completely independent. In Morocco and Algeria members are appointed by the government. In Senegal, it is a private venture.

Togo's members include two magistrates, two lawyers, a doctor, a deputy, a Red Cross official and a member of the faculty of the law school at Togo's University of Benin, each elected by their colleagues. Other members represent the workers, women, young people and the traditional chiefs.

'So what are the commission's objectives?' I asked the Maître.

'To intervene directly with the administration in order to discover and put an end to any violations of human rights; to have access to police records and documentation bearing on any violations and to ascertain for itself the condition of the victim and to enlist the support of the superiors, including members of the government, of anybody perpetrating violations,' he said. If the chairman himself could not put a stop to violations, the commission was authorised to refer the case to a special tribunal, the parliament, or even the head of state.

The fact that, as a lawyer, he had been elected by the commission as their first president was a tribute to the Togolese Bar Association and the independence of the legal system in the country. Maître Agboyibor said he was planning to launch a campaign to make the whole population aware of their rights.

As I got back to the court, the judge was giving his verdict. The clerk of the court closed his book. Everybody stood. The judge left, the clerk came down to talk to the lawyers. The fans stopped turning, people shuffled out into the sunshine. The women were doing a roaring trade in sweetcorn. The high court in Lomé had finished for another day.

I woke up suddenly. I could hear drums. It was still dark but the sky was beginning to break. I was in Kara, the second city of Togo. I got dressed quickly and went out into the streets. There were crowds everywhere. The sky became brighter, the music louder.

The whole world was drifting in: the Lesso from Niamtougou nearby and the Kotokoli from Sokode 100 kilometres away; the Tchokossi from Mango and the Moba from Diapong had been travelling for days by car and on foot. Women dressed in boubous had been driving for hours on mo-peds, babies tied behind their backs. Gradually everyone surrounded an area the size of a football pitch marked out on the plains just outside the town. Groups of singers and dancers maybe 100 strong began running round the pitch waving assogoes or maracas in the air, blowing whistles and trumpets; women were blowing the nyefe, a special flute that they alone are allowed to play.

It was now eight o'clock and the sun was beginning to get hot. Guests were arriving led by local chiefs in colourful boubous, some wearing medals gained fighting in the French army in places like Vietnam, one a British army medal. A few had umbrellas to protect them from the sun, one old German army binoculars. Women began selling tchoukoutou, a local home-made wine made from millet; others were preparing kimilie and tolo tolo, traditional chicken and turkey dishes. Girls were setting out cassavas and yams for sale.

Singers and dancers were pouring in. One group were chanting, 'Evala, Evala' as they ran round the pitch. The music was getting louder. I asked what they meant by Evala. 'If you don't take part in the Evala you can still have a wife and children, but you are not considered a man,' a sixteen-year-old student of French, English and German at Pya Technical College told me. He was taking part for the first time.

Every year, for nine days non-stop, over 1,000 young Kabyes take part in the Evala, or la Lutte, a red-raw, open-air, no-holds-barred wrestling competition, the biggest sporting event in Africa. Known as the iron men of the north, they come from studying or working in London, Paris, New York, Douala, Montreal and Accra to take part. And, of course, in their thousands they walk across the plains, over the hills and along narrow sandy tracks from Sonde, Kagninde, Agbande and all the other tiny villages in the area. Senegal's grande lutte might be tougher, and for old professional fighters, but it is a sideshow compared to this.

The Evala marks the different stages of initiation for young men into the close-knit hierarchy of the Kabyes. Nobody is excluded: sons of government officials and farmers take part as well as boys from traditional soukala houses made of clay and straw. Even the seventeen-year-old son of Togo's President Eyadema comes back from Paris for the event. Not to take part could mean exclusion from the life of the Kabyes, Goehrer's favourites in all of French West Africa.

The young men are now grouped in two small armies either end of the pitch. The witchdoctor comes on to the field; the fighters follow. The chanting becomes more intense. There are shrieks from the crowd. The wrestlers, wearing only red or white shorts and barefoot, begin running round the field in one heaving, swirling mass. The atmosphere is electric. At a signal from the witchdoctor they drop to the ground and kneel around him. He blesses them and consecrates the field. The Evala is ready to begin.

The fighters return to their places. The local chief, who will act as referee for the day, takes the centre of the field. All day young fighters will come forward from their teams four at a time. First the Hausas, boys of fifteen–eighteen; then the Evalu, who can be anything up to thirty years old. Each of the four selects his opponent from the opposing team, an enormous roar goes up and the fighting begins.

Some eye their opponents cautiously as they circle each other, trying to spot an opportunity. Others are laughing all the time. One drops to his knees to gain the advantage, another tries a quick grab at his opponent's legs. Others are trying to snatch the other's hands. Suddenly one pair are rolling over and over in the red sand and long grass – screams come from everywhere – it's the first score of the day.

The Evala has few rules. Slapping and boxing are not allowed, nor must you hit your opponent on the back of the neck or throw sand in his eyes. The object is to get his back on the ground.

Another four fights are over, another four begin. Two are now bowed over head to head circling the pitch. Suddenly one flicks his opponent over his head and he lands with a dull thud. There are no winners as such, it is taking part that counts. The week starts with boys from Walde challenging the boys from Pyade, or Tchitchao and Bohon fighting it out. But instead of the winning team going into the next round, they combine teams and go on, with fights getting longer and longer until the end of the festival.

The morning wears on. A helicopter flies overhead, part of a US $160 million programme backed by satellite communication systems to fight blackfly, the tiny insect responsible for causing river blindness over vast areas of West Africa. In the past as many as 60 percent of wrestlers and spectators would have gone blind. Today, thanks to the space-age control strategy developed in Togo, probably only 0.6 percent will be infected. Monitoring equipment in rivers linked to satellites immediately pick up any changes in water level or rate of flow or the possibility of flash floods. Any of these could mean millions of blackflies being washed downstream to infect new areas. As soon as the information is beamed down the alert goes off and helicopters are despatched to spray the danger spots, Evala or no Evala. It is expensive, although it works out at less than US $1 a year for every person protected, which must be fantastic value for money.

At Avetonou agricultural research centre further south Togolese scientists are working on another solution: panicum maximum. While trying to find ways of boosting its meat production – Togo imports over 250,000 tons of meat a year – by developing new breeds of cattle, they hit on a new strain of grass: panicum maximum. To boost meat production you must go in for large-scale ranching. For this you need cattle which grow faster than their indigenous beasts, and are resistant to trypanosomiosis, the animal equivalent of sleeping sickness caused by the same tsetse fly which causes river blindness. By crossing the small trypano–tolerant Baoule cattle from Côte d'Ivoire with the larger trypano–sensitive Zebu and Ndama, which you see all over the Sahel, they produced their own Rau crossbreed.

They had the right animal, but discovered the best weight gains were achieved by animals born in the dry season, when you don't have the grass. So they developed a strain of grass that grew so quickly you didn't have to worry about the dry season. Take a bow, panicum maximum, which not only produced maximum weight gain, but minimum problems with the tsetse fly. Plans are under way to introduce panicum in all areas affected by blackfly to see if that combined with intensive grazing will solve the problem.

Another Hausa comes out to fight, chewing grass and trying to look sinister. Within seconds he is on the ground. Another has bandages on both arms and legs but wins with a flourish. The score is 30–25.

Now there are three swaying, surging crowds of singers and musicians running round the outside of the pitch. The tchoukoutou is beginning to take effect. I'd never tasted it, so decided to treat myself to half of half a gourd's worth. It's not as strong as I was expecting; it seems to affect the stomach more than the head. It's also grainy. I have a second one which, of course, tastes better. One of the worst African maize beers I've ever tasted was in Burkina Faso. It turned your stomach just to look at it, and that was before I was told they couldn't get wild yeasts so got it to ferment by getting the old women of the village to spit into it. The acid in their spit gave it the necessary boost.

Now the Hausas were giving way to the Evalus, the fighting getting rougher and more spectacular. Suddenly one Evalu lifts his opponent above his head and dashes him to the ground. He gets the biggest cheer so far. Then he helps his opponent up and they walk back arm-in-arm. Others walk back clutching an arm or a leg. One even has blood running down his face.

Now Kpatcha Toi and Yobudema Nabliwa hold the centre stage, both twenty-four, over six foot and nothng but muscle. They have had no training, no equipment; they have trained themselves. They circle each other warily. One tries a grab. The other avoids it easily. Kpatcha rushes at his opponent trying to make him lose balance. Yobudema steps aside. Now there's a flurry of hands. One of them is lifted off his feet, but escapes easily. Yobudema gets a neck hold. Now he drops to the ground. Kpatcha is fighting back. They roll over and over, out of sight. The crowd leap to their feet. The referee rushes over. It is too late. Kpatcha is on his feet. He helps his opponent up and they walk back together. As they push through the crowd I ask how they keep so fit. They tell me they work on a sixteen-hectare farm at Kega just outside Lomé which is behind the growing boom in indoor plants which has made crotons – Joseph's Coat – a best-seller throughout Europe. They supply over 10 million cuttings a year as well as a further 2.5 million ficus, dracaena, and schefflera cuttings – many grown in special conditions because consumers do not like the natural colours – to commercial growers. The fully grown plants end up on sale in flower shops, garden centres and major retail outlets such as Marks & Spencer as well as department stores throughout Europe.

The farm, Atlantic Produce Togo, is also experimenting with

scindapsus, better known as devil's ivy, an indoor climber; philodendron; the sweetheart plant; a green-leaf climber and avocados. Trial plantings have taken place. Everything depends on the next season. Later I discover that the farm, the only specialist tropical plant breeding and production centre in West Africa – Togo is the nearest tropical country to the EC – was started by a Dane, Anders M.D. Moller. He had been managing director of Scan Shipping in Ghana where he was also Danish Consul when he saw the possibilities of supplying cuttings and tropical plants to the European market and decided on early retirement to put his theories to the test.

'I knew nothing about growing plants, but I'd been in business all my life, running big companies. I wanted to try something different,' he told me when I went to see him. 'I could see the demand for houseplants growing all the time. I could also see that commercial growers in Europe were having problems. It was costing them a lot of money heating greenhouses. I thought, if I supply them with cuttings it will enable them to switch the space they devote to producing their own cuttings to faster, more profitable plants, requiring less energy.'

And it worked. Instead of keeping plants in a hothouse for six to nine months, growers are now bringing in cuttings from Togo and potting and selling them within just five to eight weeks. With purple pseuderanthemums it's even shorter. From leaving Togo to appearing as a backing plant in a bowl of mixed houseplants in Marks & Spencer takes just three weeks.

British growers reckon it takes a litre of oil to grow the average pot plant, which constitutes 30 percent of the costs. Retail prices, however, have only risen by around 4 percent in recent years compared to a staggering 180 percent increase in the price of oil. One major British company closed its pot plant division with the loss of 120 jobs, having incurred losses of over £1 million over the past three years. Mr Moller is filling the gap. His turnover is over US $1 million a year. He is also in demand in other countries giving advice on establishing and managing tropical plant production centres. Today he employs nearly eighty people. 'Quality is the key thing. We've got to be as good as European growers if not better. We've even built special temperature-controlled packing and storage rooms to ensure first-class cuttings,' he told me. So confident is he of their quality, he offers a free replacement service to growers if cuttings or plants arrive out of condition, or even if they suffer from problems created by the customer.

Speed of course is vital. The whole farm is geared to the regular Friday evening KLM flight from Lomé to Amsterdam. 'The cuttings are taken on Fridays, packed in special boxes and delivered to the airport. By Saturday they are in Europe. Sunday afternoon they are in Heathrow. They are delivered to growers Monday morning. Monday afternoon they have been potted,' he said.

But there was one problem they had not yet solved – snakes. 'We have to irrigate our plants a lot – we use over 100 tons of water an hour – and the wet conditions attract vipers and spitting cobras. We've issued everybody with boots, but we are still trying to think of how we can stop them interfering with production,' he said.

It is now mid-afternoon and the heat is intense. Flies are everywhere. The fighters are perspiring wildly. I notice none of the spectators are trying to escape from the sun. 'Why don't they shelter under the trees?' I asked someone.

'Too sticky,' he said. 'Under the trees it's sugary sweet. Some kind of insect.'

The problem, I discovered, was a mealybug which was threatening to destroy West Africa's entire US $100 million fruit production. The story began in 1981 when mango trees started to develop a black fungus. Farmers at first did nothing and hoped the problem would go away. Then a few started chopping trees down in desperation. Some tried chemicals and sprays, but in vain. Then the fungus was discovered on other fruit trees; plaintain, mandarin, guava, breadfruit and citrus. It was even spotted on ornamental garden trees and shade trees lining streets.

'The fungus was caused by a fluffy white mealybug that was sucking the sap from the veins on the underside of the leaf. The mealybugs created droplets like honey which dripped down on the leaves underneath and the fungus developed on this,' I discovered later from Dr Horst Fischer, the German aid agency director at Togo's National Plant Protection Service just outside

Lomé. 'This had two very serious effects: first it cut production, in some cases by up to 80 percent. Second, it began affecting social life.

'Mango trees create a lot of shade. People rest under the trees, and they use them for shops and hairdressing. They even hold village courts under their branches. With this honey-dew falling all over the place, they couldn't use trees any more.'

As fruit production fell, transport companies had less fruit to take to market, market traders had less to sell, children were no longer getting those vital vitamins supplied by fresh fruit. Farmers tried chemical sprays, but apart from the prohibitive cost no spray could be 100 percent effective. In desperation more farmers began chopping trees down and looking for alternative crops.

Dr Fuseni Adam, Togolese director of the Plant Protection Service, called a biological control conference with the assistance of the Food and Agriculture Organisation. CAB International Institute of Biological Control, one of the world's leading authorities, was asked to tackle the problem. They soon discovered – with the aid of the British Museum – that the cause of the problem was a mealybug from India which had mysteriously arrived in West Africa probably on plants or fresh fruit brought in by visitors. Dr Doug Williams, a CAB taxonomist and world authority on mealybugs, discovered it was a new species and named it *Pastrococcus invadens.*

Now the problem was to find the parasite that controlled it. Of course there was no such parasite in Africa, where the mealybug was a new immigrant, but entomologists in India eventually tracked down the appropriate mealybug-killer, which they called *Gyrannsoida tebygi.* In October 1986 the first group of Indian workers arrived at CIBC headquarters in England, sealed in a box the size of a chocolate bar. The future of fruit production in West Africa rested on their voracious appetites and ability to multiply rapidly.

All the tests proved satisfactory. There were no problems with quarantine as the parasites attacked the mealybug and nothing else. After another international conference the decision was taken to introduce them in the affected areas. In October 1987 the first 300 recruits arrived at the National Plant

Protection Service. Given plenty of plants and plenty of mealy-bugs, within twenty-four days they had started multiplying. In November 500 were released on a badly affected mango tree. For four weeks nothing happened, then research staff noticed that the mealybugs were disappearing and the tree was starting to recover.

'We released them all over Togo, five to six thousand, all produced from the original 300,' said Dr Fischer. And the parasites won every time. In Togo alone it means that over 250,000 mango trees are now safe, as well as the other fruit trees. And if Togo is safe eventually all of Africa's fruit plantations will also be protected. 'This form of biological control is far cheaper than continuous spraying, much more effective and causes no harm to the environment,' said Dr Fischer.

The referee now steps in to stop two wrestlers. They have fought long enough without either gaining ground. They shake hands with that special click of the fingers as a sign of friendship and walk away with equal honours. Nobody can remember the score any more. The crowd is as enthusiastic as when they arrived, shrieking with every throw. Small boys rush on to the pitch somersaulting every time their team wins. An old water truck draws up and everybody rushes forward for a drink, then back to their place.

Suddenly the referee steps back and waves his black umbrella. The individual fighting is over, now it is one team against the other. Hundreds of young Kabyes invade the pitch and, at a signal from their chief, begin fighting. There are arms and legs everywhere.

After over eight hours, hundreds of contents and thousands of gallons of tchoukoutou, the Evala is over for today. But the singing and dancing will continue into the night. Tomorrow it takes place at another village – more singing, more dancing, more fighting. And tomorrow and tomorrow and tomorrow for nine days.

ZAIRE

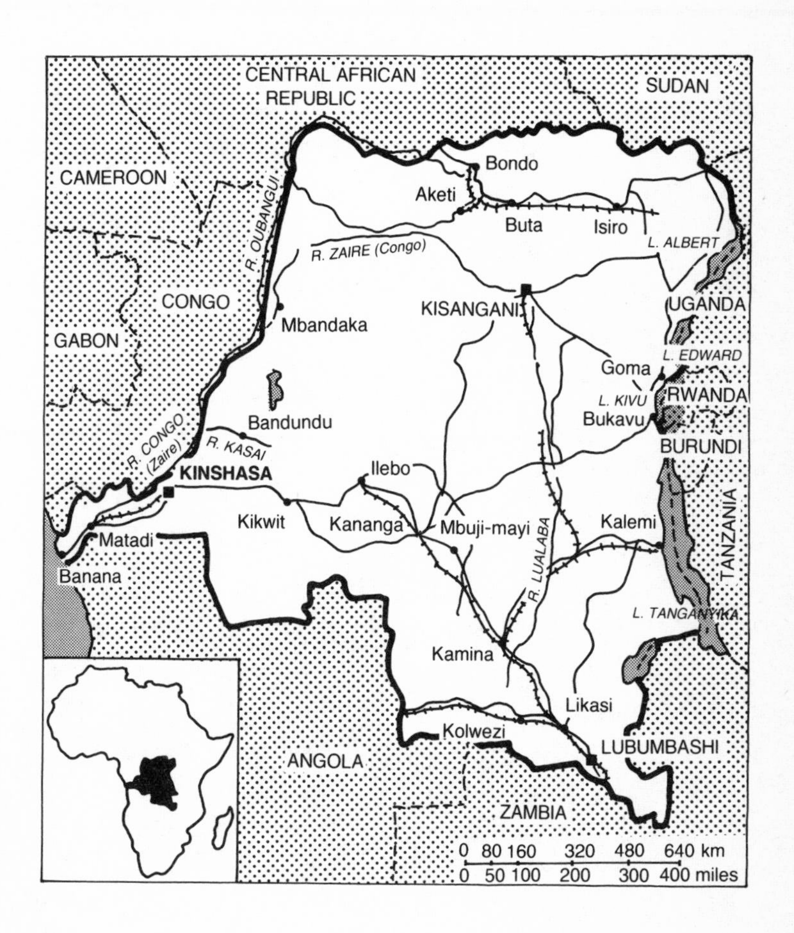
CENTRAL AFRICAN REPUBLIC
SUDAN
CAMEROON
R. OUBANGUI
Bondo
Aketi
Buta
Isiro
L. ALBERT
R. ZAIRE (Congo)
CONGO
KISANGANI
UGANDA
GABON
Mbandaka
L. EDWARD
Goma
L. KIVU
RWANDA
Bandundu
Bukavu
R. CONGO (Zaire)
R. KASAI
BURUNDI
KINSHASA
Ilebo
Kikwit
Kananga
Mbuji-mayi
R. LUALABA
Kalemi
Matadi
TANZANIA
Banana
L. TANGANYIKA
Kamina
Likasi
Kolwezi
LUBUMBASHI
ANGOLA
ZAMBIA
0 80 160 320 480 640 km
0 50 100 200 300 400 miles

Everything about Zaire is big; the country, the people, the problems, and the rumours. Especially the rumours.

The country, covering 200,000 square miles, is the third largest in Africa, eighty times the size of Belgium, its former colonial power. Its resources are enormous. It is the world's largest producer of cobalt and industrial diamonds. It supplies most of the world's radium. The River Zaire – country, currency and river all share the same name – is the biggest in the world in terms of volume and the seventh longest in the world. Wildlife? They have over 1,000 species of birds, the largest concentration of hippopotamus in the world as well as the rare white rhinoceros. They have a mountain, the third highest in Africa, actually on the equator, which is covered in snow. They have volcanoes and lakes and over a million square kilometres of tropical rainforests, more than the rest of the world put together, most of them in the coastal plains and around the Zaire river basin where rainfall can be as much as 100–200 mm an hour.

Industrially, it is potentially the richest country in Africa. Kinshasa, the capital, has a large food industry as well as big shoe, textile and plastic industries and even a vehicle assembly plant. Lubumbashi, the capital of Shaba province, has large weaving mills. So has Kisangani, a big cotton-producing area. Likasi has everything from sulphuric acid and explosive factories to big cement plants. But the biggest industry of all is – the rumour industry.

'The bank manager's wife told me the minister's secretary is also a director of every company where he is chairman.'

'A man at the Chamber of Commerce said the Americans have had to bail out that new computer company.'

'Did you hear the ambassador's been recalled to Paris? They say Mitterrand is hopping mad the contract went to the Germans.'

'Just heard from the Senegalese Mobutu is going to build a cathedral. He wants it to be bigger than Houphouet's at Yamoussoukro.'

Wherever you go, whoever you talk to – even the man who gets in the lift at the third floor and out at the sixth – has a tale to tell, about the president, some minister, the wife of a minister, the secretary of an ambassador, the daughter of the manager of the French bank in the high street. Most of them are pure gossip, some are malicious, some libellous. Some are even true. Zaire being Zaire, many are about somebody having AIDS and being rushed to Paris/Brussels/Nice/Rome to have a complete refill of fresh blood.

One of the best places to pick up the gossip is at an expats' party, a cross between a Women's Institute open meeting, a local Tory party management committee and the Young Farmers. Half of me loves them, especially if I can stir things up and drop in the occasional scurrilous item. The other half of me thinks they are the most boring thing on earth. It probably depends on how much there is to drink.

I went to one memorable expat party when Kinshasa was host to another big regional conference on AIDS. Over 200 specialists from 43 African countries were in town. Wherever I went people were talking about AIDS. Tiring of the subject, I decided to have an early night. As I got to the lift an old English Africa hand stumbled out dressed in pinstripe and regimental tie. 'Just the chap,' he said. 'Been looking for you. You're invited to a party. Let's buzz.'

'So how's business,' I said as we climbed into the oldest car in Africa, which had a shattered windscreen, torn seats and looked like the inside of a sick bag.

'Terrible. They're killing it with the commissions they want.'

'So how much did they want?'

'Sixty percent.'

'But that's crazy.'

He shrugged. 'That's Zaire. I told him it was crazy, I said it would upset all the figures.'

'It didn't make any difference?'

'No. He said everybody was paying 60 percent.'

We ended up in the hills overlooking the city in a grand, spacious house. An enormous black dog behind bars snarled and growled as we came in – a form of household insurance popular among certain expats anywhere south of Virginia Water.

'What will you have?' I was asked as soon as I set foot on the balcony.

'I'll have a whisky and soda, please.'

'Sorry. No whisky. God. Haven't you heard what happened to Nigel? Had a smash. Some car came up on the inside. Hit him hard. Right by the driver's seat. Trapped in there for half an hour. Nasty. He was going to bring the whisky. Sorry. No Nigel, no whisky.'

'That's all right. I'll have wine.'

'Then they wanted to take him to hospital. Wouldn't go, insisted they took him straight to the airport. He was in a bit of a mess. Wanted to get straight out.'

'God. You can't blame him. All those filthy needles. Use them three or four times. My secretary said her friend was admitted to hospital. Doctor came in, wiped the syringe on his jacket then stuck it straight in. God. You don't know what could have been on it.'

A little old lady now came up. She'd been in Africa for years and knew her way around – especially around the cocktail circuit, I was told later. 'It is very dangerous now,' she said, butting in. 'The French and Belgians refuse to go anywhere unless they have their blood plasma with them.'

'You mean they carry their blood around wherever they go?' I asked.

'Everywhere. They say it is too dangerous without it. Anything can happen in the streets. This morning I saw a motorbike come down the street the wrong way, against the traffic. Cars were swerving everywhere but they didn't seem to mind. The police didn't do anything –'

'Par for the course,' grunted a military type. 'Only good for two things this bloody country: AIDS and bilharzia.'

'Heard the one about the man who was taken into hospital here. Doctor said he had to have a local anaesthetic,' a burly Canadian interrupted. 'No. No, I don't want a local anaesthetic,' he said, 'I want an imported one.'

I asked the driver to drive home very slowly that night.

'Out of order,' said a greasy notice on the lift. My meeting was on the eighth floor, and it was very hot. But there was no alternative. About five hours later I arrived dripping with sweat and panting like a bull. 'Excusez-moi,' I panted. 'Lift doesn't work.'

'What do you mean?' said the secretary, an old-fashioned Belgian matron.

'There's a sign saying –'

'And you believed it.' She laughed out loud. 'That's just one of Ngandu's tricks. He's always switching the lift off and saying it's out of order so he can make money from people asking him to switch it on.'

As I got my breath back, she called Voyage Immo, the best travel agents in Zaire who always manage to get me on flights other companies cannot reach. I noticed she kept saying 'Aviation' the old French colonial word for airport.

Her boss told me he had been in Kinshasa since it was Leopoldville, when he had worked with Population Blanche, the Belgian office which issued visas and passports to tourists. Now he was in the middle of the 'campaign of hate and hostility', launched against Mobutu by Belgian Prime Minister, Wilfried Maertens, who wanted to write off US $30 million of Zaire's debt. The Belgian press had erupted with fury. Zaire's foreign minister hit back. Mobutu ordered all Zaireans in Belgium to sell up and come home.

In many ways, Belgium and Zaire have never got on. From the moment in 1877 when King Leopold of the Belgians decided to get his share of the 'magnificent African cake' with the help of Henry Morton Stanley, who approached him after being turned down by Birmingham Chamber of Commerce the Belgians seem to have been a disaster.

Stanley saw the country's enormous natural resources and recognised its economic potential, but nobody was interested in it. In desperation he signed treaty after treaty with various tribes and virtually gave it to Belgium on a plate. At first it was the personal plaything of King Leopold, then in 1908 it became a proper Belgian colony – not that that made much difference. The Belgians plundered the country remorselessly for its mineral wealth. They ran virtual slave camps to keep the rubber plantations going. Whole villages would be razed to the ground if a single worker caused trouble. People didn't count. No Africans were ever promoted into the civil service. There were no Africans in the army. Hardly any were literate.

The old Zairois will tell you they had a tough time. The Belgians made everybody, including women and children work. When the Africans tried to form trade unions, they were banned. Similarly political parties. It was only just before the Second World War that they set up a Conseil de Gouvernement but even then the Zaireans were represented by missionaries, civil servants and so on. In the mid-fifties they started thinking of handing over power in, say, thirty years. Even then many Belgians thought this was rushing things a bit.

'So what's going to happen?' I asked the Belgian businessman as we set off for lunch.

'This time it's more serious,' he said. 'Zaire can now afford to throw us out. The South Africans can no longer supply the Angolan rebels through Namibia. The only way through is from Zaire. The Americans want to keep up the supplies. Mobutu knows this; he can push us around because he knows the Americans will give him whatever he wants.'

'So what was it really like under the Belgians? Everybody I talk to, all the books I read, say it was terrible.'

'Pas du tout,' he said, shaking his head. 'Okay they didn't have their freedom, but what is freedom? Are they free today? Some of them hardly eat. Is that freedom? At least with us they could eat.'

'But they say the Belgians plundered the country; that there were slave camps, no local officers.'

'You read too many books.'

'Well, what was it really like?'

'Heavenly. Everything was neat and tidy. The Regina Hotel was a dream. They would wake you in the morning with tea; by the time you had drunk it your shoes were so clean you could see yourself in them. You could sit in the sun drinking wine. There were flowers and grass everywhere, and properly tended. There were no mosquitoes. Every morning we had a helicopter fly over the town spraying DDT. We lunched at the governor-general's palace. Exquisite.'

Laurens van der Post, who was in Leopoldville ten days before the 'Belgian scuttle', as he described their independence, paints a similar picture in his book, *First Catch your Eland*: 'The hotel was air-conditioned. Even the air of Africa was rejected. Everywhere I went I was offered ... the wine and dishes served every day in Brussels. An efficient air service supplied the Belgians with produce picked in Belgium in the afternoon and delivered to the Congo the following morning. It was easier to get escargots bourguignons in Leopoldville than an honest African yam or sweet potato ... In the night-clubs one heard not African but inferior white musicians playing the latest European and American hits. It was all due to a kind of nostalgia, of course, but infused with an insolence that was staggering when one considered how minute was the presence of the Belgians and how great and mighty the environment of Africa.'

'But what was it like for the Africans?' I asked. 'Didn't they have to carry passports, a bit like South Africa and their pass laws?'

'Yes, but it applied to blacks and whites. We had to have identity cards. We had them in Belgium. So what was the problem?'

'But weren't Africans banned from the centre of town, like in South Africa?'

'But we were also banned, as you say, from the African part of town. What's the difference? There was also a curfew. Nobody, black or white, was allowed out on the streets after seven o'clock at night. We were all the same.'

'What was the black part of town like?'

'It was nice. I was an official so I could go there. They had big houses and small houses, all with gardens. The place was crawling with children, of course, but it was clean.'

'You sprayed it with DDT as well?'

'Of course. There would be no point in spraying only one half of town. The same way we had free hospitals for them. The last thing we wanted was people with diseases living in the same town. I had a friend working in the Population Blanche as a secretary who lived in the black part of town. He was earning £50 a month thirty years ago. He got a loan from the government to build his own house. We paid the taxes: they got the loans and subsidies and benefits. Was that wrong?'

'So why have you got such a bad reputation?'

'Newspapers,' he said. 'And, of course, we didn't hand over the country very well. We just left them. Here one day gone the next. We didn't train them, but then we thought we would have more time. But we were doing all the right things – guaranteed minimum wages, free health service, everybody had somewhere to live. Not like today.'

Maybe the books were all wrong.

I wanted to ask about the events of 1959: the demonstration on January 5 which left fifty Africans dead and 300 wounded; the Round Table Conference in Brussels; the election campaign where politicians promised to raise people from the dead and repay all taxes paid to the Belgians. I wanted to ask about Belgium's sudden announcement in January 1960 that they would be gone in six months. How within a week of independence the Force Publique mutinied and the Belgians fled, sabotaging everything in sight and taking even the light bulbs. How Moise Tchombe and the province of Katanga seceded. How Zaire was pitched into a bitter civil war. But he said he had to go, and suggested I spoke to an old Zairois about the old days.

Outside the restaurant I was surrounded by taxi drivers fighting over me. I selected the smallest and weakest, on the basis that if it came to a fight I might stand a chance, checked that the fare wouldn't be more than £2.50 for a five-minute trip, climbed over the front seat because the rear doors didn't work, closed my eyes and prayed. Twenty-three minutes and two heart attacks later we screeched to a halt outside a friendly house, having overtaken a BMW on the near side at over

70 kph on a two-lane road, flattened a billboard and missed by millimetres a girl with no legs, swinging herself along on her hands the wrong way round a roundabout.

It was worth it. The old Zairois was fascinating. He had studied at Birmingham University from 1947–1953, and gone on to qualify as a chartered accountant. We sat in his study surrounded by dusty English books and files. Two girls kept running in and out with bundles of accounts which he would pore over, correct and initial. He seemed to be private financial adviser to everybody in Kinshasa. In between, he told me about working for the Belgians.

'Very good people, very efficient, very good managers,' he said. 'When I came back from Birmingham my father told me to see M. Jacquier, the Belgian who was running a big trading company here. He was a big man, very strict. There were over 400 people in the company, all over the country. He ran everything with two other Belgians. I went in to see him. I didn't have to wait. He said he wanted a general manager, was I interested? I was only thirty-two; I thought, 400 people. But I was young and ambitious. I thought, why not?'

This surprised me because everybody else says the Belgians kept everything to themselves and never thought of giving the Africans responsibility.

M. Jacquier said there were only two rules. 'If anything was routine I should do it without consulting him, even if it meant spending a million francs. The other rule was that under no circumstances should we disagree in front of other people. If he disagreed with me, he would tell me in private. If I disagreed with him, I should talk to him in private.'

'And did you always agree?' I wondered.

'Once,' he said, 'one of the managers said he needed a car. I checked the records and saw that the company had bought a car for another manager. I thought it was routine so I authorised it. I spent 900 francs. M. Jacquier asked to see me. The managers were complaining because I had bought this manager a car. I explained what I'd done, and M. Jacquier said the previous case had been an exception. I apologised and offered to pay him back from my own pocket. M. Jacquier said the money wasn't important; the important thing was that we were not seen to disagree. He would tell the other managers it was my decision and he agreed.'

'And did he continue to let you decide everything?'

'He said it was my job; he always agreed with me. He was a very good man to work for. Even after independence.'

'You mean he stayed on?'

'He was arrested by the government. I went into his office and found his secretary with all the chequebooks out, crossing out his signature. I asked what he was doing and he said M. Jacquier had been arrested. I said, You can't do that. His signature was accepted by the banks with my signature. If he crossed the signatures out we couldn't get any money. He said the new director had told him to do it, some army general. I found the general in the boardroom looking very important.' He sniffed and sat up very straight. 'The general said he would set up a committee to investigate the matter. I said that would take months, that we had a business to run and needed money to finance it. The general said, Your family is rich, you pay for everything. The government will pay us back if it decides there has been a mistake. I said, That's not how you run a business. But the general said that was democracy. I was so angry. I got all the chequebooks that had been crossed out and drove to M. Jacquier's home. There were soldiers everywhere. I didn't care. I drove straight for the gates and the soldiers opened them for me just in time. M. Jacquier came running out. I told him what they had done to the chequebooks and what the general said. Do you know what he said?'

I was scared to reply. At the time, in a country bereft of political experience and organisations, Patrice Lumumba had become prime minister. But everything was against him. The army was practically a leaderless mob. The civil service had fallen apart. Katanga, the great mining province, obviously backed by the Belgians, broke away. Another province followed. Lumumba was at his wits' end. He turned to the United Nations. He wanted to be independent of both West and East. To the United States, the great simplifiers of complicated issues, this meant he was 'soft on Communism'. That decided, suddenly everything clarified. A mineral rich country like Zaire had to be kept in the Western camp. Who was the

West's man? General Mobutu, a one-time army commander, who conveniently had most of the army under his control, and who looked a winner. Deals were no doubt done. Lumumba made a sudden dash to Stanleyville, now Kisangani, in a bid to rally supporters. He was seized by the army, despatched to Katanga and executed.

His supporters set up their own government in Stanleyville. The UN marched in. Katanga came back into the fold. The UN left. Another rebellion took place and, quickly changing sides, Tchombe became prime minister. But not for long. Come November 1965, General Mobutu came to power and has stayed there ever since.

'Do you know what he said?' he repeated. 'He said he would re-sign all the cheques, explain to the bank why his signature had been crossed out and tell them that in future they should only honour the cheques with my signature. Don't you think he was a gentleman?'

This was nothing like the picture other people had given me of the Belgians. 'So did you run the company for the general?'

'No. He was an impossible man. I left.'

'Wasn't that dangerous?'

'Yes, but I wasn't going to work for a fool. Not after M. Jacquier.'

'What happened to M. Jacquier?'

'He went back to Belgium. I tried to trace him, but he had left the company. Nobody knew where he was. He was a good businessman.'

We then talked about Zaire's label as the sick man of Africa. Malnutrition is widespread, literacy is amongst the lowest in the world, wages are minimal. It has been declared virtually bankrupt goodness knows how often. Despite its enormous mineral wealth average income is less than $300 a year. It is, many claim, the most corrupt country on earth. Admittedly there have been problems: the collapse of the copper price; the Shaba Wars; the closure of the Benguela railway; rising oil prices; huge investments in unproductive public projects. But still it survives. Still it works. Still it has the overwhelming support of the West, principally the US. It remains stable and at peace.

A friend of the family dropped in, and I left.

*

'A pig farm built by the Israelis! I don't believe you.' I was wandering around President Mobutu's big farm at Nsele. We had just left one of the pig houses full of happy, grunting pigs with dozens of piglets. Everything was clean and organised, unlike many pig houses I've visited in England. My guide was Citoyen Mutombo Zabo, a vet and a senior official in the ministry of agriculture. He was a great anglophile; spoke very good English – the language of Newton, he said – and was Zaire's number one fan of James Herriot.

I told him about the author's latest book, a collection of his favourite dog stories, and promised to send him a copy. We were now in a second pig shed, again clean and efficient; here the pigs had their own spearate yards where they could run, roll in the sun and enjoy themselves. We had organised our pigs at home on a similar system. That way they ran off the fat and produced better quality meat.

'It's a good system this. We got our pigs up to 100–120 kilos this way,' I said to Citoyen Zabo. 'And you get fewer health problems.'

'It is a new idea for us. In Zaire not many people have pigs, and when they do, they normally keep them inside.'

'What gave you the idea of keeping them in the open? Mr Herriot?'

He laughed. 'No, the Israelis were our advisers.'

'The Israelis! A pig farm! Zut alors!' I was amazed.

'It's true. They are very good with pigs. They have special kibbutz in Israel specially for raising pigs.'

'Kibbutz raising pigs? C'est une grande contradiction.'

'I've seen them, they are very good. They've given us a lot of help.'

When I mentioned this to an Israeli diplomat who travels throughout francophone Africa trying to persuade governments to establish diplomatic relations with Israel, he wasn't surprised. There were a number of kibbutz pig farms, he told me, in Israel.

'But how come?' I asked him. 'Isn't it against the law?'

'When they first started there was an enormous row,' he told me. 'There were riots. Fundamentalists demanded that they be closed down. We had a special committee of inquiry, then the government decided.'

'What? To go ahead?'

'No,' he replied. 'The government said the fundamentalists were right; pig farms should never be built on the soil of Israel.'

'So how come you've got pig farms?' I asked.

'They are built on platforms,' he said, smiling and tapping his nose. 'They're not on the soil of Israel.'

I admired their herd of Friesians. Milk production was just possible – about 10 litres a day, desperately low compared to our milk production at home, but then they are not pushing so much into their cattle. Mortality rates, however, at 5–7 percent are much lower than I would have expected – but the Zairois are good farmers.

We strolled across the yard; beautifully concreted with metal gates and barriers, it would have been a credit to any technical or agricultural college. But the dairy was a different story. It was obviously well scrubbed, but the pipes were rusty, the stalls broken, some of the milking equipment was in tatters. Water was pouring across the floor. The milk separator was not working. It was a shame.

'We can't get the spares. We haven't got the money,' said the herdsman looking dejected.

'And if we had the money, you probably wouldn't give us the spares,' added Citoyen Zabo.

It was depressing. They were obviously good farmers but the system was against them. The country had enormous debts, everything had to be rescheduled. World Bank experts were trying to put together a structural adjustment programme. A loan would help restore confidence; confidence would mean more loans; more loans would mean more repayments; more repayments would be less money for the dairy.

'But you've had a lot of help in the past. What did the Israelis do, for example?'

'They were very good. They helped us develop pig production, planted crops. All this,' the vet said sweeping his hand across the burnt countryside, 'was once fruit plantations.'

All I could see was rough scrub with the occasional tree or wrecked car. A precarious corrugated iron shack. 'Something must have happened,' I said.

The vet and the farmer grimaced and shrugged. I didn't feel like pursuing the point. But that unfortunately is the case in Africa – once the experts leave, the projects collapse. Not always; some projects are run and operated by Africans, but not too many, and not too many in the public sector.

'But I thought you had some good trees here in Zaire?'

'We have, especially palm trees,' said the good doctor, brightening up. 'Zaire palm trees come from very good stock. Lots of varieties have been developed from them that are now growing all round the world. Zaire is a good country for farming.'

Less than 4 percent of the country is under cultivation and it's not enough. The population is growing rapidly and they still have to rely on imports to top up most things. Besides, what they've got is not operating efficiently, with the exception of tobacco. And wasteage is enormous because of the size of the country and the almost complete lack of communications. To get the tobacco crop from the farms to the factories takes between four and six weeks. When they get it to market, the prices are high because of the transport costs.

'We are determined to do everything to develop our country,' said the vet. 'We have made it the most important part of our national plan. We want to feed ourselves.'

'Won't you have big problems with the traditional farmers, getting them to produce more crops, manage their land better?'

'Farmers' education is a big priority. The commercial farms are very professional, but they only account for 5 percent of production. Our priority is the small farmer, the peasant. We are the most advanced country in the world in farmer communication. Few farmers can read, so we have developed a library of cassettes on farming. It is very modern,' he said, glowing with pride.

I ambled out to reception – nobody runs in Zaire – and climbed into the car. I wanted to find out what it's like doing business in Zaire.

My first appointment was with Unilever, but the administrateur délégué was still up country trying to get back. I called at the local offices of Barclays and Grindleys Banks. Both managers had been summoned to other meetings. I went to the Chamber of Commerce. Deserted.

My next call, however, was perfect. I arrived on time. The marketing director was there. I went into his office on the dot. 'So what's it like doing business in Zaire?' I asked. He laughed. 'Different?' I said.

Suddenly his office door opened and in came three men, dressed in what was obviously once some kind of official uniform. We all shook hands.

'Mbote mookirdsi,' I said. Any excuse to practise my Lingala.

'Sangoninny.'

'Excuse me. Ten minutes. I'll be back,' the director said wheeling the men down the corridor. He was gone for twenty minutes. 'Sorry about that,' he said, 'but they were from the telephone company. I always make a fuss of them and pay on time. Without them we'd be lost.'

'You mean they come round every quarter and collect the money?' I said.

'Every week. It's the only way they get their money. If you don't pay up they cut you off.'

'That's fair,' I said.

'But what's worse is that when you pay they give you a new number.'

'You mean every week you have a new telephone number? How can you do business if your number is changed every week?'

'You can't. It's impossible. They say it's the only way they can make people pay their bills. No money, no number.'

'But it's almost as bad as not having a number.'

'I know. I keep telling them to get people to pay a deposit or a quarter in advance then leave them with the same number. They say they tried it but it didn't work. Nobody would trust them. Everybody said that if they paid in advance, they would keep the money and not give you a telephone. Nobody trusts anybody here.'

'So you're trapped.'

'But at least I can make calls. In Zaire you learn to be grateful for small mercies.'

'So tell me about doing business here.'

'Oh. As I was saying –' he looked at his watch. 'I'm sorry, I must go. I've got the electricity people coming. I'm sure you understand. Go and see Louis da Gama. He's Portuguese. He'll tell you what it's like doing business in Zaire.'

Louis da Gama turned out to own a string of companies, some public, some private, some quoted on the Lisbon Stock Exchange, others in Paris. His office was in what looked like a deserted building on the river, but inside it was full of oak panelling, deep leather furniture, computers, satellite-linked telephones, telex and fax machines. He wouldn't tell me the details of doing business in Zaire, but he told me about South Africa.

'It's two hours away by air. If I need spare parts or equipment I go to South Africa. If they say they will do something, they do it. And they are cheap.'

'So there are no problems in Zaire doing business with South Africa?'

'How can I afford not to go to South Africa? I've got a business to run. God knows that's difficult enough in a country like Zaire. What am I supposed to do? Close down? The South Africans are good. They drive a hard deal, but if they say yes, they mean it. You can't say that about many people today.'

The francophones are more polite about South Africa than the anglophones. Côte d'Ivoire allows them to land at Abidjan to re-fuel although plenty of people will swear they have seen passengers boarding the plane. South African cargo ships regularly use francophone ports. There are South African goods in most marketplaces, though not in Congo, of course.

A former Zairois minister joined us and we went back to his apartment at the Intercontinental. 'Aren't you worried about doing business with South Africa?' I asked our host as he poured Dom Perignon into beer glasses.

'We don't like their system. That's politics. We are fighting them very strongly, politically. But we have to do business to survive. Maybe if our economy was more developed, if our telephones worked, if we could get foreign exchange, if we could import goods freely – maybe then we would be stricter about South Africa. But it's not possible. In any case, politics will not change the South Africans. The whole world has been against them for so long they don't care. But maybe by doing business with them, we will make them change their minds. I often think that business will make the South Africans treat the black man as an equal. Money is more influential than politics.'

'You mean, once upon a time the black was only allowed to sweep the floor ...'

'Exactly,' he said pouring more champagne. 'The black man would still be sweeping the floor in South Africa except the businessman now wants him operating a computer, because the more black men they have operating computers, the more money they are going to make. I'm exaggerating, of course. But South Africa's economy is growing. A growing economy needs people. In the old days the whites could run the economy themselves. Now they need blacks as supervisors, storemen, computer operators, accountants. Not yet as directors, but that will come. And they also need blacks as consumers. The consumer is king. In South Africa, there are more black consumers than white. The black consumers will win.'

'If that's true why doesn't the rest of Africa do business with South Africa?' I asked.

'But they do,' he laughed. 'We're just the only ones who talk about it.' We all laughed and the former minister ordered another bottle. Talking politics in Zaire is always fun.

'But seriously,' I persisted, 'Some countries, Congo for example, are very strict about South Africa.'

'Congo, I think, is serious. They're the exception. But how serious is Zimbabwe? One day they are condemning them to hell, the next they are buying trains from them. How serious is Zambia? KK [President Kenneth Kaunda] says a lot, but what can he do? He's running a poor country. Botswana? They do nothing. If we really wanted to bring down South Africa we could do it. We all have our armies; we could support the guerillas. We could be serious about sanctions; stop all trading, all contact with them. But it would be war. Did you carry on trading with Nazi Germany during the last world war? Of course not. Neither should we have anything to do with South

Africa: trade, banking, finance. But we have too much to lose.'

'Too much what?'

'Too much money.'

'You're joking. You mean money is more important than freedom?'

'It depends whose money you're talking about.'

'And whose freedom.'

'That's unfair,' he said, 'but it's also very true.'

'You mean Africans have so much money in South Africa they don't want to risk losing it?'

'No, not in South Africa, in the US, in Europe and in Africa. The fear is that once we start anything we don't know where it will end. We like security. That's why we put our money into buildings, into land. You can't see shares. We think that if we start something with South Africa it will lead to problems elsewhere. We don't know the implications. That's why we are fighting them with words and not with weapons.'

'Do you think you'll win?'

'Eventually yes, partly by politics but mostly by economics. It will take time, but we will win.' The ex-minister poured more champagne.

Zaire is Britain's biggest trading partner in French-speaking Africa, but we don't seem to enjoy the amicable relationship Zaire has with so many other countries. Which is doubly odd because if it hadn't been for Zaire, or at least Zaire gold, Britain might not have won the last war. For the Belgians lent Zaire gold to the British to enable them, in the dark days when they stood alone, to buy armaments from the States.

When the Germans invaded Belgium in May 1940, King Leopold III went one way and parliament the other. The king as commander-in-chief of the military surrendered. Parliament, however, wanted to continue fighting from French soil, and did until the French surrendered at the end of June. The king then told Pierre Ryckmans, the governor-general in Leopoldville, to remain neutral. Parliament and the colonial minister, however, told him to stay in. Ryckmans, luckily, decided to throw in his lot with Britain. He devalued the currency, introduced exchange controls and banned all imports from countries blockaded by the British. He also ordered maximum gold production. People in Zaire loyal to the king and profits objected. Shipping goods and especially gold to Germany via neutral countries, they argued, would generate even higher profits. But Ryckmans stood firm. He banned any changes in production or sales policies without his permission. He made it illegal even to discuss business with anybody from the occupied countries.

The British consul general in Leopoldville, Mr E.J. Joint, was 100 percent behind him although the foreign office in London, as always, was split. Some wanted Zaire's raw materials at all costs. Others were frightened of what Commonwealth producers would say. In the end Lord Hailey, Britain's leading expert on Africa, was sent to sort things out on the spot.

At the time Britain was on its own. Germany controlled most of Europe. The Italians were beginning their push throughout the Mediterranean. The Russians were attacking Poland. And the Americans were still standing on the sidelines.

Hailey arrived to find the governor-general virtually running the country to meet British war requirements in spite of a mass of different opinions and demands swirling around him. Officials were pleading to quit and join the Allies but being refused permission because they were told they were more useful to the war effort if they remained where they were. Officers in the Force Publique, the internal security forces, were insisting they be allowed to fight alongside the Allies in North Africa. Between the two was a growing band of royalists demanding neutrality. There were even rumours of a coup led by Colonel A. Mauroy, a regional commander in the north east, to replace Ryckmans. The British, amazingly, moved fast. They decided Mauroy had to be removed. The head of the British Military Mission and the commander of the Force Publique were sent to Stanleyville to dismiss him. Which they did peacefully thanks to the military attaché, Duncan Smith. Instead of telling Mauroy they were going to arrive at 3 pm he told him they were coming at 6 pm, so that they were met by machine guns everywhere – but no soldiers. They were all at siesta. Mauroy agreed to step down. The crisis was over without a shot being fired. Zaire remained loyal to Britain.

Or at least the colonial establishment did; the Zairois had no choice. They were squeezed to produce everything they could for a war they had probably no interest in. At first they acquiesced. Then there were rumblings. Finally, they could contain themselves no longer. They closed the giant Union Minière down in 1941 with an all-out strike igniting a virtual rebellion in Kassi in 1943. Both were pretty forcibly crushed by the Belgians. But maybe, thanks indirectly to the British, the writing was on the wall. The Zairois had shown they were prepared to be pushed so far and no further.

But today Britain is just another country on the list of countries trying to be friendly with Zaire, because in spite of everything it is stable, pro-West and chock-a-block with vital material resources. President Mobutu visits London from time to time, but I can't imagine Zaire feels the same towards Britain as she does to, say, Canada, some Scandinavian countries and France, all of which go out of their way to cultivate Mobutu. Not to mention Belgium who in spite of the rows retains its favourite nation status and still opens its department stores late at night whenever Madame Mobutu flies into Brussels in her DC10.

I was in Kinshasa once when a British minister stopped over for a quick visit. There was a new representative of the European Development Fund in Kinshasa and he invited the minister to dinner. The minister didn't speak any foreign language apart from Latin – he kept bragging about the gerania in his garden – and he wasn't interested in meeting the locals. I was asked to make up the numbers. The minister asked me to collect him at 7 pm. I found him in the bar of the Intercontinental, cursing because he didn't dare risk putting water in his whisky. I assured him that I'd visited the laboratories of the local water company and that the water was perfectly safe. I even drank a whole glass, neat, to show him, but he remained unconvinced. He didn't trust the food either, not even the fruit and vegetables. 'Don't know who chopped them up,' he grumbled sourly. It was going to be a great evening.

The Savile Row suit and regimental tie, he of the 60 percent, came into the bar and sat by the piano. I took a drink across to him. 'So you've done the deed?'

'In the bag. Signed, sealed and delivered.'

'To Switzerland?' We laughed. I pointed to the minister, slumped over the bar.

'No, not Switzerland, but you're close,' he whispered. 'It's the biggest contract we've ever had.'

'Even though you're paying 60 percent?'

'Not 60. Forty-six,' he whispered.

'So it was big business. And the commission?'

He whistled through his teeth. 'Big. But worth it.'

'I'll ask him about a Queen's Award,' I said as we shook hands, and I returned to my charismatic companion.

'What do you know about Mobtu or Mootooboo or whatever his name is?' the minister suddenly asked me. 'Tough chap, I gather.'

I told him what I knew about President Mobutu or, to give him his full name, Mobutu Sese Seko Ngbendu wa za Banga. He stands head and shoulders over the country. He is one of the most cunning, professional and slickest politicians in Africa; and, according to many people, one of the richest. Foreign bankers and aid officials will tell you that he owns houses and castles in France, Monte Carlo, Switzerland, Italy. And his personal worth is supposed to run into international telephone numbers. I once asked a Zairois official what he thought of the president's wealth. He told me, 'In our culture, our leader is God. God cannot steal because he owns everything. The land, the air, the sea. And Mobutu is our God.' The minister grunted.

A former journalist and minister of information, Mobutu was a very shrewd and successful political operator, I continued. For he had taken an enormous country like Zaire and welded it into a unified nation. Admittedly, there had been mistakes, even disasters. Admittedly the country was in an unholy economic mess. Admittedly after thirty years of independence their GNP is lower than Ethiopia which has nothing like their riches. But the big, political fact remained: Zaire was now a single country. And Zaire was at peace.

A burly, impressive man, Mobutu in public always wears his leopard-skin hat; indeed you hardly recognise him without it. Similarly the famous Mobutu jacket, the sophisticated, haute couture Mao Tse Tung coat, which he introduced as part of his 'authenticité Zairoise' policy in 1971 and which is now the uniform of his supporters – i.e. 99.99 percent of the population. In Zaire, he is rarely seen except in Party circles or on televison. In Togo, which he visits regularly, and other parts of Africa, he is like a kindly uncle dropping in for a chat or maybe a tutor examining his students. In Paris and at francophone summit meetings, he is the elder statesman, having survived more crises and disasters than any other francophone leader.

After the death of Lumumba, I explained to the minister, the country fell apart. Lumumba's followers established a government in Stanleyville to rival the government in Leopoldville. Things simmered until 1964 when Lumumba's followers attacked the Leopoldville government. Uprisings took place all over the country. General Mobutu moved in with his army, backed up by Belgian and American troops and foreign mercenaries. He put down the uprisings and the following year, having crushed the Lumumbaists, dissolved the Leopoldville government and declared himself president.

'Hm,' muttered the minister, playing with his empty glass. I bought him another neat whisky.

'Shortly after he seized power he formed his own party, the Mouvement Populaire de la Révolution,' I continued. 'He gave the country a new name, a new constitution. He renamed the towns and cities, even the streets, and insisted that everyone became citoyen or citoyenne. He seized over 1,500 foreign-owned companies and gave them to Zaireans, who proceeded to milk them for all they were worth and run them straight into the ground. And that's virtually where everything has stayed ever since.' Another hm from the minister.

'I've seen Mobutu a number of times,' I said. 'He is unfailingly courteous, almost shy, although I don't believe that's the real man. Anyone who can hold a country like Zaire in his grip, not to mention the World Bank and most of the West, for so long has got to be a tough politician. But at one of his eleven residences – at Nsele, for example – he is the old-world statesman burdened with the cares of office.'

Last time I went to Nsele, one hour by very fast car from Kinshasa, we assembled in the big open-air pagoda. At the top was a large table covered in green baize like an altar. Either side facing inwards like choir stalls were chairs for the honoured guests. The rest of us sat in the congregation on metal chairs. And we sat and we sat and we sat in the sweltering heat.

He arrived over an hour late, smiling quietly, murmuring 'Merci bien' to gauche et droit. As his bodyguards spread out over the Chinese garden he sat down at the top table, brimming with health. The fountains were switched off and we waited for him to speak.

He read his speech slowly and carefully, following every line with his finger, emphasising the key phrases, although it didn't sound like the work of a journalist. He spoke for ten minutes; we applauded warmly and were ushered up for a private interview. He is so pleased to meet us that we are all invited to lunch on one of his boats. The whole state protocol department practically has a heart attack, but within twenty minutes we are drifting up the Congo and the president is first in the buffet queue.

'Mobutu, I reckon, has more Italian blood in him than anything – a natural descendant of Machiavelli. He is also the world's leading expert on Venice,' I went on. 'There are no haves and have-nots in Zaire today, no lords and commoners, everybody is equal. Unless, of course, you catch the eye of Mobutu – or wish to catch it. Then you are immediately subject to the rules even down to what you wear. If you are called upon to serve the state, you serve the state. If your services are required in Outer Mongolia, you go. If – and this happens many times – you are called upon to run your office or department or even an overseas embassy at your own expense, you do so. Many of today's Zairois diplomats are not much different from the old Venetian nobles "begging for alms in tattered crimson suits".'

'More like Louis Quatorze,' grunted the minister.

'Neither are you allowed to say no or worse, fail. Refuse a posting and you are out. Fail and you will probably never be heard of again. On the other hand, it can be just as dangerous to be a success. Steer the middle course and you can lead a long and happy life.'

Mobutu is not the first tough leader to rule the country. Powerful kingdoms such as the Lubas and the Lundas on the

Sheba plateau existed in Zaire as far back as 1500. In the eighteenth century the Lundas were ordered by their king to establish colonies along the Luapula river in what is now Zambia. Zaire has also been home for some flamboyant traders. Take Msiri. He was born in 1880 in Shaba, the son of a porter. He quickly saw there was more in life than carrying copper and ivory for other people, so he moved to Lake Mweru where many of his own tribe were trading and became a trader. Then, like many businessmen, he went into politics. He recruited men from surrounding tribes, equipped them with guns and started conquering villages. By 1869 he had crowned himself mwami or king of his own Garenganze kingdom between the Lualaba and Luapula rivers with his capital at Bunkeya. The local king, Kazembe, was naturally not amused by the competition, but Msiri wasn't worried. He promptly severed communications with the Lunda empire in the west. He then went back to business and sent caravans of ivory, copper, rubber, wax and even slaves from Bunkeya over 1500 kilometres to the Benguela on the Atlantic coast as well as to Bagamoyo opposite Zanzibar.

Or if you prefer, take Tippu Tip, an Afro-Arab who came from Zanzibar to Yetela, the ivory region in the east of Zaire, in the 1870s. He had worked on his father's plantations and been in the caravan trade but he wanted to break into the big time and knew it would be difficult. So he claimed he was a descendant of a Tetela princess, and was accepted. To make doubly sure he defeated the Lubas who had been troubling them for some time. The king resigned on the spot and handed the kingdom over to Tippu-Tip. Now instead of having to buy ivory, he exacted it as taxes. He established himself at Kasongo on the Lualaba river and built roads and enormous plantations. He stamped out all battles and wars within his own empire but encouraged his generals to raid everybody else in order to supply him with slaves. In 1890, defeated by new rulers, he returned to Zanzibar, one of the most successful caravan traders of all time.

I could tell by the way the minister had his eyes closed that he was absorbing every word. 'We'd better be going,' I said. 'We're expected at eight.'

*

Jump into a car with a government minister in Brazzaville or Yaounde or Lomé and he will ask his chauffeur to put on the latest cassette by Tabu Levy and his Orchestre Afrisa, or Franco, who specialises in writing songs about everyday subjects like the problems of polygamy, or songs in praise of Mobutu and his cultural revolution. Then he will ask the chauffeur to turn it up loud.

At any state banquet in francophone Africa your ears will be shattered not by diplomatic confidences being broken but by stars like Tshala Muana, 'La Reine de Mutuashi', or Radji Salamatou, 'une starlette de la chanson nationale' belting it out so loud the sound equipment practically melts. I was at a banquet once attended by the heads of all the francophone governments throughout the world; in Paris, London or Washington it would have been a sombre, black-tie affair but this was a rip-roaring party with otherwise respectable statesmen standing on their chairs screaming for more.

Switch on Radio Voix de Zaire, Radio Togo or Radiodiffusion Nationale de Burkina Faso and chances are you hear the flamboyant Papa Wemba who runs a football team in his spare time. Turn on the television and you will see top bands like Bobongo Stars or, if you're lucky, Zaiko Langa Langa, formed in 1968 when Mobutu was launching his campaign for authenticity. Zaiko Langa Langa brought Zairean authenticity to the country's music. Out went brass instruments, in came local drums. Out went the old harmonies, in came those catchy, haunting, rumba-like folk rhythms like the cavacha. They've never looked back. In Zaire they are treated much as the Queen Mother is in England.

For in francophone Africa, and especially in Zaire, musique Africaine is 'un art en evolution et non une mode', and les musiciens africains are the heroes of the new age. They are fêted by presidents, treated like VIPs and continually reported in the press. Francis Bebey, for example, a Cameroonian whose orchestra, Africa Plus, is another force en Afrique, is hailed as an 'homme de culture, chanteur, cineaste, musicologue et poète'; he writes learned articles on 'Les milles secrets des harpes africaines' or 'La Sanza: Le petit piano portatif africain' and lectures as often in French cultural centres as he performs on stage.

In Kinshasa musicians are treated like old-time Hollywood stars. People even throw money at them. Go to a concert and throughout the evening members of the audience climb on stage and give them sweets and even money.

'What are they doing?' I asked the first time I saw it. 'Didn't they buy a ticket?'

'It's our custom,' I was told. 'If you like an artist or a singer you give them a gift.'

'Do they declare it to the tax man?' A crashing cavacha drowned the reply.

Everybody told me Kinshasa, or rather Zone Matonge, was the birthplace of Zairean music; the heart (or soul perhaps) of the Zairean musical colonialisation of Africa. It was New Orleans, Liverpool and Bayreuth rolled into one. It was where the action was. There would be stalls and markets everywhere, and hundreds of bars, restaurants and nightclubs operating around the clock. It would be music, music, very loud music, twenty-four hours a day.

'Without Matonge, Zaire would explode,' a Zairean journalist told me.

'Without Matonge, Africa would explode,' a Zairean politician added.

Naturally, therefore, purely in the interests of art, I decided to spend an evening in les boîtes de nuit de Matonge.

I'd been to visit the Inga Free Trade Zone and got back to the hotel late. Outside the boys who sell cigarettes or newspapers or clean your shoes or your car for next to nothing were blocking the door, laughing and cheering. I spotted the one who always insisted on cleaning my shoes and teaching me Lingala if I ever had three seconds to kill waiting for a taxi.

He was about fourteen, very thin, wearing the same dusty jeans and old T-shirt as always. Some days he wore sandals, other days nothing on his feet. As well as cleaning shoes he sold cigarettes.

'Somebody's had a good day,' I said.

'Fantastic. He's just sold his whole packet of 100 cigarettes in one go,' they all cried.

'Is that a record?' I asked.

'Never been done before,' they all chimed back. 'One of the guards came out, said the minister wanted cigarettes quickly. He bought the lot.'

'Is it really that unusual?' I said to the shoeshine boy.

'Sure. Nobody wants to buy. They all say they have no money. It takes a long time.'

'So why not try something that sells better, faster?'

'The patron tells me to do it,' he replied, suddenly quite seriously.

'You all work for the same patron?' When you think about it, it's obvious. How can a boy who hasn't got a regular pair of sandals afford to buy 100 cigarettes and go into business? It's probably more money than his family sees in a year.

'So how does it work?' I asked. 'The patron gives you the cigarettes and tells you to sell them.' They all nodded. 'How long does it take?'

The answer ranged from two days to a month. It depended on your pitch. Outside the ministries seemed to be a good bet; people were going in and out, most had to face a long wait. What better than a cigarette to pass the time? One tough-looking boy said his pitch was outside the court building, and he had no trouble selling 100 cigarettes in two or three days. 'But if I sell cigarettes to people going into court, I make certain I get the money first,' he said, 'in case they don't come out again.' At this everybody collapsed with laughter which was probably what made him a good salesman.

'What else do you sell?' I asked.

'Everything,' they laughed. 'Jewellery, watches, shoes, cassettes . . .'

'Bange,' said the tough lad.

'Shirts, newspapers, books.'

'What's bange?' I asked.

'Some girls sell food, drink . . .'

'Brushes, shirts . . .'

'Shoes . . .'

'What's bange?'

'I used to sell ties.'

'So did I.'

'Pictures, make-up . . .'

'So how do you decide what to sell?'

One boy who hadn't spoken before said, 'We don't. We do as the patron says.'

'You mean one day shoes, the next cigarettes?'

'No, you graduate. The quiet boy now seemed to be the spokesman. 'First, we clean shoes. The patron then tells us to sell oranges or cigarettes. Then we can sell watches or cassettes or jewellery. Maybe even ivory.'

'You mean Cartier watches?' I asked. The boy nodded.

All over Africa there are 'genuine' Cartier watches for sale on street corners, in airport lounges and hotel lobbies. Occasionally I have been offered Rolex or Christian Dior or Piaget; other visitors have told me about Dunhill, even Gucci watches. The prices: anything from US $20–25 up to $75–100 for a real lookalike 'gold' Rolex Oyster. I wanted to know where the watches came from, how they got into the country, where all the money went and how much these poor boys made.

'You sell many Cartier watches?' I tried to ask casually. They all nodded. 'And cassettes?' I added. 'I bet they're easy to sell. Would you like to sell them?'

'Yes, please,' they chorused.

'Why?'

'Because everybody wants cassettes. Not everybody wants cigarettes,' said the spokesman. 'You can sell fifteen in a day.'

'Is that the record?'

'No,' they laughed. 'Over fifty. A tourist coach came to the craft centre. They all buy them.'

After watches, cassettes are the biggest counterfeiting problem. Some estimates claim over US $100 million worth of pirated tapes are sold throughout Africa every year by boys like these. In some countries they can account for more than 50 percent of cassette sales. In numbers, they total 40–50 million single tapes. And the profits to the pirates are enormous; they pay no fees, their recording costs are minimal, their sales costs pennies. And they run no risk at all. The damage they do to the countries is staggering. First, the recording artists move away. There is little point in staying and recording if they get nothing in return. They drift off to Europe and hope to record there.

Their tapes will still get back to Africa, and they will make some money out of them.

Second, countries with recording facilities just close them down. Lomé used to boast a twenty-four-track recording studio, the biggest in West Africa, which drew artistes from Ghana, Benin and Nigeria, and as far away as Cameroon, Congo and, of course, Zaire. Ghana and Côte d'Ivoire both had eight-track studios, Nigeria had a sixteen-track one. But the Lomé studio, built at a cost of $5 million, had cornered the market.

When I visited it there was no shortage of business. 'It's always very busy towards the end of the year,' the director, Ouyi Tassane, told me. 'Everybody wants to have new releases ready for the beginning of the year.'

The studio's most famous recording artiste is Nigeria's Sunny Ade, the supremo of juju music. Others include Manu Di Bango, the saxophone, piano and vibraphone player from the Cameroons, as well as Sammy Massa, Tchico, Lokassa and Mombassa, all from Zaire. With sales averaging 1,000 to 5,000 copies per record, the studio had no problem keeping up with demand. It boasted the most modern pressing plant in West Africa, capable of producing 120 discs an hour. But now it is closed down.

'Our big problem is counterfeiting,' Tassane told me. 'Shops will put records onto cassettes for you – you can get six or seven records on one cassette. The quality is not always very good but people don't mind. It's cheaper.'

Third, recording companies refuse to invest in Africa. Most want to get into this booming market, but they want protection. They are trying to do deals with governments: give us copyright protection and we'll invest, they say. Côte d'Ivoire has already agreed and others will follow. Some are even trying to beat the pirates at their own game. The Société Ivoirienne des Disques, for example, sells its tapes at about the same price as the pirates. As the director, Catherine Oro, told me, 'Something is better than nothing.'

To these boys, however, cassettes were a means of surviving, so in some ways I suppose Madonna, Prince and Stevie Wonder are doing more for Africa than War on Want, Oxfam and the US Peace Corps.

We'd been talking for over an hour; now for the two crunch questions: how much money did they make? Could I meet their patron? The answers were simple. In a month they reckoned they could make between US $6 and $10. Sometimes, if they hit the jackpot $20. At first it seemed nothing, but when you realise that average salaries throughout Africa are around $20 a month, it isn't so bad. They were less certain about the overall financial picture. Their cassettes they usually sold for around $2 each; their patron gave them around 10 cents per sale. Again it sounds like nothing, but in these countries millions are surviving on 10 cents a day or less. A bowl of rice costs less than 5 cents. For a couple of cents you can drink as much maize beer as you like. Two children selling cassettes could support a family. Where the rest of the money went was something that had not occurred to them.

The patron, a very friendly, relaxed type in lunettes, I met in a dingy shed behind the Hotel Yaki in Matonge. He seemed genuinely pleased to see me, not suspicious at all and eager to talk business. Supplies, he said, were always late, prices were high and staff were always a problem. It was much the same conversation you have with any businessman anywhere.

He came from Senegal but had been living in Kinshasa for five years. I asked how he got into the pirate business. 'Needed a job,' he said simply. He had been a teacher. Salaries had not been paid for months. He had his family and parents to look after. Another teacher gave him the name of somebody to talk to. They met, he took the job. He wouldn't tell me how much money he made, but he kept laughing and shaking my hand.

I asked about his children. They were aged sixteen, fourteen and twelve. 'Do they go to school?'

'Of course. I am a teacher. I know school is important.'

'Where? Here in Zaire?'

'Of course not. Here you don't have schools.' He pulled himself to attention, smiled a broad smile. 'In Oxford,' he said. 'The Dragon School, Oxford,' he repeated savouring every word.

My shock and embarrassment obviously pleased him.

'They are going to be English gentlemen,' he said.

I told him I hadn't been to Oxford, which pleased him even

more. 'You are obviously a rich man,' I said although judging by his house you would never think so.

'I am a poor man. I have lots of responsibilities,' he said. 'But –' swelling to attention again, 'but my children will be rich. Like all English gentlemen. Come,' he said, 'we will go and celebrate. I'll take you around Matonge.'

We went from one bar to another; into one boîte de nuit and out into another; into one café and out into another. And all the time, everywhere, there was music; very loud music.

At the Hotel Sanda we met one of the musicians, immaculately dressed in the latest designer kitende fashion. Nothing like the canaille who pass as English musicians nowadays. He told me he was a member of the Société des Ambianceurs et Personnes Elégantes, a bit like Dandies Anonymous, where the beautiful young men of Kinshasa congregate to compare designer labels. He ordered champagne.

'So what is Zaire music?' I shouted at him.

'Rumba and sookous,' he yelled back, smoothing his black velvet Mobutu jacket. 'Rumba is the slow, rhythmic beat. Sookous is the faster, more up-tempo beat. Most Zaire music is sookous. It is part of us, part of our country.'

'But surely that's true of every country?'

'Sure,' he said adjusting his silk cravat. 'But Zaire music is the only real popular music of Africa. You have traditional music, village music – music is very important in Africa – but Zaire is the home of modern African music. Zairumba.' He studied his reflection in his highly polished shoes. Our music started in the mines in Katanga. People came from all over to work in the copperbelt – from Congo, Angola, Mozambique. They brought their music with them and over the years they developed a new sound. When they went back home they took the new rhythms with them.'

'So what instruments did they play?'

'Everything; traditional African instruments as well as modern instruments. That is why our music is both traditional and modern.'

'For example?' (I'd given up shouting long questions.)

'The drum, the lamellaphone, a special kind of thumb piano, and bells. They provide that authentic sound, that special rhythm. We also use bamboo flutes made by the pygmies. And if we can't get that special sound we make our own instruments.'

'And modern instruments?'

'The electric guitar. Zaire music was developing slowly until the arrival of the acoustic guitar. Then –' he waved his hands, 'it exploded. They were made for each other.'

'So who are the greats of Zaire music?'

'Mwenda and Wendo. Mwenda is the king of maringa.'

'What's maringa?'

'Everybody knows maringa. It is our dance.' And he gave me an example, which seemed extremely complicated. 'In Zaire we dance with the hips. In Cameroon they dance with the shoulders.'

I hadn't noticed. 'And Wendo?'

He sat down again. 'Wendo was a sailor, up and down the Congo. He collected music from all over the country and from other sailors. He introduced lots of new rhythms into Zaire music.'

'So all these different influences, from the mines, from the ships, from sailors all helped to create modern Zaire music?'

'And the missionaries. They made us sing, and they brought guitars and trumpets and accordions. We had never seen them until they arrived.'

'So all the music and nightclubs and bars are the fault of the missionaries.'

He creased with laughter, kept shaking my hand, nearly slipped off the chair and ordered drinks all round all at the same time.

Downstairs at La Patience, Pepe Kalle, the enormous 'elephant' of Zairean music, was belting it out in his deep gravelly voice, a bit like Louis Armstrong with a sore throat, when I swear I heard languid Oxford accents penetrating the decibels. 'So you know old Chuckers? Independently wealthy is he?'

'Double first Oxford, then Greece.'

'Got to support them all. Also dear old pater.'

'Civil service was he?'

'Got kicked by a horse when he was forty-five. Never did a day's work after that. Spent all his time fishing.'

'Haven't played golf since October.'

In the flickering light it was difficult to see anybody. It must have been either Lord Lucan and a chum or the sons of a Senegalese counterfeiter.

Across the road in Le Carrefour, I met a group of French military advisers and diplomats. 'So who's got the best army in francophone Africa?' I bawled at them.

'Zaire,' said a crewcut diplomat. 'Mobuto keeps them on their toes at home as well as sending them off to help keep the peace in the Central Africa Republic and Chad. But the best soldiers in Africa are Gadaffi's personal bodyguard,' he shrieked. 'They're all women. I asked them once if they could kill a man. Yes, they said, but it would take three weeks.'

Staggering into L'Epique I bumped into a Belgian who runs a big trading company in town. A fully paid-up member of the Société des Ambianceurs et Personnes Elegantes approached us. 'Would you like a bange?' he smiled through his gold teeth.

'Give him a poing sur le nez,' said the Belgian avec émotion. 'Il est drogue.'

'But why?'

'They're drugs. Take them and you're in big problems.'

'You mean cannabis?'

'No, it's the local stuff. They call it l'herbe Zairois.'

'One smokes it?'

'Yes. They make it here, in the villages. It's big business. But it's dangerous.'

Not being particularly attracted at that moment to une mauvaise vie or the attentions of the Zairois police, I politely declined. Three more whiskies later I turned to the Belgian. 'So how are you two getting on now?' I asked. Zaire and Belgium are always falling out, but like married couples they seem to enjoy the rows as much as the making up.

'Friends again,' he replied, 'until the next time.'

'Doesn't it create problems?'

'Not at all,' he said. 'It's good for business.'

'How can constant rows be good for business?'

'Europeans,' he groaned. 'They don't understand African business. 'We fall out with Belgium, d'ac? The president tells us to break off all relations with Belgium, d'ac?'

'D'ac. So you have to find other sources of supply.'

'Right. Then what do we do?'

'You do business with them.'

'Wrong. We use the prices we've got from other suppliers to get a better deal from the Belgians.'

'You mean better prices.'

'No, better commissions.' He smiled. 'Better prices are not important. This is Zaire. If we can push commissions up from 20 to 25 percent, its been a good crisis.'

'And if you can't?'

'What do you mean, if we can't? Of course we can. The Belgians need us more than we need them. They always agree in the end.'

'But if not?'

'Then we arrange things. We switch everything from our French subsidiaries to our Flemish subsidiaries. The Zairois don't know. They only speak French, not Flemish.'

Inside L'Epique I found I couldn't tell a rumba from a sookous; I felt as if my ear drums were melting and running down my collar. I had had enough, I pleaded for mercy. My Senegalese protector relented and suggested a nightcap. We went back to his house, where he clapped his hands and in came three little girls carrying trays and tea pots and glasses.

He told me about his family and asked me about books and poetry. Shakespeare, he said, was his favourite. He had also read Robert Louis Stevenson, but had never heard of Dickens. This was heaven after Zairumba, but I still wanted to know about counterfeiting and kept trying to drift the conversation back to cassettes and watches. But he wouldn't let me. That was work, he said, and work had finished for the day. In any case, friends do not discuss business. He wanted to show me his house. The kitchen and bedroom were tiny. There were no floor coverings anywhere, just bare concrete. The walls were breezeblocks painted dull cream. We passed one door which had a key in the lock.

'The house of secrets,' I said.

He gave me a shy look. 'Lots of secrets,' he said and unlocked the door. Inside were nothing but shelves piled high with cassettes, thousands of them.

'For my children,' he said. 'This is what I have to do to make them English gentlemen,' and he looked a little sad.

'I've never seen so many cassettes,' I said. 'How long will it take to sell this lot?'

'A week, two weeks.'

'That's fast-moving. How many do you sell in a year? A million? Two million?'

'Maybe.'

He was equally evasive when I asked whether he was the biggest dealer in the country, and who might be bigger. Nor would he tell me anything about where the tapes came from or how they entered the country. He gave me the impression, however, that he wasn't Mr Big, just one of the distributors. He was certainly making a lot of money, although obviously somebody else was making a lot more.

'Could I become one of your agents?' I asked.

'You want to sell watches?' he said seriously.

'Sure. Maybe I could then pay to go to Oxford myself.' We laughed.

'I'll show you something else,' he said. 'Maybe you can help me.' He took me out to the garage, which seemed bigger than the house, took a brick out of the wall and pulled out a handful of – passports.

'You can help me sell passports. Passports make really big money.'

Now I was nervous. Chatting to a pirate in a house full of counterfeit tapes in a country which doesn't take piracy too seriously is one thing; talking to a man with a garage full of false passports is different.

'But that's dangerous.'

'Sure,' he said, 'but highly profitable.'

I had talked with ministers of the interior throughout Africa about passports so I knew a bit about the subject. I also know how seriously every country takes its passports and how harshly they deal with anybody peddling counterfeits or fakes. Counterfeits are passports printed illegally; fakes are genuine passports which have been doctored – photographs replaced with substitutes, fake immigration stamps and so on. Most of the fakes are printed in China or North Korea. Years ago both governments were trying to make friends in Africa and offering to supply passports to governments free of charge. Naturally a number of governments facing big printing bills from their regular suppliers took up the offer and have regretted it ever since, for the passports have about as many security safeguards as a book of football tickets – no special papers, no security inks, no watermarks, no permanent bindings, not even numbered pages. They are the easiest thing in the world to play with. I've seen passports printed in Peru which are a dream, others from Israel, some from France, which are not much better. The big centre for faking passports is supposed to be Freetown in Sierra Leone, the biggest distribution points, Accra and Lagos. But all the passports come from Côte d'Ivoire, Burkina Faso, Benin and Togo because their passports are easy to fake and because customs authorities in anglophone Africa are less familiar with francophone passports.

'So how much will a fake passport cost me?' I said.

'Around US $5,000, maybe $10,000.'

'Who can afford to pay that?'

'People who want to get out the country; big businessmen, people who are against the government, people who want to get gold out, or drugs.'

'Who supplies them to you?'

'People from Ghana, Nigeria, sometimes Sierre Leone.'

'By courier?'

'No, by post,' he laughed, which made me even more nervous.

'So what do you do?'

'I take the orders. Someone says they want a passport and I supply it – with immigration stamps.'

'You do that as well? How much?'

'For an African country, $1,000. For London and Paris $10,000, Italy about $5,000.'

'Amsterdam?'

'About $2,500.'

'Birmingham?'

'We've never done a Birmingham stamp. Maybe we should try. You see how you could help us.'

'No thank you,' I said quickly. 'Cassettes maybe, passports never.'

'You don't want to send your children to Oxford,' he said. He put the passports back into the wall and we returned to the house. It was now late and I was genuinely nervous. It had been a fascinating evening, but I didn't want to be caught in a house with fake passports. I thanked him again and fled. I fell into my car, shattered. It was almost 6.30 am. I was desperate for peace and quiet.

'Notre Dame, s'il vous plaît,' I muttered to the driver. 'It's bound to be quiet.' And I nodded off. As we swung into the gardens I woke up. I crept into the back of the church, which was filling up rapidly. Belgian priests in open-necked shirts were hearing confessions, Sisters from the convent and the school poured into the side chapel. Mass was about to begin. A bell tinkled gently in the distance. We all stood up. The priest and his altar servers walked slowly along the aisle. Outside birds were singing. An old lady in front of me sneezed, a boy dropped his prayer book. The church was full of a beautiful silence. After a night in Matonge it was the music I longed to hear.

The procession halted in front of the altar, the priest stepped forward and – the whole church erupted into a staggering, ear-splitting Zairumba which must have rocked heaven to its foundations. Zaire, I know now, is the only country in the world permitted by the Vatican not only to celebrate mass with traditional music and musical instruments. It is also the only country where they allow the priests to dance. I fled back to the car.

Little, Brown now offers an exciting range of quality titles by both established and new authors. All of the books in this series are available by faxing, or posting your order to:

Little, Brown Books,
Cash Sales Department,
P.O. Box 11,
Falmouth,
Cornwall,
TR1O 9EN
Fax: 0326-376423

Payments can be made as follows: Cheque, postal order (payable to Little, Brown Cash Sales) or by credit cards, Visa/Access/Mastercard. Do not send cash or currency. U.K. customers and B.F.P.O.; Allow £1.00 for postage and packing for the first book, plus 50p for the second book, plus 30p for each additional book up to a maximum charge of £3.00 (7 books plus). U.K. orders over £75 free postage and packing.

Overseas customers including Ireland, please allow £2.00 for postage and packing for the first book, plus £1.00 for the second book, plus 50p for each additional book.

NAME (Block Letters) ....
ADDRESS ....
....
....

☐ I enclose my remittance for ....

☐ I wish to pay by Visa/Access/Mastercard

Number ☐☐☐☐☐☐☐☐☐☐☐☐☐☐☐☐

Card Expiry Date ☐☐☐☐